THE BLUE SENSE

THE BLUE SENSE

PSYCHIC DETECTIVES AND CRIME

ARTHUR LYONS AND MARCELLO TRUZZI

THE MYSTERIOUS PRESS
New York • Tokyo • Sweden • Milan
Published by Warner Books

 A Time Warner Company

To Piet Hein Hoebens

Copyright © 1991 by Arthur Lyons and Marcello Truzzi, Ph.D.
All rights reserved.

Mysterious Press books are published by
Warner Books, Inc., 666 Fifth Avenue, New York, NY 10103.

A Time Warner Company

The Mysterious Press name and logo are trademarks of Warner Books, Inc.
Printed in the United States of America

First Printing: February 1991

10 9 8 7 6 5 4 3 2 1

Library of Congress Cataloging in Publication Data

Lyons, Arthur.
    The blue sense : psychic detectives and crime / Arthur Lyons and
Marcello Truzzi.
        p.   cm.
    Includes bibliographical references and index.
    ISBN 0-89296-426-X
    1. Parapsychology and criminal investigation.   I. Truzzi,
Marcello.   II. Title.
BF1045.C7L96   1991
133.8—dc20   90-13356
                                                      CIP

Book design: H. Roberts

Contents

1 Blue Sense or Nonsense? *1*
2 Psychic Sleuths in History *12*
3 Science Fact or Science Fiction?
The Search for Legitimacy *37*
4 The Psychic Spectrum *57*
5 A Psi of Relief: What Psychic Sleuths Do *70*
6 Gerard Croiset: The Scrying Dutchman *93*
7 Peter Hurkos: The Clown Prince? *107*
8 Lies, Fraud, and Videotape:
Lessons from the Pseudo-Psychics *129*
9 Psychic Success Stories *155*
10 The Spook Circuit: Psychic Espionage *189*
11 The Blue Sense and the Thin Blue Line *222*
12 The Blue Sense and the Law: What Lies Ahead? *239*
13 Psychics, Criminal Investigation and
the Limits of Science *251*
Notes *258*
Bibliography *303*
Index *309*

ONE

Blue Sense or Nonsense?

On April 24, 1983, Mary L. Cousett, age twenty-eight, left her home in the small town of Alton, Illinois, in the company of her boyfriend, Stanley Holliday, Jr. She was never heard from again.

Three days later, Holliday was arrested in New Jersey and shipped back to Illinois, where he was charged with murder. Through evidence they had developed, Alton police were sure Holliday had done away with the young woman, but because her body had not been found, their case was shaky. By November, frustration was mounting, as the time allowed by state law to go to trial after filing charges was nearing expiration. In a last-ditch desperation effort, Alton Detective William Fitzgerald called in Delavan, Illinois, psychic Greta Alexander.

Alexander, who claims to have received her powers of second sight after being struck by lightning, ran her hand over a map, then circled an area where the police should conduct their search. The area had been gone over many times before, so the investigators were pessimistic about turning up anything, but decided to give it one more try. This time, searchers found the woman's skeletal remains.

Fitzgerald went on to cite twenty-two "hits" Alexander had made concerning the finding of the body. Among them: the head and a foot would be separated from the body, that the letter S would be important in the discovery, and that the man who found the remains would have a "bad hand." The skull was found five feet from the body, the left foot was missing, and the auxiliary policeman who found the body, Steve Trew, had a deformed left hand, the result of an accident. "I was skeptical to begin with," Fitzgerald told the press, "but I guess I'm going to have to be a believer now."[1]

In 1978, Lompoc, California, psychic Dixie Yeterian was contacted during her local call-in radio program by distraught teenager Owen Etheridge. Etheridge's father had disappeared and he wanted to know if Yeterian could help find him. Following her instructions, the boy brought his father's watch and ring to the radio station after the show (many psychics allegedly obtain impressions by handling objects belonging to those they are trying to "track," a process known as psychometry). After handling the jewelry, Yeterian immediately "saw" that the elder Etheridge had been shot in the head—by the boy in front of her.

Yeterian promised Owen she would try to help, and when he had left she called Lompoc Homicide Detective Mel Ramos, with whom she had worked before. She relayed her impressions that the man was buried somewhere east of town, wrapped in a green sheet and with a green cloth wrapped tightly around his neck.

Ramos confronted Owen with the information Yeterian had supplied. The shocked boy confessed, and led investigators to his father's grave. The body was wrapped in a green sheet. A green cord was tied around the neck. "It was an outstanding case," Ramos told us recently during a telephone interview. "We used Dixie on more than one occasion."[2]

These are not accounts from the *Sun* or *Star* or any of the other supermarket tabloids that report UFO landings and sightings of Elvis's ghost with predictable regularity. These cases were carried by local newspapers and wire services and verified by the police officers who worked on the cases.

In recent years, hundreds of such stories have appeared in the print and electronic media, stories of psychics aiding police in finding bodies or missing persons, clairvoyantly recreating crime scenes and providing detailed descriptions of suspects. Segments on psychic sleuths have been featured on prime-time television news magazine shows such as *20/20* and *48 Hours*; news-as-entertainment shows like *Hard Copy* and *Unsolved Mysteries* have presented simulated recreations of psychic crime-busters at work; tabloid talk shows such as *Donahue* and *Geraldo* have showcased psychics along with relatives of victims and police investigators who attest to the truth of the seers' claims.[3]

Critics of the stories, such as stage magician James Randi and the Committee for the Scientific Investigation of Claims of the Paranormal (CSICOP), have dismissed the claims of the psychics, usually putting them down to self-serving publicity, self-delusion, and in some cases outright fraud. They argue that the predictions and clairvoyant visions of the psychics in virtually all of the cases are vague and self-fulfilling, often odds-on guesses, the significance of which is only colored in later by gullible cops, ESP advocates, and a public that wants to believe. This built-in wish to believe is fed by the media, they say, which have a tendency to report psychic claims in a positive manner because "sensational sells."

It is true that positive newspaper accounts about psychics far outnumber critical articles, and that on television skeptics are normally given short shrift. As a typical example, on one recent October 1989 *Geraldo* show, "Clairvoyant Crime-Busters," three psychics and their police supporters were interviewed for almost an entire show. To ensure "journalistic integrity," as Geraldo put it, a sole cop-skeptic was allowed two minutes to relate his recent unsatisfactory experience with a psychic.

Another obvious problem in getting at the truth is that much of the public perception has been molded by the accounts of the psychics themselves. Scores of biographies and autobiographies have been published in recent years, all touting the incredible accuracy of psychics such as Peter Hurkos, Gerard Croiset, Marinus Dykshoorn, Doris Stokes, and Dorothy Allison. Often the accounts in these books are offered without substantiation; some are distortions of fact, while others are flatly untrue. In virtually all of them, the psychics' many documentable failures are blatantly ignored.

In light of the criticism, many—if not most—police departments remain understandably skeptical of psychic claims, saying that relying on information provided by a psychic can only lead to a misappropriation of man-hours and tax dollars and lends a circuslike atmosphere to an investigation. "We continue to get antecdotal reports, but no additional data has emerged to suggest we should use psychic detectives or that we should take more time to research the matter," says Dr. Martin Reiser, head of the Los Angeles Police Department's Behavioral Science Services Section. "The use of psychics is wishful thinking. Roll the bones and invoke the gods when all else fails. Sloppy detective work is one thing, psychic detectives another."[4]

Los Angeles Police Department detectives apparently agreed with that assessment when Etta Louise Smith, thirty-nine-year-old mother of three and worker at Lockheed Aircraft, showed up at the Foothill Division in 1980 and told them she had had a psychic vision of a murder. And it cost them. Smith's "vision" was of Melanie Uribe, a nurse who had vanished while going to work at a hospital the previous night. Smith "saw" the canyon where the woman's body lay, and after much soul-searching went to the police. On a map, she pointed out an area in Lopez Canyon and told detectives she thought the nurse had been raped and killed with a blow to the back of the head.

Because Ms. Smith's vision included facts about the killing privy to the police, she was given a polygraph test, then told she was being booked for murder. After being held four days, she was released without being charged. Later, three men were arrested and convicted of the kidnapping-murder. Smith sued the city of Los Angeles for the trauma she had suffered at the hands of the police, and in March 1987, a jury awarded her $24,184 for lost wages, attorney's fees, and pain and suffering.[5]

The fact that many police officers view department use of psychics less than enthusiastically should not be surprising, according to some experts, "since police organizations are typically among the most conservative of social institutions . . . [the] introduction of a paranormal investigative technique not only raises the specter of the occult, but is often perceived as damaging to the credibility, expertise, and professional prerogatives of the police. In a sense, it is an embarrassment."[6]

But there is considerable evidence that this attitude is changing. Articles have begun to appear with increasing regularity in police and legal publications, investigative manuals, and criminology textbooks over the past few years, discussing the use of psychics in criminal investigations and how these "sensitives" might best be employed for maximum effect. One 1979 survey conducted by the California Department of Justice found that of eleven police agencies reported by newspapers to have used psychics, eight reported that the psychics had provided them with otherwise unknown information they considered helpful. In three of the cases, missing bodies were found in areas described by the psychics. The report of the survey concluded that "a talented psychic can assist you by helping to locate a geographic area of a missing person, narrow the number of leads to be concentrated upon, highlight information that has been over-looked, or provide information previously unknown to the investigator."[7] The paper went on to recommend the cautious use of psychics as a supplement to normal police investigation methods for unusual or difficult cases.

Psychics have been invited to lecture at the FBI Academy at Quantico, Virginia, as well as to other national law-enforcement organizations. Members of local, state, and federal law enforcement have, on their own or at the behest of their departments, attended lectures or seminars on the use of psychics in criminal investigations. As summed up by one undersheriff after attending an ESP seminar hosted by the Sonoma County, California, Sheriff's Office: "Five years ago, you could not acknowledge attending a seminar such as this."[8]

According to psychologist and psychic researcher Dr. Louise Ludwig, "In every police department, there is at least one cop who is in contact with a psychic."[9] At least one police department in the country has formally acknowledged that assertion by putting into effect a written department policy for the use of psychics. "We came out of the closet when we formulated our policy," says Lieutenant Kurt Longfellow of the Pomona, California, Police Department, who authored the policy under the guidance of Dr. Ludwig. "Even though they'd never admit it, LAPD has been using psychics for years. As police agencies become more open-minded, you'll see more [use of psychics]."[10]

Vernon J. Geberth, squad commander with the New York (City) Police Department, acknowledges that "police officers are naturally skeptical of psychics and psychic phenomena. However, from an investigative point of view, anything which has proven to be success-ful in one investigation should certainly be considered in other cases. It should be noted that information provided by the psychic may not always be accurate and in some instances may have no value to the investigation. However, this should not discourage authorities from using a psychic, especially in homicide cases where there is limited information. The use of a psychic can be considered as an additional investigative aid."[11]

Some in law enforcement go even further. In a 1989 article in *Policing* magazine, Des Plaines, Illinois, Chief of Police Joseph Kozenczak advocated that police departments consult psychics on a regular basis, citing impressive information given to his department by psychics Carol Broman and Dorothy Allison during the 1978 investigation of homosexual serial murderer John Wayne Gacy. "While the fate of a case must never be left to rest on psychic intervention alone, the use of psychics does not have to be limited to those incidents where there are few or no leads. Rather than as a last resort, psychics could be helpful on a more practical basis."[12]

The use of psychic crime fighters has not been limited to local law-enforcement agencies. Superstar psychic Uri Geller, who made a splash during the 1970s on late-night talk shows with his feats of spoon-bending and watch-stopping, claims to have worked for the FBI on several espionage and kidnapping cases, as well as being on retainer by several international corporations, just in case any of their executives get snatched by terrorists.[13]

After a ten-year quiescence, during which he allegedly became rich by psychically locating mineral deposits for mining concerns, Geller stepped back into the public spotlight in 1988, when it was revealed that he had been performing his feats of mind reading and psychic spoon-bending at gatherings of Washington shakers and movers at the behest of United States Senator Claiborne Pell (D–Rhode Island), chairman of the Senate Foreign Relations Committee. The belief in Geller's abilities by some influential politicians is so great that during U.S.–Soviet arms-reduction talks in Geneva, the flamboyant psychic was reportedly asked to beam thoughts of peace to the Russian negotiator. The next day, Geller asserts, the Soviets offered to eliminate medium-range missiles from Europe.[14]

Although the FBI denies that it has ever employed a psychic on an official basis, Bureau spokesmen admit that some of its agents may consult psychics "on their own." "We don't endorse the use of psychics, but we don't totally dismiss it," says Kenneth Lanning of the Bureau's Behavioral Science Unit in Quantico, Virginia. "I personally don't buy it, but I've run across a couple of things I can't explain."[15]

Two of Lanning's colleagues confessed under oath having witnessed similar inexplicable events when they testified in behalf of psychic Noreen Renier. During a 1986 libel trial brought by Renier against writer John Merrell, who had penned an article dubbing her a fraud, special agent Mark Babyak testified that Ms. Renier had successfully helped him locate a crashed plane. Robert K. Ressler, a seventeen-year veteran with the Bureau's Behavioral Science Unit, confirmed that Renier had done unofficial "assessments" for another Bureau agent on several cases, including the Atlanta child-murders case. He also corroborated her contention that she had predicted the attempted assassination of President Reagan during a lecture at the FBI Academy in January 1981, months before the event, terming her predictions "uncanny in their accuracy." Apparently convinced by the testimony, the jury awarded Renier $25,000 from Merrell.[16]

It is no secret that military and intelligence circles have had a longtime interest in psychic phenomena and their practical applications.[17] Although the CIA is particularly tight-lipped about the subject, the Agency admitted in 1977 that it had financed a project to develop a "spook" in the true sense of the word, an agent who could "see" events and places anywhere in the world by utilizing psychic powers. CIA Director Stansfield Turner said at a meeting of reporters that the project had gotten backing after they had found a man with such abilities. The man, who, although never officially identified, was in all likelihood former Burbank Police Commissioner Pat Price, would be shown a picture and would relate what was going on there at the time. Turner would not say how accurate the psychic had been, but confirmed that the Agency had closed down the project in 1975. "He died," Turner said, "and we haven't heard from him since."[18] At the press meeting, Turner confirmed that the Russians were studying similar individuals who might be used as international armchair spies.

Since the 1970s, the Pentagon has financed "remote viewing" experiments at SRI International (formerly Stanford Research Institute) that involve the ability of people to describe locations and documents from a distance. The CIA and the Defense Intelligence Agency (DIA) keep close tabs on similar Soviet research, which is reputed to be considerably more generously funded, and congressmen like Senator Pell and United States Representative Charlie Rose (D–North Carolina), member of the House Select Committee on Intelligence, have called for more spending in the field. (The United States spends approximately $500,000 per year on psychic research, while the Soviets are reputed to spend between $70 million and $350 million annually.)

Although the Defense Department has been using psychics since the 1950s, its psychic programs have been highly classified. But at least some of the decision-makers who have access to the results must have been convinced. In 1981, when General James Lee Dozier, the highest-ranking U.S. Army officer in NATO's Southern Command, was kidnapped by members of Italy's radical Red Brigade, several psychics were secretly called in to help. When their efforts to tune in to where the general was being held failed, military experts turned to more conventional tracking devices. Through the monitoring of Red Brigade transmissions by electronic directional finding devices, and information supplied by several captured Brigade members, Dozier was eventually located and freed.[19]

The failure of the psychics in the Dozier case apparently did not dampen enthusiasm in some military circles for use of psychics; in 1980, several were employed in the planning of a projected operation to rescue American hostages being held in Iran. They were also used during a 1983 operation to try to pinpoint the terrorists responsible for the deaths of 241 United States servicemen killed in Beirut. The operations were both scrapped,[20] however, and the psychics' pronouncements were never followed up. In 1982, Major General Albert Stubblebine, head of the Army's Intelligence and Security Command (INSCOM), and fervent ESP believer, secretly employed several psychics to remote-view the house of Panamanian General Manuel Noriega. Noriega was suspected of helping funnel arms from Nicaraguan Sandinistas to leftist rebels in El Salvador. The psychics, in an operation known as Landbroker, were supposed to provide a layout of the interior of the house, as well as pick up whatever juicy tidbits of information they could about Noriega's illicit activities. The result was a two-page top-secret report laying out the rooms and their contents. Unfortunately, once again, the operation was aborted before agents could get into the house to confirm the findings.[21]

Not to be outdone by the other branches of the armed forces, the Air Force has advocated training its own psychic performers. A 1985 booklet from the U.S. Air Force Noncommissioned Officers Academy cites a recent study by Dr. John Mihalasky of the New Jersey Institute of Technology researching the use of intuition in decision making. The study, called "PSI Communications Project," advocates those who want to improve their decision-making skills to "be aware that your hunches can be valuable and be alert so that you can recognize your own ESP (extrasensory perception) when it occurs."[22]

Is the current burgeoning interest in psychic phenomena new, or are the believers simply "coming out of the closet," as Pomona Police Lieutenant Longfellow suggests?

Part of the interest has undoubtedly been spurred by the fact that psychic phenomena have lost a great deal of their occult stigma in the past twenty years and has come to be looked upon as a matter for legitimate scientific study. But recent polls suggest that popular interest in the subject runs deeper than that. As Kenneth Lanning of the FBI's Behavioral Research Unit puts it: "Police, like the public, seem to want to believe this stuff. There's a built-in will to believe."[23]

A 1990 Gallup poll indicates that 49 percent of all Americans believe in extrasensory perception, and another 22 percent are not sure about it. Gallup also found that 14 percent of us have consulted a fortune-teller or psychic.[24]

According to a 1984 national survey done by the University of Chicago's National Opinion Research Council, 67 percent of all adults report having experienced ESP, compared with 58 percent in a similar survey eleven years earlier. Up even more is the percentage of people who believe they have had contact with the dead, jumping from 27 percent in 1973 to 42 percent in 1984.[25]

The 1986 decision of a Philadelphia jury was perhaps indicative of the growing public acceptance of psychic phenomena when psychic Judith Richardson Haimes was awarded $986,000 after her attorney argued that a CAT-scan she had been given at Temple University Hospital ten years earlier had left her with severe headaches whenever she tried to use her psychic powers. Haimes contended that this in effect had taken away her livelihood as she was now unable to conduct séances, read people's auras, and help the police solve crimes. Even though the judge in the case ordered the jury to disregard Haimes's allegations of lost psychic powers, the jury came in with the million-dollar settlement. Five months later, the judge decided the jury had disregarded his instructions and overturned the award, deeming it "so grossly excessive as to shock the court's sense of conscience." A new trial was ordered.[26]

Psychic phenomena have entered the courtroom in other ways in recent years, as lawyers have begun to be converted to the psychic cause. In 1975, during the murder trial of Joan Little, an inmate in a Raleigh, North Carolina, jail, attorney Jerry Paul employed psychic Richard Wolf (as well as a psychologist and a sociologist) to try to help him select jurors sympathetic to Ms. Little's cause. Little, who contended she had acted in self-defense when she had stabbed a prison guard to death, was acquitted. After the trial, Paul praised the psychic's perceptions, saying he "wasn't 100 percent—but he was more often right than wrong."[27]

Other attorneys have since used psychics to "read" jurors' minds. In the highly publicized 1981 murder case of Scarsdale Diet author Dr. Herman Tarnower, attorneys for accused murderess Jean Harris employed well-known psychic Phil Jordan to aid in jury selection, with less successful results. Jordan was also used in a similar capacity in the 1977 New York murder trial of Lawrence Albro, Jr., who was accused of hiring someone to murder his stepmother. Although Albro was also convicted, his attorney Robert Miller later praised Jordan's judgment, proclaiming him to have been "very helpful."

Flamboyant San Francisco Attorney Melvin Belli also claims to have successfully used psychics in the past to help pick juries, saying "The psychic came up with some good ideas that gave me more insight."[28]

What is going on here, anyway? Are seemingly otherwise rational attorneys, political and military leaders, and police lapsing back into an age of superstition and witchcraft, or are we on the verge of discovering paranormal talents that have in the past simply been mislabeled? Is the current interest simply a blind groping for "magical" answers on the part of law-enforcement investigators and an anxiety-ridden public in the face of a burgeoning rate of unsolved crimes?

Most police investigators play down their belief in psychic phenomena. When interviewed, they usually say they agreed to bring in a psychic as a last-ditch desperation measure, simply because they had no leads and therefore "nothing to lose." But is that all there is to it? If two thirds of the population believe they have experienced ESP, why should cops be exempt?

It is widely believed by many psychical researchers that almost everyone has some psychic ability and that ability may be enhanced by practice. It would not be a far-out hypothesis, then, that policemen, whose very survival can depend on "gut feelings," might have developed this faculty to a heightened degree. There are, in fact, numerous documented accounts in which police officers, following their own intuitive hunches, made arrests or took self-defensive measures that saved them from injury.

Many of these hunches can be explained as the result of accumulated experience. A man wearing a long coat on a hot day, for instance, might command a policeman's attention because of the incongruity of dress and because the officer knows that robbers wear long coats to conceal guns. But sometimes the decision seems to go beyond that.

"We've had police in this department who are psychics whether they want to call themselves that or not," says Pomona's Lieutenant Kurt Longfellow. "Cops who go back to a gas station on the feeling that a robbery is in progress there, things like that."[29]

Some years ago, Dr. C. B. Scott Jones, former Naval Intelligence officer and now personal aide to Senator Pell, was in attendance at a highly classified Washington meeting at which a well-known Canadian psychic was working with a police artist on a composite sketch of a criminal suspect. As the picture took shape, Dr. Jones noted that the artist seemed to anticipate the changes the psychic would request, almost as if the two men had the same image in mind. When Jones commented on the fact, the police artist smiled and said, "That's what we call the blue sense. Good cops have it."[30]

The "blue sense," named after the common color of police uniforms, is that hunch that sends a cop back to that gas station or down an alley; that feeling of impending danger that tells him to draw his gun. It is that unknown quantity in the policeman's decision-making process, the heightened sense of intuition that goes beyond what he can see and hear and smell. Because the blue sense specifically relates to the practical application of this unknown faculty to law enforcement, we have chosen to extend the term to cover *all* those persons—police or non-police—who use psychic powers to solve crimes.

Just what is this blue sense? Who has it and how is it developed? How truly successful are its possessors in solving crimes, and are there other, less spectacular, explanations for their apparent amazing "hits?" Is it truly a paranormal faculty we do not as yet understand or merely an imaginary phantom created by a sensationalistic media and the public's wish to believe? Are our local police and federal agencies wasting their time and our tax dollars on the use of psychics, or should we be pouring more money into research and development of psychic skills, as some proponents urge?

We will attempt in this book to answer these and other questions. But since understanding events requires a knowledge of the context in which they occur, it will be necessary to provide some historical perspective.

TWO

Psychic Sleuths in History

Stories of occult and supernatural solutions to crime and practical problems date back to biblical times. The First Book of Samuel (Chapter 9) tells us that Saul was sent by his father, Kish, to find some lost livestock, a group of asses. Searching for three days across several districts, Saul and his servant finally came to the land of Zuph. About to give up, Saul's servant suggested they pay a quarter of a shekel for a consultation with the local "seer," Samuel, a holy man who never failed to respond correctly to questions. They found Samuel near a shrine, and he correctly informed Saul that he could stop his search, that the missing animals would turn up three days later.

Tales of ghosts who returned to name their murderers are found in the folklore of many countries. The Roman orator Marcus Tullius Cicero[1] wrote of two Arcadian travelers visiting the city of Megara. One of them stayed with friends while the other went to an inn for the night. The former was awakened by a vision of his friend telling him that he needed help, as the innkeeper planned to get rid of him. Though alarmed by the seeming reality of this vision, the traveler shrugged it off and went back to sleep. Soon after, he had another vision in which his friend told him that he had just been murdered and hidden in a dung-cart that would leave through the city gates early that morning. Impressed by this vision and his dead friend's demand that his death be avenged, the traveler went to the city gate to watch for the dung-cart. When he saw such a cart, he stopped it and found that his murdered friend's body was indeed concealed there. The authorities were notified and the innkeeper was tried and executed for murder.

A similar tale, typical of this genre but culturally far removed from Rome, is the ancient Chinese story[2] of a *Kuei* (evil spirit), wherein a traveler, Ku, obtained lodgings in a Buddhist temple in a suburb of Ch'ang-chou. He was left alone by the priest and his disciples, who were holding a funeral service that night. At midnight, Ku heard a knock on the door and a voice loudly calling for entry. Ku opened the door and a strange man entered a few steps, fell on the floor, and proceeded to reveal to the startled Ku that he was the dead man whose funeral was being held at that very moment. "My wife has poisoned me," the dead man said, "and you must avenge me. Ask for an inquest to examine my remains and that will prove what I tell you." Just then, the priest and his disciples entered. They told Ku that the corpse over whom they had been praying had suddenly vanished. "He came here," said Ku, and relayed the dead man's message. An examination of the corpse showed bleeding from the eyes and nose, indications that the man had been poisoned, and the matter was turned over to the district magistrate.

Such stories, with many variations, exist throughout history and geography. In 1693, in his classic French survey *Occult Physics or a Treatise on the Divining Rod*, Pierre Le Lorrain tells us of a peasant, supervised by the police, who used a divining rod to follow the murderer of a wine merchant and his wife in Lyons. In our own era, the late Dutch parapsychologist Dr. W. H. C. Tenhaeff, who specialized in the study of such psychic sleuths (whom he called paragnosts), wrote of a remarkable practice described to him by the then Minister of External Affairs, a Swiss engineer called Alfred Ilg, appointed by the Emperor Menelik II of Abyssinia. According to this informant, Abyssinian authorities regularly used young children as "thief-catchers" (lobasjas). Placing these children, not over twelve years old, into a state of narcohypnosis, they reportedly were able to track thieves and murderers clairvoyantly.[3]

Many of the themes found in early spiritualist tales, such as the two above from ancient Rome and China, are repeated in later stories of crime solutions through occult visions, or dreams, and, later still, through dowsing or second sight or psychic powers. The history of these narratives tends to follow the same pattern found in the general history of psychical research. But whereas in earlier tales the source of the information which led to the solving of the crimes was believed to be outside the person—the revelation usually coming from a spirit or a ghost—the more frequent pattern today is to locate the source within the person who "sees" it. Though we still hear of occasional crime tales involving ghosts, and reports of crimes solved through dreams remain frequent, today's reports are more likely to be about people allegedly gifted with some means of "mystical knowing" that allows them to solve crimes that have baffled the police.

During the fifteenth and sixteenth centuries, it was common practice for victims of theft and those who sought the recovery of stolen goods to seek divinatory help from what were called cunning men and wise women. A broad range of occult techniques was used by these thief-catchers. Some employed everyday objects like a sieve and a pair of shears or a key and a book (usually the Bible) as simple detection devices that worked because of unconscious body movements by those who held them (similar to the movements produced by those asking questions of the modern Ouija board). Others used complex forms of divination like astrology, geomancy (interpreting patterns of dots in random doodling made by the wizard during a state of semi-trance), or scrying by looking into mirrors or crystal balls. Many wondrous tales were recorded during this period. In one 1662 account in the *Mirabilis Annus Secundus*, when a servant was blamed for stealing some goods, he sought help from a "cunning man." The wizard, using an evil spirit, managed not only to identify the real thief but also brought him back from fifty miles away.[4]

In a brilliant analysis of this period, historian Keith Thomas points out that "until at least the later seventeenth century, the verdict of a village wizard on questions of theft or similar crimes was a matter of some consequence. Officers of the law are known to have apprehended the supposed culprit on the basis of such identifications;

indeed it was sometimes thought worth bribing a cunning man so as to secure an arrest."[5]

As Thomas describes the episodes, these early wizards acted much as may many modern psychics. The cunning man's search for the thief usually did not begin from scratch. It typically began with a list of suspects supplied by the client, from which the wizard had to isolate the guilty party. The real problem for the diviner in such cases was to ascertain then whom the client most strongly suspected, confirm those suspicions, and enable the client to act upon them. The point was not so much to produce new evidence as it was to help the client know his own mind.[6] Thomas cites a revealing case that indicates this process was at least partly understood by the clients. In 1590, a client whose house had been set on fire engaged the services of the cunning man Thomas Harding. He later testified he had come to realize that Harding was a fraud when Harding "refused to accuse any of the persons he suspected of firing his house, even after he had pointed them out to him."[7]

The cunning man or wise woman's counsel might also help the client who had no suspicions or ideas of where to begin. Even if they had no ideas of their own to offer their clients, their divinations "legitimised random behaviour by enabling men to make a choice between different courses of action when on rational grounds there was nothing to choose between them."[8] In addition to using psychology on their clients, these wizards also often enhanced their reputations through the use of fraud. For instance, Thomas observed, the wizard's clients might wait in a room where he could overhear them converse. The wizard could then come in and display a seemingly miraculous knowledge of their problem and personal affairs. Or he might otherwise obtain information secretly, which he could then casually mention and thereby astound his clients. He could also sometimes arrange the future as well as predict it, especially where amorous matters might be involved.[9]

Thomas points up that these rituals of "thief-magic" (occult activities directed against thieves) also acted to intimidate the guilty, who usually shared the supernatural beliefs involved. This common perspective made it possible for the cunning man to provide a deterrent and a means of detection. A major goal on these occasions was the production of so much fear in the thief's mind that he might give himself away and perhaps even return the stolen goods.[10] In most of these cases, an element of bluff was probably involved. And if a person were falsely accused, he or she would then have an incentive to find the real thief. This often escalated community involvement and thereby brought more resources to bear on finding the culprit. When such magical detection was best done, it was quite practical.[11] Moreover, it must often have been an exciting affair. As Thomas observes, "The act of divination could be a very alarming business when conducted before all the parties concerned. In spirit, it was much like the last chapter in the modern thriller where the detective reconstructs the crime before the assembled suspects, while strong men wait to prevent the guilty party from bolting for the door."[12]

One of the earliest celebrity psychic detectives was Jacques Aymar, who achieved widespread publicity throughout France. On July 5, 1692, in the city of Lyons, a wine merchant and his wife were robbed and brutally hacked to death with a butcher's cleaver by an unknown assailant. Police were stymied, and public fear and pressure for a solution grew daily. Aymar, a wealthy peasant from Saint Marcellin in the province of Dauphiné, claimed he could trace fugitives through the use of a divining rod. He was summoned to Lyons by the king's procurator and taken to the scene of the crime. Apparently guided by the rod, Aymar announced that three fugitives were involved and led three police officials to a prison in the town of Beaucaire. There, from a lineup of thirteen prisoners assembled by the cooperating warden, Aymar singled out a lame convict who had been jailed only an hour before for petty larceny. Though the man denied any knowledge of the Lyons crime, Aymar declared that this prisoner had played a role in the murders. They took him back to Lyons where he broke down and confessed his participation, confirmed all the details that Aymar had described as having taken place, and named the two other men who had hired him and, he claimed, had actually committed the murders. Aymar, now granted legal powers and escorted by a troop of archers assigned to help him, continued his psychic search for the men. He managed to trace them to an inn at the port town of Toulon, but Aymar and his men arrived a day too late. The perpetrators had escaped the day before by taking a small boat to Genoa, safely outside of French jurisdiction.[13]

Aymar reportedly repeated similar feats in other jurisdictions, and this led to his being again summoned to Lyons, where his abilities were successfully tested on September 3, 1692, before distinguished visitors including the physician Pierre Garnier, who published a 108-page report on the results of these trials. This led to Aymar's being brought to Paris for further tests, all of which he failed miserably. As folklorist Andrew Lang noted of Aymar's performance: "He fell into every trap that was set for him; detected thieves who were innocent, failed to detect the guilty, and invented absurd excuses; alleging for example, that the rod would not indicate a murderer who had confessed, or who was drunk when he committed his crime."[14]

Because the history of psychic detection has paralleled the development of psychical research in general, we first need to understand something of that context. Britain's Society for Psychical Research was founded in London in 1882 and the American Society for Psychical Research soon thereafter in 1885. The major stimulus for these groups, which included many well-known scientists of their day, was a concern for investigating the phenomena claimed by Spiritualism.

Modern Spiritualism is usually said to have begun with the advent of the Fox Sisters, Kate and Margaret, who, starting in 1847, claimed to hear spirit rappings in their home in Hydesville, New York.[15] The sisters would sit at a table and ask the visiting spirit—Mr. Splitfoot—questions, and it would respond by rapping—once for "no," twice for "yes," and three times if the question could not be answered. The sisters became a national sensation, spurring the proliferation of mediums across the country, until Margaret scandalized the Spiritualist movement in 1888 by confessing that she had produced the rappings by cracking a joint of her big toe. (She later recanted the confession.)

In addition to being the twin mothers of modern Spiritualism, the Fox sisters were among the first modern psychic detectives. In 1848, the "spirit" rapped in code that he was a thirty-one-year-old peddler who had been murdered for his money and buried in the cellar of the Hydesville house by someone with the initials "C.R." That summer, the cellar was dug up, and human hair, some bones, and part of a skull were found. One Charles B. Rosana, a previous tenant who had moved to Lyons, New York, was immediately suspected. Rosana, however, vehemently denied the allegations of the slanderous spirit and produced a certificate signed by forty-four persons attesting to his good character. There the matter rested until 1904, when excavation of a wall in the house revealed most of the rest of the skeleton, along with a peddler's tin box. This affair, because of its many loose ends, constitutes a prototype for many modern cases of alleged psychic detection.

The early history of Spiritualism includes occasional reports of crime-solving mediums.[16] One such medium was Charles Foster of Salem, Massachusetts, who was in vogue during the 1860s. In a typical case, Foster cleared a young man accused of embezzling seven hundred dollars from his employer, a New York carriage manufacturer.[17] During the séance, the "spirits" revealed that the real culprit was one of the young man's fellow clerks, who was in a desperate financial jam. The suspect was named only after the employer agreed to reprimand and not prosecute the thief. Thus, in typical Victorian fashion, the story ends with the innocent man being cleared, while the life of an erring but otherwise well-disposed man was salvaged through forgiveness.

One of the most widely circulated and investigated early tales of psychic detection involves the alleged identification of the notorious murderer Jack the Ripper by the London medium Robert James Lees. The full story of these murders, as well as the question of Lees's actual involvement, is extremely complex and remains hotly debated among the many students of these crimes, frequently called Ripperologists; there is not even complete agreement on who all the victims were. The following is a simplified outline of the events.

On August 7, 1888, the first of six (though many have argued only five) similarly vicious murders took place in the Whitechapel district of London's East End. At least five of the six victims were prostitutes, and all the victims' bodies were horribly butchered. The murders took place over a mere ten-week period; the last victim being attacked on November 9. Because of the similar pattern of mutilation, the crimes were attributed to a single unknown murderer who was soon nicknamed Jack the Ripper. His identity is still officially unknown, and literally dozens of books and several television shows have been produced offering analyses and proposed solutions.[18] Many different identifications of Jack have been offered over the last hundred years by a host of Ripperologists, but few have been as intriguing as that put forward by Lees.

Though some critics have claimed that the Lees-Ripper story only surfaced in 1931 in London's *Daily Express*, the first published account of Lees's revelations probably appeared in Chicago's *Sunday Times and Herald* on April 28, 1895, and there is an earlier reference to Lees in a July 25, 1889, letter to Scotland Yard from someone signing himself "Jack the Ripper." The letter read: "Dear Boss, You have not caught me yet you see, with all your cunning, with all your 'Lees,' with all your blue bottles."[19] So the story of Lees's involvement was apparently widespread at the time. Further, in 1935, Edwin T. Woodhall, a former Scotland Yard detective-sergeant and later a member of the British Secret Service, published a memoir, *Crime and the Supernatural*,[20] in which he tells us the Lees-Ripper story was related to him as true by several older members of the Yard. Many somewhat different versions of the story have been collected, including an account left by Lees to be opened only after his death (which occurred in 1931), which was relied upon for the account of the case given by Fred Archer in his *Crime and the Psychic World*.[21] Despite many discrepancies among the various accounts, the descriptions contain a common core that has intrigued the many writers on this infamous case.

Robert Lees was a medium well known for producing alleged spirit photography and other phenomena, but he also worked as a journalist and authored several spiritualist books. Lees seems to have enjoyed royal patronage from Queen Victoria and was highly respected by those who knew him. He did not seek publicity, he always avoided association with anything unsavory, and he had an unblemished reputation throughout his life.

According to the basic story, Lees had a clairvoyant vision when the Ripper murders were at their height. The vision so disturbed him that he related it to Scotland Yard, who dismissed him as a crank. The following night, another murder took place much like the one Lees had described to them from his vision. Lees later had another vision of a similar murder, this time involving the ears of the victim being cut off. He again went to the Yard but this time was taken more seriously, particularly after they learned that a card signed "Jack the Ripper" had just been delivered to the police that included the threat that he planned to cut off the ears of the next victim. Just before the last Ripper murder, Lees had a third vision and again went to the Yard. This time, they were so impressed with the clarity of Lees's description that they took him to the scene of the crime, from which he led them "almost like a bloodhound" to the door of a much-respected West End physician. From interrogating the physician's wife, they learned the doctor had been curiously absent from home during the Whitechapel murders, suffered from brief periods of amnesia, and seemed to have some sort of split personality. He was described as usually gentle and kind but at other times became a cruel and sadistic monster. Further investigation led to the physician's being certified insane by twelve London doctors and being secretly committed to a private asylum. Lees refused ever publicly to name the physician, but much of his description of the doctor and his home fits Sir William Gull, someone who a number of Ripperologists, most notably the late Stephen Knight,[22] independently concluded might be the real Jack.

The story of Lees's involvement has been contested by some researchers, most notably the eminent criminologist and psychical specialist Dr. Donald J. West[23] and writer and British Broadcasting Corporation researcher Melvin Harris.[24] Dr. West concentrates his criticism on the version of events given him by Lees's daughter, Miss Eva Lees. He points out that the three major elements in the story, (1) Lees's correct impression of the ears being cut off, (2) his visits to the police and their utilization of his powers, and (3) the identity and fate of the mad doctor, all lack adequate supporting evidence. West points out that Lees could have known about the letter regarding the ears since it was first received by the Central News Agency and Lees had access to it as a journalist prior to its receipt by Scotland Yard. Secondly, when West inquired of the Yard about Lees's involvement, the commissioner denied it entirely, and said the Yard had no records whatsoever about Lees. Thirdly, West argues that the evidence fails to support the story of the mad West End physician and points out that other suspects were arrested by the police well after the doctor was supposedly secretly institutionalized through their efforts.

Defenders of Lees grant the possibility that Lees could have known of the ear-cutting threat in advance but insist he did not. And since Lees's story claims that a cover-up existed, it is possible that poor coordination of police efforts may be the the answer explaining the Yard's denial of Lees's involvement and their later arrests.

Harris concentrates his criticism on Lees's own posthumous version of events and upon Lees's diary. He points out many deviations there from the actual chronology of events. Supporters of the Lees-Ripper story note that Lees's version of the events was written perhaps forty years after the events, and the fallibility of human memory might easily account for his errors in detail. They also argue that there is some evidence suggesting Lees's diary may have been later altered. Thus, they argue, Lees's own account may actually be less reliable than the earlier versions. In addition, Lees's defenders point to other snippets of evidence, like the July 25, 1889, letter and a June 1987 interview a relative of Sir William Gull gave to Peter Underwood telling him that "according to a family legend" he was a descendant of Jack the Ripper.[25]

Sir Arthur Conan Doyle, the creator of Sherlock Holmes, was a firm believer in psychic powers and spent the last ten years of his life lecturing and crusading on behalf of Spiritualism. Like his great fictional detective, Conan Doyle was personally involved in successfully investigating several crimes. In fact, in two well-known cases, his own sleuthing resulted in freeing unjustly imprisoned innocent men (George Edalji in 1906 and Oscar Slater in 1927).

Conan Doyle believed there was great potential in the use of psychic ability as an aid to the detective. He regretted that, though it was often used by the French and German police, British law enforcement used it only sub-rosa. It is likely that Sir Arthur was familiar with the Lees-Ripper story, but he personally thought the Ripper might have been a man disguised as a woman. Nonetheless, he wrote to Lees on November 6, 1928, urging that Lees write the "remarkable story of the late Queen and your psychic experiences" for the historical record since "it would be good to leave a clear record behind."[26] Lees seems not to have answered Conan Doyle's letter, but it may have caused him to produce the posthumous document later publicized by Fred Archer.

Conan Doyle's belief in psychic phenomena continued until his later years. In 1926, when mystery novelist Agatha Christie suddenly disappeared, setting off a national manhunt, Conan Doyle called in psychic help to try to solve the mystery.

The police had found Christie's abandoned car on the edge of a chalk pit with its motor still running, and they suspected foul play. Sir Arthur consulted a medium well known for his accurate readings, made by holding some object previously connected with the person inquired about, a skill called psychometry. Sir Arthur then wrote a letter to the *Morning Post* in which he tells us what happened:

> In this case, I obtained a glove of Mrs. Christie's, and asked an excellent psychometrist for an opinion. I gave him no clue at all as to what I wanted or to whom the article belonged. He never saw it until I laid it on the table at the moment of consultation, and there was nothing to connect either it or me with the Christie case. The date was Sunday last. He at once got the name of Agatha. "There is

trouble connected with this article. The person who owns it is half dazed and half purposeful. She is not dead as many think. She is alive. You will hear of her, I think, next Wednesday."[27]

Christie was located some days later, registered at a hotel spa in northern England under the name of her husband's mistress. She claimed to be suffering from amnesia, but there was much speculation in the press that it was all an act to attract publicity. The full truth will probably never be known, but credibility is added to the tale of amnesia by the facts that just prior to her disappearance, Christie had behaved hysterically over the recent death of her deeply loved mother and was told by her husband, Colonel Archie Christie, that he loved another woman and wanted a divorce.

Despite the public debate, Conan Doyle credited his psychic's reading as being on the mark:

> Mrs. Christie was found on Tuesday night, but it was actually Wednesday when the news reached us, so everything in the reading, so far as I could test it (there was a good deal about character and motives which was outside my knowledge), proved to be true. The only error was that he had an impression of water, though whether the idea of a Hydro [a spa] was at the bottom of this feeling is at least arguable. I sent the report on to Colonel Christie that evening.[28]

There were numerous well-publicized cases of psychic detection in England during this period, many of which were recounted by Edwin T. Woodhall in his popular memoir.[29] Especially noteworthy is his description of the December 1921 assault and murder of Irene Wilkins, a servant girl who was lured to a meeting with her killer in Bournemouth by a bogus telegram offering her an attractive position. Miss Wilkins's body had been thrown into some furze bushes and the murderer left no clues. The main suspect, cleared by the bizarre events that followed, was a young man who was a close friend of Irene's. With no evidence and at their wits' end, several members of the Bournemouth police force were to attend a séance at which the trance medium, Mrs. Charlotte Starkey, seemed to be possessed by the dead victim. Incredibly, the police attended further séances over the next five months, during which the medium seemed to describe the crime fully, even supplying the name of the murderer, Thomas

Henry Allaway.[30] Allaway had recently been arrested on a false-check charge, so was already in police custody. Guided by the medium's revelations, the police made further inquiries that produced evidence and a case against Allaway which led to his conviction for Wilkins's murder.

Even the trial had its bizarre elements, for at one point a witness for the Crown forgot a critical date that needed to be established. He claimed that a spirit called "Pat" who had been at a séance appeared to him while he gave his testimony and seemed to hold before him a piece of paper with the correct date of January 6 written on it in large letters. According to Woodhall, "This is the only instance within my knowledge of material evidence being supplied to a witness, while under cross-examination, by psychic means."[31]

In *Crime and the Occult: How ESP and Parapsychology Help Detection*,[32] Paul Tabori described many publicized European psychic detectives operating during the 1920s. Unfortunately, Tabori's descriptions of many of these cases is unreliable and reprehensibly omit much that might weaken his claims of psychic successes. One of Tabori's prime psychic sleuths was August Drost, whose trial in 1925 received much publicity in Germany. Tabori correctly wrote that Drost was acquitted of charges that he had misled people to obtain illegal financial advantage, but his description of Drost's cases, many of which were discussed during that trial, contains many errors or omissions. As the investigative journalist Piet Hein Hoebens pointed out,[33] Tabori misdescribed Drost as a teacher and clairvoyant when he was actually a hypnotist who used female mediums.

A principal case cited by Tabori concerned Drost's attempt to solve a November 1922 burglary at the home of a Dr. Danziger in Ballenstedt. At the trial, Dr. Danziger testified that Drost's medium had been unsuccessful in solving the case. However, during a séance on November 30, 1922, she had clairvoyantly revealed that there had been a theft of a checkbook, something which Dr. Danzinger said he had not yet discovered. What Tabori failed to mention was that the original police files, later consulted by the skeptical criminologist Dr. Albert Hellwig, showed that in fact Dr. Danzinger had reported the missing of his checkbook on November 11. Drost had been given a list of those stolen items prior to the trance revelations he obtained through his medium. When Hellwig confronted Dr. Danziger with this evidence, Danziger admitted that he must have been the victim of an extraordinary lapse of memory.[34] Tabori similarly misrepresents the two other cases involving Drost, both of which Hellwig also demystified in detail.

Another prominent psychic sleuth during this period, also discussed by Tabori, was Dr. Leopold Thoma, a retired superintendent of police. In 1921, Dr. Thoma founded an Institute of Criminal Telepathy in Vienna, where he worked with a hypnotized female medium publicly identified only as Megalis ("mother of secrets"). They became very well known in Vienna as a result of many sensationalist newspaper stories telling of their successes in criminal investigations. Tabori, relying in part on the diaries of his father, who knew Dr. Thoma,[35] reported Thoma and Megalis were highly successful with many cases not only in Austria but elsewhere in Europe, including one case in Poland. An Austrian police superintendent, a Dr. Tartaruga, often cooperated with Dr. Thoma and Megalis and even wrote a book endorsing psychic criminology.[36]

A far more critical view of their efforts was offered by Hellwig, who found Thoma's experiments lacked adequate controls to prevent Megalis from cheating. More significantly, Hellwig found that Megalis also made "fantastic statements, often contradictory, that do not correspond to the real facts" and that she usually made vague statements that spectators sometimes "interpreted" as being "striking." As with other cases Hellwig examined, he concluded that "the mediums fail as soon as they are requested to indicate where the booty can be found or to identify the culprit in such a way that he can be arrested."[37]

Tabori discusses other psychic detectives from this period, including those of psychographologists (handwriting analysts) Raphael Schermann (an Austrian) and Michael F. Fischel (a Hungarian), hypnotists Alfred Pathes (a Hungarian) and Georg Mittelman (a German), Madame Luce Vidi (a French clairvoyant), and W. de Kerler (a German who called himself a psychocriminologist). We should not necessarily dismiss the claims for these sleuths, but given the scarcity of Tabori's documentation for their alleged successes, his gross misreportings in the cases of Drost and Thoma, and the lack of independent reports on these cases, there remain serious doubts about Tabori's claims for them. [38] However, Tabori does discuss one psychic sleuth for whom we have found some independent and intriguing corroboration.

Janos Kele was among several European psychic detectives prominent during the 1930s. Little known outside his native Hungary, he established a remarkable reputation there as a counselor. He spent parts of his career, in the years immediately after World Wars I and II, in Germany, where numerous authors who wrote about him were greatly impressed by his extraordinary perceptions. His strongest endorsement, however, comes from Budapest's Deputy Police Chief Dr. Stephan Szimon. In an interview given to London's *Daily Mail* in January 1936, Dr. Szimon said that after Kele had returned to Hungary from Germany when Hitler rose to power (Kele was not Jewish but was strongly anti-fascist), a special police department section was set up largely to trace missing persons and would-be suicides. He claimed that Kele demonstrated an average psychic accuracy of eighty percent and added, "There are days when he is one hundred percent accurate."[39]

Perhaps Kele's most publicized success was his long-distance location of a missing person in Argentina, some six thousand miles away. Sandor Sebok, an eccentric Hungarian refugee in San Vicente, Argentina, had disappeared, as had the former owner of his house, another Hungarian named Kandiko. The police searched for them both and concluded that they probably had simply left the country and gone to Uruguay. Istvan Tahi, a friend who had received one of two strange and confused letters Sebok sent him just prior to his disappearance, had heard of Kele. Tahi sent Kele Sebok's letter. Kele promptly wrote back saying that Sebok had written his letter under "evil pressure" and afterward had been murdered. Kele then gave a detailed description of where Sebok was buried, about one hundred feet from his house. The police easily located Sebok's body where Kele had told them to look, and they soon located Kandiko in another provincial town. Kandiko confessed to forcing Sebok to write the letters, to shooting and burying him, and then stealing his valuables.[40]

When Kele was tested at Leipzig University, Professor Hans Driesch and his colleagues classified him as an "extraordinary psychic" and "classic clairvoyant." And a few years before Kele died in 1957, Dr. Karlis Osis, then at Duke University's parapsychology laboratory, examined his diagnostic abilities by sending him samples of writing. Kele is reported to have successfully described the writers' temperaments and situations. Yet despite such endorsements and the many stories of his revelations, Kele always denied that he was a clairvoyant. He repeatedly asserted, "I am only a good psychologist."

In addition to such reports from urban areas, United States

newspapers in the 1920s and 1930s occasionally published stories about psychic sleuths in rural areas around the world. For example, according to the *Chicago Tribune* of October 15, 1925, Sigrid Schultz, a schoolteacher and medium in Bernburg, Germany, was put on trial, charged with occultism. Townspeople protested so strongly on her behalf that the trial was delayed for two years. Defense witnesses testified how she had helped them recover stolen geese, sheep, linen, and jewelry. And the *Milwaukee Journal* for July 9, 1936, contained a half-page article by A. B. MacDonald reporting an Ozark "Mystery Woman" in Roaring River, Missouri—Jean Wallace—who was able to counsel her neighbors and the sheriff successfully on where to look for missing objects.

An especially notable rural case from this period was a Canadian episode involving the Vienna-born mentalist Maximillian Langsner.[41] Dr. Langsner claimed he had studied with Sigmund Freud in Vienna and then journeyed to India, where he received his Ph.D. degree from the University of Calcutta. Langsner, who then resided in Vancouver, British Columbia, claimed many past psychic successes in solving crimes during his days in the Orient. His obituary stated that "he had solved mysteries for the Shah of Persia, the King of Egypt, and had helped the British government in Asia."[42]

In 1928, Langsner was consulted by Inspector William Hancock of the Provincial Police Department at Edmonton, Alberta, who had reached an impasse in his attempt to solve a quadruple murder on the Mannville farm of Mrs. Henry Booher. Hancock had charged her son Vernon Booher with the crime, but Booher gloated that he would not be convicted without evidence of the rifle or his confession. According to the reports, Langsner went to Edmonton and silently sat near Vernon Booher's cell for five hours, refusing to exchange any words with Booher. He then went to Inspector Hancock and drew a sketch describing where the rifle could be found in a clump of bushes about five hundred feet from a farmhouse. They drove to the Booher property and found the rifle where Langsner said it would be. Soon after he was confronted with Langsner and the rifle, Booher confessed and was duly tried, found guilty, and hanged.

A remarkably similar Canadian case took place in Beechy, Saskatchewan. On December 10, 1932, an off-duty Royal Canadian Mountie, Constable Carey, went to an entertainment featuring a Professor Gladstone, who billed himself as "The Phenomenal Mind Reader." Carey and the audience were astonished when Gladstone focused on a man in the audience, Bill Taylor, and said Taylor was thinking of his friend Scotty McLauchlin. Gladstone announced that McLauchlin had been brutally murdered and that he saw blood on the snow. Gladstone then turned and pointed at Carey, boldly stating that Carey would be the one to find the body and that Gladstone would be with him when he did. All were stunned. McLauchlin, a popular figure in the community, had mysteriously disappeared one January three years before.

Carey contacted Detective Corporal Jack Woods of the Criminal Investigation Bureau of the RCMP, and the case was reopened. Gladstone, invited to help, eventually led Woods to the buried body, and so shocked McLauchlin's partner Schumacher with his knowledge of the murder's details that Woods was able to obtain a confession from him. Schumacher was sentenced to a long term at Prince Albert's Penitentiary.[43]

Not all the stage mentalists who became psychic detectives during this period were obscure performers in remote regions. One Czechoslovakian psychic entertainer who became particularly well-known in England and who claimed numerous successes informally working with police in Europe was Frederick Marion (born Josef Kraus). Marion is one of the few stage performers who allowed his abilities to be extensively tested by several prominent psychical researchers.[44] According to the *London Forum* of June 1934, Marion's abilities led to the conviction of a man police suspected of having murdered his brother in the town of Ulm (Württemberg). Marion had visualized the murder and "saw" the man being attacked from behind with an ax, which was later tossed into a pond. Police reportedly then located the ax in the pond Marion had described, after which the suspected brother made a full confession.[45]

Marion discusses several of his criminal cases in his autobiography, *In My Mind's Eye*, but corroborative details are scanty. More impressive, however, is the reproduction of the text of a document confirming Marion's successful testing at the Apeldoorn Depot of the Royal Dutch Constabulary on November 17, 1930. The formal statement is signed by the officers who were present, including the depot commandant, Major A. P. H. Hoellard.[46] Marion was given a small box containing an automatic pistol in the presence of three officers who had no knowledge of the crime associated with it. He then gave a description of the crime, said the pistol had been shot three times without killing the victim, and that the suspect had a name beginning with the letter *L*. This conflicted with the testimony of an officer who had knowledge of the crime, which had occurred three years before. According to the officer, the suspect, a jealous farmer named Luttikhuizen, had fired at his wife six times, but had failed to kill her. Further examination of the facts, however, turned up that the policeman's memory had been faulty and that, indeed, only three bullets had been fired. In addition, all the other facts that could be checked fit Marion's account.

Marion wrote that "working with the police is a very thankless task." He found that if a psychic succeeded, police were "unwilling to admit that any psychic guidance is responsible," but if the psychic failed, the police would abuse him with ridicule and blame.[47] In any case, Marion felt there were important limitations to a psychic's usefulness to police: "I do *not* believe extrasensory impressions can be used evidentially in criminology. I do believe that they can be used as directives for scientific investigation, as they may well open up avenues not previously considered by the police."[48]

In marked contrast to Marion's experience with police, one of his vaudeville competitors, psychic Gene Dennis, frequently got full public credit from the police. Born in Atchison, Kansas, Eugenie Dennis's fame started in high school when she achieved some remarkable results locating lost articles.[49] At the age of fourteen, word of her abilities came to David P. Abbott, well-known among magicians as an exposer of fraudulent mediums and authors of the debunking classic *Behind the Scenes with the Mediums*.[50] Abbott always insisted that he could expose anyone with such powers as Gene Dennis claimed. He began by intending to expose her as a trickster, but after testing her for four weeks, Abbott concluded that she had "a God given ability."[51] Two years later, when she was sixteen, Abbott became Dennis's manager and set up a tour for her through the western states, which turned out to be an enormous success.

During her travels, she reportedly helped police in several states with minor cases. She traced fifteen stolen bicycles in Joplin, Missouri. She gave police officers in Chillicothe, Missouri, the address of a house in St. Louis where they could catch a parole violator. In Omaha, Nebraska, she was credited with the recovery of twenty-three vanished diamonds.[52] According to Gene's mother, her exploits in the West "brought her more than 800,000 letters asking for help in finding lost persons and articles and for assistance in locating oil wells and gold mines."[53] Her fame grew so great that in late 1922, when she was but sixteen, Gene Dennis reportedly signed a three-year movie contract (for the then whopping figure of $52,000 per year) with the Corono Pictures Corporation in Wichita, Kansas.[54]

At the age of seventeen, Dennis created a sensation in New York City when she was tested by top officials of the police department including Deputy Commissioner Joseph Faurot. Case after case was put to her, and, according to the *New York Times* of February 28, 1924, "for two hours Miss Eugene Dennis amazed the officials by recounting information that had never left the department files." It was reported that she further demonstrated her abilities for a reporter present by describing his relatives and friends and reciting the text of his will which was "locked up in a place to which she had no possible access." And when she told Commissioner Faurot that she would be happy to cooperate with the police during her stay in New York, he told the *Times* that "he would avail himself of the offer and expressed the hope that some of the cases which detectives have been unable to solve may be cleared up." Two days later, another story appeared, this time telling of Gene Dennis's help given to a detective agency "in obtaining a clue to stolen jewels valued at several hundred thousand dollars." According to the story, "Miss Dennis described all the circumstances of the robbery, gave the names of three persons implicated in it, and confirmed the belief of a detective that he was working on the wrong clue."[55]

Dennis's name hit the papers again in March when Mrs. Mary Foley brought charges against Gene and her mother for fortune-telling. Mrs. Foley claimed Gene had demanded and received a payment of twenty-five dollars for what turned out to be misinformation about the whereabouts of Mrs. Foley's son, who had disappeared but later returned.[56] Gene defended herself saying that she had not demanded the fee and said she never made positive statements but always referred to her intuitions as "guesses," since she realized she was sometimes wrong. *The New York Times* published an editorial about the case saying that the whole episode demonstrated the city's credulity.[57]

Though the editorial asserted that Gene Dennis was not really psychic and that the police wasted their time on her, it also defended her by saying that "to call her a fortune-teller strains the definition of that word in all except sternly judicial minds." To the surprise of many, when they appeared in court, she and her mother were accompanied not only by Hereward Carrington, a prominent psychical researcher who endorsed Gene's powers, but also by Harry Houdini, the great magician and debunker of psychic sham.[58] Also there to testify on her behalf that she had aided police in locating missing persons was Police Captain John Ayers of the department's Missing Persons Bureau. The judge, taking all this into account and saying that he felt Gene had been exploited for commercial gain, fined Gene and her mother each twenty-five dollars, a very lenient judgment given that the maximum sentence could have been two hundred dollars and six months in jail.[59]

Her stage performance consisted simply of answering questions asked by people in the audience. In 1922, David Abbott wrote a brief description to his friend Joseph F. Rinn, another renowned magician and a renowned debunker of supernatural pretensions. Rinn reprinted the letter in the memoir of his debunkings: "Miss Dennis puts on a mental act. Many of her answers appear miraculous. No doubt you will hear more of her as time goes on if she does not go into tricking. She is not a medium or a spiritualist, but a good percentage of her answers appear miraculous. Now mind you, she does not get all the lost articles or people. Maybe one in five or ten. Some she tells entirely wrong."[60] On the surface, this may seem a tepid endorsement, but given the reputation of Abbott and Rinn as debunkers, this acknowledgment that Gene Dennis was not "into tricking" and that she got what appeared to be miraculous hits with her guessing "a good percentage" of the time, is remarkable praise indeed.

Gene Dennis continued her tours and frequently became involved with police cases. One of the most publicized took place during her 1934 tour of England when she became involved with a sensational crime known as the "No. I Brighton Trunk crime." On June 17, a luggage clerk at the Brighton railway station discovered a trunk containing a woman's torso. It had been deposited in the cloakroom on Derby Day, eleven days before. Though the crime was never solved, Gene gave an estimate of the age and height of the victim and said she was pregnant. This was confirmed by the postmortem examination of the eminent pathologist Sir Bernard Spilsbury. She also predicted that another crime would be uncovered related to this one. A few weeks later, after a house-to-house search, a second trunk containing another corpse was found in a locked and empty lodging house.[61] Over the next ten years, Gene Dennis continued to perform occasionally in theaters but also reportedly acquired many well-known film stars and celebrities as private clients. She died in Seattle, Washington, on March 8, 1948. She was only forty-one.[62]

In marked contrast to the flamboyant, young, and attractive Gene Dennis was her contemporary, Mrs. Florence Sternfels. Known publicly merely as Florence, this psychic sleuth was a plump and warmhearted grandmother who worked with police without pay for over forty years. Mary Ellen Frallic, secretary of the American Psychical Institute,[63] claimed that Sternfels "has probably read more people and solved more crimes, in cooperation with the police, than any medium who ever lived."[64] Florence was held in high esteem in her small community of Edgewater, New Jersey, where she lived in a storybook house overlooking the Hudson River.

Edgewater's Mayor Henry Wissell frequently recommended her services to police in other communities, as did Chief of Police Edward Pickering, who confirmed that her help had been sought not only by agencies in the United States but from foreign countries.[65] According to Police Chief Robert Fink, who worked with her on a Boardman, Ohio, case in 1963, she even corresponded with England's Scotland Yard and France's Sûreté.[66] Florence also claimed she had solved thefts for insurance companies and private investigators.

Her public endorsements by police officials were quite remarkable. In 1964, Edgewater's Police Commissioner John A. Nash said, "Florence has helped police in New Jersey for over thirty years." And Captain John Cronin of New York's Missing Persons Bureau was quoted as saying, "I've known Florence twenty-five years. She's right seventy-five percent of the time."[67] Perhaps her most unusual indirect endorsement was by her telephone company. Though the Bell Telephone Company had a policy against such listings, Florence so personally impressed the company's manager when she told him where he had misfiled some lost papers, she was allowed to be listed in their Manhattan and New Jersey directories simply as "Florence, Psychic."

One man who perhaps should have heeded Florence's counsel was a notorious New York gangster Dutch Schultz. According to Sternfels, Schultz visited her for a reading on October 21, 1935. She said she did not like his manner with her and told him so. Nevertheless, she warned him to stay out of Newark. He apparently ignored her advice, for two days later she read on the front page that he was killed in the back room of a Newark bar.[68]

During World War II Sternfels was involved with two military cases. On one occasion, she reportedly told authorities at the Army installation at Iona Island, New York, near West Point, that a worker with dynamite in his dinner pail was planning sabotage. They searched and found a worker who fit the bill.[69] Another incident from this period was related to a reporter by Colonel (then Major) Arthur Burks. Dolly Miller, the seven-year-old daughter of a marine officer at Parris Island, South Carolina, was kidnapped and brutally murdered. When Dolly was reported missing, they searched for her for weeks without success. Then Burks contacted Florence. She told him Dolly was dead and correctly described a place in a swamp where they could find her. After they found Dolly's body but came up with no clues as to who did it, Burks again contacted Florence. She then fully described the murder and named Dolly's killer as being Joe Keller. Keller was a civilian, not a marine, and he had been conspicuously and seemingly earnestly involved in the earlier search for Dolly. When Keller was confronted with Florence's detailed description, he confessed. He was tried and sentenced to life imprisonment.[70]

Testimony to Florence's successes is abundant. Lieutenant Nathan Allen, head of detectives for the Bergen County, New Jersey, Prosecutor's Office, said she correctly identified the first name and initial of the last name of an employee who had stolen a purse with a diamond in it.[71] Police Chief Gifford Whitmore of Kinnelon, New Jersey, in 1964 told a reporter, "Florence was correct in all the information she gave us." This was in regard to the case of Dr. Phoebe Dubois, seventy-nine, who fell in the woods and died of exposure. According to the report, police searched unsuccessfully for her for fifteen days until Florence told them precisely where Dr. Dubois could be found, even correctly mentioning that the missing woman would have ten dollars rolled up into a ball on her person.[72]

Police Captain George F. Richardson, former assistant chief of police for Philadelphia, told of a case of two missing boys from another city in Pennsylvania. Florence had told the police there that the boys could be found at a Philadelphia street address. The police searched but found no such street existed, so they returned home frustrated and convinced Florence had sent them on wild-goose chase. Florence, however, felt so certain she was right that she went to Philadelphia at her own expense and there met Captain Richardson. Luckily, Richardson remembered that such a street used to exist but that the name had been changed, so they checked old street maps. They went to the location Florence had indicated and found the boys.[73]

Florence was consulted on two unusual cases during the last months before she died. Police Chief Robert Fink of the Boardman Township in Ohio wrote of fruitlessly searching for fifteen months for the whereabouts of seventeen-year-old Carol Ann, who had disappeared in August of 1963. Skeptical but desperate, he and his wife went to see Florence on November 8. She asked him if the name Marge meant anything. He could only recall that a sign near the place of Carol's disappearance had said "Marge's." Florence told him Carol was alive and well and that he would have word of her in less than two weeks. Captain Fink thought it was all nonsense, assuming that since they had heard nothing from Carol in fifteen months, word in the next weeks was unlikely. Nonetheless, he marked the date "November 22" on his calendar. On November 23, he was telephoned by Carol's girlfriend, who he had forgotten was called Marge. Marge had just received a letter from Carol in California, explaining how and why she had left and that she was now married and had a new baby boy.[74]

The second case concerned the whereabouts of missing ten-year-old Mary Ott. Interviewed for Baltimore's *News American* on July 24, 1964, Florence gave Peter Schneider and Mitchell Clogg a description of Mary's location, which the police ignored. After the police found the child on September 15, 1964, Peter Schneider wrote a follow-up article pointing out that Florence's correct description of the location should have been heeded and would have saved the searchers six weeks.[75]

According to her obituary in the *New York Times*, Florence, born in Fishkill, New York, died on April 19, 1965, at the age of seventy-four. She quietly lived in Edgewater most of her life, where she offered the public readings for one dollar. Her door was open and she had a sign outside that said simply "Florence, Psychometrist. Walk In." People came for her meetings, usually starting about 8 P.M. and sometimes going on, with her giving readings, until 2 A.M. She said she was neither a fortune-teller nor a spiritualist. "In fact," she said, "if I ever saw a real ghost, I think I'd faint from sheer fright."[76]

Even the Soviet Union has had its psychic detectives. The great psychic entertainer Wolf Messing, who became a superstar in Russia, was reportedly an occasional sleuth. Messing, born in the small Jewish town of Gora Kalvaria in Poland in 1899, toured most of the world's major capitals demonstrating his remarkable abilities as a hypnotist and mind reader. In 1939, just after Hitler's army invaded Poland, Messing fled to the Soviet Union. Three years later he was so successful as a performer there that it is reported that he was able personally to buy and present two fighter planes to the Soviet air force.

According to his autobiography, *About Myself,* published in the Soviet Union in 1965,[77] Messing was able, rather like Walter Gibson's fictional creation, the Shadow, to "cloud men's minds" through a mysterious hypnotic ability. According to Messing, Josef Stalin twice successfully tested Messing's incredible claim that he could control the thoughts of others and make them see what he wished them to see.[78] Despite general hostility to claims of the paranormal among Soviet scientists during this period, Dr. Nikolai Semenov, Russia's Nobel Prize–winning chemist, in 1966 wrote in *Science and Religion:* "It is very important to scientifically study the psychic phenomena of sensitives like Wolf Messing."[79]

According to writer Vladimir Reznichenko, during his long career, Messing "shed light on a number of involved criminal cases."[80] The best known is said to have taken place prior to World War II and concerned Poland's wealthy Count Czartoryski. His family jewels were missing, and police and detectives had fruitlessly searched for them for months. Count Czartoryski requested Messing's help and had him flown to his castle. Messing asked to see the room of a small boy, the son of one of the servants. Inspecting the boy's room and toys, Messing asked the count to have the child's large toy bear opened up. Cut open, it revealed all sorts of pieces of glass bottles, Christmas-tree ornaments, and the missing family jewels. Attracted by anything that glittered, the little boy had apparently packed all these shiny objects into the stuffing of his hear, including gems worth 800,000 zlotys. According to the story, Messing was offered a reward of 250,000 zlotys but refused it. Instead, he asked the count to use his influence in the Polish government to abolish a law that infringed on the rights of Jews. Within weeks, the law was removed.[81]

Finally, some mention should be made of Erik Jan Hanussen (born Hirschel Steinschneider). Hanussen was perhaps the most villainous psychic in this century. Stage hypnotist, mentalist, occultist, and charlatan, Hanussen became highly influential among leading members of Germany's Nazi party. According to Adolf Hitler's biographer John Toland, Hanussen even gave Hitler some early private lessons in oratory. Perhaps Hanussen received the greatest international publicity over his prediction of the 1933 Reichstag fire. Hanussen became enormously successful and powerful. Frequent newspaper attention was given to his opulent fourteen-room "Palace of Occultism" in Berlin and to his lavish white yacht, which the press called The Yacht of Seven Sins. There he lavishly (and orgiastically) entertained many of the notorious but powerful Nazi elite. And there he was able to learn much about their sexual secrets and private intrigues, knowledge that he used to assist his own rise to power.

Incredibly, by 1932, Hanussen, who was himself Jewish, had his own troop of twenty-five Nazi storm trooper bodyguards and sometimes even dressed in a storm trooper uniform, complete with swastika armband. This "Rasputin of the Reich," as he sometimes called himself, apparently pressed his luck (and his blackmail efforts) too far. On March 24, 1933, four SA men snatched him away between performances at the Scala theater. He was taken to the woods about forty-five miles south of Berlin and shot five times. His body was found thirteen days later, decomposing and partly eaten by animals.

Earlier in his career, Hanussen became involved in several episodes of psychic detection. He joined the Austrian army in 1914, and by the time he attained the rank of sergeant in 1917 had achieved some fame as a hypnotist and dowser. He was said to have found about one hundred springs in mountain areas where water was scarce, and he reportedly solved a murder in the army camp by hypnotizing the suspects.[82] After deserting from the army in late 1917, he changed his name from Steinschneider to Hanussen and began his career as a vaudeville entertainer.

Initially merely an above-average performer, he eventually gained national publicity by revealing the presence of an embezzler in a large Berlin banking corporation. According to some reports in the press, Hanussen accused the embezzler in a face-to-face confrontation, and the culprit broke down and confessed.[83] Another, probably more accurate version,[84] is that Hanussen learned from a friend about the embezzler's stashing of money in a steam tunnel below the Austro-Hungarian mint's print shop. Hanussen then went to the police and offered to locate the stolen money through his psychic powers. He led them to the money, without divining the name of the thief, and was given a reward of four thousand kronen plus a letter of thanks. In this version of the affair, the embezzler subsequently confessed.

Hanussen later became famous throughout Europe, especially as a result of the immense international publicity for his trial in 1930 on charges of fraud in Czechoslovakia. Hanussen performed several demonstrations of his seemingly psychic abilities for the jury. Among his feats he located a key hidden on an outside window ledge and "read" the contents of folded billets. On May 27, 1930, the jury acquitted Hanussen, and the judge dismissed all charges against him in his 131-page opinion.

In September 1958, a remarkably similar trial took place in a Berlin courtroom. Gerhard Belgardt, a mentalist who billed himself as "Hanussen II, Germany's No. 1 Mind Reader," was charged with fraud. This psychic detective had obtained money from clients to whom he claimed to give news about missing relatives. Like Hanussen, Belgardt demonstrated his ability at reading questions apparently secretly written by six courtroom spectators on folded papers that were then handed to the judge. The judge ruled that his claim to being a mind reader had a certain validity and dismissed the case.[85]

What are we to make of such extraordinary reports? On the one hand, these cases are qualitatively striking and seem to have no apparent "normal" or alternative explanations. It is understandable that many writers have viewed them as convincing evidence for psychic powers. Scientists, however, insist that evidence should be of a strength equal to the claim being made. They insist that such extraordinary claims demand more than ordinary proof.

It must be remembered that evidence is always a matter of degree and that all these tales are based mostly on anecdotal reports. Their validity *as scientific evidence* depends upon human testimony, and psychologists who study human behavior recognize that perception and memory are frequently filled with error. This substantially reduces the value of such case reports for scientists. However, many researchers think it would be foolish to dismiss these cases completely just because as scientific evidence they are weak or lightweight. Instead, those scientists have tried to find ways to produce and examine stronger and even quantitative evidence for psychic abilities. We will consider the results of those efforts in the next chapter.

THREE

Science Fact or Science Fiction? The Search for Legitimacy

Because claims of psychic detection have always met with varying degrees of skepticism and even outright denial, psychics have always had to find ways to gain acceptance or legitimacy for their claims. To do this, they have usually appealed to the dominant belief system in their culture. However, societies' criteria for truth have varied through human history and across cultures. In some times and places, the truth of a statement might be measured against an absolute truth believed to come from some divinely inspired revelation. At other times, the criteria society use to judge truth may be quite different. In our present society, for example, we may demand a scientifically controlled experiment for validation. In contrast, cunning men and wise women hired as thief catchers in the seventeenth century would normally claim their powers derived from the supernatural. This might have both advantages and disadvantages for the psychic, depending on whether he or she was perceived as being in league with God or Satan. During the Inquisition, a person claiming to possess the power of second sight ran the very real risk of being tried and executed for witchcraft.

Even in today's secular world, many spokesmen for fundamentalist religious sects contend that any involvement with occult or psychic powers is evil—whatever benefit for society may superficially seem to be present. Thus, in 1983, after psychic Greta Alexander was publicly credited by the Alton, Illinois, Police Department for helping them find the skeletal remains of murdered Mary L. Cousett, Madison County State's Attorney Don W. Weber, a fundamentalist Christian who acknowledged his own belief in psychic powers, issued a prohibition to his staff forbidding any future consultation with psychic detectives. Invoking Scripture (reading from Deuteronomy, Chapter 18, Verses 10 and 11, in a Bible he referred to as "my Oral Roberts version"), Weber said God's followers were forbidden from "using divination, or an observer of times, or an enchanter, or a witch, or a charmer, or a consulter with familiar spirits or a wizard or necromancer." He went on to say, "You shouldn't be dabbling or experimenting or doing anything on the fringe of occult powers. I don't think that, ultimately, anything good ever comes of it . . . I feel the success of this office in the courtroom is the result of the Holy Spirit, and I don't want to allow another spirit to undo any of that."[1]

Modern episodes like these are uncommon, however, and there are even some today who endorse what they call "good Christian psychics." This is apparently done in specific counterpoint to the diabolic picture put forth by Evangelicals who like to remind their followers that Satan may be everywhere, and, they often assert, nowhere more comfortably than among secular humanists and New Age advocates.

Despite the fact that the origins of psychic detection are rooted in occultism, magic, and supernaturalism, most of its proponents today seek explanations more compatible with the naturalism of modern science. Although some modern-day psychics invoke theology or metaphysics to explain their abilities, many contemporary psychic sleuths see their talents as natural skills that can be developed and perhaps ultimately understood by science. This seems to be true not only for those whose reputations stem mainly from tests in the laboratory, but also for those whose reputations come from practical successes in the field. These attitudes have research implications as well, for the psychics' own views and their attitudes toward science often determine whether or not they are willing to cooperate with those trying to assess objectively their extraordinary claims.

The fact is that the vast majority of psychic detectives and their cases have simply not been subjected to scrupulous scientific examination. It is the rare psychic (especially one who has been involved with detection) who has participated as a subject in a controlled scientific experiment. Notable exceptions include Eileen Garrett, Pat Price, Dr. Keith Harary, Dr. Alex Tanous, Gerard Croiset, Peter Hurkos, and Olof Jonsson. Not all their tests have produced positive results, however, and where laboratory evidence for psychic abilities has been presented, critics contested the objectivity and rigor of such experiments.

Whereas psychics in earlier times might have feared being branded as witches, to be tortured and killed by a hostile church's Inquisition, critics' negative sanctions today are far milder. Detractors nowadays are likely to be satisfied with calling psychics publicity seekers, frauds, or scam artists. Although this might result in litigation, as well as a loss of income or social reputation, that is a far cry from burning a psychic at the stake. So, while the rewards for being a successful psychic are probably about the same (income and fame), severity of punishment for lack of success has greatly diminished. This alone could possibly account for the apparent increase in psychic sleuths around today compared to two hundred years ago. Like many other aspects of the occult revival, the increase in modern magical practices is mainly due to much less powerful sanctions against them from orthodox religious communities. [2]

But religious fundamentalists are not the only social faction antagonistic to even such purportedly socially beneficial uses of occultism. Dogmatism can assert itself in the name of science. On December 10, 1982, the Committee for the Scientific Investigation of Claims of the Paranormal (CSICOP), a Buffalo (New York)–centered group that some equally zealous critics have described as a "New Inquisition" defending a dogmatic "Scientism,"[3] held a press conference blasting police departments for their use of psychic detectives. With no evidence offered indicating that these "skeptical inquirers" had contacted any of the police departments who used psychics to ask on what basis they had made their decisions to engage a psychic, CSICOP "issued a strong statement" criticizing them for using psychics "without any evidence that they are effective."[4] The press release goes on to quote CSICOP's chairman, Professor Paul Kurtz, as asserting that "there is no hard data that self-proclaimed psychics have been able to help detectives in unearthing criminals or lost persons."[5] Note Professor Kurtz's more restrained reference to "no hard data" as opposed to the initial charge that the police blindly acted "without any evidence." Presumably, too, CSICOP set itself up as the arbiter for just exactly what data we should consider to be "hard." These guardians against what they apparently prejudged to be irrationality went on to decry: "Calling in the occult to assist in what should be serious, important work, is a step back into the Middle Ages, and is dismaying to witness in today's enlightened world."[6] Going even further, a Texas anti-pseudoscience offshoot of CSICOP issued a press release on April 27, 1983, in which a psychology professor, Dr. Dennis McFadden, asserted: "Psychic crime-solvers often misidentify persons as being murderers, and innocent people's reputations are damaged."[7] No specific evidence to support this charge of frequent malpractice by psychics is given here, nor are we given any comparison rates for miscarriages of justice that have resulted from conventional police practices.

Between the extremes of religion and scientism, the True Believers and True Disbelievers, the more agnostic path of skepticism (doubt rather than denial) has been represented by the advocates for psychical research. Contrary to common belief, the British and American Societies for Psychical Research have no corporate views. Many well-known critics as well as proponents of psychic phenomena have numbered among these organizations' members.[8] For an objective assessment of the claims of our psychic detectives, it will be helpful to look first at some of the key ideas and methods developed by these early investigators.

Psychical research has generally concerned itself with the study of allegedly *paranormal* rather than *supernatural* phenomena. Whereas the term "supernatural" is essentially a theological/philosophical term that refers to miraculous intrusions into the materialistic universe—e.g., by the intervention of a deity or spirit—the idea of the "paranormal" refers to processes and laws that are observable in nature, but which have not yet been scientifically explained (but are not scientifically unexplainable). Thus, psychic functioning is seen as an unexplained biological sense, rather than necessarily communication with a spirit world. Unfortunately, critics of psychic research have intentionally and unintentionally blurred the distinction between the supernatural and the paranormal. For their own purposes, they have used "paranormal" to refer to any public beliefs generally considered wild, crazy, or tinged with the supernatural.[9] Such semantic confusion has led to a situation where psychic research has been denounced by both scientific and religious fundamentalists.[10]

The modern scientific approach to psychic phenomena is a child of the scientific and technological evolution that took place in the late nineteenth and early twentieth centuries. The purely scientific field of study dealing with the claims of psychical research, especially through controlled laboratory and quantitative studies, is called *parapsychology*. This name originated with psychologist Dr. William McDougall in the mid-1920s[11] and was popularized starting in the mid-1930s through the writings of McDougall's protégé Dr. Joseph Banks Rhine.[12] Unfortunately, the label "parapsychologist" is freely used by many so-called students of psychic phenomena who have no relevant scientific credentials whatsoever.[13] This badly misleads the general public in that many prominent so-called parapsychologists, who write books on the subject and appear on television talk shows, simply adopt the label without credentials. Many persons claiming to be psychic detectives also call themselves parapsychologists, even though very few of these psychics have credentials that would allow them membership in the Parapsychological Association. Also, many public psychics—especially many psychic detectives—claim to have been tested by parapsychologists when in fact no qualified investigator has examined their claims of psychic powers.

Dr. J. B. Rhine introduced the term *Extra-Sensory Perception* in his classic 1934 book of that title.[14] Soon commonly shortened to ESP, it describes any means of knowing outside the channels of normal sensory-motor communication. Whether or not such extraordinary channels for communication exist is far from resolved among scientists.[15] But there is some evidence for a growing acceptance of ESP among many scientists, despite continuing strong opposition from psychologists.[16]

Rhine divided ESP into three areas: *telepathy* (direct mind-to-mind communication), *clairvoyance* (knowing about something elsewhere in space), and *precognition* (knowing about the future). In addition to ESP, Rhine later added the concept of *psychokinesis* (usually shortened to PK), which refers to a direct influence of the mind upon matter (as in experiments which report that freely tossed dice can be influenced by a subject's volition). As a practical matter, it is often difficult to know which of these four processes is occurring. For example, if a psychic tells a policeman something about a homicide, is she "seeing" the scene of the crime through clairvoyance or is she simply looking into the mind of the policeman and "reading" his thoughts via telepathy? To avoid some of this confusion, in 1942 parapsychologists B. P. Weisner and R. H. Thouless suggested that the theoretically more neutral term *psi* (pronounced "sigh") be used as a term that lumped ESP and PK together.[17] Today, parapsychologists commonly use the term *psi* in this manner. So shall we, but keep in mind the distinction between telepathy and clairvoyance, for, as we shall see, it may have special significance for our understanding of what psychic detectives may be doing.

Many proponents of psychic detection, especially popular writers and many television presentations on the subject, have greatly overstated the scientific acceptance of the evidence offered by parapsychology. In a recent manual for law enforcement on the use of psychics in criminal investigations, for example, the authors state that "considering the evidence for psychic phenomena . . . it is obviously far more unreasonable to deny its existence and validity than what many consider the 'unreasonable' belief in psychic phenomena."[18] But is such doubt "unreasonable"? Has the scientific case been convincingly made for ESP?

The fact of the matter is that although a serious scientific case for psi does exist, the general scientific community has remained unconvinced. Nowhere is this antagonism from mainstream science more sharply found than in the National Research Council (NRC) study *Enhancing Human Performance: Issues, Theories, and Techniques,* released on December 3, 1987, and published by the National Academy of Sciences.[19] This report included a section on parapsychology that purported to examine the best arguments and evidence put forward by parapsychologists for the existence of psi. The study harshly concluded that it found "no scientific justification from research conducted over a period of 130 years for the existence of parapsychological phenomena."[20]

Unfortunately, many scientists critical of psi have probably exaggerated their own objectivity, the credulity of psi's scientific proponents, and have confused opposition to psi with opposition to parapsychology itself.[21] The most informed researchers in parapsychology are actually rather conservative and frequently quite skeptical. Contrary to apparently widespread popular opinion, by no means all parapsychologists believe in the reality of psi. Though most parapsychologists may personally believe psi exists, most do not think that the scientific case for psi has been established beyond any reasonable doubt.[22] In fact, the official position of the Parapsychological Association is that the existence of psi is still a hypothesis and not a proven fact.[23]

In general, psychical research has concerned itself with two types of extraordinary events, those that occur as *spontaneous phenomena* (in natural or field settings, usually unexpectedly) and *laboratory phenomena* (which are experimentally produced under carefully controlled and usually somewhat artificial conditions). Laboratory experiments conducted in the hope of producing significant paranormal results probably fail more often than they succeed. Far greater success rates are claimed for some of the newest experimental protocols, but this is still being hotly debated.

On the other hand, subjective reports of spontaneous paranormal experiences are remarkably common and may actually be on the increase. Polls in the United States, Italy, England, Iceland, and Hong Kong all indicate high rates of psychic experiences.[24] Impressed by the quantity of such reports, psychical researchers in the late 1800s began compiling case reports from the general public. Great Britain's Society for Psychical Research in 1894 conducted a *Census of Hallucinations* that included interviews with 17,000 persons. And in Durham, North Carolina, the Foundation for Research on the Nature of Man (the successor to Duke University's famous Parapsychology Laboratory), has more than 14,000 cases on file.[25] So there seems to be an almost unlimited supply of reports of spontaneous psychic phenomena, and researchers have accumulated vast data bases of them for study. It is important to remember that experimental laboratory studies on psychic phenomena were largely initiated to obtain greater insight and understanding of such reports. Though the modern scientific debate has properly been mainly around the experimental laboratory studies, we should not lose sight of their conceptual background, which lies in the reports of spontaneous cases. We should also keep in mind that even if all reports of spontaneous paranormal phenomena turn out to be due to human error and fraud, their surprising frequency and pattern remain a mystery in need of scientific explanation.[26]

Because most parapsychologists recognize the scientific demand that extraordinary claims like those for psi need a commensurately higher level of proof than do ordinary claims, most of their work has been confined to the laboratory, to the neglect of spontaneous phenomena. A major exception is found in the analyses of Dr. Louisa E. Rhine, Dr. J. B. Rhine's wife and co-worker, who largely concentrated her own research efforts on reports of spontaneous psi. She felt that "they can give tentative hints on which the slower methods of experimentation can capitalize." She also noted that for those who believe they have had psi experiences, case studies can be examined to find such hints or insights into the psi process. Nonetheless, she recognized their limitations and reminded us that "case studies must always be peripheral. They never *prove* anything by themselves. They only suggest."[27]

Though there have been a few experimental efforts to study the accuracy of psychic detectives (studies we shall soon examine in detail), almost all the information we have about psychic sleuths comes from spontaneous case studies. The need to concentrate our attention on such field studies raises special methodological issues, especially between those trained in the physical rather than the social sciences. This is especially true among psychologists, where we find many hostile critics of alleged psychical phenomena. Most *experimental* psychologists, identifying with the so-called hard-science tradition, insist on the need for optimum controls. Because they wish to avoid interpretations that might be based on error or fraud, many such scientists simply dismiss most—if not all—evidence from spontaneous cases as unworthy of (too weak for) serious scientific attention. However, many *clinical* psychologists, like most other social scientists (such as sociologists and anthropologists), come from a tradition that regularly deals with spontaneous or non-experimental human phenomena. These scientists seem generally more willing to consider and weigh the kind of "soft" data traditionally found in psychical research. On the one hand, reports of spontaneous paranormal phenomena are especially difficult to validate because of the constant possibility of erroneous interpretations based on coincidence, poor observation, faulty memory, and deliberate fraud. On the other hand, critics of laboratory studies argue that psi may best be observed under natural field conditions. They argue that the situation may be similar to that in zoology.[28] Ethologists have observed that animals in their normal field conditions will demonstrate behaviors one might never see them exhibit in an artificial setting such as a laboratory or a zoo. There may be similar problems in getting human subjects to produce observable psi phenomena. As has been the case in other areas of science, it may be that gains in description and theoretical understanding can—at least at first—only be obtained at some cost in precision.

Aside from the issues of fraud and perceptual error which plague reports of spontaneous psychic phenomena, a major problem that experimental work seeks to overcome is the fundamental difficulty in judging just exactly how extraordinary (and therefore perhaps due to paranormal abilities) a surprising phenomenon really is. Let's take the common example many use to argue they have had a psychic experience: getting a telephone call from someone you have not heard from in a long while right after you thought of that person. Since we don't usually keep track of the occasions we think of people and they *don't* call us, we may remember the successes and not the failures. Also, some would consider such a call a psychic "hit" even if the call came only the next hour, the next day, or maybe even the next week. We might also consider it a hit if we saw our friend on television or ran into him in the grocery store after we thought of him. In this context, almost *any* event could be considered a hit, depending on the amount of slack one is willing to cut. [29]

A better example to demonstrate the point, and one closely related to the problem with stories of psychic detection, might be a newspaper story telling of a pet lost fifty miles from home but somehow managing to find its way back. [30] Such stories suggesting a possible psychic homing ability in dogs or cats have appeared in papers many times over the years, and several parapsychologists, including the Rhines, investigated them. [31] Even if we can confirm that it is indeed the same dog or cat that appeared back at home (something not often easily done, but convincing evidence is available for some cases), should we really be surprised? We don't know how many pets are abandoned or lost fifty or more miles from home each year, but it seems likely that quite a few are. Assuming that they all start walking in random directions, we might expect a few of them actually to return to the sites from where they originated. So, if enough animals are left to roam, we should expect a few to return home. Since we don't know how many pets may be abandoned over, say, a ten-year period, we really have no rational basis to make a judgment as to just how surprised we should be if one manages to get home without any special psychic or homing powers.

The same sort of problem exists with psychic detection. Let's say many psychics regularly tell police that a missing person can be found "near water and a tree" or that a single psychic tells that same thing to many police looking for many persons over many years. Surely we would expect an occasional hit even in the absence of anything supernormal going on, just as we expect an occasional pet to find its way home. But as with the pets, we don't know how many psychics have given incorrect descriptions to police. We simply have no baseline for what is "normal" so we could make a rational judgment about what may be "paranormal." None of this is to say that we can be sure that the psychic hits we read about are merely due to chance. As one philosopher neatly put it: "Absence of evidence does not imply evidence of absence." Nonetheless, even though we should not confuse *non*proof with *dis*proof, in science the burden of proof is on the claimant. Science is not simply neutral. A verdict of "not proved" gives scientists a proper reason to reject a psychic claim. [32]

One creative early study of spontaneous psychic detection—in this case through dreams—was conducted in which researchers explicitly tried to control against the chance factors we just discussed. [33] In March of 1932, just days after the Lindbergh baby was kidnapped, Harvard psychologists H. A. Murray and D. R. Wheeler published a request in the daily newspaper for readers' descriptions of dreams relative to the kidnapping. They received over thirteen hundred (three of which the writers said had occurred prior to the kidnapping) and then categorized the dreams according to their content. After the dead child was found and the court had rendered its verdict against Bruno Hauptmann, Murray and Wheeler compared the dreams with the facts. They found that in 5 percent of the dreams reported did the baby appear to be dead, and only seven dreams suggested the actual location of the body, its nakedness and the manner of its burial. Of these seven, all described the child as dead; five had it lying in a grave, and four had it located among trees. Murray and Wheeler noted that the possibilities were limited since "the child must be (a) either dead or alive; and if dead it must be (b) either in water, above ground, or below ground; and if below ground it must be (c) either in a cellar, in an open space or in the woods." [34] Surprisingly, they concluded: "It appears that on the basis of pure chance one should expect a great many more dreams than were actually reported which combined the three crucial elements." [35] Thus the result actually suggests that some avoidance factor— something like a negative-psi factor—was operating, since only four correct dreams out of thirteen hundred is substantially *below* what we should predict if chance alone were present. [36] Just as people turn away from a gruesome view of an accident, do they also "tune out" unpleasant psychic visions?

In addition to seeking to control against the chance effect, early experimental work sought to control for the elimination of all non-psi factors (usually called "sensory leakages") that might actually produce what merely looked at first like psi phenomena. Most of these early experiments conducted by Dr. Rhine and his associates, then at Duke University, involved what are called *forced choice* tests. Subjects were asked to choose between several possible outcomes predesignated by the experimenter. Typically, subjects were asked to guess the faces of playing cards with special symbols on them: circles, squares, triangles, wavy lines, and stars. These were called Zener cards, after Dr. Karl Zener, a colleague of Dr. Rhine who suggested those particular symbols.

These experiments produced what all agreed were highly artificial test conditions, but such targets made controls and quantitative analysis relatively simple. Some successes were reported by Rhine and others, but much controversy ensued. Researchers reported that even the best subjects showed a loss of psi over time. While critics argued that this was merely the result of statistical movements toward expected chance, proponents argued that it represented a *decline effect* just as fatigue produces a decline in other kinds of performances. ESP experimenters claimed that some cases of seeming failure actually indicated success. When a subject performed consistently below what might be expected from pure chance, that indicates he somehow must unconsciously perceive the target he avoids. This the parapsychologists called *psi-missing*.

What skeptics viewed as signs of failure, proponents sometimes saw as signs of success. Parapsychologists often searched the data for indications of psi in ways that critics felt were statistically impermissible and sometimes even ludicrous. For some cases where a subject failed to name the cards correctly, evidence was reported that success could be found if one compared the guesses not to the card being targeted by the experimenter but to the card before or after the targeted card. Patterns of this sort were demonstrated to be present in the data, but such alleged *displacement effects* (as these are called) raised new issues about the statistical appropriateness of such analyses. And while parapsychologists felt they were dealing with a complex process, critics saw them as making excuses for failed results. Martin Gardner, one of psi research's sharpest critics, at one point wrote of parapsychologists' resorting to a kind of Catch-22. Gardner called it Catch-23 and said it "asserts that psi powers are negatively influenced by complexity."[37]

To explain disappointing lab results, believers have argued that the Rhine-type experiments produce highly artificial laboratory atmospheres that are rarely conducive to the production of psi. Both subjects and analysts have complained that such highly artificial and limited targets are quite unlike the spontaneous episodes found among the field reports collected by psychical researchers. Guessing cards is a far cry from a mother rescuing her child after somehow "knowing" that the child was in imminent physical danger. Much of the qualitatively most striking evidence in psychical research consists of such spontaneous and mostly unquantifiable data. Because the validity of these reports so strongly depends upon always fallible, frequently unreliable, and sometimes highly suspect human testimony, most critics simply dismiss them as mere "anecdotal evidence"; and for some critics, such reports do not even qualify as "scientific evidence" at all.

In partial answer to these complaints, parapsychologists have initiated a number of new research directions. In the early years, the focus of psi researchers had been nearly exclusively spent on trying to convince critics and those without psi experiences that psi exists. Their efforts had been geared toward creating what they hoped might be definitive demonstrations of psi's validity. Others, less concerned with such *demonstration-oriented research,* concentrated instead on *process-oriented research,* experiments that seek to establish possible correlates and conditions for the production of psi. By finding the conditions under which psi is more likely to manifest itself, they also hope to set the stage for more convincing demonstrations. Those still particularly interested in demonstration, however, have accepted the critics' challenge and have sought to design a standard experiment that could repeatedly produce psi even if conducted by skeptics.

Two types of experiments recently developed by parapsychologists are particularly noteworthy because of the high rates of repeatable success claimed for them. Over 50 percent of these experiments have obtained statistically significant psi results. The first of these, the ganzfeld (German for "entire field") procedure, was developed out of research into so-called altered states of consciousness at the dream laboratory at Maimonides Medical Center in New York.[38] In the most sophisticated of the ganzfeld experiments, the test subject is placed in a soundproofed, electromagnetically shielded, bathysphere-like room, in a comfortable position (often reclining). Halved Ping-Pong balls are placed on his or her eyes, onto which a diffused light (frequently red) is projected, and unstructured sound—such as "white noise"—is played in the subject's ears. The purpose of all this is to provide homogeneous, unpatterned sensory stimulation, the theory being that human receptivity to psi is interfered with by normal everyday sensory distractions. In another room, the experimenter selects at random a slide or videotape which is shown to a "sender" in the third room, who tries to transmit the image telepathically to the test subject. The test subject's impressions are recorded and compared with the images sent.

The second new type of experiment, called remote viewing, was the product of two physicists, Dr. Harold Puthoff and Russell Targ, who developed it in 1974 at the Stanford Research Institute (today called SRI International).[39] In the experiments, the "sender" or "beacon" is dispatched to random locations from which he (or she) tries to beam back what he is seeing to the test subject back in the lab. The subject then sketches what he is receiving, and the sketch is later compared to the actual target sites by judges (most recently through a system of computerized evaluation). According to the SRI scientists, both subjects and experimenters had no knowledge of what sites would be chosen until after the experiments were completed. Some of the SRI psychic "stars," like Ingo Swann and Pat Price, were reported to have made startling hits—far too startling to be attributed to chance—but critics have attacked the experiments for using inadequate controls to prevent cheating.

The criticisms are far from resolved, but the important point for us here about both the ganzfeld and the remote-viewing experiments is that they did not involve forced choices or artificial targets. They involved open-ended decision making by the subjects, thus following a naturalistic pattern similar to what has traditionally been reported in spontaneous cases. For that reason, these lab studies have special relevance for our appraisal of psychic detectives who are asked to perform similar tasks.

The debate about the validity of these experiments is ongoing, but there seems to be general agreement that some progress has been made. In a joint statement issued by parapsychologist Charles Honorton, the leading ganzfeld researcher, and psychologist Professor Ray Hyman, the leading critic of the ganzfeld work and a prominent member of CSICOP, the two agreed that further and improved experiments in this area should be conducted and that "there is an overall significant effect in this data base that cannot be reasonably explained by selective reporting or multiple analysis."[40] Of further significance is an admission made in the otherwise negative NRC study, *Enhancing Human Performance*, acknowledging that, for the best of the parapsychological experiments they examined, "We do not have a smoking gun, nor have we demonstrated a plausible alternative."[41] That study also recommended that work in parapsychology should continue to be monitored and enhanced by expert advice from both parapsychologists and critics.[42]

On the heels of this controversial report, in 1988 the Congressional Office of Technology Assessment (OTA) assembled a special workshop where psi researchers and their critics discussed the issues.[43] The researchers argued that this admission by the above panel constituted a vindication of their position (despite the negative conclusion drawn).[44] Psi proponents also called attention to a new statistical approach called *meta-analysis*, which has added strength to the case for psi.

Meta-analysis is a means of looking for patterns in groups of experiments rather than at individual experiments themselves, and researchers now claim that by applying it to a large group of similar experiments, they can demonstrate important consistencies and counter earlier arguments against the existence of psi.[45] Critics of the ganzfeld experiments, for example, argued that the largely successful results were invalid because experimenters were sloppy and used inadequate controls to prevent leakage or cheating. From this conclusion, one would logically expect that the more sloppy and loose the controls, the more successful the results would be.[46] In other words, the more a test subject could get away with cheating, the more he or she would cheat, and therefore the better would be his or her test scores. But applying meta-analysis to the experiments, this was surprisingly found not to be true. If test subjects were getting more opportunities to cheat, they obviously were not taking them.

In the remote-viewing experiments, meta-analysis might be used to discredit the "file-drawer" argument often posed by critics. That criticism contends that possibly only the studies which show positive results are published, while those with negative results remain unpublished and are hidden away in the experimenters' file drawers. Meta-analysis might show there would have to be literally thousands of such unpublished negative experiments to counteract the statistical results published.[47]

As noted earlier, the rigorous experimentation of the sort we have been discussing has rarely included subjects who work as psychic detectives. These controlled studies are mainly important in so far as they lend scientific credibility to everyday claims of psychic experience, including those claimed by psychic slueths. Nonetheless, a few researchers have sought to bring in experimental test conditions (with varying degrees of methodological rigor) to evaluate feats of psychic detection. In general, these reports reached negative conclusions, but it is important to note that little critical analysis has been given to these studies by those who have cited them as gospel. Whereas parapsychologists often attack one another's methods, critics of psi seem rarely publicly critical of one another. It seems both reasonable and fair to demand of critics that they apply the same rigorous scientific canons to experiments whether those report the presence or absence of psi.

The earliest of what best might be called a semi-experiment to test psychic detection was conducted in the Netherlands by a police officer, Filippus Brink.[48] Though his full 1958 report is in Dutch, Dr. Brink summarized his study in English in an article he wrote for the official journal of INTERPOL.[49] He and his police colleagues obtained the cooperation of four clairvoyants—all of whom had previously made their talents available to police, two of whom advertised their services in the press, and one of whom was internationally known.[50] The tests involved showing the psychics randomly derived photos and objects (weapons, keys, fingerprints, et cetera), which the psychics were allowed to handle. Some photos and objects were drawn from files of a criminal records office, while others were quite unconnected with criminal events. The psychic descriptions given by the four were then examined. These tests were conducted over a one-year period and were done in a wide variety of settings, including a laboratory, a criminal registry office, the clairvoyant's own waiting room, and even the living room or study of one of the experimenters. Dr. Brink and his colleagues concluded that "the results invariably proved to be nil," and had not "evinced anything that might be regarded as being of actual use to police investigation."[51] Because Brink gives us so few details of his method and analysis in this report, the strength, if not the value, of his conclusions really cannot be evaluated.

Another semi-experiment was conducted in 1984 by anchorman and reporter Ward Lucas and the investigative news team at station KUSA television in Denver, Colorado. Reporting on this effort in an article in *Campus Law Enforcement Journal*,[52] Lucas describes how a group of psychics known for their contacts with various law-enforcement agencies in Colorado agreed to give psychic descriptions in answer to questions about a dozen unsolved and solved criminal cases. The psychics asked for and were allowed to examine original evidence from these cases, such as photos, clothing, and other items. As a control group an unspecified number of Auraria College students were asked to make "wild guesses" in answers to the same questions the police asked of the psychics. Lucas reports that "each group scored according to chance."[53] Unfortunately, Lucas's article does not detail exactly how this conclusion was reached, since we are not told the basis used to establish what should be considered a chance level of performance. Presumably the psychics in this study did no better than the students. If so, that would only demonstrate that the professional psychics had neither more nor less psi than the perhaps equally psychic students. It also is quite unclear as to how hits versus misses were assessed, especially for the unsolved cases presented to the subjects.

The deservedly most widely known and carefully designed experiments testing psychic detectives were conducted by psychologist Dr. Martin Reiser and his colleagues at the Behavioral Science Services Section of the Los Angeles Police Department (LAPD).[54] The first was published in 1979 in the *Journal of Police Science and Administration.*[55] In this study, twelve psychics (eight professionals and four amateurs) looked at evidence from four crimes, two solved and two unsolved, and gave their psychic reactions to each. These reactions were then tabulated to obtain the frequency of verifiable hits in various categories. Looking at the frequency of these hits in terms of their statistical likelihood, Reiser and his colleagues concluded that "the usefulness of psychics as an aid in criminal investigation has not been validated."[56]

This study is actually very limited in terms of the scientific conclusions that can be drawn from it. Although some critics trumpeted news of this experiment as categorical evidence against the police use of psychics,[57] our conversations with Dr. Reiser indicate that he fully recognizes the limitations of his study, and the article explicitly states that "further research in this area would be desirable."[58] First, it is doubtful that this group of alleged psychics is truly a representative sample from what may be the universe of genuine psychics. The criteria for their selection can be reasonably questioned.[59] More importantly, however, we can methodologically question this study even for what it says about this group of psychics. Only 50 percent of the information provided by the psychics was deemed verifiable and was actually included in the final analysis. The information considered unverifiable included such things as statements about "accessories to the crime, lifestyle of the victim and/or suspect, and psychological traits of the victim and/or suspect."[60] Clearly, such statements might not lend themselves to *easy* verification, but they are not unfalsifiable and certainly could be useful toward the solution of a crime should they be true. But even for those statements treated as verifiable, these experimenters failed to distinguish between cases where the psychic provided incorrect information and those where no information at all was provided. Silence may not be a hit, but the study treats it the same as if it were a miss. This makes its statistical analysis questionable. In addition, by concentrating on a limited quantitative analysis, some qualitatively high psychic reports may have been undervalued. For example, in one of the crimes where a church historian was killed, the study indicates a psychic indicated his strong feeling that a church was somehow connected with the crime.

Realizing the shortcomings of his first study, Reiser decided to conduct a second experiment.[61] In this study, two groups of psychics (four in one and eight in the other) were compared to two control groups, one consisting of eleven college students, and the other of twelve homicide detectives. Again, four crimes (two solved and two unsolved) were considered by the subjects and their descriptions were scored by categories for hits much as in the first study. The results showed no statistically significant differences between the psychics, students, and detectives, and the experimenters concluded that "the data provided no support for the belief that the identified 'sensitives' could produce investigatively useful information."[62] Despite some improvements, the same criticisms we raised about the first study also apply to this one. Reiser and Klyver acknowledged this at least in part when they also concluded that "it is recognized that the samples utilized in this study are limited and may not be generalizable to all psychics or to all cases.[63] Further, proponents might argue that comparing these particular psychics to students and detectives and finding no differences may simply indicate that the students and detectives have more psychic ability than we usually assume.

It has been argued by some parapsychologists that much of the current anti-psi sentiment on the part of the mainstream scientific community is rooted in philosophical, rather than purely scientific, grounds. These advocates say that simply because psychic functioning does not fit into any known paradigm of scientific thought, the dogmatists refuse to acknowledge the validity of *any* parapsychology experiment, no matter what the result, and eagerly cite studies like the Reiser study, which is actually scientifically imperfect. But all that could change with a shift in scientific theory, just as the universe was forever changed by the discoveries of Galileo and Newton. Once the laws of physics are no longer seen to be violated by psychic functioning, advocates say, resistance would give way, and what is now seen as impossible may become highly probable.[64]

Relativity, recent developments in quantum mechanics, and theories in physics about alternative and parallel universes have introduced concepts about physical reality that assault common sense and have turned traditional materialistic science on its ear. These new theories have persuaded some physicists that psi is not only possible but likely and may even be a key to the problem of consciousness. The principal work along these lines is being done at Princeton University by the Engineering Anomalies Research Project (PEAR) under the direction of Professor Robert G. Jahn, formerly dean of Princeton's College of Engineering and Applied Science.[65]

Though most such theory has little relation to our concern with evaluating psychic detectives, one important part of such theoretical efforts for our purposes may concern the special attention they give to issues in the modern physics of time. Scientists like Professor Jahn at Princeton and especially Dr. Edwin C. May, who headed psi research at SRI International, have been particularly interested in precognition.[66] This may have special relevance to our understanding of psychic detection. Though we usually think of a psychic detective in terms of simple clairvoyance or telepathy, in fact this is seldom done in present time. The psychic detective usually claims to tell us what is seen as happening at some former time, when the crime actually took place. Thus what we seem to be dealing with are claims of *retrocognitive* psi. In fact, some psychics, like Dorothy Allison, often tell police they work with that their impressions of a past event may actually be of some present or future one. This makes falsification of their claims often impossible, but advanced theoretical ideas about time in quantum physics have been cited by some advocates as endorsement for such an empirical possibility.

The second alternative road to that of producing a scientifically convincing experiment is being pursued by some parapsychologists who merely seek a useful application for psi. The concern here is with *applied parapsychology*, or what some of its proponents have called *psionics*.[67] The history of science demonstrates that sometimes a phenomenon gains scientific acceptance even in the absence of theoretical understanding if a practical enough use exists for it. A good example is anesthesia in medicine, the physiological mechanisms for which are still largely mysterious. A small minority of parapsychologists argue that if psychic "guesses" can be shown to be practical or cost-effective, pragmatic areas like business will adopt them, and science will simply have to follow belatedly with new theories and eventual acceptance. For many advocates, this pragmatic approach is at the heart of the case for psychic criminology. If psychics are found to be useful in solving crimes, any scientific explanation for their successes may be secondary to their achievements. Similar arguments are put forward for many other areas where psychics have entered the practical marketplace. Psychics like Uri Geller and "Doc" Anderson claim to have brought great wealth to themselves and to the clients who consulted them about using psychic abilities to locate oil and minerals.[68] Some psychics, like Beverly Jaegers or Dr. Keith Harary, have reportedly made money for clients by accurate predictions in financial markets.[69] Show business has even gotten into the act. Between 1978 and 1980, psychic Beverlee Dean was on ABC's payroll, predicting viewer ratings for its new seasons' television shows.[70]

As we have seen, parapsychologists have mostly concerned themselves with laboratory experiments rather than field investigations into claims of spontaneous psi. Thus very few scientists have carefully examined the case studies of psychic detection. Most parapsychologists seem to view an emphasis on alleged applications of psi to be premature. They contend it is comparable to trying to develop a technology before any basic physics has been worked out. Though they often feel that cases of psychic detection are interesting and strongly suggestive, most parapsychologists recognize the scientific weaknesses in most of the evidence that has been put forward to validate such claims of successful sleuthing. So they, like the general critics of psi, have not shown much inclination to examine these cases. Only a very few parapsychologists, most notably Professor Hans Bender, Dr. Karlis Osis, and especially Professor W. H. C. Tenhaeff, have shown any continuing interest in psychic criminology. However, several so-called star subjects who have undergone repeated lab tests by parapsychologists—for example, Pat Price, Ingo Swann, Keith Harary, and Uri Geller—have also occasionally been asked for help with police cases.

But just as few parapsychologists have examined these episodes, criminologists have also paid scant attention to them. This is perhaps surprising, since several eminent criminologists, most notably Italy's Professor Cesare Lombroso (often called the Father of Modern

Criminology) and England's Professor D. J. West (Director of the Institute of Criminology at the University of Cambridge), were extensively involved with psychical research. But even these two scholars wrote little if anything about the interface between the psychical and criminological.[71]

In dealing with attempted practical applications of psi, such as its use in criminal investigations, there are special problems for the analyst. Participants in these psychic efforts—both clients and police—may be reluctant to reveal information to outsiders due to embarrassment, fear of publicity, or other personal motivations. The psychics themselves, in seeking to enhance their reputations, self-esteem, and incomes, may exaggerate claims and intentionally or unintentionally distort facts. Media reporters, seeking a spectacular story, may embellish accounts or repeat allegations without adequate investigation to determine their truth.

The "real world" usually presents us with different priorities than the laboratory, and in trying to evaluate such cases, scientists must avoid two opposite kinds of errors. In statistics, these are called Type I and Type II errors. Type I error occurs when we conclude something special (like psi) is happening, when in reality nothing special (merely chance) is. Type II error occurs when we think nothing special is happening, but actually some rare or infrequent event (like psi) is. Scientists critical of parapsychology are usually particularly careful to avoid a Type I error, but tend to ignore the Type II error. In dealing with a lot of sloppily recorded and clearly false cases, they assume *all* cases are false, thus perhaps throwing out the baby with the bathwater. But sometimes it may be extremely important to avoid Type II error. Take the deaths caused by Tylenol tampering in the mid-1980s, for example. If we believe that only one bottle of pills out of hundreds of thousands is poisoned, we may still act to remove all the pills from the pharmacy shelves. We don't want to make a Type II error that might kill someone, even though the odds are much against the next customer's getting a poisoned bottle. Many parapsychologists feel that the importance in finding psi is theoretically similar. In like manner, proponents of psychic criminology argue that if even one murderer might be brought to justice, even if many psychics' guesses fail, it may be good to try using them. Even if the use of psychics for criminology is a long shot, may their use not prove to be socially cost-effective? It is that question we need to examine.

FOUR

The Psychic Spectrum

I n spite of the fact that a majority of Americans feel they have experienced ESP, the two words that probably pop most frequently into the public's mind in association with professional psychics are "charlatan" and "kook."

Psychologist *and* psychic Dr. Keith Harary blames this popular image largely on movies, television, and the news media, arguing that "the images of psychic functioning that are depicted in mass media quickly lead you to believe that only very strange people have psychic experiences and abilities, or that psi is experienced by normal people only under the most bizarre circumstances."[1]

It is undeniable that the oddball stereotype of the psychic has been exploited in film and on television. Images of swarthy, smarmy swamis and white-haired, gypsy crones foretelling the future in portentous, thickly accented tones abound in the movies of the thirties and forties. But at least part of the blame for this stereotype must be laid at the feet of the psychics themselves, and it is hard at times to determine whether the movie images were art imitating life or vice versa.

The truth of the matter is that spiritualism and psychic research in general have attracted some oddball types confused about their own identities, as well as con men eager to exploit the human anxieties these fields have sought to assuage.

Tea-leaf readers, palmists, and crystal-ball gazers have traditionally donned unusual garb and have taken exotic-sounding names, like Madame Zeena or Zorah or whatever, to cultivate intentionally a "different" image. During the first half of the century, every traveling carnival had a resident psychic who dressed up like a gypsy and spoke in a foreign accent thick with mystery. It was all part of the pitch. A person claiming to possess such strange, mysterious powers usually tried to look and act the part.

Stage mentalists, too, eagerly adopted the "exotic" stereotype. Rajah Raboid, whose real name was Maurice P. Kitchen, one of the top mind readers of the 1920s and 1930s, wore a jeweled turban and claimed he had picked up his powers of second sight while traveling in mysterious India.

Internationally famous Erik Jan Hanussen cultivated a hypnotic Svengali personality on stage, as did America's premier mentalist, the dominating Joseph Dunninger. Dunninger spoke with such authority while performing that when he mispronounced a word, you thought—magicians say—that the dictionary must have been wrong.

The content of movies has changed over the years, but not the oddball-fraudulent images of the psychic. The unscrupulous con man, à la Tyrone Power in *Nightmare Alley,* has remained, although his pitch may have changed. And those "genuinely" possessing psychic powers—from Sissy Spacek in *Carrie* to the squeaky-voiced midget exorcist in *Poltergeist*—have only added to the repertoire. In many of these films, psychic powers have been depicted as a curse and a danger to those unfortunate enough to be plagued by them. Several films, such as *The Evil Mind* and *The Night Has a Thousand Eyes,* combined the two psychic types into one, having the main character start as a phony mentalist and wind up receiving true psychic "flashes." In the latter film, everything Edward G. Robinson sees is tragic, and for a while he lives in an abandoned mine shaft to avoid these visions. When he abandons his reclusive life, his visions of tragedy lead to his own death.

While lamenting the depiction of psychics in such films, Dr. Harary admits that some "people with serious psychological problems also often cast themselves as 'psychics' complete with whatever personality quirks they have learned to associate with this role as a result of their exposure to film and television fiction. These individuals may claim that the problems they have in relating to other people are purely the result of their being 'special' people, 'psychics' misunderstood by those who are less 'aware.' The strong need they feel to validate their delusions sometimes leads them to make extreme claims . . . as a means of attracting public attention."[2]

This, according to Harary, is where the so-called objective news media contributes to the distorted public image, for as the function of the news becomes increasingly to entertain, it becomes less able and willing to handle subtleties.[3] News reporters will seek out stories to amaze and confound their audiences, and if that fails, to titillate and shock with a juicy case of fraud. Outlandish claims by publicity-seeking charlatans and delusional neurotics are eagerly reproduced by the media *because* of their outlandishness.[4] Thus, in 1987, news wires carried a story that Houston police had filed harassment charges against self-styled psychic Deanna Reams, who had repeatedly called up detectives demanding they open an investigation of the death of Howard Hughes. According to Reams, the ghost of the billionaire had risen up from the ground and told her he had been murdered.[5]

The media also got some mileage out of the 1979 Chicago murder trial of Allan Showery, who confessed to murdering co-worker Teresita Basa after detectives heard the dead Ms. Basa accuse Showery by speaking through the body of another woman in her native Philippino language. Although it was speculated by some involved in the case that the "medium"—a co-worker of both Showery and Basa—had suspected Showery all along and had only pretended to be "possessed" to convince police, the media had a field day with the arcane aspects of the case.[6]

If the "con man fruitcake" image of the psychic has been promoted by the media, it is also true that the media has been responsible in recent years for helping to break the stereotype. Aside from the paranormal powers they claim to possess, the people who appear on talk shows to talk about their feats of psychic crime-solving seem to be perfectly "normal," just like the neighbors next door.

With her hair austerely pulled back, donning horn-rimmed glasses and conservative dress, Nancy M. Czetli's appearance is more stereotypical of a schoolmarm than a psychic. The forty-three-year-old mother of three and wife of the editor of a weekly Pittsburgh newspaper has appeared on numerous television and radio shows talking about her psychic police work.

Born in Warwick, New Jersey, Czetli grew up abroad—her father worked for the State Department—and although she was aware of her psychic abilities as a child, she refused to accept them for fear of being dubbed "kooky." It was only in her mid-twenties, after she began to read up on the subject, that she did decide to drop the pretense. She began lecturing to student groups, women's clubs, and police departments, and it was at one such meeting in 1976 that she later picked up a believer in Colonel Irvin Smith of the Delaware State Police. Smith asked her to work on one of his cases, and since that time, Czetli says, she has been involved in over two hundred police investigations in twenty states.[7] Not too shy to toot her own horn, Czetli claims an 80–90 percent success rate, and says that in the past fourteen years she has "provided valuable evidence in every case I've worked except three."[8] Aside from police work, she does meditation training, holistic counseling, and psychic healing for private clients.

Bill Ward of Lockport, Illinois, is another psychic who challenges the stereotype. An employee at a Lockport printing company, the rugged-looking Ward is a decorated Vietnam war hero. Ward credits his wartime experiences with triggering his psychic powers. The witnessing of so many violent deaths while serving as an Army medic, he feels, put him on "another level of consciousness." Ward, who has been deputized by several Illinois county sheriffs' offices, claims to have worked on more than four hundred cases since 1971, with 80 percent accuracy, although he admits that accuracy can vary greatly from case to case. Among the tools Ward uses to catch crooks is astrology—both the Chinese and Western varieties. By charting a person's biorhythms from his date of birth, Ward claims he can determine a person's guilt or innocence on the date of the crime in question.[9]

Greta Alexander, of Delavan, Illinois, ran a secondhand store and cleaned chickens before being struck by a bolt of lightning in 1961. Ever since then, she has had visions—sometimes of angels and the Virgin Mary, sometimes of more unpleasant things. It has been the latter that have gained the hefty, fifty-seven-year-old mother of five widespread fame as a psychic sleuth. Aided by her daughter, Greta says she handles about a hundred cases for police agencies a year, but keeps no tally of her hit rate, pointing out that she does not always get feedback from the police about the resolution of the cases on which she works.

In addition to detective work and private psychic consultations (among her clients are Debbie Reynolds and soap-opera actress Ruth Warrick), she is actively involved in charity work, especially her House of Hope, a Ronald McDonald–type home for sick children, which she supports with her income from private readings. She has also been participating in experiments with doctors concerning the psychic diagnosis of disease, by "reading" patients' palm prints. Alexander's reputation has become so widespread that the Springfield, Illinois, Convention and Visitors Bureau rates her as an area tourist attraction second only to Abraham Lincoln's home. [10]

Superstar psychic Dorothy Allison claims to have given police and the FBI valuable leads in the Son of Sam, John Wayne Gacy, and Atlanta child-murders cases, as well as the Patty Hearst kidnapping. In her twenty-two years of working with the police on hundreds of cases, she claims to have been unable to come up with clues in only five.

One of thirteen children of Italian parents who immigrated to New Jersey, Allison married at fifteen and never held a job outside her home. The short, plump Nutley, New Jersey, housewife allegedly first became aware she was psychic when she dreamed her father's sudden death before the event. Her mother, who, she tells us, was also psychic, brought her up to accept her gift as part of her life.

Allison's police work began in 1967, after she had a vision of a blond, blue-eyed boy stuck in a bent drainpipe, drowned. Nearby, she saw a school with an "8" on it. A month later, according to her autobiography, she related the dream to Nutley Police Chief Francis Buel, who told her such a boy indeed was missing. Later, the boy turned up in a drainpipe exactly as she had described. [11] Allison's blue sense keeps her busy, as she often works on five or six cases at a time. When she works, she usually takes along one or more police detective friends to "interpret" her psychic impressions.

Some policemen are more than interpreters. Phil Jordan, a deputy with the Tioga County, New York, Sheriff's Department, made national news in 1982 when he psychically pinpointed the whereabouts of lost five-year-old Tommy Kennedy, for whom police had been searching for seventeen hours. [12] Jordan, a schoolteacher before going through the police academy, has since been consulted by police departments across the country and has done work for criminal attorneys assessing prospective jurors.

Tom Macris has used his blue sense in his job as police artist with the San Jose Police Department, enabling him to put together suspect composites when information from witnesses is scanty. He believes he is psychic "only to the degree everyone is," and thinks that the intuitive part of the mind, what people normally label "psychic," is something that can be developed through practice. Macris works frequently with well-known psychic Kathlyn Rhea, sketching Rhea's impressions, and although his work is not endorsed by his own department, the duo has been used over the past ten years by several San Francisco Bay Area police departments, as well as the local office of the FBI.[13]

Before his retirement and subsequent death in 1975, Patrick Price, whose remote-viewing abilities were tested intensively at SRI in the 1970s, was police commissioner of Burbank, California. He asserted that while commissioner, he used his abilities "to track down suspects, although at times I could not confront the fact that I had these abilities, and laid my good fortune to intuition and luck."[14]

Sacramento psychic Judy Belle, forty-eight, was sworn in as a deputy coroner in 1980, although she has never officially worked in that capacity. She went through her police training as a "legal cover" so that she could handle evidence in criminal cases without jeopardizing the cases in court. The evidence she handles is dead bodies, or parts of them, from which she "experiences what the dead person saw, feels as they did when they died." She originally became aware of her psychic abilities as a child, but only developed them later, after becoming bored with her role as "Little Susie Homemaker" and enrolling in an ESP class. When a cop attending the class asked her to help out on a case, her blue sense came to the fore. "I have a cop mentality," she says.[15]

Retired detective Ray Gros, dubbed "Captain of the Kook Patrol" by his co-workers at the Torrance, California, Police Department, has written an unpublished book about his psychic experiences as a cop. He says he acquired his powers after a near-fatal car accident at the age of twenty. Early in his career, Gros had to make up reasons for how he would know beforehand what was going to happen. He limited the use of his powers on cases, however, because he was "afraid" of them. Gros worked on over a dozen cases with Dutch psychic Jan Steers, the most famous being a 1971 double homicide—the Rolling Hills Theater case—about which Steers was allegedly so accurate that he himself became a suspect. In the end, another suspect was arrested, but committed suicide before the case could come to trial.[16]

Steers is only one of a disproportionate number of psychics to hail from the Netherlands. In fact, some of the world's most famous psychic detectives are natives of that tiny country, including not only Peter Hurkos, Gerard Croiset, and Marinus Dykshoorn, but also several psychic sleuths less well-known in the United States, like Steers, Gerard Croiset, Jr., and Cor Heilijgers. Indeed, the growing phenomenon of psychic crime-busting is not confined to the United States, but is truly international in scope. Swedish psychic Olof Jonsson, who conducted telepathy experiments with astronaut Edgar Mitchell during the Apollo 14 lunar expedition, claims to have helped police solve murders in both the United States and Sweden.[17] In the 1970s, Swiss psychic Clothilde Napflin was reportedly consulted in investigations by police departments in several countries, including France. The white-haired widow's specialty was trying to locate missing persons by holding a gold ball on a chain over a map. Britain has had more than its share of seers, among them Doris Stokes, Nella Jones, Frances Dymond, Robert Cracknell, Flora MacKenzie, and Patrick Barnard. Hailed as one of Greece's greatest psychics, Maria Papapetro now lives in Los Angeles, as does Dutch-born Lotte Von Strahl, who has been consulted in numerous criminal cases, and Jamaica's Ernesto Montgomery, who claims successes in psychic espionage.[18]

With the advent of *glasnost*, increasing accounts have begun to reach the West about Soviet dabbling with psychic detectives. One Moscow psychic, fifty-three-year-old Dina Nazarenko, has received particular media attention for her assistance to Moscow police in several criminal investigations. During one recent investigation of a missing cabdriver, Nazarenko was reportedly consulted by stymied detectives after she saw the murder of the man in her coffee grounds. According to investigator Shamil Alghinin, Nazarenko accurately told him how the crime had been committed, as well as described the location where the body would be found. The Moscow psychic also provided sketches of the faces of the four murderers, which police distributed nationwide.[19]

In addition, many psychics have been summoned across international boundaries to work on cases. Gerard Croiset participated in criminal investigations in Australia, and Peter Hurkos received considerable publicity for his involvement in psychic crime-busting in Southeast Asia. Dorothy Allison claims to have worked on cases in Latin America, and Noreen Renier was recently flown to Hong Kong for consultation in a kidnapping case. Los Angeles psychic Jim Watson has reportedly been psychically successful in Japan, appearing on Japanese television in conjunction with a case in which he reputedly located several bodies on Mount Fuji.

Considering that there are several hundred professional psychics in the United States alone who claim to have participated in criminal investigations, the number across the globe must be closer to one thousand. In the last ten years or so, many of these psychics have begun networking and forming groups devoted to crime-solving, apparently on the principle that two or more psychic heads are better than one.

One such group is the Psychic Detective Bureau, also known as the U.S. Psi Squad. Founded by licensed private investigator Beverly Jaegers in 1971, the Bureau is headquartered in St. Louis and has twenty-five members in one state and two regional groups.[20] Daughter of a policeman and mother of six, Jaegers took up ESP research in 1962, after reading about Russian experiments. Jaegers believes that ESP is a skill that can be learned and does not accept spiritualists, mediums, or occultists in the group. The Bureau does not accept cases unless asked by the police, and does not seek publicity, although it has received quite a bit over the past nineteen years. Lately, Jaegers has de-emphasized her police work and has devoted more attention to predicting business trends and has told us that she has now mostly retired.

The North Texas Parapsychology Association, based in Richardson, Texas, was formed in 1984 by John Catchings. The group, which consists of five psychics, meets irregularly with police seeking their aid. Catchings, who was featured in 1981 and 1982 segments of *That's Incredible* for his success in finding dead bodies, has worked on cases from coast to coast and claims to have helped send at least fifteen people to jail since 1980. Like Greta Alexander, Catchings alleges his powers are the result of being struck by lightning.[21]

Professional Psychics United in Berwyn, Illinois, headed by Edward S. Peters, was founded in 1977 and claims 350 members in eleven state groups.[22] Aside from its main objective—helping police solve crimes—the group will also provide psychic rescue teams to assist locating missing persons, do research, sponsor psychic fairs, and conduct lectures on ESP.

Los Angeles's Mobius Group, the brainchild of Stephan Schwartz, former special assistant to the Chief of Naval Operations, was formed as a nonprofit corporation in 1977. Working with groups of seven to eleven psychics, Mobius is primarily a research group trying to explore the practical applications of psi and expanding the boundaries of human potentialities. Although detective work has only been an occasional sideline for Mobius, the group has worked fourteen cases.[23] Although he feels they were "wildly successful" in many of the cases, Schwartz decided to phase out criminal work three years ago, due primarily to police methodology. "We're a parapsychology group and are interested in testing," Schwartz says. "We've tested thousands of psychics. But testing is a very specific process. The police don't do meticulous enough research for our standards."[24] That is too bad, Schwartz adds, because "properly done, the use of psi would be quite fruitful for law enforcement." Lately Schwartz, who co-produced a 1989 prime-time television show for ABC called *The Psychic Detectives,* has turned Mobius's efforts to locating lost archaeological treasures psychically.

Many other groups have come and gone over the years: the Society for Psychic Investigation, the San Diego Sheriff's Psychic Reserve, the Nick Nocerino Group, the Canadian Society of Questors, the Canadian Psychic Systems Research Group. Most recently in 1988, Los Angeles psychic Fred Hansen founded United Sensitives of America in a similar effort to pool psychic resources into a network to help law enforcement.[25]

One group no longer in existence, but important enough to deserve mention, is PsiCom, which was active in California from the late 1970s through the middle 1980s. Consisting of five members, all college professors or administrators, PsiCom was described by its founder, psychologist Dr. Louise Ludwig, as a "professional behavioral science organization seeking to provide service to law enforcement personnel seeking new investigative techniques." Before its dissolution, the group helped police in the state work on dozens of cases, with varying degrees of success, but its main goal was to help police departments develop their own psychics within the force.

One police force that worked with PsiCom in this capacity was the Pomona Police Department. For four years, from 1979 to 1983, PsiCom conducted seminars attended by Pomona detectives in an effort to get them to think less analytically. Lieutenant Kurt Longfellow, then chief of detectives, wanted to train his officers to develop their "right-brain thinking"—to use their intuition and imagination. In exchange for this training, PsiCom members were allowed to go out on homicide calls with detectives. Although Longfellow says that the information the psychics provided on these calls for the most part was "not useful," he insists that he was "not interested in having them solve crimes for us. What we used them for was to help our own investigators be more intuitive," and in that respect, Longfellow feels the program was moderately successful. Also, out of the association came a written departmental policy for the use of psychics, which Longfellow feels is a model for other departments.[26]

In addition to the professional psychics, there are on record many instances of spontaneous, isolated experiences of ESP by individuals who would not otherwise consider themselves psychic. The literature is full of cases in which a relative or spouse has had the "feeling" that a loved one had died or experienced major trauma some distance away, or in which a person had a detailed precognition of some major disaster in the future. One such recent isolated case that received national attention was the "dream murder" of Steve Linscott.[27]

One Friday night in October 1980, Linscott, a twenty-six-year-old Bible student, described as the "All-American husband and father," had a dream in which he saw a man beating someone to death with a blunt instrument. That night, less than half a block away, nursing student Karen Phillips was beaten to death. After agonizing with his wife, Linscott related his dream to the police, who immediately suspected Linscott. When several hairs consistent with Linscott's were found in the dead girl's house, the Bible student was arrested for murder. Linscott was convicted—largely on the hair evidence—but seven years later a new trial was ordered after an appeals court ruled that prosecutors had misled the jury and distorted the physical evidence to get a conviction.

In light of the publicity received by cases like Linscott's, which was covered on the August 6, 1987, edition of ABC's *20/20*, and that of Etta Louise Smith, whose "vision" of murder led to her arrest by police in Los Angeles, it is not unreasonable to theorize that many more people have had such experiences but have not reported them for fear of becoming suspects.

Many professional psychics express a reluctance to get involved in police work for that very reason. Others avoid it—and some quit doing it—because of its inherent unpleasantness. (Many psychics say that they "relive" the event, experiencing the pain, emotional trauma, and even deaths, of the victims.) Still others are reluctant to work on felony cases out of fear of reprisals by the criminals they are stalking. Many psychics say they have been threatened or shot at while working on police cases. Two years ago, in Alaska, Dixie

Yeterian was pistol-whipped, shot seven times in the head, and had her throat cut, in what was apparently a hired hit. Remarkably, she survived, but the experience understandably soured her on police work, saying she has "literally been in hiding for the past two years."[28] But for those professionals who are seeking to build up a large and lucrative list of private clients by building a reputation, the allure of publicity of a sensational criminal case may always be too attractive to ignore.

Working habits of the psychic sleuths vary widely. Some, like Yeterian, find it helpful to walk over the crime scene, while others, like Greta Alexander and Noreen Renier, work primarily at long distance, over the telephone. Many like to handle an object that has been in close proximity to the victim or the suspect; others say they only need a photograph and a name; some work with topographical maps.

A few have their own unique "wrinkles." Just as Marinus Dykshoorn goes over crime scenes with a loop of piano wire, which he says acts like an antenna, picking up vibrations of the events that have taken place there, some—like Ted Kaufmann and the father-and-daughter team of Louis and Ginette Mattacia—dowse for criminals, much as Jacques Aymar did in the seventeenth century.[29] Others, like Bill Ward and Dorothy Allison, combine astrology with their psychic efforts. One of the more flamboyant in the field is Dallas's Frances Baskerville, who specializes in finding missing children. Billing herself as the "world's only singing psychic," Baskerville has embarked on a second career as a country and western singer and Dolly Parton would-be look-a-like.[30]

Some psychics say they get visions of the crime from the eyes of the victim. Nancy Czetli says that she links her mind with the victim's "but it's as if I'm standing alongside him." Judy Belle claims she sees the event through the victim's eyes and that details are all relative to that. If the suspect was taller than the victim, for example, she finds herself looking up at him; his height, then, can only be gauged by measuring the height of the victim. Others, like Allison and Bill Ward, claim they experience events from the perpetrator's point of view. "What I do," says Allison, "is hop on the killer and stick with him every minute of his life."[31]

Although the point of view and content of the images may differ, there seems to be a general point of consensus among psychics as to the form the images take. Allison describes the pictures she gets as a "flickering TV screen." Bill Ward says he receives his images, "faces, areas, just like you get on TV." Greta Alexander describes the process as "a television signal and I become the antenna and pick up the picture." Dina Nazarenko describes the critical moment of when she visualizes a crime as "cinema." The television description is one commonly bandied about by psychics. But where is the signal coming from?

Explanations by psychic sleuths for the source of their powers vary, but they seem to break down into three main groupings: (1) genetic disposition; (2) physical trauma or near-death experience; and (3) learning, either on one's own or by instruction by another psychic.

Those who say they were born psychic usually say they came from a family that accepted the existence of psychic powers, and often had one or more parents who were also psychic. Sometimes, they say they tried to deny their talents, for fear of being looked on as weird by their peers, but eventually came to accept them as a part of maturation. Many of these lifers, such as Irene F. Hughes, a well-known Chicago psychic who claims to have solved dozens of murders for police, view their psychic talents as divine dispensations, and claim to be acting as "channelers" from the spirit world. Others, like Nancy Czetli and Dorothy Allison, take a more naturalistic approach, explaining their psychic functioning simply as an acute extension of their natural senses. Allison claims she knows nothing about telepathy or clairvoyance, saying, "It's just natural to me." According to Czetli, "Simply put, all of my senses are acute and extended. I process on the conscious level information that most people store on the unconscious." Czetli derogates esoteric explanations for psi, saying, "Having 'spirits' talk through one is part of the folklore of parapsychology."[32]

One common explanation offered by many psychics of what they do is "right-brain thinking." According to current biological theories, the right hemisphere of the brain is the seat of creativity, intuition, and pattern-recognition, while the left hemisphere is responsible for analytical thinking. Many psychics claim their abilities lie in their ability to switch into a right-brain mode easier than other people. "Psychics aren't analytical or organized," says Noreen Renier. "We're into this emotional, intuitive side."[33] For this reason, many psychics prefer to be referred to as "intuitives."

The second common category of explanation given by these sleuths for their powers is trauma or near-death experience. Peter Hurkos (head injury from falling off a ladder), Ray Gros (automobile accident), Kelly Roberts (near-fatal drowning), and John Catchings and Greta Alexander (hit by lightning), all claim to have acquired their psychic abilities in this manner. Great emotional trauma, such as Bill Ward's wartime experiences, is also occasionally cited as having triggered the emergence of psychic abilities. Biological theories have been offered by some believers that such shock or physical injury in some way alters brain chemistry, causing the brain to function at another level. But again, some psychics have more metaphysical theories. After being struck by lightning, for example, Greta Alexander claims she had a vision of the Virgin Mary and began hearing "angels" talk to her. Alexander also claims to receive messages from the spirits of dead victims of crime, asking her to solve their murders.

The third category of psychics are the taught. Beverly Jaegers teaches courses through which she says anyone, through the practicing of certain mental exercises, can learn ESP. Those with high IQs are the quickest learners, she asserts, and especially cops, because they are used to playing hunches. Judy Belle and Noreen Renier are two others who discovered their skills through classes and honed them by practice. In her early days as a professional psychic, Renier worked nightclubs dressed as a gypsy and charged five dollars for a twenty-minute reading, just for the practice. "You have to practice continually," she says. "It has to be part of your life . . . I try to show people that I'm not something special. This ability, it's not something to fear. It's something we all have that with work, with practice, we can develop."[34]

Kathlyn Rhea, who owned a modeling school before she turned professional psychic, also says practice makes perfect. "I'm not something special," she says. "Everybody is intuitive. You just have to learn to educate your feelings. A baby has eyes, but it has to be educated to what it is seeing. It's the same thing with intuition. You have to learn to interpret what your feelings are."[35]

While theorizing that everyone has some psychic ability that can be developed by conditioning, Dr. Louise Ludwig asserts that ESP is a talent, like any other artistic talent, and that a psychic cannot explain the source of his talent any more than a virtuoso pianist or a great painter.

"Psychics need an explanation in their own minds as to how they are doing what they are doing," Ludwig says. "They try to explain it to themselves to make themselves feel more secure. So they come up with a lot of different explanations as to how their power works to assuage their inability to explain. Most of the time, they're wrong. The fact is, they don't have the slightest idea of how it works."[36]

FIVE

A Psi
of Relief:
What Psychic
Sleuths Do

As in other fields of professional endeavor, there are specialists in the psychic detective business. Some specialize in finding dead bodies, others search for missing children or lost pets. Some say they work best recreating crime scenes, describing events, and pinpointing motives. Still others are adept at working with artists, providing police with faces to link with crimes.

Texas's John Catchings has achieved a nationwide reputation for finding dead bodies. Although not on target one hundred percent of the time, Catchings claims he has helped "turn up information" in almost all of the hundreds of cases he has worked on across the country and that his input has helped put at least a dozen criminals behind bars. Much of his business, he says, comes from referrals within law-enforcement circles.

In 1985, for example, Catchings was called in on the search for seventy-four-year-old Mayme Knight, who had wandered away from a Hempstead, Texas, convalescent home. After local police and hundreds of local residents had searched for the woman for days, Catchings led police to a swampy field two miles from the home. Although nothing was found on that day, Catchings insisted he had a "strong feeling" the woman was nearby. Her body was found two days later, less than fifty feet from where the psychic had been searching.[1]

In a similar case in 1981, Catchings was credited by Wilson County, Texas, Deputy Sheriff Basil Cate for finding the body of seventy-four-year-old Edna Imkin, who had wandered away from her car near San Antonio. Six weeks later Mrs. Imkin had still not been found and her frustrated children called in Catchings. Arriving at the scene of the disappearance carrying the missing woman's ring and penknife, Catchings walked over the adjoining fields trailed by several television reporters and cameramen. After four hours, he pointed to a portion of the field and told Cate to search there. The deputy recalled in an interview: "I just threw up my hands in disgust because I had been searching there for six weeks."[2] Swallowing his skepticism, however, Cate re-searched the area and within ninety minutes had located the woman's remains, less than one hundred yards from where Catchings had indicated. She had apparently died of exposure.

Greta Alexander says that for some reason she has more luck locating drowning victims than others. One example, which is often cited as one of her greatest hits, was the 1979 case of Ramon DiVirgilio, who police had presumed had drowned during an outing at a Saylorville reservoir near Johnston, Iowa. Seven weeks after he had been reported missing, Johnston police called Alexander and asked for help in locating the body. While talking to Alexander on the phone, an officer relayed messages by radio and walkie-talkie to another policeman who was wading in an area Greta had suggested. She told the searcher he would walk by a tile pipe trickling water (he did), would have to step over some fallen trees (correct again), that he would see a barrel in the water (no barrel, but a piece of painted plywood was seen, later interpreted as a hit), and that he would spot the body nearby tangled in a pile of brush. The body was there.[3]

Another psychic who has made a reputation for finding bodies is Kathlyn Rhea of Cupertino, California. Ms. Rhea, author of *The Psychic Is You*, says that since 1970 she has been consulted on hundreds of cases by the Secret Service, the FBI, and dozens of local police forces. In 1979, she received considerable publicity when she told police where to find the body of eight-year-old Victoria de Santiago, who had been abducted in Fresno, California. After handling a photograph of the girl, Rhea allegedly told the girl's parents that the child was dead, and described the actions of her kidnappers. In the presence of a Fresno police detective, Tim McFadden, Rhea said that the suspects had driven down a road that ran through farm fields and was elevated above the fields. There, they had raped and murdered the little girl, leaving her unburied body clad only in white socks. She also told the detective that there would be a sign nearby bearing only the letter S.

McFadden recognized the area described by Rhea and, following her directions, located the body, which was wearing only white socks. A few feet away was a mailbox on which was written the single letter S. McFadden was so impressed by Rhea's vision that he submitted a copy of the transcript of her statement to the California Department of Justice.

Since then, McFadden has worked with Rhea on five cases involving missing children, the last one in August 1989. According to the detective, information she provided was accurate in four of the cases, while the fifth one has yet to be solved. "She told us right from the git-go whether the children were alive or dead," McFadden says. (In one case, the child was found alive.) "She has been right every time. I believe in her one hundred percent."[4]

Locating dead bodies constitutes a majority of publicized hits by psychics. The success rate in finding *live* missing persons, however, seems to be considerably lower. Because live people have volition and can move around, locating them can be a tricky affair, especially if they do not wish to be found. Even guessing whether they are alive or dead can be tricky, although a psychic has a fifty-fifty chance of being right either way.

Requested by Manalapan, New Jersey, police, in May of 1977 to aid in finding fifteen-year-old Brian Timmerman, who had been missing for more than a month, Dorothy Allison told investigators that the boy had been murdered, that she had seen him "suffocating." Her clues were a church, airplanes, construction equipment, a lot of digging, a yellow brick house, gold, and some kind of camp or park. The police spent a lot of time searching a scarcely populated area of Manalapan, where there was a small airstrip, a Jehovah's Witness meeting hall, and a Scout camp, to no avail. On a tip from a high school guidance counselor, Timmerman was found, not dead, but in front of New York's Pan Am Building, peddling religious tracts. He had been living with the Moonies. Allison explained away her error by saying she had been confused because the boy was "spiritually" dead. Her airplane clue she rated as a hit because the Pan Am Building then had a heliport on the roof.[5]

Similarly, in April 1981, Kathlyn Rhea announced that Jeana Rodriguez, a young girl who had been missing for two months, had been kidnapped and murdered by a Mexican man. The following August, an Anglo male was arrested for the kidnapping by police after Jeana returned home safely.[6]

When Patty Hearst was kidnapped in 1974, Allison was flown out to California by Patty's father, Randolph Hearst, to help in the hunt. Allison's taped impressions were of no help in locating the fugitive heiress, but after Hearst's capture, Allison claimed her miss was a "hit," saying that she had notified the FBI in 1974 that Patty was in Pennsylvania at a time when the fugitive was hiding out in Scranton. There is no record at the Bureau of whom she talked with, or indeed, if she ever talked to anyone, but Allison has since implied that her "lead" might have led to Hearst's capture, if the Bureau had followed it up.

Another of the dozens of psychics to get into the Hearst drama was Peter Hurkos. In 1975, Hurkos announced that the missing heiress was in Wisconsin and would be taken without a shoot-out. Following the pronouncement over the UPI wire, the FBI reported it was swamped with calls from Wisconsin residents who said they had seen Hearst.

Colleen Dibler of Galveston, Texas, claims to have assisted the U.S. Army Special Forces, the FBI, and police departments across the country in finding missing persons and alleges that through her association with the Smith-McIntire-Howard Foundation of Fayetteville, North Carolina, she has searched for POWs and MIAs in southeast Asia. Ms. Dibler, who explains her ability to "leave her body . . . and find people" as a "gift from God," says that her prisoner-of-war work has taken her to Hong Kong and Manila. She does not explain why, if she can leave her body, she would need to fly corporally to Hong Kong, or just how many documented MIAs she has found, although she claims a "ninety percent recovery rate in locating people."[7]

One psychic who seems to have had some documented success finding missing persons is Phil Jordan. In 1982, after five-year-old

Tommy Kennedy of Owego, New York, wandered off from a picnic site at Empire Lake, Tioga County sheriff's deputies searched the area fruitlessly for seventeen hours. Knowing that Jordan had successfully located another missing boy the year before in Bradford, Pennsylvania, after a two-day police and bloodhound search had failed, the psychic was called in. After fingering the boy's T-shirt, Jordan drew a map depicting a lake, some overturned boats, a house, and a rock, and told Kennedy's distraught parents that the boy was all right, asleep under a tree. The next morning, Jordan accompanied deputies on their search. Fifty-five minutes later, the boy was found asleep, in an area that looked startlingly similar to the map Jordan had drawn. "It was no coincidence," Sheriff Raymond Ayers told reporters. "Phil Jordan simply used some kind of paranormal talent the rest of us don't have."[8]

In one case that has never been publicized, Los Angeles Sheriff's Homicide Detective Stanley White verified in an interview that Peter Hurkos had been responsible for precisely locating a suicidal policeman, thus saving his life. According to White, the officer, who was facing indictment on several criminal charges, telephoned several of his co-workers to announce he was going to kill himself, but refused to tell where he was. In a desperation effort, Hurkos was contacted by phone, and the psychic proceeded to relay a motel name and room number. Following the lead, White and several colleagues rushed over to the motel and found the cop, unconscious from an overdose of drugs. While White dismisses most psychics as "fruitcakes," he admits he remains bothered by Hurkos's prediction. "How the hell can you explain away something like that?" he asks.[9]

Interestingly, this story was virtually duplicated by another source, except with a different psychic as the hero of the day. In an article that appeared in the October 1979 issue of Fate, Captain Jim Shade of the Downey, California, Police Department credited Dutch psychic Jan Steers with pinpointing the location of a fellow police officer who was dying of self-inflicted injuries somewhere in the Los Angeles area. According to Shade, Steers gave him explicit directions to the dying man, who, he said, was "five miles away at a motel with a red door." Half an hour later, the wounded man was located and rushed to a hospital in time to save his life. "I don't think police should take as gospel the information psychics give us," Shade was quoted as saying, "but at the same time—and I know I'm in the minority when I say this—I don't see how trained investigators can continue to ignore altogether what psychics say."[10] "Suicidal Cop Saved by Psychic"—true story or variation of a modern "urban legend"?

Psychics are not only called upon to locate people. In 1989, Pat Huff, who operates the Parapsychology Center of Toledo, Ohio, was employed by a distressed cat owner to help find three stolen pedigree Persian show cats. The psychic found one of the purloined Persians, leading police to a storage shed in the woods near a spot where the animal's cage was found.[11]

Huff is not the only psychic who has claimed to be able to communicate psychically with animals. In 1978, Dean Goodman was killed when his car left a canyon road in Los Angeles. When the wreck was discovered nineteen days later, Goodman's German shepherd, Prince, was found alive with his master's body, which was missing various anatomical parts. Goodman's mother, assuming Prince had kept himself in the pink by dining on her son, decided to have the dog destroyed, but was stopped by the intervention of Hollywood psychic Beatrice Lydecker. After "interviewing" the accused canine culprit, Lydecker concluded that Prince was innocent of the charges. It seemed that the dog had relayed to her through telepathy that coyotes and wild dogs had carried off Goodman's body parts in spite of Prince's efforts to drive them off. "I have this ESP with animals," she told police investigators. "Prince had been traumatized by the accident. All Prince could talk about was his dead master."[12] As a result of Mrs. Lydecker's revelations, Prince's life was spared.

Missing and stolen goods have also been the objects of psychic searches. According to his autobiography, Dutch psychic Marinus Dykshoorn in 1958 solved a theft case in Duisburg, Germany, by long-distance telephone, identifying the thief and giving police very specific instructions where the booty had been hidden.[13] The Duisburg police, however, flatly deny the claim, insisting that the case was broken through normal methods. As will be pointed out in a later chapter, considering the dubious nature of many of Dykshoorn's claimed hits, it is not unlikely that the police version is correct.[14]

In 1971, Gary, Indiana, clairvoyant Anne Rose announced in the Chicago *Daily News* that she was going to find $98,000 worth of buried gold that had been taken during Indiana's last great train robbery in 1968. Five days later, according to Rose's instructions, a tin box was exhumed from the Hobart, Indiana, city dump. It contained some tintypes, a penknife, a small canvas money bag, and $20.30 in Confederate money.[15]

After thieves broke into the Kenwood House Museum in London on February 22, 1974, and made off with the priceless painting *The Guitar Player* by Dutch artist Jan Vermeer, British medium Nella Jones mystified Hampstead, England, police when she phoned them with what turned out to be an accurate description of where they would find the painting's discarded frame. Ms. Jones related to investigators from Hampstead and Scotland Yard that she had been watching the BBC broadcast of the museum robbery and gone into a trance during which she had "seen the whole picture." Police were reportedly further impressed when the medium led them to a spot behind Kenwood House where part of the alarm system protecting the painting was found half-buried in mud. After telling investigators that the painting was hidden in a cemetery and was under surveillance, presumably by the thieves, Jones led police to Highgate Cemetery, where they pursued a "suspicious man" who eluded their chase. A search of the cemetery failed to locate the painting, but later Jones allegedly had another vision, that the painting was being moved. After accurately predicting that a ransom note would soon be delivered, along with a piece of the painting, Jones told investigators that the painting would be found and would be all right. On a tip from an informant, *The Guitar Player* was found in Bartholomew Cemetery, some six miles from Highgate, in good condition. Although Ms. Jones's "visions" did not lead to the recovery of the painting, Hampstead Police Detective David Morgan credited information provide by the psychic as "leading the investigation forward."[16]

In 1982, Greta Alexander was called upon by the Springfield, Illinois, Convention and Visitors Bureau to help locate a missing bronze statue of Abraham Lincoln, which had been stolen from nearby Wilkinsburg. Alexander gave a description of the place where the statue was hidden, which later was proclaimed by her fans and some newspaper accounts as generally accurate, but which was far too vague to be of any help to the police in pinpointing its location. The statue was eventually recovered, but as in the case of the Vermeers masterpiece, through an informant's tip and not through the psychic's pronouncements.[17]

Headed by former Naval Intelligence officer Stephan A. Schwartz, Los Angeles's Mobius Group has developed methods for pooling the efforts of several intuitives for their ventures into psychic criminology. In 1979, they used a similar approach in an attempt to apply psi to archaelogical exploration. After reportedly locating five investors to put up collectively $500,000 for the project, Schwartz and his fellow researchers—including two of the six psychics he had used in his criminological experiments—ventured to Alexandria, Egypt, to search for ancient treasures.

At a January 1980 press conference, Schwartz issued a statement that seemed to imply that the Mobius explorers had discovered the "palace of Marc Antony . . . and ruins which may well have been the Ptolemaic Royal Palaces where the legendary Queen Cleopatra lived." This press release, later retracted, was almost immediately attacked by two on-site Egyptian scholars, Dr. Shehetta Adam, head of Egypt's Department of Antiquities, and Dr. Mostafa El Abbadi, whom Schwartz had listed as a "research associate" on the project. Schwartz replied that his critics had failed to note qualifying statements he made in a paper given a month later, and by 1983, when Schwartz's book *The Alexandria Project* was published, he had toned down the spectacular Antony-Cleopatra claims substantially. In the book, however, he asserted that his group had managed to locate an extension to the ancient city of Marea, and in a 1988 interview he credited the project with providing "profound clues to the location of Alexander's [the Great] tomb," which his psychics pinpointed as being beneath the Nebi Daniel Mosque. No proof was ever unearthed to substantiate Schwartz's claims, however, and the "profundity" of this psychic's "clues" remains in doubt.

Mobius continues its efforts in historical psychic sleuthing and raising funds for psychic treasure hunts, among its various projects. Between 1985 and 1988, one such endeavor, the Mobius Banks Project, searched the waters along the Bahama Banks for sunken treasure. Using guidance from twelve psychics, eleven sunken ships were located, some of special interest, but none contained the riches the project's sponsors had hoped for.[18]

Some psychics specialize in finding other kinds of treasure. When not working on criminal cases, Los Angeles's Ron Warmouth dowses for oil and gas.[19] Ingo Swann, famed for his remote viewing successes at SRI in the 1970s, has also been paid by corporate heads to hunt for oil.[20] In 1977, Equity Service Corporation hired an unnamed Dutch psychic to pick out sites to drill oil wells, but the effort backfired when the Securities and Exchange Commission (SEC) stated in a civil suit filed in Philadelphia that investors in the company were not so informed.[21]

One of the few psychics who claims his psychic powers have made him rich is Israeli Uri Geller. During the early 1980s, several large mining concerns, including Britain's Rio Tinto-Zinc, Ltd., Zanex, Ltd., and South Africa's Anglo-Transvaal Mining, paid handsomely for Geller's psychic services in pinpointing oil and mineral deposits. Geller works for himself now, having formed Uri Geller Associates, a London-based company that unites Geller's talents with those of engineers and geologists.[22]

Geller's apparent financial success notwithstanding, documented accounts in which a psychic has successfully and specifically located missing objects or contraband seem to be in short supply. A significant exception reportedly took place in the summer of 1974, when, according to dowsing historian Christopher Bird, Vietnamese authorities lost track of a Thai junk suspected by Interpol of carrying six tons of raw opium. Captain P. M. Khue, assistant chief of the Vietnamese Navy's Sea Operations, allegedly brought in Captain Vo Sum, a dowser whose recent location of a crippled Vietnamese patrol boat had created a sensation in Vietnamese naval circles. After suspending a pendulum over a map of the area, Vo Sum pinpointed the junk's location and pronounced that the opium aboard the junk would be seized by 6 A.M. on June 27. Based on Vo Sum's information, Khue's forces were able to pinpoint the junk on radar and it was pursued and boarded. After an intensive search, 2.1 tons of opium was found hidden aboard—at 5 A.M., on June 27! Vo Sum, who now lives in San Diego, California, told Bird that he had hoped that his success would bring him a substantial portion of the reward money, but the Vietnamese Customs Directorate, apparently less impressed by Vo Sum's tale than Bird was, only sent him a check for ten dollars.[23]

Some psychics explain away their lower success rate for locating contraband by saying they function best in cases involving intense emotions, such as murder. Emotions such as terror, hate, fear, create lingering vibrations, they say, that are picked up by the psychic, who acts as an antenna. "My mind works on violence the best," says Bill Ward. "The more violent, the better." Since theft is a more calculated crime and objects have no emotions, burglars and booty are more difficult to track.

Some psychics do not even attempt to find things—living or inanimate. "I can't find anything," admits Judy Belle. "I only deal with feelings. Just once, I would love to get a name, or an address number—1330 Scott Street—but I never do."[24] What Belle and many other psychics do is recreate scenes and events surrounding a crime. Belle considers her best hit a double homicide in Tulare County, California, in which a mother and her two-year-old son had been stabbed to death. The police's principal suspect in the case had an alibi, but by seeing the events prior to the murder through the eyes of the dead victim, Belle was able to place the suspect's car at the scene. Later, an eyewitness was turned up who confirmed her vision. Unfortunately, the witness could not put the suspect at the scene, only the car, and no arrest was made. Corcoran, California, Detective David Frost, however, who handled the investigation, remains "ninety-nine percent sure we had the right man in mind. She [Belle] gave us a feeling of what went down, where the vehicle was parked."[25]

Sergeant Mark Anderson, of the Amador County, California, Sheriff's Department, used Belle in a murder case in which they had a suspect in custody and a lot of circumstantial evidence, but no body. Belle could not find the body, but recreated the murder scene for investigators. "Her accuracy was tremendous," says Anderson. "She had never been to the house, never been in Amador County, so she couldn't have known about it. She gave us an idea what had happened in the case."[26] (Eventually, the suspect cut a deal with prosecutors and pleaded guilty, but not as a result of anything Belle had turned up.)

Former Delaware State Police Superintendent Irvin B. Smith has described Nancy Czetli's ability to reconstruct crime scenes as "fantastic." She has also been called upon by police to sort out motives in difficult cases. One case in which Czetli was not only able to supply a motive but also a suspect, was the 1979 stabbing murder of sixty-two-year-old Leonetta Schilling in Rivera Beach, Maryland. One month after the killing, the police had a list of thirty-two suspects, but nothing definite to go on. They called in Czetli. The psychic told detectives that the killer knew Mrs. Schilling very well; that, in fact, she had been his baby-sitter. She said that he was a drug abuser and that the murder had resulted from an argument over money. Out of a stack of photographs, Czetli picked one she thought had a "thought pattern . . . most similar to the killer's."[27] The picture turned out to be of Mrs. Schilling's nephew, Allen Glenn Finke, whom the dead woman had baby-sat when he was a child.

Further investigation turned up evidence and witnesses that led to Finke's conviction for the murder. According to Sergeant James Moore, one of the detectives on the case, "it would have taken us six months to get statements from those thirty-two suspects and then verify their alibis. Finke was way down at the bottom of our list. We wouldn't have gotten to him for months, and by that time who knows where he might have gone?"[28]

Another way psychics are used by police is to provide descriptions of unidentified criminal suspects. Frequently, this is done with the assistance of a police artist, as in the teaming of psychic Kathlyn Rhea and San Jose police artist Tom Macris.

One particularly significant case involving such a collaboration occurred in 1978, in South Gate, California. After five days of investigation had turned up no leads in the disappearance of seven-year-old Carl Carter, Jr., South Gate detectives William Sims and Louie Gluhack contacted a psychic named "Joan," at the suggestion of a retired Torrance police detective. Joan immediately told the investigators that the boy had been murdered by a man who had killed before. With the aid of LAPD police artist Fernando Ponce, a composite sketch was made of the killer from Joan's impressions. When the sketch was shown to the missing boy's parents, they both said that it looked like Harold Ray "Butch" Memro, a thirty-three-year-old boat-company worker and acquaintance of the family. Sims and Gluhack questioned Memro, and on the basis of his statements and the fact that he was on probation for child molesting, placed him under arrest. Memro confessed to the Carter murder as well as the unsolved throat-slashing murders of two other young boys in nearby Bell Gardens in 1976. Weeks after the arrest, Sims would say that the sketch looked so much like Memro, "it was spooky." But Memro's attorney argued that the drawing "looked more like me—like forty million males—than Mr. Memro . . . The parents had a feeling it was Butch, so they said it looked like him."[29]

At the trial, Memro's attorneys attacked the legal basis of the arrest, since "probable cause" had evolved solely from the psychic rendering. But in a landmark decision, Los Angeles Superior Court Judge William McGinley disagreed, ruling that the use of the psychic in the case was merely an "investigative tool . . . that may be used to follow up additional leads."[30]

Not all psychic renderings are done with pencil and paper. Frank Bender, an artist-sculptor from Philadelphia, does it in clay. Bender, who claims to be able to reconstruct psychically the faces of decomposed bodies, first discovered his talent when being given a tour through the morgue by a policeman friend. Bender's reconstructions have been credited by the Philadelphia Medical Examiner's office with helping solve several difficult cases, including the 1978 homicide of Anna Mary Duval. After a poster was made of Bender's rendering, the Arizona woman was eventually identified.[31]

In 1977, Dixie Yeterian provided Fontana police not only with faces, but with a couple of names in connection with the sexual assault and homicides of a teenage couple in that California city. In several interviews with the authors, Homicide Detective Frank Donlon, a thirty-year veteran, confirmed that among other startling hits, Yeterian told him and his partner that the two juvenile victims had been killed by four black men, two of whom were brothers, both with the name Al. Working according to Yeterian's instructions, composite sketches of the suspects were made up. Months later, when normal investigative work resulted in the arrest of four black suspects, Donlon would be amazed by the likenesses, terming them "the best composites we ever did." Two of the suspects were brothers—Alan and Albert. "I get goose bumps when I talk about it even now," says Donlon.[32]

Yeterian's hit is not a common occurrence among psychics. According to Whitney S. Hibbard and Raymond Worring, two Montana private investigators who have not only worked with psychics but have written an operations manual for the use of psychics in law enforcement, "Sensitives seem to be generally most accurate in describing personality and physical characteristics of perpetrators . . . Very seldom are correct names given."[33] That is perhaps due to the fact that descriptions, and even sketches, offered by psychics often tend to be vague, generic, their "accuracy" being filled in later in the mind of the believer. Names, however, are another story. Either a name is correct, or it is not, which is perhaps why not many psychics eagerly produce them.

One of the few who reportedly did so frequently was Peter Hurkos. After going over the gore-splattered site of one of the century's most infamous crimes, the murders of Sharon Tate and four others, Hurkos allegedly named "Charlie" as the man responsible for the killing of actress Sharon Tate. If true, this hit would seem to be doubly significant, as there were two Charlies involved in the murders of Tate and the others—Charles Manson and Charles "Tex" Watson.[34]

British medium Nella Jones asserts, in her book *Ghost of a Chance*, that eighteen months before police arrested Peter Sutcliffe—the Yorkshire Ripper—in 1981, she gave the police a sketch of the killer along with the name "Peter," as well as Sutcliffe's address! There are discrepancies between the psychic's claims and the facts, however. Although the house number she says she gave for the Ripper—6—was correct, the name of the street was not. Her sketch of the killer, moreover, bears no resemblance to Sutcliffe. Still, she did come up with the name Peter. Unfortunately, her pronouncements were never published in advance, so that one only has Jones's account to go by.[35]

Dorothy Allison is another psychic who frequently comes up with suspects' names. Perhaps the most well-publicized instance is her claim that she gave Atlanta police the name "Williams" as the killer of numerous black children in that city in 1980.

An investigation by the authors indicates that she may indeed have mentioned the name Williams—along with every other name in the Atlanta telephone directory. Atlanta Police Chief George Napper claims that the much-publicized name Mrs. Allison gave his department was *not* Williams. Two witnesses Allison claimed could verify her amazing "hit" also waffled on the assertion. One, a reporter with WGST in Atlanta, remembered no mention of the name. The other, a Baltimore detective, seemed to remember her naming Williams, along with several other names, apparently not giving it any special attention.[36]

But even if she did give police the name Williams, what good would it have done their investigation? How many Williamses are there in the Atlanta area? When police have no suspects in mind, particularly in cases of motiveless murder, such as serial killings, what help will the name Peter or Charlie be, even if correct?

In actual practice, the psychic sleuth is typically called upon to look clairvoyantly into the past (or the present if a missing person is sought)—in effect, to use his or her blue sense to recreate some prior crime scene. This process, *retrocognition*, is actually the opposite of *precognition*, or psychic glimpsing of the future, which, despite the popular equation of "psychic" and "fortune-teller," is seldom demanded of the psychic detective. (One possible exception might be in trying to anticipate some future action by the criminal perpetrator, perhaps to avoid an anticipated murder or crime.)

Most psychics, however, claim they can use their psi to look either forward or backward in time. In fact, this can present special problems for criminal investigators. For example, psychics often say they cannot be sure if the feelings or images they receive about the crime refer to something in the past, present, or future. It may even be the case that some psychics are better geared to looking backward, rather than forward, in time. If so, those with the strongest blue sense may be less gifted as prognosticators than is usually assumed. The optimum blue sense might involve a kind of psychic specialization.

Nevertheless, the most traditional function of the psychic in society has been to predict future events. Shawn Robbins, listed by the *National Enquirer* as one of America's "top ten psychics," claims in her autobiography, *Ahead of Myself*, that early in her career she worked as in-house psychic for a large cosmetics company, predicting market trends and conducting corporate espionage on the competition. She also claims in that 1980 book to have predicted the crashes of two Boeing 747s in the Canary Islands, the crash of a Turkish Airlines flight from Paris to London, the 1974 IRA terrorist bomb attack on Parliament, the 1975 bomb blast in LaGuardia Airport, the assassination attempt on the Pope, and the capture of Patty Hearst. The problem with the predictions is that most of them were made on radio shows and cannot be verified. One prediction she made in the book does stand out, however: that Indira Gandhi would flee India as revolutionary groups sought to overthrow her. Gandhi was assassinated. Among Robbins's 1988 predictions were that Malcolm Forbes would wed Liz Taylor, that Fawn Hall, Donna Rice, and Jessica Hahn would team up for a "bimbo squad" TV series à la *Charlie's Angels*, and that the Soviet Union would wage psychic warfare on a northern California town, causing nausea and fainting spells among the populace.[37]

Professional psychic Clarissa Bernhardt, a former copywriter from Texas, claims that she accurately foresaw the attempted assassination of President Gerald Ford by a woman dressed as "Little Red Riding Hood."[38] When Lynne "Squeaky" Fromme, ex–Manson Family member, was arrested trying to shoot Ford, she was dressed in a red cape with a hood. But it is Bernhardt's impressive record in predicting earthquakes that has gained her national attention and earned her the sobriquet the "Earthquake Lady." Her string of hits began in 1974, when, on a San Francisco Bay Area radio program, she predicted to the minute a 5.2 quake in the Hollister area of northern California. She accurately predicted two 1975 quakes in the Azores and Hawaii, and, in 1976, notified the Earthquake Information Service in Denver that on June 26, 1976, a magnitude-7 quake would hit in the Pacific, south of Japan, saying she saw "naked natives and mudslides." On June 26, a quake of 7.1 hit Indonesia, leaving six thousand buried under mudslides. Bernhardt says that her predictions come true when she feels a "change in the intensity of vibrations . . . or sometimes I just see a calendar in my mind with a date circled and earthquake marked."[39] She was off, however, when she said during that same radio interview that 1978 would start a ten-year period of seismic turmoil which would transform San Francisco Bay into an inland sea, leave Los Angeles and San Diego offshore islands, and convert Phoenix into a seaport.

An audience of police officers and FBI agents witnessed Noreen Renier's 1981 prediction of the attempted assassination of President Reagan. At first, Ms. Renier said that she felt Reagan having a heart attack, then clarified the statement by saying it was a sharper pain than that, it was a gunshot. She went on to say that Reagan would not be killed, but would become stronger in office because of the sympathy the shooting would get him; only that sympathy would be short-lived, as he would be assassinated the following November. She described the assassination, saying Reagan would be killed in a hail of machine-gun bullets on a parade stand surrounded by many people wearing foreign uniforms and brandishing automatic weapons. The prediction did not come true for Reagan, but that fall, Egypt's President Anwar Sadat was gunned down in a fashion that remarkably conformed to Renier's prognostication.[40] Apparently, Ms. Renier just got her Presidents crossed. She also got them crossed two years before, when she said that President Carter would be assassinated on the White House lawn after his reelection and that Vice President Mondale would commit suicide.[41]

If Noreen Renier was half-right in 1981, Chicago's best-known psychic crime-buster, Irene Hughes, was not when she predicted that by the end of that year, the United States would launch a satellite that would somehow generate enough energy to solve the world's oil crisis.[42]

A prediction by Linda Davis in the summer of 1989—that her husband was going to try to kill her—resulted in her shooting the man to death. The thirty-two-year-old psychic, known professionally as Kelly Roberts, was known by local authorities before the fatal incident; she had helped Escondido and San Diego police in several homicide and kidnapping investigations and she had been consulted by law-enforcement agencies as far away as Kansas. Aside from her police work, Roberts counsels clients and conducts private readings at her San Diego–based Parapsychology Research Center, which she started in 1984. Roberts claims to have developed her psychic powers after she was nearly drowned at the age of fourteen.

Roberts's prediction, however, may have been due more to her "black-and-blue sense" than to any psychic feelings. According to her later testimony, over the months prior to the shooting, her husband, James Davis, had become erratically violent and had threatened her life. In August 1989, her fears for her own safety precipitated her to buy a handgun and carry it at all times. On September 10, after agreeing to a divorce, Davis attacked her from behind with a baseball bat in an apparent homicidal rage. After taking several blows to the head and face, Ms. Roberts shot him to death. A review of the case by the District Attorney's Office declared the shooting to have been in self-defense and charges were not sought against the psychic.[43]

A prediction in 1974 by Greta Alexander made a believer out of Washington, D.C.'s, Chief of Homicide Arif Mosrie. When consulted on the telephone about the unsolved murder of Barbara Myersburg, Alexander told Mosrie that the man responsible for the murder would be shot in the leg by a policeman while running away from the scene of another crime. She went on to say that the man would be charged with the crime he was fleeing, and police would not suspect him of murdering Myersburg until later. The man who was eventually convicted for the murder was shot in the leg and arrested while fleeing from a robbery.[44]

Police are not the only part of the criminal justice system to use psychics. "Seeress to the Stars" Kebrina Kinkade, who claims to have solved over twenty murders and forty-two missing-persons cases since her rise to national prominence in the early 1970s, was used in at least one homicide case by a deputy district attorney in Los Angeles. Reportedly, she gave the prosecutor unpublished details of a 1975 murder by handling the suspect's fingerprint card.[45]

Another Hollywood psychic crime-buster who was consulted by the LA District Attorney's Office was former baroness Lotte von Strahl. In the mid-1970s von Strahl, whose movie-star client list included Glenn Ford, Goldie Hawn, Ann Sothern, and George Hamilton, was consulted by Deputy District Attorney George Kennedy in the stabbing assault of a man at a wedding-turned-brawl.

According to Kennedy, the six-foot, white-haired octogenarian psychic described the assailant right down to a tattoo on his right elbow and an appendix scar. When confronted with von Strahl's pronouncements, the man, who matched the description perfectly, broke down and confessed to the crime.[46]

Kathlyn Rhea says she has assisted defense attorneys and prosecutors with criminal investigations, and has advised them in jury selection. "I tell them how a certain judge is going to react in a case, what points they should stress, and what they should gloss over," she says. "I can often also tell how their expert witnesses are going to go over and what juries will be impressed by."[47]

During the 1977 murder-for-hire trial of Lawrence Albro, Tioga County, New York public defender Robert L. Miller praised Phil Jordan's input during jury selection as "very helpful." According to Miller, Jordan advised him to keep one female juror Miller was about to dismiss. The woman turned out to be the single holdout on the jury. Miller, now in private practice in New York, thinks Jordan's presence kept the jurors truthful during the selection phase. "They didn't know what he could do, whether he could see into their minds or what. I think it kept them extraordinarily honest."[48]

During the 1981 trial of Jean Harris, accused of murdering Scarsdale Diet doctor Herman Tarnower, Jordan helped pick many of the jurors and predicted that the woman would be convicted if she was allowed to testify. (Of course, she might have been convicted even if she had not testified.)

Jordan claims his success in "reading" prospective jurors comes from his ability to see "auras," colored emanations said to surround human beings, which are supposed to originate from the central nervous system. "Red means a person is frustrated or upset," Jordan says. "And if an aura jumps, the person may be lying."[49]

Famed attorney Melvin Belli has used psychics to help pick juries on several occasions. In one such case, a wrongful death suit, he won a large reward for his client. "I thought he [the psychic] was very good."[50]

Some attorneys even claim to be psychic themselves. Madison, Wisconsin, trial attorney Jack McManus claims he can read the minds of witnesses. "A light goes on and I have knowledge of thoughts beforehand," he says. McManus also claims to have waged psychic warfare on other attorneys who themselves have paranormal abilities.

"I just put up my mental defenses, become a trickster, make them think the power is backfiring."[51]

One anonymous female attorney from a small midwestern town recently told a reporter for _Omni_ that her ability to read minds during cross-examination led one colleague to try to have her prosecuted for witchcraft. Another was quoted as saying that he was fired for confessing to his boss that "disembodied voices" had led him to crucial evidence in a case.[52] Still others claim to be able to affect the minds of jurors favorably, an assertion that, if true, would seem to constitute a breach of judicial ethics.

While working for attorneys, psychics inevitably come in contact with the investigators they use. Sometimes they even make converts of them. Kathlyn Rhea has worked with many private investigators on assorted cases from arson to missing persons. Former Winchester, Virginia, sheriff, now private detective, Carroll K. Mauck, has used Nancy Czetli on cases in the past and is a believer in her crime-busting talents.

Raymond Worring, a licensed private investigator and forensic hypnotist from Helena, Montana, has co-authored a manual for law-enforcement use of psychics. With Captain Keith Wolverton of the Cascade County, Montana, Sheriff's Department, he runs Investigative Research Field Station, which provides seminars and courses for law enforcement in the testing and use of psychics, as well as the development of the intuitive powers of police investigators. Worring also recommends and acts as a liaison between psychics and police, who often do not know how to deal with a sensitive. Often, says Worring, police do not know how to ask a psychic the proper questions in the proper way, and due to their regimented thinking, investigators feel more comfortable dealing with someone who has the same kind of law-enforcement training. Although he has run across only a small percentage of psychics who can be of any use on a case, Worring claims he has known some who "get into unusual states of awareness during an investigation . . . Like search dogs, they see an invisible landscape others don't see. There's a parallel between a good investigator and a good intuitive. They can both pull together information not available to the ordinary senses."[53] Worring charges for his services and claims to have had requests for help from as far away as China.

As in the ranks of attorneys and police, there are psychic sleuths in the echelons of private-eye-dom. Whereas a vast majority of the licensed private detectives in the country are men, however, there seems to be a disproportionate number of females of the psychic variety.

Frances Baskerville, the "World's Only Singing Psychic," who heads the Baskerville Foundation for Psychical Research in Dallas, Texas, claims to be a licensed private detective specializing in finding lost children. In a recent letter to the authors, she credits herself with having found over "five hundred persons," although she regretfully states that she "only has the right" to name three, due to fact that she neglected to get "release forms" from the other four hundred and ninety-seven. She also claims to work with attorneys in several states helping to select juries.

St. Louis's Beverly Jaegers, head of the Psychic Detective Bureau, got her investigator's license in 1975 so that she could testify in court as an expert witness. Lately, however, she seems to have neglected her crime-fighting pursuits in favor of investment counseling.

Jenita Cargile, from Cypress, California, has been a licensed PI since 1973. She works mostly through personal referrals and does a little work through attorneys. She claims to use her blue sense to help track down missing persons, which are a majority of her cases. "Anyone in the investigative area learns to follow his feelings, hunches when there's no evidence to go on," she says. She claims to be able to home in on the people she hunts by psychometrizing their pictures. "It may take a while, she says, but eventually I get a strong feeling that the person I am looking for is in a certain area. I am seldom wrong."[54] Unlike many psychics, Cargile usually turns down cases in which she feels the missing person is dead, not wanting to deal with the negative emotions involved.

In 1984, Los Angeles entrepreneur-businessman Leslie Lewis founded Psychic Enterprises, a company whose major specialty seems to have been giving psychic business forecasts on junk-food trends. A sideline of the company, however, was to provide firms with security problems a psychic investigations report—for the modest sum of $2300. One of Psychic Enterprises' clients was Hugh Whitman, owner of Quality Sound, a stereo shop in Denver, who hired Lewis to ferret out the company thieves who were ripping off the store's expensive equipment. After going over all the store employees' handwriting samples and personnel files and giving them each a psychic, astrological, and graphological examination, Lewis came up with descriptions of two suspects that led to the apprehension of both culprits responsible for the thefts. Whitman was so pleased with Lewis's results that he posted a large sign on the premises: THIS STORE IS UNDER PSYCHIC SURVEILLANCE.[55]

How prevalent is the use of psychics by police? In the few surveys conducted in the field, less than 10 percent of the departments polled say they have ever used a psychic, and of those that had, considerably less have reported their use successful.[56] One 1987 survey conducted by the United Kingdom *Police Review* of 40 percent of England's police forces verified that most of them had received unsolicited offers from psychics, but concluded that "it was commonly accepted that none of the information supplied assisted in any significant way in the solving of crime and there were no instances reported of successes which could be investigated."[57] *Criminal Investigation and Interrogation,* a law-enforcement textbook on investigative techniques, lists among "ten popular fallacies . . . regarding homicide investigations" that "clairvoyants, fortune tellers, and mediums can give valuable information with respect to a murder."[58] That line is echoed by Dr. Martin Reiser, head of LAPD's Behavioral Sciences Service Section: "We continue to get anecdotal reports, but no additional data has emerged to suggest we should use psychic detectives or that we should take more time to research the matter."[59]

Such official denials are common, but perhaps misleading. For one thing, few police departments would officially admit using psychics for fear of looking incompetent, or because of the worry that such an admission would raise a public protest from certain fundamentalist religious elements, which see psychics as practitioners of the black arts. In addition, there is always the worry that the publicity generated by a psychic's involvement might irreparably damage a case. Because of that, police often demand strict confidentiality on the part of a psychic before he or she is brought into a case. Often, this wish for confidentiality cuts both ways. Researching this book, we ran across many psychics who told us they purposely avoid publicity for fear of criminal reprisals.

Many police investigators are reluctant to admit their belief in psychic phenomena, *even privately*. Police artist Tom Macris says that he has not found fellow officers to be particularly "forthcoming about the subject of psychic phenomena. There is a reluctance to take a public stand for fear of being ostracized. Personal attitudes or experiences are held close to the chest."[60]

But there are indications that the use of psychics may be gaining in acceptance among certain police circles, at least unofficially. According to Macris, "The idea that you're offbeat because you believe in psychics is on the way out. There was a time when I first joined the force [twenty-three-years ago] that I wouldn't have breathed a word of it. Now, it is seen, even by hard-nosed skeptics, as a matter of opinion."[61]

By far the majority of cases in which psychics are brought into the investigative process are homicides and missing persons. Usually, they are called in by the families of the victims, and their presence is merely tolerated by the police. Noreen Renier reports that 70 percent of her cases originate from families and 30 percent from police agencies. Kathlyn Rhea, on the other hand, says most of her work comes from police. She has been deputized by several northern California law-enforcement agencies and claims to have an entire Rolodex of police she advises. Fontana, California, psychic Armand Marcotte, who claims to have worked on over three hundred criminal cases across the country, works *exclusively* with police departments. He refuses to work with bereaved families, saying, "They always refuse to believe the worst, that their son is a drug addict or their daughter is a little loose."[62]

In several police surveys, quite a few of the police officials polled said that they would not rule out the possibility of calling in a psychic in a dead-end case. The February 1979 *Criminal Information Bulletin* of the California Department of Justice, for instance, concluded that "some psychics have provided valuable assistance to law enforcement on specific cases." It went on to say, however, that the psychic must function as an "investigative tool," and not "replace sound investigative techniques."[63] Similarly, an article in a 1979 issue of the prestigious law-enforcement magazine *Police Chief*, after discussing the skepticism many law-enforcement officers have about the use of psychics, states that "despite these concerns, individuals with bona fide psychic ability offer a unique and potentially valuable investigative skill."[64]

U.S. Department of Justice statistics indicate that less than half of the violent crimes committed in the United States are likely to be solved by arrest. The solution rate for crimes against property is much lower, around 20 percent. And things are not likely to get better in the near future. According to the U.S. Department of Justice's *Report to the Nation on Crime and Justice* (1988), it is calculated that "at current crime rates . . . an estimated five sixths of us will be victims of attempted or completed violent crimes during our lives."[65] A burgeoning crime rate, combined with the limited availability of resources to deal with the problem, will undoubtedly place additional pressure on already overburdened police agencies to perform.

Rather than leading to increased performance, however, such public pressure is more likely simply to produce frustration on the part of police. Studies have shown that to make an arrest, investigators rarely exploit other than the most direct types of evidence—catching the suspect at the scene, identification by the victim, information provided by an informant, et cetera. Furthermore, it has been demonstrated, particularly in theft crimes, that follow-up investigation is often almost entirely ineffective. It is perhaps not surprising, then, that police would be amenable to experimenting with developing new investigative tools that would enable them to tap otherwise unattainable information.

This willingness to experiment was exemplified in a 1981 memo from Pomona, California, Chief of Police Donald J. Burnett. In discussing his department's decision to be the first law-enforcement agency to establish an official policy for the use of psychics, Burnett stated, "Like many Police Departments, we face an increased demand for service without the ability to proportionately increase our resources to meet the demand . . . The use of psychics as an investigative tool is now emerging nationwide. It is noted that law enforcement agencies have used psychics for years in a limited manner . . . It is believed that this new tool—development of nonconventional clues by psychics—will provide additional information the Investigative Officer needs in successfully completing a difficult assignment."[66]

There is also a psychological dimension that must be considered. In certain dead-end cases, calling in a psychic, particularly at the urging of the victim or victim's family, might serve as a method of assuaging public anxiety by showing that investigators were leaving "no stone unturned."

According to one criminology textbook: "Many police officials assert that the _appearance_ of dedicated efforts on each case contributes positively to public confidence in the police. Even when the general public effort is discounted, extra investigative efforts (such as interviewing witnesses, dusting for fingerprints, neighborhood searches) are often used to placate particular victims rather than in hopes of solving the crime."[67] Most police investigators who admit they allowed a psychic to be brought into a case say they did so only because they had "nothing else to lose."

But *is* there nothing else to lose? Man-hours and money can be squandered foolishly in the pursuit of psychic visions. After Judy Belle was brought into the still unsolved 1983 investigation of the disappearance of teenager Cindy Bringhurst by the missing girl's parents, Pocatello, Idaho, Chief of Detectives Lynn Harris instituted a strict "no psychics" policy. "She wasn't the only psychic who called us up," Harris told us. "Ten others called up saying they could give us information on the case. We spent hundreds of man-hours running around where these people were telling us to go. At the same time, we weren't doing the things we should have been doing to bring the case to court."[68]

Homicide Lieutenant T. C. Swan of the Fort Worth, Texas, police, says he never uses psychics, because of the "circus atmosphere" they create. "They call you on sensational cases, not on cases where some wino is stomped to death in some back alley."[69] He also states that a psychic can often give false hope to survivors who are emotionally vulnerable.

Some psychics agree with this viewpoint. Nancy Czetli says, "My feeling is, if you can't get precise detail, you're no use whatsoever to the police because they've got to have really concrete stuff. The rather harsh fact of it is that very few psychics are capable of getting the kind of detail and having the stamina to do police work properly."[70]

Ingo Swann, whose remote-viewing experiments at Stanford Research Institute in the 1970s brought him international recognition, will not do police work for just that reason. Swann reports that out of twenty-five criminal cases he worked on between 1972 and 1979, three were successes, the other twenty-two "flops." Swann stopped participating because "the rate of success is far too low to justify arousing the hopes of families regarding missing family members, and to justify the dollar/man-hours the police use to follow up on empty psychic leads."[71]

Most police departments officially echo this line. Talking privately, however, many investigators express a willingness to suspend disbelief if no other solution is readily available. Says Detective Robert Mallwitz of the Sturtevant, Wisconsin, police, who consulted Greta Alexander in a particularly bothersome hit-and-run killing, "I talk to cops from all over. They *all* use psychics. It's about time this part of the country woke up."[72]

SIX

Gerard Croiset: The Scrying Dutchman

Called "The Wizard of Utrecht," "The Man With the X-Ray Mind," and even "The Mozart or Beethoven among Clairvoyants," Gerard Croiset is the best-known—and many would argue the best-authenticated—modern psychic detective. When he died on July 20, 1980, obituaries in newspapers and magazines around the world noted his passing, echoed the stories of his work with allegedly hundreds of police departments around the globe, and the German publication *Esotera* featured a cover story on him as "the clairvoyant who never disappointed." According to his supporters, Croiset's talents were diverse, a kind of Leonardo Da Vinci of the paranormal. It is claimed that he solved many of the century's most puzzling crimes, found scores of lost objects and hundreds of missing persons. He is said to have performed hundreds of paranormal healings and occasionally demonstrated extraordinary powers of precognition by correctly foretelling future events. But here we had no exotic modern-day Nostradamus, no strangely occult figure of mystery. Even Croiset's fellow Dutchman and sharpest critic, Piet Hein Hoebens, a reporter and editor for Amsterdam's important European newspaper *De Telegraaf*, acknowledged that "Gerard Croiset was respectable. Many educated Dutchmen who profess disbelief in ESP have managed to hold the simultaneous conviction that Croiset, for one, was genuine."[1]

Born on March 10, 1909, in the small artists' town of Laren in northern Holland, Gerard Croiset came from a theatrical family. His father, Hyman, toured throughout Holland and Belgium playing leading roles in productions by Shakespeare and Ibsen, and his mother was a wardrobe mistress. Gerard's younger brother, Max, continued in that tradition and became a renowned Dutch actor. Gerard displayed a theatrical manner himself later in life, and some who worked with him said he could be "a real ham in front of the camera." He had little home life and was placed with the first of six sets of foster parents when he was eight. He was nearly drowned that year, and some have contended that this may have in part accounted for his later high rate of success in locating drowned children. He quit school at thirteen to work on a farm and went on to a wide variety of odd jobs, ranging from shop assistant to sales representative to helper in a grocery. At twenty-five, he married Gerda ter Morsche, and the next year, 1935, their first son, Hyman, was born. He borrowed money from his in-laws to start a grocery story in Enschede, but he proved a terrible businessman and soon declared bankruptcy.

It was during this period of dejection that he briefly joined a local spiritualist society and soon thereafter began the demonstrations of his—until then apparently latent—psychic talents.[2] The eminent Dutch parapsychologist George Zorab tells us that when he first met Croiset in 1936, "he showed no indications of possessing great ESP gifts" and "was more interested in stage-hypnosis than in extrasensory perception."[3] Nonetheless, Croiset tells us that in 1935 he gave a strikingly accurate psychic reading for Henk de Maar, a watchmaker in nearby Borne, and that news of his abilities soon began to spread as people came to him seeking his psychic help for their problems. As he told his biographer, Jack Harrison Pollack, "I forgot about my grocery-store failure and started to think of a new career." From then until the end of World War II, however, Croiset remained a relatively obscure local psychic, mainly supporting himself and his family with "unorthodox healing" by making so-called magnetic hand passes over his patients. His reputation as a healer grew steadily, and by 1949 he was known locally as "the miracle-doctor or Messiah of Enschede."[4] Though he eventually became wealthy from his healing clinic, so far as is known Croiset never took any payment for his services as a psychic detective (though he did accept occasional fees from some individual clients for private consultations).

In December of 1945 Croiset attended a talk given in Enschede by a visiting parapsychology lecturer from the University of Utrecht, Dr. Wilhelm H. C. Tenhaeff. Croiset told Dr. Tenhaeff about his abilities and asked to be tested. Over the next several months, he underwent extensive examination in Utrecht. Tenhaeff had previously tested and studied many other psychics, most notably a Mrs. van den Bos-Theunissen of The Hague, with whom he had worked for the fourteen years between 1926 and 1940. Tenhaeff concluded that Croiset was one of the most remarkable subjects he had ever found. As for Croiset, the nearly illiterate psychic accepted Tenhaeff as his guide and mentor. Over the next eight years they established an informal partnership that would bring them both fame and a degree of fortune. Tenhaeff presented vivid endorsements of Croiset through his many research reports and generally acted as Croiset's publicist as well as his scientific sponsor. At this point, despite his reputation, Tenhaeff was only a free-lance lecturer at Utrecht State University (an unsalaried position) and had financially survived mainly from the small royalties from his books. In large part as a result of the widespread publicity he and Croiset attracted, in 1951 the fifty-seven-year old parapsychologist was officially appointed a teacher at the university, and in 1953 he was given a full professorship. This was the world's first academic chair in parapsychology, and Tenhaeff was also appointed director of the university's new Parapsychology Institute. Despite these prestigious titles, Tenhaeff's annual university salary was an extremely low 15,000 guilders (about $4,200).[5] According to journalist Norma Lee Browning, Tenhaeff's salary was actually paid by the Dutch Society of Spiritual Healers, an organization headed by Croiset.[6] So Tenhaeff was at least indirectly on Croiset's payroll and probably owed his academic position to Croiset.

In 1961, journalist Jack Harrison Pollack published two articles about Croiset and his police work in the Sunday supplement *This Week Magazine*,[7] which he followed up in 1964 with the highly successful biography *Croiset the Clairvoyant*.[8] Translated into both

French and German editions, Pollack's book was largely responsible for Croiset's international reputation, and despite its journalistic style can be examined as part of the record of evidence, since it was fully authorized by Tenhaeff and Croiset. In Pollack's Acknowledgments, he thanks Tenhaeff for having "indefatigably double-checked the facts in my manuscript," and Tenhaeff wrote in the journal of the Dutch Society for Psychical Research (the *Tijdschrift voor Parapsychologie*) that the book "was written on the basis of information which I supplied and also under my supervision."[9] Pollack surveys over seventy cases to which Croiset brought his psychic acumen. They cover everything from discovering murderers in sex crimes and finding missing children to identifying an African fossil and locating a lost pig—he even became involved with trying to find the legendary Judge Crater.[10] Altogether, they create an impressive picture of psychic power, all of which we are told was carefully documented by the scientifically meticulous Dr. Tenhaeff.

Croiset's reputation continued to grow, and Tenhaeff took him on visits to meet with other parapsychologists in Austria, Italy, France, Germany, and Switzerland. Croiset was soon reputed to have solved mysteries psychically in many countries, ranging as far away as Australia and Japan. For example, on May 3, 1976, Croiset arrived in Japan to appear on a television show about the occult. While in the studio for rehearsal, Croiset saw another program that showed the distraught father of a seven-year-old schoolgirl, Miwa Kikuchi, who had been missing since May 1. According to a spokesman for Nippon Educational Television, Croiset was shown an old picture of Miwa "and then informed his television audience that she was dead on the surface of a lake near her home." He drew a rough map, and staff members, led by the television show's director, went to the area indicated. They found the girl's body floating in the water just as Croiset had described.[11]

The scope of Croiset's involvements, both geographic and topical, was itself amazing. It was not uncommon for newspapers in other countries to call him for his psychic opinions about local unsolved mysteries. Thus, in 1978, headlines appeared in Australia's *Sunday Sun* telling how Croiset "saw" a missing anti-drug crusader, Donald Mackay, as having been executed six months before by three men, including a VIP Croiset said was well respected in social and political circles. Croiset said Mackay had learned too much about the illegal drug market.[12] And in 1964, Pollack tells us that Croiset was consulted by phone about the murder of three Mississippi civil rights workers and obtained what he said was useful information that was given to the FBI.[13] Tenhaeff said he tried to tape record Croiset's telephone consultations but complained he was only able to do so for about 30 percent of them. The sheer volume of Croiset's cases makes any exhaustive assessment impossible. Tenhaeff quotes Croiset as saying that relatives of missing persons contacted him on an average of ten to twelve times per week, and this lasted for nearly forty years.[14] So, during his lifetime, Croiset probably dealt with over 20,000 cases!

Though Croiset made himself available as a subject almost exclusively for Tenhaeff's research, he also was tested by several other European parapsychologists, most notably Germany's Professor Hans Bender, Sweden's Dr. Martin Johnson, and George Zorab, the Dutch parapsychologist who discovered him some years before Croiset allied himself with Tenhaeff. When Dr. J. B. Rhine visited Holland in 1951, he met Croiset and offered to test him. Croiset declined, saying that he did not like to guess cards and needed to be emotionally involved in his cases. Croiset declined testing by Rhine again in 1962, when invited to come to Duke University by Dr. Johnson, who was then studying with Rhine. This time Croiset indicated his lack of interest in purely statistical tests, but said he would work with Rhine on qualitative experiments if they could be under the direction of Tenhaeff.

While the world outside the Netherlands received glowing tales of Croiset's successes, the reaction within Holland seems to have been rather different. Unfortunately, most of the critical works appeared in Dutch, were not read outside the Netherlands, and seem to have been ignored by Pollack and Croiset's other supporters. For example, during the 1950s, the Dutch skeptic Ph. B. Ottervanger fired several well-aimed salvos at Croiset and Tenhaeff.[15] In 1958, Dr. Filippus Brink published his critical study of several psychic detectives he investigated,[16] one of whom was Croiset. Whereas Pollack and Tenhaeff described Croiset as never "fishing" for information from his clients,[17] Brink reports he heard Croiset do little else. In 1959, a Hamburg police officer published a scathing report entitled "Mr. Croiset, You Are Not Psychic."[18] And in 1960, a Dutch police journal carried an article by Utrecht's police commissioner that cataloged many of Croiset psychic goof-ups,[19] including a December 1957 case of a missing fourteen-year-old. Croiset told his parents the boy drowned, and they then contacted an undertaker to arrange for his funeral. The boy was found alive and well a few days later, hiding in a haystack.

Because few outside of Holland read these criticisms, most parapsychologists knew little of the case against Croiset's claims until 1981—when the investigative reporter Piet Hein Hoebens revealed the details of his and others' investigations, publishing his exposés not only in Amsterdam's *De Telegraaf* but as articles in American, British, and German magazines. Many who had relied on Pollack and Tenhaeff for their information were understandably surprised to learn that "the successive Utrecht chiefs of police have been notoriously skeptical of Gerard Croiset," and that as late as 1980, Hoebens was officially told that "none of Croiset's attempts to locate missing persons or solve crimes in his home town [now Utrecht, where Croiset moved in 1956 to be nearer Tenhaeff's Institute] had ever been successful."[20]

Typical of Hoebens's examinations of the evidence was his double-checking of one of the cases where Pollack tells us he was present. On May 21, 1960, Pollack says Croiset took a call from the neighbor of an Eindhoven family whose four-year-old child was missing. Pollack tells us the police had no clues. Croiset told the neighbor that "the outlook isn't good" and that a search should begin immediately, but he feared the child's body would be found in about three days in a canal close to a bridge. Curiously, Pollack does not tell us how he understood any of this since he spoke no Dutch and Croiset spoke no English. Pollack goes on to tell us that the child was found exactly as Croiset had predicted in his presence. Twenty years later, Hoebens contacted the Eindhoven police's public-relations officer, Mr. W. Jongsma. Jongsma checked the police diary and located the only case fitting Pollack's description, the drowning of three-year-old Anthonius Thoonen, an entry dated May 20, 1960. Contrary to Pollack's claim, the police had more than just clues: The mother had been told by his playmate, John, that her son had fallen into the river, and she had even seen "something" floating some distance from the bank. For some reason, she then waited until her husband came home, and he reported it to the police. Whatever the "something" floating there had been, by the time the police arrived, it apparently had drifted off somewhere; it was no longer visible. Little Anthonius's body was found on May 23, where it had floated up near a playground, and there is no mention of Croiset in the police report.

As Hoebens points out, Croiset's remark that "the outlook is not good" hardly constitutes a striking hit, and the advice to search the area immediately is common sense. Mr. Jongsma told Hoebens that most bodies of drowned persons surface after "about three days"; as for the nearby bridge, there are so many bridges over the river from Eindhoven, it would be remarkable if a drowned body could be found that was *not* near one of them. [21]

While sifting through the available evidence for the most prominent claims made for Croiset, Hoebens soon began discovering damaging new facts. For many of Croiset's cases where a paranormal solution was offered, Hoebens found alternative and more mundane explanations were readily available. For some cases, he found that even if Croiset might have demonstrated some psychic abilities, for example, by telling police or relatives things they already knew, such revelations had no consequences for the police investigation. Frequently, Hoebens found significant omissions in Tenhaeff's and others' descriptions of Croiset's alleged successes. Sometimes he found apparently intentional misrepresentation of the events, and, in a few instances, wholesale fabrication of facts.

Hoebens also found many unpublicized cases of Croiset's striking failures, some of which produced rather extreme consequences for those involved. Here are a few examples:

When in Viareggio, Italy, in 1969, Croiset said he "saw" a missing thirteen-year-old, Ermano Lavorini, falling into the water while playing. It turned out the boy was killed in a quarrel with a friend and his body was found in the dunes. [22]

Croiset stated in May of 1956 that a missing man from Rossum, Holland, was alive, well, and living in Germany. Soon thereafter, his body was found in a canal in Ootmarsum, Holland. [23]

In 1966, a committee concerned with locating three missing children brought Croiset to Adelaide, Australia. Croiset said the children were buried under a new warehouse and advised its demolition. His sponsors collected the $40,000 (Australian) needed to do the job, and they dug four yards down through all the soil beneath what had been the concrete floor. When no bodies were found, Croiset insisted that they dig a yard deeper. They did, with no results at all. [24]

One of Croiset's "visions" proved unfortunate for one Mr. Senf when relatives of a murdered Chinese from The Hague consulted Croiset in June of 1973 and were told Senf could tell them more about the crime. The relatives then abducted Senf and tortured him for three hours, hoping to get a confession. Senf insisted he knew nothing. Later, when Croiset visited the recovering Senf in the hospital, he told Senf that he was now convinced Senf was innocent.[25]

Hoebens fully recognized the practical impossibilities in trying to check the details of even a majority of the cases claimed for Croiset, and clearly noted that "it is impossible to disprove each and every one of Croiset's alleged psychic feats."[26] The sheer number of these allegedly successful cases necessitates some degree of rational selection. However, having found so much of Tenhaeff's writings to be "utterly unreliable," Hoebens warned that "it is therefore hazardous to suggest possible 'naturalistic' explanations for any 'facts' presented in these reports. One may easily waste one's ingenuity on entirely spurious data."[27] To make matters worse, when Tenhaeff was directly confronted by Hoebens's request for comments on Hoebens's analyses, Hoebens tell us that "the 'stickler for complete scientific proof' flatly refused to answer any questions, shouting a number of insults before slamming the receiver down."[28]

Because Tenhaeff asserted he kept meticulous (and what would have to be enormous) files of tape recordings and affadavits to document Croiset's marvels, many hoped these materials would eventually allow an impartial sorting out of the facts, which would reveal the full story of Tenhaeff's work with Croiset. Roy Stemman, one of Croiset's admirers, wrote that "the Utrecht archives must contain some of the best-authenticated accounts of clairvoyance on record," and commented that despite Croiset's death, "the records on file at Utrecht University of the world's most tested psychic will continue to intrigue and baffle scientists for many years to come."[29] Alas, these records seem another chimera, for when Hoebens made inquiries at Utrecht State University in 1981, he was told that "the whereabouts of Dr. Tenhaeff's celebrated files are a mystery," even to Tenhaeff's successor, Dr. Henri van Praag, the new special Professor of Parapsychology.[30]

In light of these serious problems for any objective evaluation, Hoebens concentrated attention on those cases Tenhaeff himself put forward as the strongest scientific evidence for Croiset's powers. Perhaps the best such examples were the three major cases presented by Tenhaeff to impress his fellow researchers at the First International Conference on Parapsychological Studies at Utrecht State University in the summer of 1953.[31] After first pointing out that the information psychics provided to police often did not advance the crime investigation but still "proved interesting in terms of parapsychological research," Tenhaeff went on cite three prime examples of cases he felt demonstrated "where the contribution of Mr. Croiset was of concrete use to the police and the courts of law." The first of these was the Wierden case, one which Tenhaeff repeatedly cited as a prize case in his later writings. The case was widely cited in newspaper articles, is in both Pollack's and Enkelaar's biographies of Croiset, and was even the subject of a dramatized TV documentary in Italy.

According to Tenhaeff's account, a young girl returning home near Wierden, Holland, was assaulted by a man who leaped out from behind a stone storehouse and hit her with a hammer on her neck and arms. Police contacted Tenhaeff, who went with Croiset to the station. They did not see the girl because she was in the hospital. Croiset picked up the hammer and described the assailant: "He is tall and dark, about thirty years old, and has a somewhat deformed left ear." He further said the hammer did not belong to the assailant but to a "man about of about fifty-five whom the criminal visits often at a small white cottage . . . near here. It is one of a group of three cottages, all the same."[32] Months later the police picked up a twenty-nine-year old man on another morals charge. He had a badly scarred and swollen left ear, which led to his being questioned about the attack. He confessed and said he had indeed borrowed the hammer from a friend in a white cottage, exactly as Croiset had described. Tenhaeff claimed he had full documentation authenticating this version of the events.

This case was later investigated by Professor C. E. M. Hansel, a psychologist at the University of Wales and a leading critic of parapsychology. When he contacted the Wierden police, the mayor (burgomaster) from that period, E. D. Van Maaldrink, wrote Hansel that Tenhaeff's description was false in nearly all its details.[33] There was no stone storehouse in the neighborhood. The girl was struck twice on the head and never on the arms or neck. She did not have to go to the hospital. The police did not call in Croiset. He was consulted by the landlord of the girl's sister, who obtained the hammer from the police when he asked if he could borrow it to consult Croiset. The assailant's name actually came up early in the case because several people had noticed he seemed a sexual exhibitionist. But, most important, the assailant actually had two quite normal ears, and the police were never able to find out who the real owner of the hammer was. Tenhaeff based his case largely upon a letter he had earlier received from Mayor van Maaldrink, but from which Tenhaeff later selectively quoted. He left in the mayor's initial confirmations, which resulted from distortions of memory by the policeman who reported to the mayor, but removed the passages where the mayor cited errors by Croiset.[34] The mayor had not kept a copy of his original letter and complained that Tenhaeff did not reply to his request for a copy of his own letter. After he obtained a copy (apparently via Hansel, to whom Tenhaeff had sent a Xerox copy), Mayor Van Maaldrink explained his earlier erroneous confirmations and wrote: "For the work of the police the declarations of Mr. Croiset had not the slightest value indeed."[35]

Tenhaeff's second-prize case took place on November 10, 1952. An official of Enschede's Customs Department, a Mr. A. M. den Hollander, wrote Tenhaeff about how he had shown Croiset a picture of a man suspected of coffee smuggling. Croiset made many correct statements about the suspect, including some details he told Tenhaeff were previously unknown to the police but later verified. In particular, Croiset had said the transportation of the illegal coffee took place "not across smugglers' trails, but normally through the customs barrier." Den Hollander said this was unknown at the time of his consultation, and that they later found that part of the coffee went over the border hidden in a limousine.

Hoebens tracked down the case as one involving a Mr. G. Hasperhoven, director of a coffee-roasting factory in Enschede. Hoebens noted some discrepancies between the story as reported by Tenhaeff and later by Pollack and points out that Tenhaeff provides no basis for us to assume that Croiset really was a complete stranger to the case. More significantly, Hoebens found that the suspect had been mentioned in the local press, and it would have been easy to guess the questions were about this affair, since Mr. den Hollander was clearly from customs. Hoebens also found that on October 27, only about two weeks before, the Enschede newspaper *Tubantia* reported the customs department's staging of a reconstruction of the smuggling and the way it took place, including a picture of the limousine and the customs barrier.[36]

The third exemplary case given by Tenhaeff, and one he glowingly wrote about in at least three different papers, concerned an October 1952 attempt to murder a policeman on patrol in Woerden,

Holland. In the courtroom on what Hoebens shows must have been November 25, Croiset gave a number of apparently striking impressions about the suspect, a sheet-metal worker, just arrested but unseen by Croiset. As it turned out, and as Tenhaeff acknowledged fully in one of his last versions of this episode,[37] the suspect was innocent, so Croiset had picked the wrong man. But Tenhaeff considered the case an excellent study for psychical research if not criminological purposes. However, Hoebens traced the story fully and found out that there had been actually *two* innocent suspects arrested, and while some of Croiset's descriptions fit one, other impressions fit the other. Most important, however, Hoebens found that the full story of these two suspects, including mention of their professions, former professions, and even their fondness of fishing, appeared in *De Telegraaf* on November 20, five days before Croiset made his very similar revelations.[38]

As Hoebens points out, Tenhaeff's prize cases repeatedly fail to withstand outside scrutiny. When Utrecht's police superintendent, Th. van Roosmalen, expressed his skepticism to Tenhaeff, the latter offered to supply him with "a few cases where the police failed and where Croiset was successful."[39] He gave van Roosmalen two cases, one a murder case in municipality X, where Croiset gave so clear a description that an arrest was possible, the other in town Y, where Croiset identified a thief in a factory. Van Roosmalen checked with police in the two cities. From police in X, he was told that no such murderer could have been correctly identified by Croiset, since there had been no murder in this small town since the beginning of this century. And from city Y, police told him that Croiset had indeed named a culprit who was then arrested, but he turned out to be innocent and was released with much embarrassment and profuse apologies.[40]

In addition to Tenhaeff's many case reports, Croiset frequently offered demonstrations of his psychic abilities through what came to be known as the chair tests. Tenhaeff devised this demonstration based on similar tests constructed in 1925 by the French parapsychologist Dr. Eugene Osty. Essentially the test consists of numbering a group of chairs in a meeting hall some days prior to the audience's attending. As a demonstration of his precognitive abilities, Croiset would make tape recordings describing those who would be sitting in these numbered chairs when they were later freely selected by audience members (no chairs were reserved). His prior descriptions were then compared with the people who chose to sit in the numbered chairs. Croiset performed his first such demonstration in 1947 and exhibited his abilities in several hundred similar chair tests over the years. Tenhaeff and other supporters of Croiset, especially Professor Hans Bender, cite these "experiments" as convincing proof of Croiset's psychic powers, and he and his colleagues even conducted statistical analyses of his level of hits.[41]

These demonstrations have been regularly criticized over the years for their inadequate controls against error and fraud, especially by George Zorab.[42] It should also be noted that these tests were not always successful. For example, Zorab describes a 1957 chair test Croiset did with him in Bologna, Italy. Zorab writes that "this Bologna chair test was a complete failure! Not a single item right."[43] However, the most devastating attack on the chair tests was in a posthumously published paper by Hoebens.[44] Here Hoebens compares Tenhaeff's account of a transatlantic chair test with the independent account of Dr. Jule Eisenbud, revealing remarkable discrepancies and major distortions by Tenhaeff that call into serious question Tenhaeff's other accounts of such tests.

Going even further, in 1981 Hoebens conducted his own experiment to show the subjective difficulties involved with these tests.[45] Hoebens took Croiset's descriptions of sitters in his 1953 chair test in Pirmasens, which Dr. Hans Bender called a classic, and pretended they were fresh descriptions for "target" subjects in Hoebens's audience. Hoebens found "these results were even more striking than in the original experiment—the targets 'recognizing' descriptions of themselves—which certainly confirms any suspicion that a typical 'hit' in the chair test was the result of subjective validation rather than genuine ESP."[46]

But the most devastating accusation from Hoebens was yet to come. On November 15, 1979, Croiset was visited by Commander Eekhof, a state police officer, in the hope that Croiset might help him find an unknown arsonist who for months had been terrorizing the Woudrichem area. Writing in the German occult magazine *Esotera*,[47] Tenhaeff told of his July 1980 visit to the police to get the details of Croiset's success. Tenhaeff informed his readers that "everything Commander Eekhof told us was videotaped. The tapes were protocolled and the protocol was checked and signed by Mr. Eekhof." Tenhaeff tells us that Croiset told Eekhof that the arsonist "sometimes wore a uniform," "had something to do with toy airplanes," and "lived in an apartment building." Tenhaeff wrote that Eekhof was shocked to recognize the man Croiset described as a quartermaster in his own police group who had model airplanes, and all Croiset described was eventually confirmed.

Hoebens visited Commander Eekhof and asked him to read Tenhaeff's article. Eekhof told Hoebens that it contained "outright falsehoods" and allowed Hoebens to hear the tape recording of what Croiset really had said. In fact, the consultation with Croiset had taken place on November 15, 1977, two years before the date Tenhaeff gave. Croiset never mentioned a "uniform," nor did he mention "toy airplanes." Also, the quartermaster did not live in an apartment, and Croiset had originally identified the arsonist as someone entirely different. Eekhof told Hoebens that he could not possibly have recognized his quartermaster from the confused images Croiset gave him, and, worst of all, Eekhof absolutely denied having seen or signed any protocol.[48]

W. H. C. Tenhaeff died on July 9, 1981, only a year after Gerard Croiset's passing. And Piet Hein Hoebens, only thirty-six, died on October 22, 1984. So the debate was never fully played out, and many questions remain. George Zorab, the parapsychologist who knew Croiset longest, told Hoebens that "Croiset was at least a part-time cheat,"[49] and that he had some "evidence that Croiset sometimes employed confederates in his experiments."[50] Yet, despite all this, Zorab still concluded that when all was considered, Croiset probably also had genuine psychic abilities.[51]

What then can we conclude about this alleged Mozart of psychics? Certainly, Tenhaeff's evidence on his behalf will not bear the burden of proof science would demand of it. The case for Croiset remains unproved, but we need to remember that nonproof is not the same as disproof. When all is sifted through, how damaging is Hoebens's case against Croiset? His defenders might raise two points. First, the main thrust of Hoebens's revelations goes against Tenhaeff more than it may go toward Croiset. Some still impressed by Croiset, like George Zorab, may argue the faults lay less in the flawed psychic than in his promoter.

Second, a great part of Hoebens's criticism consists of having located previously unpublicized instances of Croiset's failures. This most certainly makes untenable Tenhaeff's claim that Croiset was a psychic who "never disappointed," but Croiset himself never claimed such infallibility. And just as critics can account for many of his publicized successes as simply occasional coincidences or a portion of lucky hits that might be expected from any psychic who makes twenty thousand guesses, so, too, can defenders argue that a dozen or so of his known failures count for only a very small percentage of his total cases. If chance can produce hits for a nonpsychic, it can also allow some misses for an imperfect psychic. Hoebens may not have demonstrated that our psychic Mozart was actually tone-deaf, but he has at least reduced him to the level of a mere Salieri. At one time, Tenhaeff apparently did have a mass of documentation on Croiset's cases; not only Pollack but others tell us they saw it.[52] Unless someone can locate and examine that missing stockpile of evidence Tenhaeff claimed he was going to leave for future researchers, we probably will never know the full tale, and Croiset will continue to have his supporters.

Meanwhile, Croiset's psychic detection work has been continued by his son, Gerard Croiset, Jr. Reports of his sleuthing occasionally appear in the press, but without a Tenhaeff to act as his publicist, his work is far less well-known.

In 1973 Gerard, Jr. received a request for help from one of the mothers of two missing girls from Folly Beach, South Carolina.[53] Though Croiset was credited with an uncanny description of where the girls would be found, they were actually located quite independently when police picked up a man on a different matter and a thread of information about the girls emerged. In another much-publicized episode, Croiset, Jr., was consulted when a plane went down in the Andes. This event later received intense press coverage when they found the passengers who were still alive and discovered that they had survived largely through resorting to cannibalism. Though Croiset, Jr., was apparently correct in some of his impressions, the interpretation placed on them misled the searchers. The parents of Gustavo Nicolich, one of the boys who was lost, said they felt animosity toward the psychic because he "sent them off on a false trail at the time when to continue toward the Tinguiririca and Soneado mountains might have saved their son's life."[54]

SEVEN

Peter Hurkos: The Clown Prince?

I f Croiset was the king of psychic sleuths, the leading candidate for heir apparent was surely Peter Hurkos. Often referred to as "the man with the radar brain," he was born Pieter Cornelis van der Hurk on May 21, 1911, in Dordrecht, Holland. Hurkos was only two years younger than Croiset, but his psychic career only began when Hurkos was thirty, and Croiset was already well established. During his lifetime, Hurkos presented several variations on his life story, most notably in his autobiography *Psychic*[1] and Norma Lee Browning's biographies *The Psychic World Of Peter Hurkos*[2] and *Peter Hurkos: I Have Many Lives*.[3] He frequently contradicted himself, and many of the things he said about his early life were greatly embellished if not pure fabrications, so even our attempt at a short reconstruction here needs to be considered in that light.

At sixteen, Hurkos left school to become a merchant seaman, for a while helping his family with their painting business in summer and going to sea in winter. By 1935, he had worked his way up to a job as a tallyman (checking cargo and passengers) in Shanghai, but when war broke out in 1939 he lost the job and returned home. In 1937, on one of his trips home, he married a local girl, Bea van der Berg, and she soon gave him first a son, Benny, and then a daughter, Bea. He tells us he joined the underground and changed his name to Hurkos (a Hungarian name) to avoid possible reprisals against his family (an unlikely story, since he seems to have been living with them). On July 10, 1941, while helping his father paint a German airplane hangar, Hurkos fell thirty feet from a ladder onto his head and shoulder.[4] He later claimed that when he awoke in the hospital after being unconscious for four days, he could somehow pick up information about people and things merely by touching them.

According to Hurkos, one of his first visions was that a fellow patient about to be released from the hospital was a British agent. He tried to warn the man that he would be shot down on Kalver Street within a couple of days, but the hospital staff thought he was hallucinating. Two days later, the agent was indeed shot down by the Gestapo on the named street. In February 1981, as part of his investigation into Hurkos's Dutch claims, Piet Hein Hoebens checked with the State Institute for War Archives in Amsterdam. Dr. C. J. F. Stuldreher at the Institute wrote Hoebens: "It is not known to us that in the summer of 1941 a 'British' agent (either of Dutch or British nationality) has been shot by the Gestapo in the Kalverstraat in Amsterdam or any other Dutch town. It is very improbable that this occurrence really took place."[5]

Hurkos tells us he continued working with the underground in a section headed by Hert Goozens. Hurkos claims he distinguished himself through a variety of heroic acts. In his autobiography, he tells us of an episode when his underground friend Yap Mindemon was arrested by the Nazis and taken to the camp at Vught. Hurkos disguised himself as a German officer and went there, introduced himself (apparently in impeccable German), and told the camp commandant the prisoner was to be turned over to him so he could be brought to headquarters for questioning. The Germans bought his story and took him to Mindemon. When Mindemon saw Hurkos, he recognized him, and Hurkos suddenly "knew" that his friend believed he must be a traitor and was about to shout at him and ruin the escape. So Hurkos went up to Mindemon, hit him as hard as he could, and started beating him while yelling at him in German that he was a spy and a dirty dog.

Two soldiers pulled Hurkos away from the now unconscious Mindemon and said, "Please, Herr Kapitän. He is not dangerous." The soldiers then carried Mindemon to the staff car and Hurkos drove off with him past the gates of the camp and to safety with the underground.[6]

Hoebens examined this story and concluded it was most likely fictitious on three grounds. First, it is contrary to everything we know about how the highly organized Nazi bureaucracy worked. Second, the files of the Vught camp are preserved at the State Institute for War Archives (known there as RIOD) and show no indication that any such sensational escape ever took place there. And third, a Dutchman whose German was flawless enough to fool a German camp comman-dant would surely have known that in the German Wehrmacht, a soldier would not have been called "Kapitän" but "Hauptmann."[7] When asked for his opinion after checking the RIOD archives, Drs. Stuldreher told Hoebens: "The story seems to me a product of the imagination."[8]

Norma Lee Browning's biography tells us that after the war was over, Hurkos and others (presumably including his section leader Hert Goozens) were presented to Queen Juliana at the Royal Palace to receive commendations, each being given a gold medal and scroll.[9] Hoebens was unable to find any record available of this presumably public ceremony. Further, when he checked with the RIOD in 1981, Dr. Stuldreher wrote him: "Mr. Hert Goozens, 'one of the bravest men in the entire system of secret fighters' must have been extraor-dinarily fond of secrecy, for even now nothing is known about him or his group."[10]

According to Hurkos's autobiography, near the end of the war he was caught with forged papers by the Germans and sent to Buchen-wald in Germany, but his life was spared because he was not Jewish.[11] According to the version he told Browning, however, he was arrested for "cutting trees for firewood to keep his family warm" and was interned at Vught, a punitive labor camp in Holland.[12]

When liberated shortly after D-Day, he went home to recuper-ate and found that he could no longer work at his past jobs because he found his psychic abilities too distracting. People began to hear of his strange talents and requested his appearance before groups. By 1946, he had started appearing at church benefits and soon began accepting theatrical bookings. His theatrical debut seems to have been in a 1946 variety show at the *Kaas Lange* in the Hague.[13] Under the sponsor-ship of René van Straaten, a Belgian promoter, he toured Europe demonstrating his psychometry, and, he tells us, was soon helping police departments not only in Holland but in Belgium, England, France, and Germany.

It was during this period that he and his wife, Bea, divorced. He later told Browning it was because of his gift,[14] but his autobiography does not even mention Bea's existence. He reportedly married his second wife, Maria, a Belgian former beauty-parlor operator, in 1947. They had a daughter, Caroline. During this European period, Hurkos—who ran away from home and out to sea soon after he was thrown out of school for hurling an ink pot at his teacher—seems to have started calling himself "Dr. Hurkos,"[15] a title he later dropped. In his autobiography, Hurkos wrote that Maria spoke seven languages and often acted as an interpreter for him in his public and private readings. Hurkos claimed that he also spoke seven languages, including Chinese,[16] though this seems very unlikely (especially given his always terrible English), and Kobler wrote that Hurkos spoke only Dutch.[17] Maria left him sometime around 1965, and we hear little about her in Browning's 1970 biography, but she must have been an asset to his work. She also seems to have had a wry sense of humor. In the context of discussing Hurkos's ability to sense people's infidelities, writer Jess Stearn describes Maria greeting Hurkos at the airport and asking, "Are you kissing me or just checking?"[18]

Hurkos alleges his first police case concerned an October 1946 shooting in Limburg, Holland.[19] The police brought him a coat belonging to a murdered coal miner named van Tossing. Hurkos told them the killer was his stepfather, Bernhard van Tossing, and that the older man's motive was his desire for the victim's wife. The police were astonished, for they already had the stepfather in custody, but they assumed Hurkos must have obtained this information from someone on the force. Hurkos then told them they would find the gun they had been searching for by looking on the roof of van Tossing's house. They checked and found the weapon there with empty shells and the fingerprints which they used to convict the murderer. However, says Hurkos, the police would not publicly credit him for fear of ridicule by those who would criticize them for having gone to a crystal-ball gazer.

Reporters from the newspaper De Telegraaf looked into this case in 1958 when news spread about plans to shoot a film about Hurkos, and some citizens of Limburg expressed concern about their city being associated with a dubious occult success. The journalists checked with Hurkos, who repeated his story, and then with the Limburg police. They were informed that what Hurkos had actually told the police was that the gun could be found not on the roof but in a brooklet. The cops dragged for the gun and found nothing in its waters. The weapon was found on the roof only the next year, and, contrary to what Hurkos claimed were the killer's motives, the victim's wife played no role whatsoever in the case.[20]

Hurkos tells us of another much-written-about episode during a trip to England in January, 1951, soon after the Stone of Scone was stolen on Christmas Day 1950. As was already widely suspected, Hurkos told the police the Stone had been stolen by Scottish nationalists and transported to Scotland. He said it was in Glasgow and went there but failed to find it. As it turned out, the Stone had been hidden in a ruined abbey in Arbroath, not at all near Glasgow. Despite Hurkos's claims that he gave information to the police that consisted of a number of striking "hits" that the embarrassed police "covered up," Scotland Yard formally denied that Hurkos or any of the several other psychics who offered their services had been of any help whatsoever. Upon his return to Holland from Britain, Hurkos suffered a further indignity he avoided mentioning. The Dutch newspapers were highly amused to report that customs officials at Schiphol Airport searched his luggage and found a substantial amount of contraband.[21]

That same year, Hurkos became involved in the case that has most frequently been mentioned about him and which many have called his clairvoyant masterpiece: his alleged discovery of the mysterious pyromaniac of Ooijpolder, Holland—Piet Vierbloom, the seventeen-year-old son of a wealthy and respected Nijmegen family. Supposedly, Hurkos pointed to the unsuspected youth and shocked the police chief, Captain Cammaert, who simply refused to believe it. They reluctantly had the boy brought in for interrogation. He denied the charges until Hurkos did the questioning. The young arsonist could not resist Hurkos's penetrating gaze and gave a full confession. In examining the actual records of this case, Hoebens found that in fact the mentally deranged boy had been suspected almost from the beginning, because of an earlier fire where he worked. And on August 14, at the site of one of the fires, they found wrappers from a brand of sweets of the kind the boy had bought just before at the local candy store. He was arrested on August 17. Hurkos did not even enter the case until August 18, and the public prosecutor, Baron

Speijart van Woerden, told Hoebens he was quite unimpressed by Hurkos's managing to pick the boy out of a picture of his family, a stunt he might have accomplished through the well-known trick of muscle-reading.[22] To cap off his debunking, Hoebens obtained a photostat of a June 23, 1956, statement signed by Captain Cammaert, put out for the state police of the Nijmegen district, in which it is categorically denied that any psychics were ever successfully employed by them in any criminal investigation.[23]

In 1952, when Hurkos was in Madrid, he claims he told the newspaper reporters about a vision he had of Adolf Hitler in which he saw Hitler traveling through Spain disguised as a monk. "Hitler is alive," he told them. "I will stake my life and reputation on it."[24] Hurkos further claimed that the night after the story came out, he was visited by two fascist leaders who warned him to stop speaking of it. Writing about this in 1961, Hurkos tells us: "I don't know whether Hitler is alive today, but I knew that he was living at that time."[25]

In his book *The Occult Explosion*, Nat Freedland wrote that Hurkos had received a written commendation from the Pope for solving the Amsterdam murder of a priest and also for not letting it be known that his murderer was the mother of his illegitimate child.[26] In 1982, Hoebens checked this claim with both Father Solleveld, the 1945–1964 secretary to the Roman Catholic diocese of Haarlem (which district includes Amsterdam), and the police. Both indicated the story was impossible, since no priest had been murdered in Amsterdam since the war. The secretary told Hoebens he would "certainly have heard of such an incident" and that it was also "highly unlikely that the Pope would have written a commendation without having informed the diocese. This was further confirmed to Hoebens by Father Solleveld's successor as diocesal secretary, Father Landsdaal.[27]

In 1954, Hurkos supposedly was invited to give a private demonstration for her husband and some guests by a Mrs. "Mevrouw R.," the wife of "one of Holland's richest, most influential, and renowned patriots." Hurkos says that when given Mr. R's cigarette case, he was suddenly hit by a terrible vision of sixteen Dutchmen being shot. Hurkos could not restrain himself and cried out, "He is a traitor! He was honored by our country as a patriot, and he betrayed us—sixteen men—shot—sixteen Dutchmen shot—and all his fault! He made a deal with the Nazis; they ran his factories and he controlled them." Mr. R. had blanched with fear at Hurkos's first words, then stiffened in his wheelchair, choked out some words, and tried to step toward Hurkos but then collapsed on the floor. His now hysterical wife yelled at Hurkos, "He's dead, he's dead—and you killed him! Liar! Liar!" But Hurkos says he spoke the truth, and "five long, lonely, haunted years" later, it was finally established that Herr R., the highly honored patriot, had indeed actually been a collaborator with the Nazis.[28] When Hoebens checked into this story, he found that "the enormous files of the RIOD do not contain the slightest indication that this drama, or anything like it, ever took place. Nothing is known there about 'one of Holland's richest, most influential, and renowned patriots' who has posthumously been exposed as a traitor." As with Hurkos's other stories of his World War II heroics, Dr. Stuldreher told Hoebens this story was purely from Hurkos's fertile imagination.[29]

When interviewed by the *De Telegraaf* journalists in 1958, Hurkos told them of another 1955 episode when forty-three coal miners were trapped in a Limburg mine for seventeen hours because their lift system had been sabotaged. Unless the culprit could be found, the miners threatened to strike. The chief of the mine police consulted with Hurkos, who took him straight to the saboteur's house. The man confessed. When they checked this tale, the reporters found the failure took place in an *unmanned* lift, was due to wear rather than sabotage, and, of course, no one was arrested since no crime had taken place.[30]

Hoebens tried to investigate several other alleged Hurkos hits, but for many of them the descriptions by Hurkos were simply too vague or undetailed to follow up adequately. For others, he simply could find nothing to back up Hurkos's story. For example, Hurkos tells of his great (but undated) success in locating the body of the drowned son of a Captain Folken after the boy fell from his father's ship into Rotterdam Harbor. Hurkos informs us that the newspapers described his psychic detection in this case as "phenomenal."[31]

Hoebens enlisted the aid of a Mr. Bouwamn of the Rotterdam municipal police force, who went through volumes of police reports and interviewed current and several retired policemen who might recall the case. He found that there seemed to be no documents, no such newspaper stories, and nothing in the memories of any of the policemen he consulted that would back up Hurkos's story.[32] Hoebens cautiously reminds us that though his failure to unearth corroborative evidence does not disprove Hurkos's claims, it certainly does constitute a good basis for our skepticism. Given that the burden must be on Hurkos to establish such extraordinary claims, and in light of his apparent history of fabrications, Hoebens's caution here is surprisingly generous to Hurkos.

In 1956 neurologist and parapsychologist Dr. Andrija Puharich, then director of the Round Table Foundation in Glen Cove, Maine, which he founded in 1948, brought Hurkos to the United States and ran tests on him there for over two years. Altogether, Puharich collected laboratory and field materials on Hurkos for about seven years. (Years later, this same Dr. Puharich would similarly introduce the Israeli psychic Uri Geller to the United States.) The Round Table research was primarily funded by William Henry Belk, the American retail tycoon. Hurkos told his biographer that he sacrificed much financially to come to the United States to be Puharich's experimental guinea pig. He claimed he gave up yearly retainers from several large European industrial firms[33] and that he could have made far more money by continuing in Europe with his private readings and public performances.[34] Browning wrote that he could have achieved great wealth and fame by staying in Europe and working as a stage telepathist,[35] but the fact is that as a stage mentalist, he was decidely third-rate. This was quite evident to many magicians we interviewed who saw both his early and later nightclub and talk-show appearances.[36]

Hurkos wrote in his autobiography that he left the Round Table Foundation in 1958 "when it became apparent that the foundation was dissolving—after the death of Mrs. Alice Bouverie, its most interested patron."[37] It seems more likely that his departure was connected with the disenchantment William Henry Belk had undergone with Hurkos. Belk had followed Hurkos's advice and lost twenty thousand dollars in a uranium search in Utah, and "considerably more" by opening Belk stores in Miami and Atlanta after Hurkos predicted success for them. He said his total involvement with Hurkos had cost him fifty thousand dollars and concluded that "no man should ever trust a psychic for business purposes." But his main disillusionment came when Hurkos failed to foresee tragedy when Belk's ten-year-old only daughter drowned in June of 1957.[38]

Dr. Puharich wrote about some of his research with Hurkos in his books *The Sacred Mushroom*[39] and *Beyond Telepathy*,[40] but none of those experiments are described in adequate scientific detail to evaluate them properly. Though Browning tells us that Puharich "probably has the most complete file in existence on Peter Hurkos,"[41] and that he performed well under controlled conditions, Puharich's experimental reports on Hurkos have yet to appear in any standard scientific journals, including those of parapsychology. Puharich worked independently, and most of the results he claimed have long been regarded with skepticism even among many parapsychologists. Hurkos himself correctly observed the problem when he told an interviewer that "Dr. Puharich made a mistake by not having a lot of scientists witness his experiments. He did research for many years . . . but he did it all by himself."[42] Hurkos claimed that he had earlier been tested in Antwerp, Belgium, by Dr. René Dellaert, a psychologist at the University of Louvain, who measured his brain waves with an electroencephalograph. Purportedly, Dellaert showed Hurkos photos of strangers, some of whom were deceased while others were still alive, and found violent brain-pattern fluctuations when Hurkos viewed a photo of any of the dead persons.[43] The results of that reputed research does not seem to have been published, either.

Around 1947 Hurkos was apparently tested by a Belgian scientist familiar with conjuring methods, Professor Albert Bessemans.[44] Hurkos failed these tests miserably. According to Hurkos, Dr. J. B. Rhine offered to test him only if he would agree to take a lie-detector test first. (Rhine was openly distrustful of all stage mentalists, since he believed most were publicity-seeking frauds, but this alleged demand for a polygraph examination is quite out of character for him.) Hurkos tells us he was insulted and refused.[45] Apparently, this did not keep Hurkos or his promoters from issuing a statement in 1960 that he had been "at Duke University and had given ESP performances with one hundred percent success," and also that "Hurkos performed successfully at one laboratory in an electrically screened cage." This compelled Dr. Rhine to publish a denial saying that though he had been extended an invitation to be tested there, "Hurkos has *not* been investigated at the Duke laboratory and is not known to have given any such performance as those claimed in any university laboratory."[46] Such exaggeration by Hurkos should not have been a surprise. Even Professor Tenhaeff told writer Jess Stearn that Hurkos falsely claimed to have "received a statement from me by which I declare him to be one of the world's best clairvoyants."[47]

In April and June of 1965, Hurkos agreed to participate in two experiments designed by the parapsychologists Professor Charles T.

Tart and Jeffrey Smith. Both these tests were designed to allow maximum psychological support for Hurkos and consisted of his being given cuttings of human hair from about one hundred different persons Hurkos psychically described. It is interesting to note that Hurkos himself thought he was doing well in the experiments. Tart's and Smith's careful statistical analysis of the results revealed no evidence of any ESP in Hurkos's performance.[48]

Hurkos first came to broad attention in the United States through a *True* magazine article in 1956 by John Kobler.[49] There, Kobler acknowledged that Hurkos "has to be sure, failed—at least as often as he had succeeded."[50] By the time Norma Lee Browning first wrote about Hurkos in 1961 for the *Chicago Sunday Tribune Magazine,* his claim success rate had substantially risen to what he modestly referred to as "only 87 per cent."[51] Hurkos apparently did not feel it necessary to tell us his basis for this remarkably precise figure.

Much of Hurkos's fame stemmed from his many radio and television appearances. After moving to Miami, Florida, in 1958, he starred in the WPST-TV *Mind Mysteries* television series, and often appeared on Alan Courtney's radio show. Listeners would call in and ask Hurkos questions, and he would give them his psychic impressions. Hurkos was a master at what had been called his "sleight of tongue." As Dr. Ronald A. Schwartz showed in an analysis of some of Hurkos's radio readings, between Hurkos's heavy Dutch accent, his frequent ambiguous mispronunciations, and a great deal of vagueness in his descriptions, listeners who wished to could easily find what might seem to be hits among his many statements.[52]

A Dutch television pilot film, *Sixth Sense,* was made about his early psychic experiences. Hurkos's widespread celebrity really began in 1961, when "One Step Beyond," a film dramatizing his life, with actor Albert Salmi playing Hurkos, was broadcast as an Alcoa TV special on network television. Brought to Hollywood for the film in the spring of 1960, he met many movie stars who were impressed by him, and some of them—including Marlon Brando, Frank Sinatra, and Lucille Ball—later patronized him for his psychic advice. When Hurkos's autobiography, *Psychic,* was published in 1961, his new friend Glenn Ford bought the option to make a movie in which he would play Hurkos. Ford says the project fell through because he could not get clearances from some of the people Hurkos told about in his book. Small wonder, since many of them may never have existed.

According to Hurkos's autobiography, in 1958 he was consulted in his home, sitting at his coffee table with his fingers on the police file, after volunteering his aid to Lieutenant Tom Lipe, the head of the homicide squad, in the matter of a killing of a taxicab driver in Miami. Hurkos claims he startled Lipe by telling him that this murder had been committed by a Detroit hood called Smitty who had also recently killed another man, a retired colonel, in Key West. Hurkos said he would be picked up somewhere other than Miami after a bank robbery. Lipe checked and discovered there had been such an earlier murder. A man called Schmidt was later apprehended after a stickup in a Detroit bar. He was brought to trial and convicted when it was found that his gun matched the two bullets in the victims. Hurkos acknowledged his mistake about the bank, but asserted that he had seen Smitty near the bank he said must have been next door to the bar.[53] However, in the version of this episode given us by Browning (presumably also relying on information from Hurkos), the police were *already aware* of the similarity in the bullets; they had *earlier* theorized that the victims might have been killed by the same person; Hurkos's revelations were given while he was sitting *in the cabdriver's car;* the earlier victim was a *navy commander* in Key Largo; and the culprit's name was Charles *Smith.* Though Lipe told Browning he felt Hurkos had been helpful, he also made reference to some of his colleagues' disapproval of his connecting Hurkos with the solution of the case, so "in some published reports of the case Peter didn't rate even a mention."[54]

Hurkos's biggest fiasco came in 1959 with the Jackson Family Murders, a case he avoided mentioning in his autobiography.[55] The bodies of Carroll V. Jackson, who had been shot, and his seventeen-month-old daughter Janet, who had been beaten and then buried alive, were found on March 4, outside of Fredericksburg, Virginia. On March 21, police found the beaten bodies of Mrs. Jackson and her four-year-old daughter. Hurkos was hired for one hundred dollars a day by Dr. F. Regis Riesenman, a staff psychiatrist at Washington's St. Elizabeth's Hospital. Hurkos directed police to look for a man whose business was "either junk or garbage." Police already had a suspect, John A. Tarmon, who was a trashman. They had inadequate evidence to arrest Tarmon but were convinced they had their culprit. Mrs. Tarmon was persuaded to sign a commitment petition, and Tarmon was whisked off two hundred miles away to a mental institution for the criminally insane following a hurried lunacy hearing held at 3 A.M., with Dr. Riesenman as one of the three members of the lunacy commission. Hurkos bragged to the press, "I've done a good job here. I worked three days and cracked the case."[56]

A jazz musician and piano salesman, Melvin David Reese, was picked up by the FBI two weeks later in Arkansas, and police found his diary described his killing of Mrs. Jackson and her daughter. Reese was convicted and sentenced to death. The American Civil Liberties Union had already raised complaints about the unusual lunacy hearing and what the Washington *Sunday Star* editorially called "Crystal Ball Justice."[57] Mrs. Tarmon claimed the interrogations by the police and Hurkos had worn her down to the point where she said she had made "erroneous statements" about her husband. Once free, Tarmon brought a $25,000 suit against the police (a case which he subsequently dropped).

Despite all this, including Hurkos's acknowledgment that "I picked the wrong man," Dr. Riesenman, Norma Lee Browning, and many other writers on the occult have managed to produce a variety of after-the-fact arguments to convert this mess into some semblance of a success for Hurkos. For example, Hurkos told Browning he had the right house and that Reese had earlier lived in it.[58] It was just a little "cross-over" error. In fact, it is unlikely that Reese ever lived in it at all, and even Tarmon no longer lived in the house Hurkos described when Hurkos went to visit his wife.[59] Dr. Riesenman later claimed that Hurkos had actually been "fantastically successful"[60] and had described both Tarmon and Reese.[61] In fact, he claimed, Hurkos not only got Reese but "described him down to the last detail." He said that parts of his description "had no application at all" to Tarmon[62] and had obviously "fitted Reese to a tee."[63] If so, it apparently was not so obvious to Dr. Riesenman when he sat on Tarmon's lunacy board.[64] For those truly convinced of Hurkos's psychic powers, disenchantment by his failures may be impossible. In what may be the ultimate cop-out, Norma Lee Browning said of this case that "at least for me, it is this very fallibility that gives him the ring of genuineness."[65]

For the next six years after the Jackson case, Hurkos became less involved with crime cases and pursued other commercial ventures, including performing in clubs as a stage mentalist and consulting privately for industry and for Hollywood celebrities, contacts he probably started making around the time of his Alcoa TV show. Around 1961 Hurkos moved to Milwaukee, Wisconsin, where he tells us his new business partners, attorney John Burggraf and Miss Terrie Jacques, used his psychic abilities to help with construction work by picking sites, checking bids, and inspecting the work in progress. He also worked with Burggraf on his autobiography. During this period, Hurkos claimed he had psychically located the Lost Dutchman gold mine in Arizona. He also set up the Peter Hurkos & Associates Foundation, Inc. Hurkos seemed confident in his powers in 1961 when he wrote: "The mine is going to produce all the money I will need for my livelihood and to pursue my personal goal, the further-ance of psychic research through my foundation."[66] Hurkos was soon shown to be mistaken. Not only did the gold excavations turn out to be far below his expectations, his wife Maria threw him out of their house (as had his first wife done), and went off with the administrator of Hurkos's foundation.[67]

Hurkos told Norma Lee Browning that he then spent a few traumatic years during which he drifted out to California, where he was "a nonentity, a complete derelict in spirit, dejected, rejected and about ready to take his own life."[68] It was while Hurkos was in Beverly Hills staying in the home of his friend and patron, actor Glenn Ford, at a time when Hurkos was in the process of his divorce from Maria, that he got an invitation to participate in what was to become his most publicized case, that of the Boston Strangler.

On June 14, 1962, Mrs. Anna Slesers was molested and killed in her Boston apartment. The next eighteen months saw ten more women sexually assaulted and similarly strangled. Citizens of Boston grew increasingly apprehensive as the police searched for the elusive multiple murderer. On January 29, 1964, Assistant Attorney General John Bottomly, who was in charge of coordinating the so far unsuc-cessful search for the Boston Strangler, brought Peter Hurkos into the case. Hurkos's services had been offered to Bottomly by a concerned industrialist who said he and some of his friends would foot the bill. Bottomly skeptically read the chapters on Hurkos in journalist Jess Stearn's book *The Door to the Future*, and checked with some police officers Stearn had quoted as saying they were impressed by Hurkos. What did he have to lose? After clearing things with other police officials to make sure Hurkos would not interfere with their own efforts, Bottomly brought him aboard. Bottomly told author Gerold Frank that he felt that even if Hurkos was not psychic, it might be useful to bring in a fresh approach from someone accustomed to working with extraordinary murder cases like this one. He also indicated that even if Hurkos only succeeded in irritating Boston's detectives, that might make them redouble their efforts just to prove Hurkos a fraud, and "the increased activity might be advantageous."[69]

According to Gerold Frank, Hurkos, who arrived in Boston with his friend and bodyguard Jim Crane, initially greatly impressed Bottomly and Assistant Attorney General Julian Soshnick as well as others working on the murders, as he seemed to be able to tell them things about themselves and the case. At one point, a police sergeant handed Hurkos a letter to examine. It was from a shoe salesman[70] looking for matrimonial prospects who had written to the Boston College of Nursing for a list of their nurses. Hurkos crumpled it up in his hand then bolted upright, saying, "By God, son of a bitch, he do it! This is the one—he's the murderer!" They went to see the salesman, found him to be a psychotic and paranoid and had him committed for tests and further investigation. They took Hurkos to the mental hospital for an interview with the salesman. Late that evening, when Hurkos left Boston, he told Soshnick, "My work finished." Hurkos later claimed he was never paid; but *Time* magazine reported that "he pocketed his $1000-plus fee and left for New York."[71]

Over the next few days, the Boston *Herald* and the American Civil Liberties Union voiced complaints that the salesman's rights had been violated. Then on February 8, at three in the morning, Hurkos was roused from sleep in his New York hotel room and arrested by the FBI. He was taken to jail and was there for nine hours, until he was released on $2500 bail into the custody of Dr. Puharich. It was alleged that back on December 10, 1963, nearly two months before, Hurkos had passed himself off as an FBI agent while purchasing gas in a Milwaukee suburb where he stopped on his drive to Las Vegas to look into the kidnapping of Frank Sinatra, Jr.[72] Hurkos claimed it was all a mistake due to his bad English. He said he had been showing a bunch of his honorary police badges when he was asked if he was with the FBI. According to Hurkos: "I not tell him I FBI agent. I tell him I something *more* than that."[73]

Bottomly and Soshnick were furious. They believed it was all a politically inspired attempt to discredit not just Hurkos but the attorney general, too. In the days ahead, the press went wild with charges and countercharges. While one newpaper's headline charged

"Hurkos Framed," another mockingly said, "Psychic Sleuth Failed to See FBI on His Trail." When Hurkos finally went to trial, the judge believed his story of a mixup,[74] but by then the damage had been done. To top it all off, before the year was out, the real Boston Strangler, Albert DeSalvo, had confessed all. Though Hurkos continued to insist that DeSalvo was not actually the Strangler and that his shoe salesman was the real killer, public opinion and the weight of evidence was clearly against him.[75] As Detective Phillip DiNatale, a key figure in the Strangler investigation, succinctly put it when asked about Hurkos: "He contributed nothing to the investigation. He did nothing . . . he did not contribute one thing to the solution of the Boston Strangler murders."[76]

Browning tells us that when news of Hurkos's arrest was broadcast coast to coast, his Hollywood friends deserted him in droves and the plans for the movie based on his life were scuttled. He began to drink heavily, and, as he put it, "I was a broken wreck. It took me many months to get over that case."[77] It actually took several years, but it was during this period, in California, that he met his third wife, Stephany Courtney. Though thirty-three years younger than Hurkos, she took him in hand and, along with an aggressive new business manager, got his career going again. His ambitious young wife also eventually gave him a new daughter, Gloria Ann (Hurkos already had six children by his former wives). In 1968, Hurkos even played himself in the movie *The Boston Strangler*. And by 1969 he was able to get $2,500 for a weekend at a Lake Tahoe nightclub and $10,000 for a week at a theater in Los Angeles.

In April of 1967, Hurkos became involved in the search for James H. W. Thompson, a wealthy American known as the Thai Silk King of Bangkok, who had mysteriously disappeared into the Malaysian jungle. Thompson's sister and her husband hired Hurkos for a large fee to try and find her brother. He and Stephy went to Bangkok and other points in the Far East. Hurkos finally "saw" that Thompson was alive and well but in Cambodia and that his disappearance was part of a political intrigue. Of course, it was impossible to go into Cambodia in search of Thompson because of the Viet Nam War, something Hurkos surely might have foreseen. The vanishing of Jim Thompson remains unsolved.

On July 22, 1969, Peter Hurkos came to Ann Arbor, Michigan, with his associate, Ed Silver, to investigate a series of murders of—at that point—six young women.[78] One of us (M.T.) then lived in Ann

Arbor, and the picture of the events that followed was quite different from the version of the events later given out by Hurkos.[79] When a local citizens'-committee group invited him to come, he first asked for a fee of $2500 plus expenses. When they told him they were unable to come up with the full amount, Hurkos agreed to come just for expenses, about $1000.[80]

Hurkos's first involvement with this case had come on June 14, when he was interviewed in his home by Arnold Rosenfeld, a staff writer for the *Detroit Free Press*. Rosenfeld published Hurkos's impressions of the case on July 6. Among his many statements to Rosenfeld, Hurkos gave him the killer's name (never made public) and said the multiple murderer was a very sweet boy, kind and with a brilliant mind, twenty-five or twenty-fix years old, with a baby face, about five feet six or seven, weighing between 136 and 146 pounds, with blondish "pepper-and-salt" hair. Hurkos said the killer was a night-school student who worked as a salesman during the day and had held a variety of past jobs as a handyman. He also said that the killer liked privately to dress as a woman, was a dope addict, and had once been arrested while driving either a car or motorcycle, and that the next victim would probably be a black woman. Rosenfeld said Hurkos's complete statement could be reduced to about sixty statements. The majority of statements could not be checked at that time, but of those that could be, some were right (perhaps based on logical reasoning or information from the papers in some cases), while some were categorically wrong. For example, Hurkos told Rosenfeld that one girl was found lying on her stomach when in fact none of the victims were.[81]

When Hurkos arrived at Detroit Metro Airport he was on crutches from a recent fall in the California Sierras, where he had been searching for a lost hunter. With a theatrical flourish, Hurkos growled into the reporters' microphones: "He knows I'm coming. I'm after him and he's after me. But I'm not afraid."[82] After working for only two hours on the killings the next day, Hurkos had already greatly impressed several of the policemen working with him. Lieutenant Melvin Fuller of the Ann Arbor Police Department told reporters, "He's making me a believer," and Lieutenant William Mulholland of the County Sheriff's Office told them he was more of a believer than he had been the day before.[83] Though there were rumors that Hurkos would only stay until the end of the week because of a nightclub engagement in Los Angeles, he vowed that he would remain in Ann Arbor until a killer was apprehended.[84] Hurkos seemed pleased with the cooperation he had been receiving and told reporters that "the most help police have ever given me is here in this town."[85] Ann Arbor's Police Chief Walter Krasny seemed impressed, too, for he told reporters that Hurkos had told them things Krasny was "reasonably certain he couldn't have read about in the newspapers."[86]

On July 24, reporters were told that Hurkos had given police a name that corresponded to that of their prime suspect. Hurkos said the killer was a homosexual who had sexual relations with the victims and got satisfaction from killing them. Police Chief Walter Krasny said he was no more optimistic about a solution than before, but said of Hurkos, "The guy has got something going. You can't run away from it."[87] But the next day an impasse developed. Hurkos's associate Ed Silver told reporters that the prime suspect whom Hurkos had named had not held up under later scrutiny. When police checked his whereabouts on the night of the murder for which he was mainly suspected, he had an alibi that cleared him of all further suspicion. He also retracted his earlier prediction that Hurkos would pinpoint the name of the thirteen-year-old Ypsilanti girl whose body was found on April 16.[88] Hurkos again vowed he would remain on the case until the murderer was apprehended.[89]

On July 23, the woman who would turn out to be the next victim, a co-ed at Eastern Michigan University in adjacent Ypsilanti, had been reported missing. Now, two days later, police enthusiasm for Hurkos had already rapidly begun to cool. Interest in the new mystery displaced Hurkos from the spotlight. Officers Bill Mullholland and Mel Fuller had dutifully tagged along with Hurkos as he erratically wandered through Ann Arbor's coffee houses and centers of the youth subculture. They as well as reporters said they were getting bored with taking notes on his useless "findings." On the evening of July 25, a cryptic and unsigned note was left for Hurkos at his hotel. It said there was "something interesting" located at a burned-out cabin on Weed Road. Hurkos held the note as he psychometrized it. He said he felt something strong, that it might be the girl, and that they should go look. The police reluctantly went out after midnight in a heavy downpour and slogged around in the rain for the full length of Weed Road. They could not even find the alleged cabin there. The cops' disenchantment with Hurkos was now almost complete.[90]

The next day, Saturday the twenty-sixth, the missing girl's naked body was found in some brush by a doctor and his wife on a stroll. Hurkos had weeks earlier said that the killer's seventh victim would be non-Caucasian, either Negro or Spanish, with dyed hair, and that the murder would take place west of Ann Arbor. The white coed did not fit his description, and the body was found southeast of Ann Arbor. Ypsilanti's Sheriff Douglas Harvey was busy with a stakeout at the scene and didn't bother to notify Hurkos, whom he did not want around. On Sunday, after Hurkos heard about the find from a newsman, he got in touch with Chief Krasny, who had not been told of the stakeout. Krasny took Hurkos to the crime scene and angrily confronted Harvey. Hurkos wandered about but said he felt little because he had come too late. However, one of the few observations he did make was: "I see a young man . . . and *not* American! He got some kind of foreign money." Shortly thereafter Hurkos looked at Sheriff Harvey and the police there and said, "Hostile. No good for me. Everybody wants Hurkos to go home."[91]

Hurkos and Ed Silver left for Los Angeles that Sunday evening, complaining about the lack of police cooperation, but not before theorizing further about the case—this time giving a scenario markedly different from that his later defenders (like Browning) recalled. Now he said that the killings were done by a gang of from three to five men, a kind of "blood cult" that believed they were ridding the world of dope addicts or hippies.[92] When he departed to return home, now in Studio City, California, there was some speculation that he might soon return to Ann Arbor. He never did.

On August 1, less than a week after Hurkos's departure, twenty-two-year-old John Norman Collins, an education major at Eastern Michigan University, was arrested and eventually convicted for the Ann Arbor murders. Though some few elements in Hurkos's various descriptions matched Collins, the vast majority did not. For example, he was dark-haired, about six feet tall, not a night student or salesman, and was markedly heterosexual (in fact, several friends described him as "oversexed"), with no evidence of his ever having been either homosexual or a closet transvestite. As for Hurkos's later statements, Collins was not foreign, and no evidence was ever produced suggesting the involvement of others in any supposed blood cult. It also turned out that Collins had once been near Hurkos and gone unnoticed by him. A girlfriend of Collins later told Edward Keyes that in the middle of Hurkos's investigation, John Collins went with some friends to the restaurant-lounge in Hurkos's hotel and managed to get seated at a table right next to that of Hurkos and a group of reporters. Collins eavesdropped on Hurkos's conversation as the psychic told reporters personal things about themselves. Collins told his friend that he thought Hurkos was just a big clown.[93]

Less than two weeks after Hurkos got back from Ann Arbor, on August 9, 1969, four followers of cult leader Charles Manson entered the Beverly Hills home of film director Roman Polanski. Charles "Tex" Watson, Patricia Krenwinkel, Susan Atkins, and Linda Kasabian sadistically shot, stabbed, and clubbed to death Polanski's pregnant wife, actress Sharon Tate, and four others: coffee heiress Abigail Folger, writer-producer Voyteck Frykowski, hair stylist Jay Sebring, and eighteen-year-old Steven Earl Parent. Two nights later, Manson's followers similarly butchered Leno and Rosemary La Bianca. Hurkos offered his help to the Los Angeles Police Department, but they refused his assistance.[94] Hurkos later told the press that he had identified the killers to the police. But according to Vincent Bugliosi, the Los Angeles prosecutor who successfully prosecuted the case: "If Hurkos did identify the three men to the LAPD, no one bothered to make a report of it. All publicity to the contrary notwithstanding, those in law enforcement have a standard procedure for handling such 'information': listen politely, then forget it. Being inadmissible as evidence, it is valueless."[95]

On August 12 Peter Knecht, Jay Sebring's friend and attorney, brought Hurkos into the case. Most of what is on record about Hurkos's involvement comes from Norma Lee Browning's purportedly meticulous notes at the time. However, she describes Hurkos as just walking into his home on August 11 upon returning from Ann Arbor and the Michigan murder case when Knecht called him.[96] This alone should make us skeptical about some of the other details in Browning's narrative.

Through Knecht and John and Michelle Phillips, singers with The Mamas and Papas group and friends of Polanski, Hurkos obtained permission to visit Polanski's home on August 16. Hurkos told the press that he had identified the killers. Knecht was later quoted as saying that Hurkos "indicated right then and there that a guy named Charlie was responsible for this. And, of course, there were two—Charlie Watson and Charlie Manson."[97] This overlooks that Hurkos also repeatedly brought up the names David, Billy, and Sally as among the killers.[98]

Browning later insisted that "if the LAPD had done more than 'listen politely, then forget it,' the case might have been solved sooner," and that "the evidence that Peter turned over to them might have helped in the capture and conviction of Charles Manson and his co-conspirators."[99] In fact, if we examine his statements to the press, Hurkos's visions were not only useless but wrong. He said that three men had killed Sharon Tate when it was one man and three women. He incorrectly said the killers had been friends of Tate and that they had been turned into "homicidal maniacs" by massive doses of LSD. Though insanity was part of the defense at the trial, evidence there showed the killings were not performed in a crazed fashion, for the killers had cut phone lines, wiped off fingerprints, disposed of their weapons and clothing. Hurkos also incorrectly claimed that the killings had erupted during the performance of a black-magic ritual known as "goona goona."[100] Perhaps it is a good thing that Hurkos never told the world what the horrible "goona goona" was.

Browning tells us that on August 20, 1969, Hurkos was suddenly and rather mysteriously "dropped from the case and warned: Hands off!" While most might view this as an indicator that perhaps there was some disenchantment with Hurkos among those paying his fee, Browning suggests that Hurkos was getting too close to terrible truths that some people, including perhaps even Polanski, might not wish revealed. Thus, Browning treats Hurkos's seeming dismissal as a failure as "possibly the highest tribute that could be paid to his powers as a psychic."[101]

In one heretofore unpublicized case, Hurkos was summoned in 1974 to Palm Springs, California, by Detroit millionaire Robert Adell, whose teenage son Larry had been kidnapped. Although the kidnappers had been apprehended by the FBI, Larry was still missing, and his father was frantic to know about his son's fate. After taking three thousand dollars from Adell, Hurkos drove around the area accompanied by the millionaire, private investigators, and Palm Springs police detectives, finally homing in on a large rock pile in the desert north of town. "His body is there," he told the distraught parent. In sweltering hundred-degree temperatures, the Palm Springs police dug in the spot marked by Hurkos. They lost considerable water-weight but found no body. Years later, one of the convicted kidnappers led police to Adell's skeletonized remains, twelve miles away from Hurkos's rock pile.

Hurkos seems to have been wrong right up to the end. Although the psychic had always emphasized that he was unable to make accurate predictions about himself and could not even find his own shoes in the morning, he seems to have flubbed particularly badly when, in a recorded psychic reading, he predicted the date of his own death—November 17, 1961[102] The pessimistic prediction turned out to be premature by twenty-seven years. A few months after having his cancerous right lung removed, Hurkos had a fatal heart attack on June 1, 1988. He was seventy-seven. Since 1969, Hurkos had received relatively little further national press publicity other than that stemming from Norma Lee Browning's two books about his exploits. For the most part, for most of the last twenty years, Hurkos coasted along on his past laurels, apparently no longer finding it necessary to prove himself through newspaper publicity. Ironically, given Norma Lee Browning's stated dislike for Tenhaeff's methods, her first book on Hurkos had pretty much done for Hurkos what Tenhaeff's writings did for Croiset. To those interested in his abilities, Hurkos or his publicist could merely point to the gospel according to Browning. Hurkos continued his private consultations and occasional stage and rare television talk-show appearances. Hurkos now had many Hollywoodites and other celebrities paying for his psychic advice. Dr. C. B. Scott Jones told us that when he visited Hurkos at his home a few years before his death, Hurkos told Jones that he included then-President of the Philippines Ferdinand Marcos among his many regular clients.[103]

A particularly revealing episode took place when Hurkos appeared on a local Los Angeles TV program, *The Ashman File*, in 1975, a few months after the disappearance of Jimmy Hoffa. Host Chuck Ashman gave Hurkos some items to psychometrize, including a shirt, which Ashman identified as having belonged to Hoffa. Hurkos proceeded unequivocally and with apparently great confidence to describe Hoffa's last days, where he was, and many other details. At the close of the program, Ashman revealed that in fact none of the items Hurkos had held had belonged to Hoffa. They were all from Ashman's own closet and had never been within two thousand miles of Hoffa. A stunned Hurkos sat there while the show's credits rolled by. The next day, magician David Alexander says he contacted Ashman to ask what Hurkos's reaction had been after they went off the air. Alexander reported that Ashman told him that "Hurkos voiced a rude description of Ashman's parental lineage and stormed off the set."[104]

Anecdotal reports about Hurkos's remarkable psychic readings still abound. He continues to have some strong admirers even among police. In May of 1981, one of the authors (M.T.) was contacted by Bridgewater, New Jersey's, Chief of Police Dix R. M. Fetzer. Fetzer wrote that Hurkos gave him and his detectives a number of leads they could not have obtained using regular investigative techniques, and amazingly told them the first and last names of the perpetrator. They were only able to arrest this person two years later, when he was implicated by his partner in crime. Telephoned for more details, Fetzer said that Hurkos had even told him that the killer's gun would be found inside a wall, and police eventually did find the gun in one in a building near the one Hurkos had indicated. Alas, however, Chief Fetzer complained that the perpetrator was not convicted and that a mistrial was declared. Fetzer expressed his anger against this injustice, which he blamed on the judge and the newspapers.[105]

In 1987 Hurkos, his wife Stephany, Dr. Andrija Puharich, and Dr. Keith Harary appeared on Geraldo Rivera's television show about alleged government use of psychic powers.[106] Hurkos claimed he had been consulted by both Ronald Reagan and Lyndon B. Johnson. His brochure, which was distributed to audience members in the studio, quoted both these Presidents in what otherwise looked like form thank-you statements sent out to campaign contributors or other well-wishers.[107] Dr. Puharich also claimed that Hurkos had been regularly employed by the U.S. Navy as their chief psychic for many years. No proof was put forward for this assertion. Police Chief Fetzer, now retired, was in the audience and was briefly put on camera; he described the above case and gave a testimonial for Hurkos. It just so happened that one of the authors (M.T.) happened to also be on the show. Replying as a skeptic, he pointed out that the alleged murderer was not convicted.

After the show went off the air, Chief Fetzer, who had apparently forgotten about our past communications, came backstage and asked M.T. where in the world he had gotten the idea that there was no conviction in this case, insisting that there had been a conviction. He was urged to write about the details if this was so, and told that a public apology would be forthcoming to him and Hurkos if the case's actual outcome had been misrepresented. In addition, it was mentioned to Hurkos and his wife that they had never responded to a letter M.T. had written them in 1981, along with a copy of Hoebens's critical article and an invitation to reply in the same journal. Mrs. Hurkos said they did not recall getting the letter and asked for another copy of Hoebens's critique. Finally, Dr. Puharich promised he would send some proof about Hurkos's Navy activities. The critique was posted (this time by certified mail). Neither Puharich, Chief Fetzer, or the Hurkoses ever responded.

EIGHT

Lies, Fraud, and Videotape: Lessons from the Pseudo-Psychics

In the late 1970s, hypnotist and palm reader Naomi Randall decided to depart her native Wisconsin for sunnier California climes. Taking the name Tamara Rand, she set up her Tamara Rand Institute in Beverly Hills, where she soon built up a star-studded clientele said to include Sylvester Stallone, Tony Bennett, Bob Dylan, and Phyllis Diller, who paid up to $135 an hour for psychic readings. The blond, attractive Rand appeared on many television and radio talk shows, but she instantly skyrocketed to psychic superstardom on April 1, 1981, when a two-minute videotape was aired on KNBC Television in Los Angeles of Rand predicting with uncanny accuracy the March 30 assassination attempt on President Reagan.

On the tape, reputedly made on January 6 on a syndicated Las Vegas talk show hosted by Dick Maurice, Rand said that Reagan would go through a "crisis time" in late March or early April; that he would experience a "thud in the chest area . . . there are gunshots all over the place and it could be an assassination"; the would-be assassin would not be part of a conspiracy but would be someone "young and radical, with a fair-haired look," with a name "something like Humbly—maybe Jack." The man taken into custody for the shooting was John Warnock Hinckley, a blond twenty-five-year-old former American Nazi.

The following morning, April 2, the tape was aired on NBC's *Today* show, as well as on ABC's *Good Morning America* and on CNN, which carried the Maurice show. Rand's fame was secured—for the fifteen minutes Andy Warhol promised us all.

The fly in the ointment turned out to be Ed Quinn, the young station manager of KTNV in Las Vegas, where the Dick Maurice show was taped. Deluged with calls asking for verification of the January 6 taping date, Quinn began an in-house investigation that led him to believe that the tape had actually been made on March 31, the day *after* the assassination attempt. Quinn made a public statement to that effect, drawing fire from Rand, Maurice, and Maurice's producer Gary Greco, who all vehemently denied any allegations of fraud. The three acknowledged that Rand had made a taping in Las Vegas on March 31, but contended that that interview was a redramatization of Rand's most "noteworthy predictions." (Rand claimed to have also accurately predicted the murder of *Hogan's Heroes* star Bob Crane, the Aldo Morro kidnapping, and several natural disasters.) The tape shown on the networks, they insisted, was made on January 6.

A check of the KNTV logs showed that Rand had not been in the station on January 6, but had been interviewed, along with several other psychics, by Maurice on January 20. That tape had been aired on CNN on March 28, but Rand's prediction was not on it. (Ironically, on that show, one of the other psychics, a Professor Harvey, *did* predict an assassination attempt on Reagan, pointing up perhaps a case of psychic plagiarism.)

On April 5, after threatening Quinn and KNTV with libel suits, Maurice confessed on the front page of the Las Vegas *Sun* newspaper that the whole affair had been a hoax cooked up by Rand, himself, and Greco. Greco soon caved in, saying that Rand had approached him about making the fake tape, saying, "This could make me the Jeane Dixon of the eighties."

Rand, in the meantime, folded her institute, but stuck by her guns, saying that she had been assured by Greco that the tape she had been given—and which she, in turn, had given KNBC anchor Kelly

Lange—had been the January tape, not the "redramatization" tape made March 31. She filed a ten-million-dollar civil suit against Maurice, Greco, and KNTV, alleging conspiracy, slander, libel, and misrepresentation, resulting in her suffering "loss of reputation . . . embarrassment . . . and injury in her occupation and business." She later dropped the lawsuit and out of sight.[1]

What does an episode like Tamara Rand's mean for our view of other psychics who claim successes? Are they just other phonies, but ones who got away with it? Critics of the blue sense might properly ask: Are the kinds of misrepresentation and distortion we find in the case histories of Gerard Croiset and Peter Hurkos representative for all cases of psychic sleuthing? Many hard-line skeptics think they are. For example, professional debunker James Randi complains that "until police departments reject these charlatans as publicity-seeking clowns, the so-called 'psychic detectives' will continue to interfere with effective police work and profit from the glory they borrow from such official association."[2]

Of course, not all critics of the blue sense fully agree with one another. There is a spectrum of viewpoints among critics ranging from those who doubt and demand further inquiry (the true skeptics) to those who would dismiss all evidence for the blue sense (often calling themselves "skeptics" but who are actually *deniers* and seem more concerned with debunking than inquiry). Though many scientific critics remain more open-minded and less militant than the hard-liners, many of these debunkers are highly visible, so we need to give them some special attention here.

Just as there exist True Believers who uncritically accept nearly all alleged evidence for psychic phenomena, there are also what we might call True Disbelievers, those who may uncritically accept nearly all alleged evidence against psi. Such critics also tend to exaggerate the significance of negative evidence. As we have noted, the few actual experiments skeptics have conducted with psychic detectives have serious methodological flaws. It seems very unlikely that these otherwise sophisticated skeptics would ever have allowed those flaws to go unnoticed if the results of these same studies had favored the psychic's claims. Similarly, critics often call attention to failures by psychic detectives, but then they ignore the fact that most psychics never claim to bat a thousand. Some of these critics make much over a statement by some policeman that a psychic was of no help in a particular case. Yet, they would reject an appeal to such authority if the same cop said the psychic was helpful, as they usually do when policemen corroborate a psychic's claim. These same critics (who at other times insist on control groups for any serious analysis) also usually fail to consider the batting average of the police against whom the psychics are being compared. Thus, True Disbelievers at times behave as unscientifically as do the True Believers, and since many of these debunkers do so as scientists, this is particularly regrettable.[3]

Whereas the rational and scientific posture toward a claim with inadequate evidence must be nonbelief, many skeptics express active disbelief.[4] As we noted earlier, spokesmen for groups like the Committee for the Scientific Investigation of Claims of the Paranormal (CSICOP) and some prominent individual public debunkers have been outspoken in their total condemnation of any police use of persons purporting to give aid through psychic powers. Thus, CSICOP's chairman, Professor Paul Kurtz, wrote: "To call on the occult to assist police in what is very serious, important work throws crime-solving, and our civilization, back to the Middle Ages. By condoning the use of 'psychic detectives,' we may be turning our backs on centuries of progress."[5]

Hard-line critics typically base their condemnation of psychic sleuths on two assumptions (which they do not always state explicitly): (1) There is no validity to ESP, so any allegedly successful application of it to crime investigation must be a myth. And (2) there has been much fraud and misperception throughout the history of psychic research, so that must be what is happening in the case of reports of successful psychic sleuthing.

In regard to this first assumption, as we saw in Chapter 3, the reality of psi remains a claim still scientifically *un*proved. Proponents of the psi hypothesis have not yet produced a convincing scientific case. But we must not confuse that with thinking psi is *dis*proved. This remains an area in which reasonable scientists have differences, some of them extreme, but the issue remains unresolved. Instead of examining the evidence for the blue sense, which might produce new arguments for psi, some hard-line critics simply dismiss evidence for the blue sense on grounds that it must be in error because psi cannot exist. Such an approach puts the cart before the horse. It also is unfalsifiable and depends on one's having faith that further examination will disclose error. Worst of all, it tends to block further inquiry, considered by many a cardinal sin for any scientist.[6]

The second assumption made by hard-line critics has more merit. Given the past history of psychical research, it is not unreasonable to expect a high likelihood that ESP really may mean "error some place." But the presence of error or even fraud is an empirical question that cannot be determined prior to inquiry. Error in reports of psychic crime solution may be highly probable, but we cannot scientifically presume it is certain without concrete evidence. We should also note that the most important evidence of error or fraud in psychical research has been discovered and exposed not by parapsychology's hostile critics but by psychical researchers themselves.[7] Instead of congratulating parapsychologists for their notable past debunking efforts and recognizing they have done much among themselves to police against error, critics usually hold such episodes against parapsychology. It is perhaps bad enough that researchers get blamed when fraudulent psychics fool them (which is a bit like blaming the rape victim for "asking for it"), but when critics condemn parapsychology for having discovered fraud in its midst, it's like calling a police department corrupt because it exposed some criminality in its ranks.

Many of the psychic detectives we spoke with largely agree with their critics that there are many phony psychics operating. In fact, psychics like Nancy Czetli and Noreen Renier say that they would strongly back government licensing procedures for policing psychics. Others, like Beverly Jaegers, told us that the problem of pseudo-psychics was one reason why she wanted to help police develop their own psychic potential rather than rely on outsiders, some of whom may be scam artists. Though implementing a testing and licensing program might prove difficult, this may actually be the answer. Perhaps groups like CSICOP should stop attacking psychics and join with them in their call for licensing. After all, if the hard-line critics are right and real psi is just an illusion, and if a proper set of credential-establishing procedures could be instituted, none of the applicants, including Czetli and Renier, should be able to pass the formal exams.

There are two important principles that operate to maintain balance in science. Psychologists Leonard Zusne and Warren H. Jones called one the *principle of Laplace* and the other the *principle of Hamlet.*[8] The principle of Laplace (named after the French astronomer and mathematician Pierre Simon de Laplace) states that the weight of evidence for an extraordinary claim must be proportioned to its strangeness. In other words, an extraordinary claim requires commensurate extraordinary proof. For example, if someone tells us that he once saw Elvis Presley walking down the street, we likely would take the speaker's word for it. But if he then adds that he saw Elvis doing so this morning, we almost certainly would demand greater evidence than his mere testimony before we believed his story. Similarly, if a policeman tells us he solved a crime, that seems ordinary enough. But if he tells us he solved it through the use of psychic powers, we should demand evidence strong enough to convince us that so extraordinary a thing actually happened.

The principle of Hamlet (named after Shakespeare's hero who tells his friend that "There are more things in heaven and earth, Horatio, than are dreamt of in your philosophy") states that all is possible. In other words, though some things may seem highly improbable, science ultimately cannot say anything empirical is absolutely impossible.[9] The reason this principle is so important is that once scientists deem a dissenting position as representing something impossible, they may feel justified in closing the door on research into it. As physicist Mario Bunge—a harsh critic himself— has observed, "Dissent is the essence of the scientific process, and the occasional pressure to suppress it in the name of the orthodoxy of the day is even more injurious to science than all the forms of pseudo-science put together."[10]

Whereas the principle of Laplace is sometimes ignored by proponents of the paranormal, the principle of Hamlet is sometimes overlooked by skeptics.[11] Most scientists try to keep a balance between the extremes,[12] for both these principles must work to-gether to keep science essentially conservative but also open to new information.[13]

Despite occasional excesses by True Believers and True Disbe-lievers in implementing and balancing the principles of Laplace and Hamlet, however, the crux of the skeptics' case against the blue sense rests on a third scientific rule. This is the principle of *parsimony* (sometimes also referred to as Occam's Razor).[14] This rule states that if two adequate explanations are offered to us, we must accept the simpler. Applying this principle to our examination of the blue sense, it means we must reject any paranormal explanation *if a normal one is adequate*. So, before we can accept claims of a blue sense, we must first eliminate all normal explanations by showing that they are somehow inadequate or do not cover all the facts encompassed by the paranormal explanation. Now let's consider the most common alternative explanations skeptics have put forward to account for episodes of seeming psychic detection.

Two major alternatives might explain the seeming successes of those claiming the blue sense: (1) errors and misperceptions, and (2) fraud. The line between the two is often difficult to draw, for fraud involves intentional misrepresentation of the truth. Hard-line critics are usually more willing to assert the presence of fraud by the psychic. This raises the question not only of the *validity* of the blue sense, whether psi is present or not, but also the question of *authenticity*, whether or not the psychic believes what he or she claims.[15] It seems likely that most psychic detectives are quite authentic, even though their claims may be invalid. As psi-skeptic Kendrick Frazier observed: "Many 'psychics' . . . are quite sincere and honestly believe they possess supernatural abilities. The psychology of self-deception is a rich field. Their sincerity, of course, is not the issue."[16]

Of course, some psychic detectives are pure charlatans and quite inauthentic. Most of the psychic detectives we spoke with expressed concern about such "bad apples" in their ranks, and as we already noted, some even urged that psychic sleuths should be tested and licensed. They also liked to remind us that rogues can be found in most other professions, including law and medicine. Many psychics we interviewed insisted that critics who charge all or most psychics with fraud are engaging in character assassination (scientifically inappropriate ad hominem argument). In any case, too much concern with establishing fraudulent intent misdirects our attention from the central question of validity. It may even be the case that an inauthentic psychic occasionally gives a valid reading. Even a psychic scoundrel like Peter Hurkos, who frequently lied about his successes, sometimes seems to have produced hits that we find difficult to dismiss. We have also found that unsupported accusations of fraud too often seem a last refuge for some skeptics who are unable to provide a plausible alternative explanation for a psychic's success.

It seems likely that pseudo-psychic successes often involve a combination of error and fraud. Psychics, like all human beings, are capable of rationalization, distortion, and self-deception. Based on our experience and interviews, even psychics who believe in their own powers may sometimes try to bolster their abilities by obtaining some degree of additional information or by engaging in some psychological manipulation. Some more than others realize that professional success may involve matters like publicity and self-promotion. As with any business, the product does not always just sell itself. Keeping this in mind, let us now consider the major forms of error and misperception that might explain away apparent cases of the blue sense. After we first look at ways both the client and the psychic might mistakenly infer psi is operating, we will take a second look at cases of outright fraud.

The most frequent error in judging the success of a case of alleged psychic detection may come from mistaking a mere coincidence for a hit, that is, thinking something extraordinary occurred when it was only a result of chance. In a recent review of the sources of such errors, Harvard statisticians Persi Diaconis and Frederick Mosteller break them down into four general categories.[17] (1) Sometimes a hit is actually due to some hidden cause. For example, the success may never have happened at all or may have been due to some bit of information to which the psychic was previously exposed. (2) The seeming hit may actually be due to some psychological factor like selective memory, remembering what was accurate and forgetting what was not. (3) The hit may be the result of what are technically called "multiple end points and the cost of close." This refers to the latitude we allow statements we would characterize as hits. Thus a psychic might say that he sees water near the body. This could mean anything from the Atlantic Ocean to a pitcher to the word "water" on a piece of paper or a billboard, all of which could be interpreted as hits if anywhere "near" the body. There are really a great many outcomes (multiple end points) that would satisfy the initial statement. Or (4) the hit may not really be unusual but is actually commonplace due to the "Law of Truly Large Numbers." This states that just about any particular event is likely if there are enough total events. For example, in a given year, there may be thousands of psychics nationwide telling the police that a missing person can be found near water and a large tree. It is likely that one of these missing people is located somewhere that would fit that description. So we really should not be surprised if a few psychics actually locate a few people every year or so simply based on chance. On the other hand, if a single psychic has repeated successes, that strongly argues against the chance hypothesis.

Another common reason for public misperception of the hit rate of psychic detectives is distortion by the media. In general, the press has been far more interested in publishing stories about successes than failures. Like the old adage that "man bites dog" is news while "dog bites man" is not, reporters see little news value in psychic failure except at the local level. This is especially true for tabloids like *The National Enquirer* and *The Star*, which dedicate substantial space each year to psychic success stories. Reporters, especially those who later write commercial books about psychic detectives, seem to develop a vested interest in their subjects, and may even omit details unfavorable to their story. For example, Norma Lee Browning co-authored *The Other Side of the Mind* a few years before embarking on her biographies of Peter Hurkos. There she had some critical things to say about Hurkos and even quoted a letter from the police chief of Amsterdam in which he flatly stated that there had never been any cooperation between the Amsterdam police and clairvoyants, that Dutch police do not have any tendency to work with psychics, and that "there are no Dutch crime cases known here which were solved by clairvoyants."[18]

As Melvin Harris says, "Unfortunately, while a lie can be coined in minutes, months may be taken up in exposing that lie. And therein lies the difficulty of grappling with accounts of psychic detection."[19] Misquotes do not have to be lies to convey something not quite the truth, however, and newspapers seldom have the time or the inclination to do follow-up stories to verify or disprove a psychic's allegations, especially if those allegations are backed up by the police. Since positive accounts of psychic feats are more striking and sensational than negative ones, the tendency is to go with a "hit."

One of Nancy Czetli's recent highly touted hits was her involvement in the search for Sylvester Tonet, an elderly man from Monroeville, Pennsylvania, who disappeared on January 2, 1988, while walking home from a neighbor's house. Due to an earlier skull injury, Tonet became disoriented if he did not have medication. After he had been missing for five hours police were notified and a search was instituted. For three weeks police, volunteers, firefighters, and bloodhounds combed the woods and surrounding terrain in an unsuccessful effort to locate Tonet. Then the family called in Nancy Czetli.

Psychometrizing the old man's knit cap, Czetli immediately sensed that the man was dead—hardly a startling guess, as temperatures were bitterly cold—and that he had not been murdered. Czetli drew a map for the police indicating where she felt the body was, then told Corporal Willis Greenaway that the body would be found "at a sharp embankment, near some construction, railroad tracks, and a road."

On January 27, Czetli accompanied police to a wooded area three to four miles from Tonet's home, but the search had to be called off due to inclement weather. When it was resumed the following week, Tonet's body was found within ninety minutes, 150 yards from where the search had been discontinued.

One of the many newspaper articles, and typical of the coverage of the event, entitled "Psychic's Success Impresses Police," began: "Cpl. Willis Greenaway of the Monroeville police has never believed in psychics. 'But boy, I'll tell you, after this . . . It was close. It was really close.'"[20] Yet in a telephone interview with the authors, Greenaway's enthusiasm was considerably more subdued, saying, "It always comes out in the news different." Greenaway told us that he did not believe in psychics and had been "unimpressed" with Czetli's pronouncements, saying what she had told them was "general stuff." She had said the body would be found near a body of water and railroad tracks, but there are railroad tracks all over the area and she never specified if the body of water was a pond, a lake, or what. As for the picture she drew of the area, Greenaway told us that out of curiosity he dug another picture out of the police files that had been done by another psychic for a different case twelve years before. "It was the same trees, the same damn picture. There are always trees and a body of water. It could be a puddle or a pond."[21]

Media accounts had played up the fact that Czetli had led police in the opposite direction from where their bloodhounds had been taking them, but according to Greenaway and Detective William McClelland, who was also involved in the search and who also professes to have been "unimpressed" by Czetli, an eyewitness had put Tonet to within a mile of where his body was eventually found, and police had lately been concentrating their search there—a fact given to Czetli. Greenaway admits that the psychic did make a couple of observations that threw him. While they were walking through a heavily forested area, she asked them if they had checked in the ravine a short distance away. Searchers did not even know the ravine was there, but it turned out to be. She also said that the body was over a mountain across from them and that there was an access road to it, another fact later confirmed by searchers. Greenaway says it could have been coincidence. Still, Greenaway admits that they might not have searched the area again if Czetli had not been called into the case, since they had been over it so many times before.

Interestingly, Detective Greenaway admitted that he had possibly been "influenced" by the media accounts. "A lot of people were saying, 'Wow! She was right on!' You start to think, well, maybe she was." And the ripple effect of that influence is still being felt. Because of the publicity on the case, Detective McClelland says he gets "one to two calls a month" from police departments requesting Czetli's phone number.

Even if a police investigator is not misquoted in the media, however, and confirms his belief in a psychic's paranormal abilities, it must not be accepted as the ultimate verification of a psychic's success. In assessing the value of police opinion, investigative journalist Piet Hein Hoebens warned that it must be remembered that the average policeman is a layman, whose judgments are no more valid than the average citizen's. "In fact," he wrote, "police officers may be at a disadvantage, as they are trained to quickly discover meaningful patterns in apparently chaotic data. They are conditioned to help the conveyor of information and to encourage the witness. They may be ideal victims for the talented psychic who relies on the cooperation of a sitter. This can be a serious problem as soon as a police officer momentarily steps outside his or her role as an expert in detection and starts playing the amateur psychologist."[22]

Many policemen, he reminds us, are every bit as desirous of witnessing the "inexplicable" and proving the reality of psychic phenomena. Because they often possess the blue sense and find themselves having successful hunches whose source they cannot identify, some might even often be *more* credulous than the average person. The idea of psychic functioning can provide a way for them to provide a framework for understanding their own intuitive hunches.

On a 1984 television broadcast on WVPT, in Harrisonburg, Virginia, Rockingham County Deputy Sheriff Donald Jenkins stated that Noreen Renier gave police information in a case some years before that was "ninety-nine percent" accurate. Among her accuracies was a circle she had drawn on a piece of paper. Although Jenkins admitted the circle did not help solve the crime, it had been a "correct" clue, as it turned out the culprit in the case drove a rotating cement mixer. Jenkins's reference presumably was to a 1980 case in Staunton, Virginia, in which James B. Robinson was arrested for the rape of five women. Upon Robinson's conviction, Staunton Detective

Jack Benton also termed Renier's description of the rapist "accurate," saying that she correctly predicted that the man police wanted had a scar on his leg, wore a uniform, had been in prison, and drove a truck that went "round and round." Robinson wore green rental work clothes, which the detective said could be considered "a type of uniform," and drove a cement mixer. (Tires go "round and round," too.)[23]

Similarly, Des Plaines, Illinois, Chief of Police Joseph Kozenczak is willing to cut psychics Dorothy Allison and Carol Broman considerable slack when he praises their work in the 1978 investigation of the murder of 15-year-old Robert Piest, one of the victims of homosexual serial murderer John Wayne Gacy. Although many of the psychics' declarations seem to have had striking similarities to the facts that were later unearthed in the case, including the fact that the boy's body was found on the exact date predicted by Allison, virtually none of the "leads" given by either psychic was helpful in solving the case. In fact, considerable police manpower and equipment— including dogs, helicopters, boats, and trained divers—seem to have been wasted pursuing the psychics' pronouncements. Detailed searches were carried out of vacant lots, a boy's camp, a cemetery, and a solid waste incinerator, all for naught. Over the period of a week, then-Lieutenant Kozenczak drove Allison around for over one thousand miles, searching for the boy's body. Acting on information supplied by Broman, a dirt hill in a cemetery was excavated. Piest's body later surfaced in the Des Plaines River. Yet, while Kozenczak admits that "psychics did not solve the Gacy case," he insists that "they did lend to it in providing investigators with some pertinent information regarding the location of John Wayne Gacy's last victim. Had weather conditions not been prohibitive . . . it is possible that Dorothy Allison might have found Rob's body. During the course of the investigation the law enforcement personnel who worked the closest with information acquired from Broman and Allison came to believe in psychic phenomena."[24]

It is common to talk to police detectives who claim to have been skeptics but were converted to psychic belief after having been exposed to a psychic. Over and over again, you hear investigators say that they didn't believe in psychics before, but so-and-so was so right-on in his or her predictions that it caused them to reassess their position and become ardent believers.

As to why some cops flip-flop from alleged hard-nosed skepticism to credulity, Dr. Martin Reiser, director of the Los Angeles Police Department's Behavioral Sciences Section, says that it all depends on an individual's psychological vulnerability. "Someone who has a scientific mentality will be less susceptible," he says. "When someone professes a very strong belief one way or another, it suggests a defensiveness against the opposite—the Elmer Gantry syndrome, in which an evangelist becomes a degenerate lecherous drunk."[25]

Like born-again religionists, converts often staunchly stick by their newly found faith with blind devotion. In the case of the 1977 disappearance of Brian Timmerman, for example, Lieutenant Michael J. Rumola of the Manalapan Township Police Department still deemed Dorothy Allison's "clues" as accurate, even after Timmerman had turned up alive and living with the Moonies when Allison had said he was dead. Rumola stated that Allison had given police twelve dates—in the months of July, August, September, December, February, March, and April—as significant. The family then linked eight of the dates to some event—the death of Brian's grandmother, his sister-in-law's father's birthday, the day a traveling salesman had taken an interest in Brian. She had mentioned "meeting places" near where the body lay. Perhaps the meeting places were where the boy had been passing out his religious leaflets, Rumola reasoned. Maybe her mention of "marble and limestone" was the New York Port Authority, where he had been spotted by his former guidance counselor. She had said the boy had gone west, when he had gone north, but perhaps he had been "thinking of going west" to see his father in Tulsa. This convolution of fact was all reasonable to Rumola. "The only thing that did baffle me was why she did say he was dead," he confessed to reporters. But even for that, the detective had an out: "But which way? Biologically? Clinically? Dead tired?"[26]

Psychic stories, like fish tales, tend to change over time, even among cops. And since detectives rarely keep their notes of psychic tips, their recollections of what a psychic did say may tend to portray the psychic as more accurate as stories are retold. Take Dorothy Allison's first highly publicized case, the recovery of the body of five-year-old Michael Kursics in 1968. According to her book, Allison had a dream of a blond, blue-eyed boy in a green snowsuit, who had drowned. The boy was stuck in a drainpipe, with his shoes on the wrong feet. Her vision was so disturbing that she telephoned Nutley, New Jersey, Police Chief Francis Buel, who was stunned, because a blond, blue-eyed boy was missing, but no description of him had ever been carried by the media. One month later, the Kursics boy was found in nearby Clifton, proving in chilling detail the accuracy of Allison's vision.

Ten years later, in 1978, after Allison's fame was secured, the story was reported in both *Newsweek* and *McCall's,* and a year later in *People,* although the accounts varied as to whether the body had been found in a drainpipe or a shallow pond. In November 1979, in the northern New Jersey *Record,* and again in October 1980, in the Washington *Post,* Nutley Detective Angelo Ferrara was quoted as saying that Allison had led them to the drainage pipe. "This is where the boy is," Ferrara said she told them. "Dig here. I was with her. We dug up the pipe, cut it open, and found him. His sneakers were on the wrong feet. How the hell can a person know something like that? It shook me up."

No small wonder, if true. But actually, Allison was nowhere near the *small pond* where Kursics's body was found. In fact, neither were the police. The body was actually found accidentally by a man burying a dead cat.[27]

In a June 1968 affidavit, Ferrara stated that the investigation of the boy's disappearance was launched on the basis of Allison's information, when in actuality it had been ongoing for a least a month prior to her telephoning Chief Buel. (In her book *Dorothy Allison: A Psychic's Story* Allison states that the investigation had already been started.)[28] Furthermore, both Ferrara's affidavit and another by police officer Donald Vicaro neglect to mention the fact that the body had been stumbled upon by a civilian, suggesting by omission that her information had somehow been useful in the investigation.

Molding memories to conform to one's strongly held beliefs is not uncommon. People "remember" things that did not happen all the time. Someone tells a story so often he begins to believe it. As psychologist Richard Kammann puts it: "You have a mixture of a kind of fraud and naivete, where a person believes something so strongly he thinks it's justified in rounding off the edges."[29]

Psi-critic D. H. Rawcliffe termed the memory distortion process "retrospective falsification" and pointed out that there is a distinct sequence usually found in psychic anecdotes.[30] First, the story is told as an example of the extraordinary in the teller's experience. This fixes the pattern of the tale. Then the story is retold with embellishments, the favorable points getting emphasized and the unfavorable elements omitted. When the distorted version is part of the teller's memory, utter conviction becomes present. The original tale becomes transformed into a far more striking and inexplicable situation.

The most frequent alternative explanation skeptics offer for apparently successful psychic consultations is called *cold reading*. The term originated as part of the argot of phony spiritualist mediums in the 1920s to describe how they dealt with a client about whom they knew nothing in advance, one who walked in off the street "cold." The expression is now part of the standard jargon used by mentalists and magicians and designates a number of psychological techniques used by mediums to tell strangers seemingly remarkable things about themselves and their problems.[31] The key element to the cold reading is that although the client thinks all the information is coming from the psychic, most of it comes directly from himself, either through cues he gives the reader or interpretations he places on what the reader tells him.

Though application of cold-reading techniques usually involves calculated manipulations by the psychic, many of them may actually be used quite unconsciously. So even authentic psychics make use of them. In fact, clinical psychologists and psychiatrists have been criticized for frequently inadvertently relying on some of them.[32] This technique is not even limited to humans. The history of psychical research has included several sensational cases of alleged animal savants, including pigs, dogs, and horses.[33] The most famous of these was the horse Clever Hans, who seemed to answer through a coded series of hoof movements even the most erudite questions. The horse turned out to be responding to subtle non-verbal cues which his interrogators sent out. The horse actually would stop moving his hoof at the appropriate times by seeing a change in the movement of his questioner when the expected correct answer had been completed.[34]

The simplest technique involved in cold readings consists of having a "stock spiel." In other words, the psychic may simply memorize a number of statements that are highly general and fit many persons or situations even though the client may think the comments are quite specific to him. Psychologists have called this the Barnum Effect.[35] Classic Barnum statements a psychic might give a client include "Disciplined and controlled on the outside, you tend to be worrisome and insecure on the inside," or "Your sexual adjustment has presented some problems for you."[36] Many reports about psychic detectives include mention of the psychic's telling police impressive personal things about themselves that have nothing to do with the crime. Much of this may consist of Barnum-type statements. There also appear to be some stock elements in the psychic sleuth's descriptions. For example, when a person is missing, it is unusually common for the psychic to "see water" in the description. A good phony reader will have a number of optional stock spiels depending on the known characteristics of the client or the known parameters of the problem.

A pseudo-psychic will typically fish for information. For example, she may say, "I see the letter S." The subject may indicate some reaction, in which case the medium may go on to say something like "Shirley . . . or Suzanne," at which point the client may say, "It must be Sue Smerdly!" If the psychic is lucky, the client will remember the event as one in which the psychic initially brought up Sue Smerdly's name as though from nowhere. Thus a major element in a good cold reading consists of feeding back information to the client, usually in a different form. The client usually will not recall the original source of the information and attribute it to the psychic. Los Angeles Police Department researchers noted that "'psychics' used the information they were given about the details of the crime and prominent suspects to feed them back to police in altered form—then claim recognition for their 'abilities.'"[37]

Though these techniques may seem audacious in print, in actual practice they are rather subtle and can even fool those quite familiar with them. Several years ago, one of the authors (M.T.) visited with a friend who is now a prominent occultist. At one time the occultist had worked on a carnival as a "gypsy" fortune-teller, and being an expert pseudo-psychic, had earned his living using cold-reading techniques. On this occasion, he was a guest on a Detroit television show. A highly respected psychiatrist was also a guest on the show, and all were sharing a car to the airport after the show. In the car, the psychiatrist and M.T. sat up front while the occultist and his wife (who was also very familiar with cold-reading methods) sat in the back. After a while the doctor suddenly remarked, "Your name is Marcello, eh? An interesting name. Wouldn't it be a perfect match if your wife's name was Patricia." The occultist and his wife, knowing M.T.'s wife was indeed named Patricia, both gasped in amazement. After thinking a few moments, M.T. said to the psychiatrist, "That's most interesting, but I happen to recall that earlier this evening I mentioned her name to you." "Oh, well," sighed the eminent doctor, "it works with a lot of my patients." It is unlikely that this psychiatrist was alone among his colleagues in using such techniques. It was recently discovered that even Sigmund Freud was not above such methods. In his published account, Freud claimed he'd guessed the name of the girlfriend of his patient Ernst Lanzer (known as the Rat Man for his fear of rats) from an anagram. Through an examination of Freud's case notes, however, Dr. Patrick Mahony discovered that Freud had actually learned her name earlier and then applied it to the anagram.[38]

Another technique used by pseudo-psychics is careful observation and deduction, much in the manner of Sherlock Holmes.[39] Good readers are careful observers and excellent listeners. Thus when a psychic holds your hand, as for a palm reading, he can examine not only the lines on your hand but also such things as whether or not you are wearing a wedding ring or have the marks of one recently removed, whether you bite your nails, have them professionally manicured, and so on. Social psychologists call the reading of such cues "unobtrusive measurement," and there is now a substantial professional literature on the subject.[40] Robert Hicks, a criminal-justice analyst and police specialist with the Virginia Department of Criminal Justice who has an interest in psychic sleuths, noted of many of them that "the psychic becomes attuned to the officer's behavior and is using the officer's cues—the detective leaning forward or raising an eyebrow—to figure out things that haven't been released to the public."[41]

A critical element in a good pseudo-psychic reading is the skillful use of vagueness and ambiguity. This allows the client to project appropriate meanings into the statement. As Piet Hein Hoebens observed, "These sensitives offer their consultants the verbal equivalent of a Rorschach test. Their statements are typically vague, rambling and verbose. The accuracy of the 'readings' is evaluated post factum: 'Good' sitters retroactively interpret their ambiguous and often contradictory statements in such a way that they fit the true facts and obligingly forget the many details that were too wide of the mark. Complete failures are ignored or suppressed."[42]

As Adam Berluti, a state police spokesman in Connecticut, remarked to a reporter: "A psychic might say, 'I see a body near an old church and a pine tree.' Well, there are old churches and pine trees all over the state. Plus how do you define near? Is it a mile? Is it five miles?"[43] An excellent example of this problem can be seen in an actual statement made by one of the psychics involved in the experiment conducted by Dr. Martin Reiser and the Los Angeles Police Department: "I get a man, black. I hear screaming, screaming. I'm running up stairs and down. My head . . . someone bounces my head on the wall or floor. I see trees—a park? In the city, but green. Did this person live there? What does the number '2' mean? I get a bad, bloody taste in my mouth. The names 'John' or 'Joseph' or something like that. I am running on the street like crazy. This is a *very* serious crime. I can't hold the envelope in my hand."[44] At first glance, this dramatic statement may seem specific, but a closer look shows it is far too vague to be useful for an investigator.

In addition to using vagueness, the psychic can increase her likelihood of a hit simply by increasing the quantity of information thrown out. Researchers in the Los Angeles Police Department observed that the psychics they examined frequently threw out hundreds of clues. Some were bound to fit just because of their sheer number.[45] Investigative reporter Ward Lucas has termed this technique "shotgunning." As he concisely described the method: "Shotgunning refers to the rapid-fire delivery of a quantity of generalized information. The listener who has an interest in the outcome of the reading becomes passive. Bits and pieces of information surprise him, and he reacts imperceptibly. He cannot help it. As the psychic keys in on the nonverbal response, she becomes more specific, at some point delivering incredibly accurate information. A close analogy is the game of 'twenty questions' without verbal answers."[46]

Another technique pseudo-psychics can use involves a variation on what we earlier called "multiple end points." Based on the reactions given to a psychic's statement, he can stop or continue with qualifications or redirective comments. For example, in one of the classic stock spiel lines used by the phony reader, the client may be told, "I see from your hand that you are artistic." If the client responds favorably and perhaps even mentions his activities as an artist, the psychic can say, "I thought so." But if the client reacts verbally or nonverbally in a way suggesting the psychic is on the wrong track, the psychic can add the statement, "I don't mean that you can paint or draw. I mean that you have . . . *taste!*" (And who does not think he does?) By careful wording and what magicians call "sleight of mouth," the clever reader can use many "outs" to avoid end points that indicate failure.

The psychic's presentation of a great many ambiguous and even contradictory "impressions" has a further advantage. As Piet Hein Hoebens noted, one or more of these information bits may act as a trigger for some appropriate new hypothesis. "Police officers are forced to rack their brains to discover some signal in the noise and, presumably, will be in a state of intense concentration. A chance remark by a psychic may produce a chain of associations resulting in a lucky guess. The relevant piece of information is already stored inside the police officer's mind: the psychic merely helped retrieve it by presenting the verbal equivalent of a Rorschach tableau. In cases where the investigation has become bogged down in a morass of false trails and vicious circles, such 'brain washing' applied by a loquacious sensitive may actually contribute to the solution of a case."[47]

A related principle which may turn vagueness into success is the "self-fulfilling prophecy." If the prediction made by the psychic looks superficially specific but actually is ambiguous, the client may seek out elements in the future results that will fit the psychic's statement and make it seem an accurate forecast. Ward Lucas presented the excellent example of a psychic who says, "I see some wood, perhaps a barrel . . . no, a stick of some kind . . . it appears to be curved." This description could fit anything from a tree to a fence to a French Provincial desk. Or the psychic might say, "The body is near an object . . . it appears to be a rock . . . no, two objects . . . both of them very hard like a rock . . . perhaps an outcropping of some sort . . ." Lucas points out that a statement like this is vague but potentially very likely to be self-fulfilling. Having heard this prediction, police will likely look for "hard" objects near the body. Whether they find pebbles, boulders, or even milk bottles on the kitchen table, they can interpret such objects as confirmation of the psychic's "vision."[48]

Though the manipulative techniques involved in cold reading are important means by which the pseudo-psychic can simulate psi, we should not forget that psychic sleuths may also use quite standard methods. Piet Hein Hoebens noted that "many such psychics employ the same methods as do private detectives, police detectives, and Pinkerton employees: collecting evidence, reconnoitering, questioning witnesses, making informed guesses, and practicing the art of deductive thinking."[49] We also should not underestimate the normal range of human sensibilities. Some people have an unusually acute sense of vision, hearing, or smell, what psychologists call *hyperesthesia*. A recent example was a New Jersey doctor who was able to examine an unlabeled classical recording and ascertain the music and sometimes even the conductor just by looking at the grooves.[50] As Hoebens observed, "Some successful psychic detectives may actually be able to detect traces too faint to be discerned by the average person and erroneously attribute this ability to ESP."[51]

Quite aside from any possible hyperacuity, many psychic sleuths have actually had more experience with some forms of crime than the law-enforcement personnel they encounter. This is particularly true of their dealings with rural police departments where the crime may be the first of its kind encountered there. Sergeant L. C. Stinnet of the Maryland State Police carefully observed Dallas's John Catchings in 1984 when he came up to help search for the missing body of Mary Cook Spencer. Stinnet, who says he does not believe in psychic powers, stated he benefited from watching Catchings work. As he put it, "I think some of them [psychics] are very intelligent and would make very good police detectives . . . Whenever there was a low spot or a high spot in the woods, he directed us to dig. One of the things he taught us is that when somebody buries a body, you have to do something with the ground to hide it. If it's a recent burial, the ground will be disturbed. If it's old, the ground will sink. Also, it's hard to put leaves and sticks over the grave to make the ground look normal. So you will have a pile of brush over the grave or a pile of trash. That's what I learned from John Catchings."[52]

It must be kept in mind that although these various techniques for simulating psi are frequently used, often unconsciously, we cannot conclude that all cases of apparent psi are due to them. As the great criminologist and psychical researcher Cesare Lombroso liked to point out, just because there are wigs does not mean there is no real hair. For many critics, the term "cold reading" has become a catch-all explanatory phrase too glibly used to explain any apparently psychic demonstrations they really don't understand, just as most laymen speak of magicians using sleight of hand to explain a trick whose exact method they do not know. This can be a serious mistake. A few years ago, social psychologist and magician Dr. Daryl Bem gave a lecture to skeptics at a meeting of the CSICOP. After a preliminary talk about cold reading, Dr. Bem proceeded to show the audience what he told them would be a demonstration of some "advanced techniques in cold reading." He then proceeded to do a series of remarkable magic tricks (including a prediction effect in which a sealed chest was opened to reveal a letter locked away days before in which he had apparently predicted what card an audience member would freely select at this demonstration). After some further discussion between himself and the audience about cold reading, he informed the group that none of the tricks he had done actually depended on cold-reading methods at all but were actually accomplished through a wide variety of other conjurors' techniques. As he pointed out to the group, they "bought" what should have been an obviously false explanation for what had happened in the same way that they believed others mistakenly accepted psi as an explanation. We must be careful to examine the full details if we want an objective judgment.

Finally, we must acknowledge that even such scatter-gun techniques may actually prove useful. We already noted the possibility of a new hypothesis being triggered by something the psychic says. In addition, where the case seems to have reached a dead end, this may be the result of the police's having approached the problem in the wrong way somehow. As L. K. Summers concluded in a review for the police publication *Law and Order:* "Psychically obtained information may in many cases be no more valid than citizen's hunches, but the important factor is that the use of such information gives a new and different perspective from which to re-evaluate the evidence."[53]

Now that we have considered some of the misperceptions that can occur in assessing the blue sense, we can return to the question of fraud. In general, to practice parsimony and to avoid unnecessary questions of character, we should first try to eliminate the sources of inadvertent error. Still, the fact remains that true fraud, both small and large, has existed in this area of psychic phenomena just as it occasionally occurs in others.

The simplest sort of fraud by a pseudo-psychic is through misrepresentations of past cases. As we saw with Peter Hurkos, some psychics have simply fabricated stories about their exploits. Sometimes distortion may be unintentional. For example, most of the psychics we dealt with claimed incredibly high levels of success, some even asserting they were always successful to some degree. This sort of exaggeration may in part be the result of the psychic's own misperceptions. Also, a professional psychic may come to believe his or her own lies. Psychologist George Kelly once said that when we wear a mask for a long time, it begins to stick to our face and may eventually *become* our face. Hurkos and Croiset may have come to believe their own publicity.

A noteworthy example of what seems a calculated misrepresentation was found by investigative journalist Piet Hein Hoebens to exist in the case of the internationally known Dutch psychic sleuth Dr. Marinus B. Dykshoorn.[54] In 1974, Dykshoorn published an autobiography called *My Passport Says Clairvoyant*.[55] According to Dykshoorn, the (uncited) investigations by (unnamed) university researchers resulted in his being "allowed to practice as a professional clairvoyant."[56] This strongly suggests that in some sense he was "licensed" or "endorsed" by the Dutch government, although Hoebens found that "Dutch authorities have never licensed anybody as a practitioner of the psychic arts."[57] Further, Dykshoorn went on to assert that "I believe that my work . . . led to my claim of being endorsed by the Dutch government when I was issued a passport listing my occupation as *helderziende*—'clairvoyant.' As far as I know, I am the only psychic ever to have been so honored."[58] When Hoebens checked into this with the Ministry of Foreign Affairs in the Hague, he was officially told that Dykshoorn's claim was "rubbish." Apparently, Dutch citizens are allowed to place freely any profession on their passport that they fancy, and the government's entry of it there does not imply any sort of recognition at all.[59]

As far as obtaining information is concerned, the astute pseudo-psychic can make use of a wide variety of both professional and "underground" sources, some of which are little known even to police. These fall into three general categories. First, there are the books and articles written for private investigators, both professional and amateur. These might include do-it-yourself books like *How to Locate Anyone Anywhere Without Leaving Home* or *How to Investigate Your Friends and Enemies*.[60] There are a number of specialized manuals marketed mainly to private detectives and investigative journalists.

Second, there are a great many largely unknown small publishing houses that produce books for what may even include the criminal market. Available primarily through small mail-order houses that specialize in such works, they include titles like *How to Get Anything on Anybody*, *How to Find Anyone Anywhere*, and *How to Find Missing Persons*.[61] Unlike the books in the first category, works in this group sometimes contain illegal and ethically dubious methods for getting information. For the pseudo-psychic with bolder aspirations, there is even a small book called *How to Organize and Manage Your Own Religious Cult*.[62]

A third category of "how-to" books includes publications especially produced for private "spiritual counselors" and magicians with a special interest in the simulation of psi. These include titles like *The Art of Cold Reading, Secret Methods of Private Readers*, and *Cashing in on the Psychic*.[63] It is in these volumes that the pseudo-psychic can find many scams and gimmicks that can be used as "convincers" for their clients. For example, there is a classic ploy used by some phony "spiritual advisers" when a woman comes looking for a husband who has deserted her. The medium says he will meditate upon the matter during the week and will try to have something for her when she returns next week. On her return visit, the medium gives her an address some distance away (perhaps in Oregon if they are in Ohio) and says the husband seems to be there and that she should write him. About a week after the wife writes her husband, she receives the letter returned to her with a note on it from whoever was at the address, saying that the addressee had left there a few days before with no forwarding address. Convinced that the medium has located her errant hubby, but that she was just a little bit too late, she becomes a regular client. In reality, the address to which the woman's letter was sent belongs to a confederate of the medium.

The role of accomplices has probably been underestimated in past examinations of pseudo-psychic sleuths. It is not uncommon for local informants, including people like the hotel's bartender or even newspaper reporters on the scene, to pass some information on to a visiting psychic. A number of psychics travel with some sort of assistant. Croiset and Hurkos often arrived at a crime scene with an associate. Sometimes the companion of the psychic is even a private detective or an off-duty or retired police officer. While most eyes are on the psychic star, these associates may be in a good position to gather information surreptitiously for the psychic.

Sometimes pseudo-psychics have resorted to quite elaborate and even outrageous frauds.

David Nobel Bubar, an ex-Baptist minister and psychic from Memphis, Tennessee, lost more than revenue and reputation when he predicted weeks in advance a fire at a Connecticut rubber factory. After the Sponge Rubber Products Company of Shelton, Connecticut, burned to the ground on March 1, 1975, the FBI investigation of Bubar's prognostication uncovered that Bubar had received $50,000 to set the fire so that the rubber company could collect a $62.6 million insurance claim. Bubar and several corporate officers were convicted of arson and conspiracy in this case of pyromanic prognostication.[64]

In another outlandish case described by magic historian Will Goldston, a mind-reading act known as the Cornells was performing at a Chicago theater in the late 1920s when they had a "vision" of murder. They told their astounded audience that they could see two young men bashing in the face of an old man, putting him in a bag, and throwing the body into the river. The revelation caused Chicago police to drag the river, netting the bagged body of an old man, just as the psychic duo had predicted. Unfortunately for the Cornells, they had confided to several other people that they themselves had bought the body of a tramp from a local mortuary, bashed in his face to prevent identification, and thrown it into the river. The publicity they got was not the kind they had been looking for.[65]

Not all the fraud involving psychic detectives is targeted at the police or public, however. On rare occasions, police have actually been included in scams intended to produce roundabout justice. For example, there has been documented at least one case in which a policeman, having his own theory about a case, took the psychic into his confidence. Using the psychic as an informal ally, the cop was able to add plausibility to his views and was thus able to convince his superiors to pursue that direction.[66]

Police may also be willing to go along publicly with a psychic by claiming certain information came through the psychic which they actually got in some way they cannot betray. Thus, the psychic can be used to launder information for the police. Taking one such scenario, the police might have information from an informant. By attributing this information to a psychic source, they can keep the informant in place without blowing his cover. Another situation might occur when the police obtain information through some illegal means, for example, from a wire tap. By attributing the information source to a psychic, they can introduce into court whatever evidence it might lead to that could otherwise be disqualified under the legal rule forcing its dismissal as "fruit from the poisoned tree."

Police have also been known to use a psychic as a form of disinformation when they wished a criminal to act out of his superstitious belief. If a psychic is brought in, the believing suspect may even confess. Martin Ebon, a well-informed and careful author of many books dealing with psychic claims, told us that a former New

York City police captain, who had worked for years on the Bunko Squad, confided in him that "cops may bring in a psychic as part of their psychological pressure on a suspect, whether or not the psychic may hit the right button." The officer further indicated to Ebon that "the palaver of psychics can be clever enough to push a jittery suspect into making a confession or giving himself away in some other fashion. Likely, the psychic will claim afterwards that she/he 'helped' the police, and the cops won't contradict her—if only because she will get a certain reputation that may help in future cases."[67]

We even had one instance reported to us of a cop posing as a psychic. A New Jersey attorney, who asked us not to identify him publicly, told us of a case in which he was involved when two police officers interrogated an uneducated male suspect. One of the cops took a trick deck of cards from his desk and performed an apparent miracle for the man. The other officer told the suspect that his partner was gifted with psychic powers. The suspect was so impressed, he reportedly blurted out an admission of his crime.

Finally, there have probably been some cases of a publicity-seeking psychic successfully bribing some informant, perhaps even a police officer, for inside information or an endorsement. Obviously, successful episodes of this sort would remain unknown to us, but reports of unsuccessful efforts of this kind have sometimes surfaced. Because of the risks involved, it seems unlikely that many psychics would make themselves vulnerable to exposure or even blackmail by trying bribery. Put simply, a psychic sleuth would have to be pretty stupid to try bribery if unsure of the outcome. Obviously, too, if someone who refused a bribe reports it, it may enhance his reputation for honesty. On balance, then, it is wisest to weigh such reports carefully.[68] Even psychic superstar Dorothy Allison has been accused of fraud. Paterson, New Jersey, Detective George Brejack went so far as to do it on television.

In a 1980 interview on New York's WABC-TV, Brejack stated that Allison had offered him a bribe if he would publicly credit her with leading police to the body of eight-year-old Delvis Matias, who had been brutally murdered in 1979.

Brejack said Allison—who claims never to get involved in police cases unless invited—showed up at Paterson police headquarters with scrapbooks of her psychic successes and offered to help out on the case. Brejack said he went for it, although he was later sorry he did.

"She was in for seven days," he said, "but she kept making wrong predictions. We went all over the place with her, we even had fire trucks pump out an old building full of water because of her. Then she disappeared. Two weeks later, the body was found, clear on the other side of town from where she said. She said real general stuff to us, like, 'You'll find the boy in a shallow grave.' Now that stands to reason, doesn't it? I mean, if you murder someone, you don't dig a six-foot grave and buy a coffin."[69]

According to the detective, Allison immediately surfaced when news broke that the body had been found, asking Brejack for a letter on department stationery attesting to her contribution in the case. When he refused, Brejack claims that Allison offered him and his partner money to tell the media that she found the body, saying that she "needed it for her book." Although they turned down the bribe, Brejack says that Allison claimed credit in a local newspaper, which precipitated him to go public with his charges.

Allison responded by calling Brejack a liar, saying that his allegations stemmed from professional jealousy. She even has a newspaper clipping in which Brejack is quoted as crediting her with helping to find the body. Brejack claims he was misquoted.

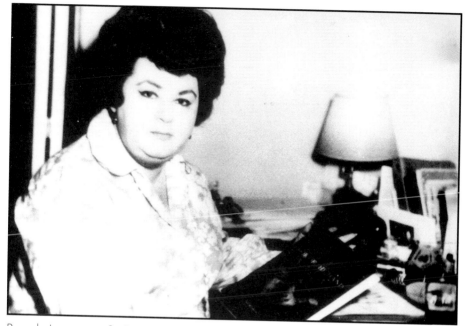

Beverly Jaegers, a St. Louis private eye-psychic detective.

Ludwig Thoma, founder of the Institute of Criminal Telepathy in Vienna, an early proponent of psychic detection.

Patrick H. Price, ex-Burbank Police Commissioner and CIA remote viewer.

Psychic performer Rajah Raboid, prototype of the public stereotype of the psychic-exotic.

W.H.C. Tenhaef, parapsychologist and chief promoter of Dutch psychic Gerard Croiset.

Harold "Butch" Memro and the psychic composite of the killer of Carl Carter, Jr. Detectives were "amazed" at the likeness, although "Joan" said at the time, she thought the face should be "longer," the nose more pugged and tilted.

Marinus B. Dykshoorn investigating a crime scene with his magic loop of piano wire.

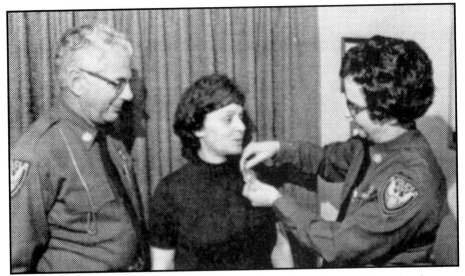

Dorothy Allison is made an honorary police officer of Washington Township by Officer Dorothy Gingrich as Chief Harold Gingrich watches.

Psychic detective par excellence Gene Dennis.

Trance medium Charlotte Starkey, who aided Bournemouth police in the 1921 murder investigation of Irene Wilkins.

Stalin's favorite psychic, Polish-born Wolf Messing, in performance.

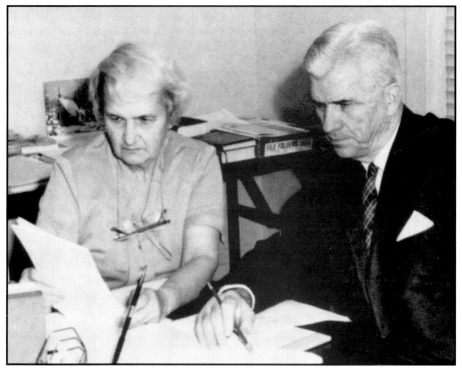

Drs. J.B. and Louisa E. Rhine, parapsychology pioneers, at work in their laboratory at Duke University. (Photo courtesy of Foundation for Research into the Study of Man)

"Rasputin of the Reich," and alleged adviser to Hitler, the infamous Erik Jan Hanussen.

Psychic Kathlyn Rhea working on a case with Fresno Police
Detective Tim McFadden.
(Photo courtesy of Kathlyn Rhea)

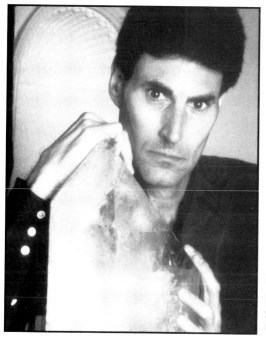

Uri Geller, world-famous Israeli
psychic, spoon bender, with his
giant crystal.
(Photo courtesy of Uri Geller)

Gerard Croiset, the
"man with the X-ray mind."
(Photo courtesy of
American Society of
Psychical Research.
Photo: Ann Johnson)

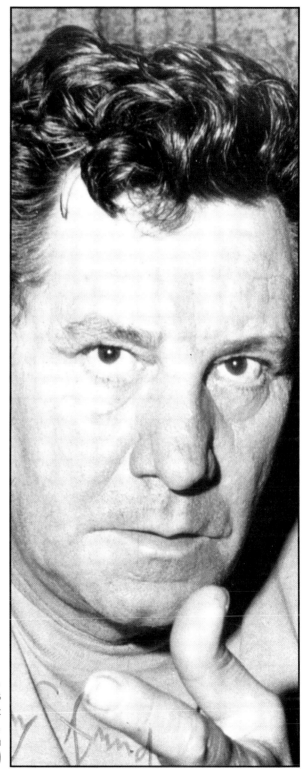

Peter Hurkos,
one of the 20th century's
most famous psychic
crime-busters.
(Photo courtesy of Norma
Lee Browning)

Dr. Alex Tanous, one of the few laboratory tested psychic detectives. (Photo courtesy of C. B. Scott Jones)

Bill Ward going over photos of a crime scene.
(Photo courtesy of Bill Ward)

Delavan, Illinois, psychic
Greta Alexander.
(Photo courtesy of Greta Alexander)

Noreen Renier, who predicted the
Reagan assassination attempt at
the FBI Academy.
(Photo courtesy of Noreen Renier)

Dolly Parton look-alike, Frances
Baskerville, the world's only
"singing psychic."
(Photo courtesy of
Frances Baskerville)

Captain Keoth Wolverton (left) and private investigator Ray Worring examine
murder site specified by psychic Harold Sherman. Following the psychic's
directions, the murder weapon was found embedded in the wooden post indicated.
(Photo courtesy of Ray Worring)

Coroner-trained Judy Belle psychometrizes clothes from decomposed body.

SRI "remote-viewing" star, Ingo Swann.
(Photo courtesy of Ingo Swann)

Dixie Yeterian, psychic
sleuth and author.
(Photo courtesy of
Dixie Yeterian)

Stage mentalist Kreskin,
who has been consulted
by police on numerous
cases. (Photo courtesy of
Kreskin)

Ginette and Lousi J. Matacia: One of the few father-daughter teams of psychic sleuths. (Photo courtesy of Ginette Matacia)

Nancy Czetli, on a crime scene, while the cameras roll.
(Photo courtesy of Steven Czetli)

NINE

Psychic Success Stories

Discounting fabrications and confabulations by psychics and their biographers, media distortions, and cases of outright fraud, there remains a considerable body of documented cases in which psychic sleuths have scored impressive and seemingly inexplicable successes.

But what constitutes "success" by a psychic? When the press trumpets an amazing "hit"? When police detectives involved in the case credit the psychic with contributing to the solution of a case? When the family of the victim publicly expresses gratitude for and satisfaction with the psychic's work? Then again, what is meant by "solved"? When a psychic's intervention leads to the apprehension of the suspect? When that suspect is convicted of a crime? When the police officially or unofficially consider the case closed?

The fact is that dozens of police detectives seem willing to deem the use of a psychic "successful" in cases which never reached court, or that did and resulted in a "not guilty" verdict.

The double homicide in Fontana mentioned earlier, in which Dixie Yeterian named the two brothers, Al and Al, as suspects, is just one example. The defendants in that case were found not guilty, but Detective Frank Donlon blames that on the ineptitude of the prosecutor, saying he was "sure" they had the right men.

This dynamic was exemplified in another double homicide Yeterian worked, this time with Montclair, California, police. In the case, a husband and wife were shot to death and their house was set on fire. In an interview with the authors, Lieutenant Marvin Goss termed Yeterian's contribution in the case a "partial success" even though his recollections of the case vary drastically from the account Yeterian gives in her book, *Casebook of a Psychic Detective,* and even though no conviction was obtained. "We solved the case as to who the players were, we just couldn't prove it," he said. "But without Dixie's information, we wouldn't have gotten that far."[1]

According to Goss, Yeterian was taken to the murder scene and "gave them an idea of what had happened." After visualizing the killer's movements, she led the investigators to a ravine, where she said, "The killer threw something down there." A search of the area turned up a can of Wizard charcoal lighter, which Goss feels had been used to torch the house. But the accelerant used at the scene was never identified, and there were no fingerprints found on the can, so the significance of the can might have been filled in by the investigators afterward. According to Dixie's instructions, a sketch of the killer was made, and when a suspect was eventually turned up through conventional police methods, Goss "noticed a resemblance." Goss says that his department only used a psychic on one other case, but "if it got to the point where nothing was happening, I wouldn't be reluctant to use one again."

These cases typically demonstrate the sorts of problems repeatedly encountered in trying to determine whether or not a psychic sleuth was successful. It soon becomes apparent that one cannot rationally make that judgment without considering factors far more complex than most proponents and skeptics have suggested. For most critics of the blue sense, the central question is whether it has scientific *validity*. But for most people directly involved with these episodes, the main concerns are about the *usefulness* of the psychic.

The central question asked is not "Are psychics real?" but "Can psychics help?"

If we view psychic detectives in purely practical terms, setting aside the question of their validity, the controversy about them takes on different dimensions. If we consider their utility, we must ask: "How and to whom are they useful?" To answer that question we first need to examine psychic detectives in relation to the different audiences that evaluate them. These include (1) the general public, (2) media and reporters, (3) informed others such as the family and others associated with the victim, (4) police agencies, (5) the courts or legal system, and (6) the scientific community. These audiences can be conceptually viewed as a series of concentric areas, and their relations are roughly illustrated in Figure 1.

Psychic sleuths perform different functions in relation to each of these audiences, and the evaluation criteria used by each audience vary considerably. In general, the criteria for success become more stringent as we move from the general public toward the inner

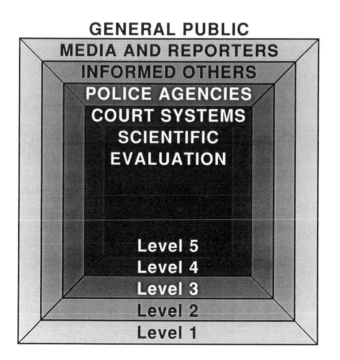

audiences, with the criteria of the scientific community (the inner-most area) being the most demanding. Also, in general, each audience tends to look at the evaluation by the next inner audience level as confirmation of the psychic's success. Thus, if the police say the psychic was useful, that is usually taken by the family and media as confirmation of the psychic's success. On the other hand, each audience on a given level will not take the evaluation by outer audiences as seriously. Thus, the court system may view police belief in the psychic as evidentially weak or even inadmissible. And even a court's conviction of a murderer based on evidence which police located through the advice of a psychic is unlikely to convince scientific investigators that the psychic used paranormal powers.

To understand better the different functional relationships psy-chic sleuths have with these audiences, let's look briefly at each. As we saw in Chapter 3, most of the general public accepts the reality of psychic phenomena, and personal experiences interpreted as "psy-chic" are widespread. Therefore, the threshold for acceptance of tales of psychic sleuthing is quite low. For most of the general public, such stories seem not only plausible but actually quite probable. These tales are probably "useful" to people on many levels. The stories provide "happy endings" to tragedies and make life seem better. The tales also reinforce what psychologists call the "just-world hypothesis" (evil loses and virtue wins out) that most of us want to believe. Since the psychic in these reports brings a criminal to justice or helps innocent victims, it suggests that things work out equitably in the end. In short, any successes by psychic sleuths, as by policemen, reinforce our faith in the social order by telling us that things are more or less in control, that "the system works." Whereas tales of psychically gifted criminals would be upsetting and threatening (and extremely rare), these are essentially stories of good triumphing over evil. They make us feel safer. Also, the stories are interesting and out-of-the-ordinary. They are enjoyable to read and talk about. They add a positive sense of mystery and wonder to our lives.

All of which might explain why we never hear tales about psychic criminals. If psychic phenomena are real and capable of being used for the purposes of good, there is no reason it could not be used for evil ends. Just as there are good and bad "normal" people in the world, why should there not be good and bad psychics? The reason, perhaps, is that such tales would be upsetting and threatening. The thought of a Charles Manson or a "Night Stalker" lurking around neighborhoods, picking out victims at random for slaughter, is disturbing enough without considering such a monster with super-human powers!

Reporters and the media especially appreciate this. Tales of beneficial uses of psychic powers sell papers and raise TV ratings. Tabloid newspapers and now television programs fully understand this and exploit such stories fully. It is no accident that most of the reports about psychic detectives appear in *The National Enquirer* or *The Star* rather than *The New York Times* or *The Wall Street Journal* or that we are more likely to see a television show about psychic detectives on *Oprah Winfrey* or *Geraldo* than on *60 Minutes*. In fact, some media actively seek out and sometimes even fabricate such reports. They understand that it may be less that "enquiring minds want to know" than it is that they "want to believe."

At the next inner audience level, those informed others close to the case—like relatives or friends of the victims—are often the source of information used by reporters and media to bring the "news" to the general public. Although many psychics refuse to work directly with the families, it is very commonly the family or friends who persuade the police to bring in, or at least cooperate with, the psychic. Most psychic detectives also provide private consultations to clients. In fact, it is common for them to refer to themselves as "quasi-therapists" and "poor people's psychiatrists." The psychic sleuth performs many similar roles for the victim's family, offering them support, sympathy, and hope. Some years ago, a critical study described much of psychotherapy as mainly "the purchase of friendship."[2] Since most psychics charge relatively small fees and many have worked on crime cases for nothing at all, supporters can argue that at least the price is right.

Since many psychics bring a quasi-religious or metaphysical orientation to their work, they can sometimes bring the victim's family some sort of "meaning" to a horrible and otherwise senseless episode. By telling of a "psychic vision" that purports to provide a scenario of the crime, its causes and perpetrators, the psychic makes "sense" of what happened, and to that degree removes some of the threat that it may happen again to anyone for no reason. The psychic's tale of what happened also may indirectly remove suspicions and feelings of guilt. By speaking of things like the victim's karma and suggesting that the horrible event plays some sort of constructive role in the general scheme of things, psychics can help those close to the victim to accept and better adjust, much as priests have done for their flocks in times of disaster. And in cases of particular horror, the psychic may give some solace to the friends or parents of the victim by saying things such as that the victim left his body before he actually died and did not feel the tortures that were inflicted on him. As Dixie Yeterian counseled in her autobiography, "If someone you love has been a murder victim, don't agonize over images of the horror and pain of that death." She reminds her clients that "the soul does leave immediately" and that "death is not terrible even in these situations."[3]

A major problem for some families of victims is closure. A loved one is missing. There is an emotional need to resolve the uncertainty about that person's fate, even if the resolution is a tragic one. As pointed up by psychologist Gustav Jahoda: "The anxiety to know one's fate is so great that often ill tidings may be preferred to an absence of information, and after a period of anxious waiting even bad news may come as something of a relief because it frees a person to adjust actively to a situation. Thus prisoners who had a chance of release were found in an American study to be under greater strain than those who had none, and were reconciled to the fact."[4]

Special mention should also be made of the fact that finding the victim or bringing the perpetrators to justice is likely to be of special psychological importance for the relatives and friends. As such, they are probably more interested than others concerned with the case not to neglect any long shot, no matter how poor the odds (thus avoiding a Type II error). They are also likely to be most anxious to avoid any further guilt feelings by trying *everything* humanly (or even super-humanly) possible. As the anthropologist A. R. Radcliffe-Brown pointed out in his examination of magical practices, when society offers a ritual solution to a problem, we may feel increased anxiety from *not* performing the magical ritual.[5] For example, if you spill some salt and you believe it is mere superstition to throw some over your shoulder to avoid bad luck, you may still perform the ritual because you have just enough doubt about its being completely foolish that you would rather reduce the small anxiety the doubt produces.

This feeling that all must be done that might even remotely be of help seems to have been especially strong for some corporate leaders in several cases where a firm's leading member was kidnapped by terrorists. Psychic Uri Geller claims he is on a retainer for several companies desiring his services should one of the executives be taken captive. If nothing else, if and when the firm gets its leader released, the colleagues of the kidnapped executive would be able to show him to what extraordinary lengths they were willing to go to save him. The feeling that you have "left no stone unturned," even when you fail, can go a long way toward relieving you of any feeling of indirect responsibility. There are times in our lives when we can take solace from saying, "I tried everything rational . . . even the irrational!"

At the next inner level—that of police agencies—as we saw in Chapter 8, there can be a variety of reasons why police may erroneously or even strategically announce that a psychic was "successful" when that may not have been the case. Such considerations need to be taken into account when we examine any police endorsements. We also need to remember that psychics—like Croiset and Hurkos, as we saw earlier—sometimes claim police endorsements that don't really exist. Thus, it is very common for psychic sleuths to claim that they have worked with the FBI or the CIA (with the psychic typically claiming all this was done with great secrecy) even though those agencies publicly insist that they have never officially employed psychics. Though we believe these agencies have used a few psychics upon rare occasions, the claim is simply too common among psychics to be taken very seriously without some modicum of reasonable documentation (which is almost always absent).

Like the relatives and friends of the victim, police are human beings with much the same feelings and natural biases. They, too, need closure and crave some degree of justice, but they also have great pressure placed upon them to resolve somehow the puzzles these cases represent. As we shall see in Chapter 11, there are many special issues involved for the police, but here we will limit our discussion to some of the general differences between this audience and the others that assess and deal with psychic sleuths.

As many criminologists have noted, policing crime is largely a clinical art, perhaps more than it is a forensic science. A successful police detective normally depends upon a wide range of skills and beliefs, few of which may have established scientific validity. Criminologist Peter K. Manning, an ethnographer of police culture, has described the myths and rituals involved in policing.[6] As Manning points out, arrests are usually matters of luck and chance, and he found that "patrolmen in private moments are quite critical of the 'Sherlock Holmes model of policing,' where diligent pursuit of clues leads to a dramatic confrontation with the suspects assembled, an accusation with pointed finger, and a sobbed confession."[7] The harsh reality, as analysts point out in *The Criminal Investigation Process*, is that "to make an arrest, police investigators rarely exploit other than the most direct type of evidence—apprehension at the scene, suspect named by the victim, street identification by victims or witnesses, et cetera."[8] What's worse, studies for some areas—like robbery and burglary, which have arrest rates of respectively 13 percent and 4 percent anyway—seem unaffected by increased amounts of investigatory effort. For theft crimes, follow-up investigations are almost entirely ineffective, and even where fingerprint evidence is available, this seems seldom used.[9] Police work is full of frustration and the anxiety that attends it. In discussing the major fallacies of homicide investigation, Cleveland, Ohio's, Detective Captain David E. Kerr cited the widespread belief that "Murder Will Out," despite the many thousands of unsolved murders known to police. As Captain Kerr sadly put it: "There is no doubt in my mind that people can be murdered and buried every single day of the year without the police having any knowledge of these crimes."[10]

In short, the storybook picture of police efficiency and success is a far cry from the realities, and we must take such background facts into account when assessing unconventional methods like the blue sense.

As with the Dixie Yeterian cases discussed earlier, we found that police frequently feel the psychic helped even if the case remains formally unresolved. Though not enough evidence was uncovered to make an arrest in the Corcoran, California, double homicide of a mother and son, Sergeant David Frost termed Judy Belle's work a success. "She just confirmed for us we were looking at the right suspect," he told us. "I'm ninety-nine percent sure we had the right man in mind."[11]

In 1981, Nancy Czetli (then Nancy Anderson) was brought into the kidnap-murder investigation of a fifteen-year-old girl from Front Royal, Virginia, at the suggestion of former Winchester, Virginia, Sheriff Carroll K. Mauck, then a private investigator. Working with maps and photos of the girl's body, Anderson sketched a parking lot where the abduction had taken place, described the car used and the location where the body had been found. Quoted in *Your Virginia State Trooper* magazine, Mauck said: "Nancy took the case and told us just about everything we already knew. Then she got into her idea of who might have done it. She picked out the suspect we had picked, the man we had clearly established as the prime suspect. She led us right up to him."[12] If they already had a prime suspect and knew what happened, why did they need Czetli? It sounds suspiciously as if they led her right up to the suspect rather than the other way around.

Because of the legal burden of proof required to obtain a conviction in a criminal case—especially a homicide case, which may result in a death sentence—police often feel frustrated by the system. The psychological feeling that a case has been "solved"—if only in the officer's mind—can alleviate some of those feelings of frustration and provide a sense of closure. Nobody likes to feel that he is beating his head against a wall and that whatever he is doing is futile. It is possible, then, that a psychic may act as *corroboration* for what the detective already suspected (much as did the sixteen-century's cunning men described in Chapter 2). He had the right man because the psychic said so.

Although the public tends to think of solved cases in terms of those judged so in the courts, police have the frequent problem of believing they *know* who did it without having adequate proof to go to trial and win a conviction. Some psychics also seize upon this difficulty as a rationale to justify their own failure to produce adequate evidence. Thus Dixie Yeterian writes, "Our laws are designed to protect the criminal rather than the victim. It's especially frustrating to me, working as a psychic consultant. . . . The men I have worked with . . . put all their heart and soul and caring into their work, in many cases just to see it blown away in court . . . The laws are so stringent that any case can be thrown out of court on some little technicality."[13] This sort of sympathetic but fundamentally rationalizing attitude probably goes a long way with some of the police with whom psychics work.

In his observational study of criminal investigators, *Detective Work*, criminologist William B. Sanders found that "nothing by itself, independent of interpretive work is recognizable as information, and the 'facts' do *not* speak for themselves."[14] Perhaps the fictional Detective Joe Friday of TV's *Dragnet* said, "We just want the facts, ma'am," but real-life detectives do not build their cases by simply linking such "facts" together. Sanders describes the investigative process as essentially one of reaching decisions that reduce an investigator's uncertainty. Sanders found that he could better understand what was happening if he made a distinction between "data" and "information."[15] Data are everywhere. The victim may have worn a size-ten shoe and perhaps he liked hot-fudge sundaes, but such data are probably going to be irrelevant to solving his murder. When data come to the attention of the investigator in a way that he thinks is likely to reduce his uncertainty, they become "information."[16] Sanders found that the process by which detectives convert some data to information is a highly complex one full of potential pitfalls. Fundamentally, a psychic brings some data to the attention of a policeman and seeks to persuade him that it is information, that is, represents a significant clue. To the degree that the policeman accepts the psychic's data as information, he will view it as helpful in so far as it acts to reduce his own psychological uncertainty.

As we saw earlier, regardless of the validity of psi, a criminal's beliefs in it may prove important. Sociologist W. I. Thomas originated the maxim popular among social scientists that "if an actor defines a situation as real, it is real in its consequences." Captain Kerr provides us with an excellent parallel case. In his discussion of the popular fallacies of homicide, he mentions the widespread belief that the image of the murderer will be permanently fixed in the eyes of his dead victim. Even though Kerr tells us there is absolutely no truth to this legend, he also notes that "many murderers accept this statement as true and give themselves up to the police."[17] As we already saw in Chapter 8, belief in the myth of the psychic has also resulted in some confessions. Even illusions can have utility.

Police goals are practical ones, like catching a murderer or finding a missing person. Such goals are not in themselves scientific ends. They are socially negotiated and set. Police no more need to understand scientifically all the means they use to fulfill their mission than a physician must fully understand the chemistry of all the pills he prescribes (and which may in some cases be merely effective placebos). The role of the police is, after all, a restricted one. Just as we do not expect the police to make society's judgment of a criminal's guilt, we should not expect them to make final judgments for us about the scientific validity of tools they may feel aid them in doing their job.

Even when failure results from trying a psychic, such unsuccessful episodes do not necessarily invalidate all claims for the psychic's abilities. Police use of psychics has hardly been systematic, and the representativeness of isolated failed (as well as successful) cases is difficult to evaluate. We need to keep in mind that most departments that have tried using a psychic have turned to them only as a last resort. And Hibbard and Worring may be correct when they claim in their analysis in *Psychic Criminology:* "All too frequently this encounter is the first and last, because a skeptical department is placing an untested psychic in a high-pressure situation which is not conducive to psychic receptivity."[18]

On the next inner audience level, that of the court system, the issue of the psychic's usefulness is typically indirect. The psychic is not considered an "expert witness," and normally information received psychically is not admissible as evidence. On this audience level, there are elaborate legal rules for admissibility of testimony and evidence with hearsay and many things permissible in everyday life (and even normal scientific adjudication) are here excluded. The burden of proof is upon the prosecution, and that burden varies from demanding a preponderance of evidence to evidence beyond a reasonable doubt, depending upon the crime and legal jurisdiction involved. It is important to remember that in British-American law, the defendant is considered innocent until proved guilty. Since our court system is especially concerned about not judging an innocent man guilty, even when his circumstances are rare or extraordinary, we can think of the legal system as more concerned with avoiding a Type II rather than a Type I error.

Though the role of the psychic is carefully circumscribed by the legal rules of evidence, psychics may play a significant part elsewhere in the court process. As we saw earlier, psychics have been used by attorneys to help in jury selection, and there have been some cases where a judge believed in the paranormal and allowed it to sway his actions.[19] When facts involving a psychic are revealed, they could possibly play a role in a jury's deliberations where individual jurors' own beliefs about such things may carry weight. Though the psychic cannot directly present psychic visions as evidence, during a trial a juror might possibly be influenced if he or she learns about a psychic's opinions from others' testimony. This ploy is not limited to the prosecutor. If the defense can somehow have it mentioned that a psychic was convinced someone other than the defendant committed the crime, it might help his case with some jurors. Even if the judge rules that such "evidence" is inadmissible and that the jury should ignore it, jurors may actually not fully do so.

Since the role of the psychic in the legal adjudication process can usually only be indirect (as when a psychic directs police to the location of the weapon used), even when there is a conviction and police say the psychic played a useful role, it may be impossible to assess that role's real contribution to the court's decision. The same is true even in cases where the psychic has been accused of being the culprit because the police (who did not believe in psi) felt such knowledge of the crime could only be had by the perpetrator. Even when the psychic in such a situation has sued for false arrest and won, skeptics argue that while such a judgment may show the police acted improperly, it does not validate the psychic's claim of paranormal powers.

Critics of psychic detectives often demand "proof" by asking for specific cases where information provided by the psychic has resulted in convictions. This suggests that such successes might act as validation for their psi abilities. As we have seen in many examples throughout this book, if testimony of police and prosecutors can be believed, such cases do exist. But in reality these episodes establish little. In the first place, skeptics can usually offer counterexplanations for the conviction, and police who earlier acknowledged the psychic's positive role often later change their minds and/or memories. In the second place, failures to convict also say little about the psychic's role. As we have seen, police "knowledge" of the perpetrator of a crime does not necessarily lead to arrest, and even arrest and extensive prosecution evidence may not lead to conviction. A prosecutor will not normally bring a case to trial unless he feels he has enough evidence to give him a reasonable chance for a conviction. Since psychics are most commonly brought into otherwise dead-end cases, it is not unreasonable to assume that their involvement may have helped in such a case's going to court at all. To make a proper evaluation of even the usefulness of the psychic's role for the outcome of their cases, we would need to find some way to compare the conviction rates in cases of not only *not* using psychics, but cases comparable in quality to the ones in which psychics have been involved. At this time, given the data available, there really is no way to do that properly.

As with our discussion of the police level, here we have considered some of the more general problems involved in trying to appraise psychics' usefulness within the court system. We shall examine further details and problems on this audience level in Chapter 12, when we consider the special legal issues the reality of psychics would produce.

The final inner audience level, that of the scientific community, is actually a continuum of views depending upon the particular scientists involved. As we noted in Chapter 3, the social or cultural sciences, which include criminology, have "softer" methodologies than those of the "hard" natural sciences. Psychology, which is intermediate in this continuum, is itself split into experimentalist (positivistic) and clinical (humanistic) wings. The positivistic psychologists remain the harshest critics of psychic claims because it is their accepted view that human communication can take place only through the normal senses, which is being challenged by psi claims. But those in the humanistic camps, not only in psychology but also in sociology and anthropology, are more open to taking reports of psychic experiences at face value. Whereas the hard-liners are often almost exclusively concerned with avoiding a Type I error (accepting a false psi claim), the softer sciences are more likely to give at least equal concern to avoiding a Type II error (rejecting psi when it really does exist).

Though all scientists place the burden of proof on those who claim psi exists, the positivists would make that burden far heavier than would the humanists. Thinking of it in terms similar to those developed by the legal system, humanistic scientists are likely to demand that psi's proponents present a *preponderance* of evidence for their side, while positivistic scientists are more likely to demand that any such proof be *beyond a reasonable doubt*. To take the legal analogy further, for scientists the psi claim is presumed to be "guilty" (that is, false) until proved "innocent" (that is, free of error). In this sense, the direction of proof science demands is the reverse of that demanded by our legal courts. The more demanding the critic, the more he is inclined to consider almost any basis for doubt as "reasonable," and some critics may be so hard-line that their threshold of doubt may itself be viewed as unreasonable and on the edge of dogmatism.[20]

Unlike the other audience levels, the scientific community is primarily concerned with the validity rather than the usefulness of the blue sense. Though social scientists may consider the criminological, social, and psychological functions of psychic detectives, there simply is no agreed-upon scientific criterion for utility. Scientists can describe how and why the various groups in society judge the utility of psychic detectives, but utility itself remains a matter for society's own cultural evaluation and is outside the scope of scientific methods. Scientists can point out that groups may be using false data for their own evaluations of psychics' utility, but the goals against which the usefulness of means is examined are cultural ends and not part of science itself.[21]

In addition to the question, "How and to whom are psychic detectives useful?" which we have just examined, we also need to consider the related question, "How useful are these psychic sleuths in comparison with the less-extraordinary or more 'normal' alternatives available?" Obviously, if other aids exist that are less controversial and more effective, those might be better alternatives for police use. On the other hand, if such alternatives are equally or less effective than psychics, the case for using psychics is at least relatively strengthened.

The major alternatives to using psychics would seem to be: (1) private investigators, (2) police psychiatrists, psychologists, and behavioral scientists, (3) hypnosis, and (4) polygraph examinations. Let's consider each of these in turn.

In our investigations, we found that police frequently view private detectives with some disdain. Sometimes retired or former cops become private investigators (PIs), and these may remain part of an old-boy network and be viewed as exceptions to the common police perception of PIs as unprofessional. But typically PIs are viewed by police as outsiders who are engaged primarily in low-status civil squabbles like divorce and in snooping operations that are not part of normal police work and which many cops view as undignified or even seamy.[22] Perhaps more important, police are centrally concerned with having control over their cases, and PIs may be viewed as unwanted intruders whose territorial encroachments add to the problem rather than its solution. Also, while PIs do not bring the authority of police to their investigations, they do have greater flexibility in them and sometimes use unorthodox and even illegal methods to obtain information while police are restricted in their available means. Though police and PIs do work cooperatively in many instances, PIs are primarily an aid for their clients, not the police. In fact, where rewards are offered or glory is to be gained, PIs may be in active competition with the police.

In any case, what slim objective evidence exists indicates PIs have relatively little success in criminal cases. In many ways, assessing their work creates problems similar to those we found in evaluating psychics, for PIs may produce information or satisfied clients without any resulting convictions. Contrasting their methods with those of psychics may largely be inappropriate, since many critics of successful psychics claim that they are actually using the same sorts of methods and are simply unlicensed or amateur PIs. Comparison is further complicated in that, as we have seen, some PIs have hired or regularly work with psychics, a few PIs themselves claim psychic abilities, and several psychics have obtained PI licenses. Since all PIs rely on intuition as well as hard evidence, it seems best to think of psychics more as a kind of amateur PI than as a completely separate and alternative aid to that available from PIs.

A notable and instructive exception may be the PI who specializes in finding missing persons. Perhaps the leading such finder now operating is Schenectady, New York's, Marilyn Greene. Greene is a self-taught PI who has located over two hundred missing persons, many of them children. At one point, she told us, she investigated the alleged psychic successes of Dorothy Allison, hoping that such paranormal techniques might further assist her. She told us she became disillusioned with what she learned after talking with officers who had worked with Allison, and after becoming involved in a Florida case that the Nutley, New Jersey, psychic was also working on.

Much of Greene's success can be attributed to her thoroughness and tenacity, but she also depends on patterns she believes exist in such cases.[23] She contends that missing elderly people are typically located about a mile from where they were last seen, whereas hikers are likely to be found about four miles away. Runaway children usually travel downhill, and first-time runaway kids are likely to do so in the company of a friend. Runaway teens from the Northeast are likely to go to Florida. And people who commit suicide outside often do so within a quarter of a mile from where they were last seen. As we suggested in Chapter 8, many psychic sleuths may actually be working from similar generalizations but unconsciously so.

Examining Marilyn Greene's statements about her methods, we were struck by other similarities with methods that successful psychics may also be using. According to Greene, one can correctly gauge the answers to questions by watching a person's reactions. Nonverbal clues, she says, ". . . the eyes, the body, the tension— sometimes tell you the answer you want without any words." Once you see a lie in the eyes of an adult, she says, ". . . if you know what the lie is, you also know what the truth is."[24] Put in these terms, these abilities may seem normal rather than paranormal. But the fact is that the mental processing Greene goes through is clearly what many others would consider intuitive judgments, for the orthodox psychological literature on reading body language and lie detection simply does not support the predictive strength of such inferences under usual conditions.[25] For example, when Greene described her detection of a perpetrator's lies to a reporter, recalling that "his manner, his body movement, his eyes told me they had gone into that wooded area and that a crime had been committed there," she clearly is making a substantial intuitive leap from a minimum of physical cues. At one point, she told the reporter that she believed that women may be better suited for her job than men, describing it as "women's intuition."[26] Clearly, Greene sees much of her own success as based on intuition rather than systematic reasoning and purely logical inference. Thus it seems reasonable to conclude that some of her own success may result from the still largely mysterious process called the blue sense.[27]

Police psychiatrists and psychologists are the experts on the criminal's mind and behavior who perform the roles most similar to those of psychic detectives. Though there are a few psychic sleuths who also are professional psychologists (most notably Dr. Keith Harary), these two roles are usually exclusive and often competitive. Behavioral scientists at times are called upon by police to assess the character and motives of a criminal based upon available evidence and to develop likely psychological and physical profiles of the culprits. The major such profiling service is the National Center for the Analysis of Violent Crime, which has become "the world's clearinghouse for the pursuit and capture of irrational, abnormal offenders, the most difficult of all criminals to apprehend."[28] According to internal studies, the Center, located at the FBI's Quantico Marine base in Virginia, reportedly "contributed significant aid in 80 percent of the more than six hundred cases it now accepts each year."[29]

Though such profiling shows great promise, comparison of this technique with the use of psychics reveals limitations and some similar problems. First of all, the profiles are reportedly effective primarily in dealing with "abnormal" and especially serial criminals. Though the profiles produce interesting differentiations such as that between the behavior and background patterns found for "organized" versus "disorganized" offenders (for example, the former tend to be intelligent and sexually competent while the latter are usually not so bright and are often overtly inadequate), such designations are not absolute. The profilings do not cover the entire range of criminal activities, including location of missing persons and bodies, as psychics allegedly do. Second, a major survey by the Center to gather data on criminals' patterns that played an important role in the Quantico profilings was based on interviews with fifty notorious inmates in the nation's prisons. Like much criminological investigation, this approach has the disadvantage of basing conclusions on a sample of convicted felons. Obviously, those criminals who successfully evaded conviction (or perhaps even suspicion) are not among those sampled. It seems likely that such a sample bias would skew the results. After all, those who were caught are the "failures," and may have very different profiles from those criminals who have been "successful."

More important than such limitations, however, may be the similar problems we found in assessing the success of profiling just as we did that of psychics. Take, for example, the "wizardly" and pioneering profile given by New York psychiatrist Dr. James A. Brussel in 1956 when he produced an "uncannily precise analysis" of a "Mad Bomber" who terrorized New York City for over ten years with homemade explosives. Reporter Stephen A. Michaud was astonished to find that "Dr. Brussel even accurately predicted that the bomber, George Metesky, would be brought in wearing a double-breasted suit, neatly buttoned."[30] Though such an inference might constitute a good guess anchored in the generalities found within the profile, such a specific prediction must surely have been based on an intuitive leap from that information, much like what seem to be similar jumps from limited information to the insights put forward by psychics. Psychology still little understands such intuition processes.[31] Dr. Brussel may have been using his own blue sense. As with the psychics, profilers seem to keep little track of their own misses and emphasize their hits. When profilers and psychics say their clients tell them they have contributed "significant aid" 80 percent or more of the time, we need to look very carefully at exactly what sort of aid that really is. As with the testimonials psychics get from police they have worked with, some of whom seem to consider very little help qualifying as "significant aid," we need to retain a high degree of skepticism toward any vague claims made about profiling success rates.

Unlike psychics, forensic and police psychiatrists and psychologists are considered part of the professional in-group. In general, their abilities are presumed to exist and are little tested. Whereas police will withhold information from a psychic as part of their tests of the psychic's credibility, they normally give all potentially useful information to the behavioral scientists they employ. To obtain a proper comparison, we need to see what would happen if psychics were given similar data and cooperation. Given this difference in current police cooperation, it seems surprising that police scientists do not perform far beyond the effectiveness cited by proponents for the use of psychics.

The solid evaluative studies of forensic psychiatry that have been done have been by and large damning. An excellent example in an area where psychiatry is frequently used concerns the prediction of dangerousness for *known* criminals. One often reads of patients being released by psychiatrists from mental institutions only to commit horrible crimes. As one major early study pointedly concluded: "Whether magic or science, the prediction of dangerousness by psychiatrists represents an excellent example of professionals who have exceeded their areas of expertise and for whom society's confidence in their ability is empirically unjustified."[32] More recently, in 1988, researchers cast serious doubts on whether or not psychologist and psychiatrists should even be classified by the courts as expert witnesses. Writing in *Science*, David Faust and Jay Ziskin summarized their survey of the evidence by concluding: "Studies show that professionals often fail to reach reliable or valid conclusions and that the accuracy of their judgments does not necessarily surpass that of laypersons, thus raising substantial doubt that psychologists or psychiatrists meet legal standards for expertise."[33]

In our interviews with police detectives, many of them expressed hostility toward some psychiatrists in terms similar to those other detectives used to denigrate psychics. Aside from doubts expressed about the scientific character of many psychiatric efforts to profile the perpetrators, several officers expressed their special dislike for those psychiatrists who worked with the department and then "grandstanded" by going on television news and talk shows (much like some psychics) and giving the public their "expert opinions" on who the perpetrators might be and what motivated them. Police told us they became especially angry when psychiatrists sometimes disclosed privileged information to the public that the police wanted kept secret. In general, police prefer psychics and psychiatrists who act as good team players and keep a low public profile, and who allow the officers in charge to maintain maximum control over their case, including the handling of public relations and any disclosures to media.

Hypnosis is another police aid that can be used as an alternative to using a psychic in attempts to reconstruct crime events. As David and Herbert Spiegel point out in their review, for the last hundred years "the primary forensic uses of hypnosis have been for the purpose of assisting victims, witnesses, and occasionally defendants in enhancing memory of a crime."[34] Many police who are skeptical about using psychics have expressed more confidence in hypnosis. For example, Captain Bill Valkenburg of the Palm Springs Police Department told us that he felt a psychic's "vision" and a cop's "hunches" are really impressions registered on the subconscious. Impressed with the results gotten from hypnosis, he says, ". . . we've had cases where witnesses have remembered license numbers and descriptions of perpetrators while under."[35] The use of hypnosis by police seems widespread. According to one text on criminal investigation methods, an estimated fifteen hundred criminal-justice and mental-health professionals representing local, state, and federal agencies have been trained to use hypnosis.[36]

Scientific research into hypnosis has had a turbulent and highly controversial history. A leading expert in the field, A. M. Weitzenhoffer, wrote as late as 1979 that "speaking of only hypnotism research done during the last forty-five years, I find much of it, and the associated writings, to have been of low scientific caliber. There has been far more pseudoscience than science in it."[37] Contrary to what the public has been told in most popular-science writing on the subject, University of Liverpool psychologist Graham F. Wagstaff's 1989 review of the research found that "the vast majority of studies show that hypnotic procedures do not facilitate accurate memory."[38] One of the strongest critics of using hypnosis to facilitate witness recall, especially for courtroom testimony, is the University of Pennsylvania School of Medicine's distinguished experimental researcher Martin T. Orne. Orne contends that today's science simply "cannot distinguish between veridical recall and pseudomemories elicited during hypnosis without prior knowledge or truly independent proof," so "testimony based on hypnosis or any other procedures that invite fantasy, diminish critical judgment, and increase the risk of pseudomemories should be prohibited."[39]

One outspoken critic of the abuses of hypnosis is the popular stage mentalist Kreskin, America's premier psychic entertainer. Kreskin has assisted a number of police departments in their investigations, and told us that he has worked on about eighty-four to eighty-six cases, most with no publicity. Though the press stories about his involvement in crime cases suggest he acted the normal role of the psychic detective,[40] his method was one that most would consider more related to using hypnosis. But in fact, Kreskin disbelieves in hypnosis as a special state, and his work with witnesses did not involve placing them into a trance. He believes everything done in a trance can be done in the waking state. As Kreskin put it to us, "There's no hypnosis or sleight of hand involved."[41] He told us that what he did was try to get people to recall more than they thought they could, drawing recollections from the unconscious. Kreskin tries to stimulate imagination and emotions through a barrage of probing questions.

While appearing on stage at Harrah's in 1976, Kreskin was approached by a Reno, Nevada, police detective who asked him to assist in the investigation of the murder of Michelle Mitchell, a University of Nevada–Reno coed who had been found with her throat cut. The detective wanted him to play the usual role of the clairvoyant psychic. Kreskin told him he could not do that but might be able to help if there were witnesses. Three witnesses came forward who happened to be driving by the front of the school as hundreds of kids were coming out of class. Kreskin met with each of them separately and had them relive their actions at the time while assuming the body positions they then had. Two of the three reported vivid recollections of the girl; both saw her walking to her car with a man they similarly described. "It was amazing," Kreskin told us. "Somewhere, unconsciously, they had both picked up stimuli and stored it." A composite sketch of the suspect was made and widely circulated. Months later, Kreskin recalled, a suspect matching the description was picked up in California for another crime, and was brought to trial. Captain Don McKillip, chief of the Reno detectives, said Kreskin's help had been valuable in re-interviewing witnesses and "freshening" the investigation.

Kreskin is very cautious in his approach and fully recognizes the pitfalls. He pointed out to us that in most cases, even if he picked up a clue, without independent corroboration such information is useless and could just be an hallucination. In one prominent murder case Kreskin told us he was consulted on, police had a suspect who, when hypnotized, showed signs of multiple personalities. Kreskin told police he was skeptical of the genuineness of the suspected personality split because the hypnotist in this case was a strong believer and had a book coming out shortly on multiple personalities. As Kreskin candidly told us: "Probably the easiest people in the world to fool, besides the retarded, are psychiatrists."

Hypnosis, like psi, has historically been entwined with various occultisms. From the late-eighteenth-century attacks on Franz Mesmer's claims of "animal magnetism" to today's denials of hypnosis as a special process, many parallels can be found between orthodox science's attacks on hypnosis and its denials of psi. While some researchers have been proponents of extraordinary claims for both hypnosis and psi, and a few have claimed hypnosis can be used to increase psi ability,[42] most scientists in the forefront of hypnosis research are likely to be among the critics of psi claims. Among the latter is Martin Reiser of the Los Angeles Police Department, who is a major proponent of what he calls investigative hypnosis.[43]

Reiser argues that though hypnosis certainly has had its abuses, critics like Orne may go too far in their condemnations, and this could result in throwing out the baby with the bathwater (making a Type II error). The issue of whether or not hypnotically recalled information should be admissible as evidence in the courtroom is quite different from that of whether such information can be effectively used as a source of materials for further investigation by police. (We should note that the same argument can be made for "information" obtained from alleged psychics.) Reiser cites considerable research data to support the effectiveness of investigative hypnosis, including a 1977 pilot study conducted at the LAPD in which sixty-seven hypnotic sessions were conducted in a broad variety of criminal cases. As Reiser summarized, "New investigative leads were obtained during hypnosis interviews in 77.6 percent of the cases," and "16.5 percent of the cases were solved during the year of the study as a direct result of the information gained in the hypnosis interviews."[44]

As a working police psychologist, Martin Reiser seems to us to be primarily interested in the pragmatic aspects of using hypnosis. Summing up his more than fifteen years of experience at the LAPD in using investigative hypnosis on serious crime cases, he remains sanguine about its potential. He writes: "Although not a panacea and as subject to abuse or misuse as any tool, the investigative hypnotic process works in a meaningful number of dead-end cases to assist the criminal justice process."[45] Our research leads us to think that a similarly conservative yet optimistic statement may reasonably be made about police use of some psychic consultants.

Lie detectors or polygraphs are another police aid that are sometimes used to obtain information as an alternative to engaging a psychic. The use of physiological measures to determine deceit goes back to ancient times.[46] For example, Bedouins until recent times made conflicting witnesses lick a hot iron. The witness whose tongue was burned was judged to be lying. The ancient Chinese reportedly forced suspects to chew rice powder and spit it out. If the powder was still dry, the suspect was found guilty. In both instances, the principle was the same. A suspect who knew he was lying would be experiencing fear, which in turn would diminish salivation, thus drying the mouth. When the tongue and palate are dry, a hot iron burns, and expectorated rice powder will appear dry. We mentioned some other folk methods used for lie detection in our discussion of the fifteen-century thief catchers in Chapter 2. Such "autonomic ordeals," as anthropologist John M. Roberts called them, have a long history and are found in many cultures; some have proved surprisingly effective.[47]

Beginning with Cesare Lombroso's studies in the early 1900s on the physiological correlates of emotions as indexes of lying, modern science has investigated a wide variety of potential lie-detection methods—the most common of which is the polygraph, which monitors changes in the subject's skin resistance (the galvanic skin response), blood pressure, and pulse. In 1985 there were over thirty polygraph schools accredited by the American Polygraph Association (APA). Most federal government polygraph examiners in the United States were trained by the U.S. Army Military Police School. Though there are APA-accredited training programs, many examiners are not graduates of such approved schools. There is no national regulation of polygraph training programs and "in about half of the states and Canada there is nothing to prevent the unscrupulous and untrained entrepreneur from purchasing some cheap recording equipment (sometimes little more than a prop) and hanging out a shingle."[48]

Polygraphs are generally used for both deception and information tests. The former are to ascertain if a person is deceiving and the latter are to determine if the subject possesses specific information that suggests knowledge or involvement with some criminal incident. These two kinds of tests are similar but make different psychological and physiological assumptions and involve different sorts of procedures for conducting and interpreting the test results.[49] In both situations, subjects can use successful countermeasures to mask their deceptions.[50] To confound matters further, a major danger with polygraphs has been what deception expert Paul Ekman termed the *Othello error,* named after Shakespeare's tragic hero.[51] This error consists in mistaking signs of fear and distress for evidence of deception, as did Othello when he killed his faithful Desdemona—again a case of what we have been calling a Type II error.

Though debate on the usefulness of lie detectors has raged for decades, there simply is no consensus today among the experts about the validity and accuracy of polygraph tests, nor is there agreement about how or even if they should be used. Iacono and Patrick conclude their review of the literature by stating it simply "will be impossible to reach a consensus with the existing (almost nonexistent) data base. The sixty-five years that have elapsed since the first polygraph test was administered have given rise to far more questions than answers."[52]

Interestingly, there are some striking parallels between what polygraph examiners and psychic detectives try to do. A study by sociologist Phillip W. Davis and polygraph examiner Pamela McKenzie-Rundle found that a good examiner tries (1) to manipulate the suspect so that he will provide something tangible to show the police that will appear to prove his unambiguous guilt or innocence (what is called a "good chart"); and (2) get the suspect to confess.[53] Many psychics, as we have seen, try to do the same thing. And, as with many psychics, there would seem to be a degree of charlatanry in the process. It is the job of the polygraph examiner to induce the suspect to produce a set of squiggly lines in response to certain answers that differ physically from responses to other questions, then *convince the police* that those squiggly lines translate into the suspect's guilt or innocence. In reality, the squiggles are only marks on paper, and may signify a host of emotional responses other than guilt, or may—in rare instances—signify nothing at all. As with the issue of whether or not psychics are useful, pragmatic arguments for the use of polygraphs are abundant, but solid scientific conclusions regarding their validity remain elusive.

As we have seen, all four major police aids alternative to psychic consultants involve some degree of controversy and questions about their validity. Proponents of each often center arguments for their use by police largely on practical grounds. Those who favor using psychics are in much the same position. Whether or not psychics are "real" may be less important than understanding how, when, and why they sometimes seem to be effective.

Until enough proper comparative data can be gathered for precise scientific analysis, the fundamental questions about the validity and accuracy of psychic detectives remain unproved. But, as we argued in Chapter 3, matters *un*proved should not be mistaken for those *dis*proved. In the meantime, while hard-line laboratory scientists may quite properly treat the undemonstrated claim as one probably untrue, we continue to get a growing number of field reports that endorse claims of the blue sense. These reports vary greatly in their quality. For most of these reports of the paranormal, it is relatively easy to suggest alternative normal explanations. We considered many such alternatives in Chapter 8. But some cases present evidence for a psychic's success which, if not absolutely convincing, strain our efforts as we search for more plausible alternatives.

Let us take one example commonly accepted by many ESP proponents as proof of the blue sense: Greta Alexander's involvement in the missing-person case of Mary Cousett.

Cousett had disappeared from her Alton, Illinois, home in April 1983. Foul play was suspected, and on the basis of information provided by an informant, Cousett's boyfriend, Stanley Holliday, was arrested for murder. The informant also told the police where Cousett's body had been dumped—on a forty-mile strip along Route 121, north from Lincoln to Peoria. Months of searching, however, had turned up nothing, and without a body, the case against Holliday was ready to fall apart. Enter Greta Alexander.

Hovering over a map of the area, Alexander poured out her visions to the police, who eagerly took them down. Then, with a pencil, she drew a circle on the map, marking an area near the Mackinaw River on Route 121. "I feel the body is here," she told them.

The circle was in the area indicated by the informant, an area that had been searched several times before. On the basis of Alexander's reconfirmation, a new search team was dispatched, and three hours later, the woman's remains were found.

Detectives later listed twenty-two out of twenty-four "amazing" scores that Alexander had made concerning the circumstances surrounding the finding of the body. "I'm a nonbeliever in this sort of thing, but this makes you wonder," Alton police Lieutenant Donald Sandidge told reporters.[54] "I was skeptical to begin with, but I guess I'm going to have to be a believer now," echoed Sergeant William Fitzgerald, also involved in the case.[55]

So, here we have it: a psychic case that is judged a success at almost every audience level. The public accepted the hit because the media portrayed it as such, quoting police, who gave Alexander credit for her contribution. The family judged it a success because the search, fruitless up to that time, ended in the location of the body. The case can even be judged successful at the legal level, where a conviction was obtained.

Only at the level of the final inner audience—the scientific—does the burden of proof in the case probably fail to meet the test for success.

In an analysis of Alexander's predictions, Ward Lucas (Denver's station KUSA-TV's reporter whose investigative work we considered in Chapters 3 and 8) found them to be vague, self-fulfilling prophecies.[56] As we saw in Chapter 8, self-fulfilling prophecies are commonly found in psychic predictions. They are predictions that appear to be specific but are actually phrased loosely enough to fit many scenarios. Thus the statement, "I see some water . . ." can mean a pond, a puddle, a river, or a water tower; "curved wood" can be a tree, a part of a barrel, a stick, or a table leg; "the word 'brown'" can be a surname, a color, part of the name of a place, et cetera. The significance of such pronouncements is only filled in later by credulous witnesses who are stunned by their accuracy.

This case is a key one for our extended analysis for two reasons. On the one hand, it is a prize case that contains many hits. On the other, it has been carefully examined by an astute critic who raised objections that convinced other skeptics and discredited the psychics in their view. Since the writings on this case are among the best found on both sides of the issue, examination of the arguments should prove revealing.

Now let us briefly examine both the twenty-four predictions Alexander made to the police in the Cousett case and Lucas's critical appraisal of each:

1. *The area where the body is has already been searched.* Lucas felt this was a common prediction for psychics to make where they had been directed to a possible location, and Alexander could assume

they had already used more conventional search methods. Lucas's explanation is certainly possible, but is it really probable? It seems more reasonable to think that if the psychic actually knew they had searched that area and found nothing, she would direct them elsewhere. In fact, the more reasonable skeptical hypothesis may be that she did not know where they had already looked and naturally picked the most likely spot (which the police must also have thought likely since they had searched there "thoroughly").

2. *During one of the previous searches, a man with funny-looking boots walked past the body.* Lucas pointed out that Alexander knew the previous searches had taken place along the muddy riverbank, where someone would normally wear boots and could later be claimed to fit the bill. But if not all the searchers wore boots, this remains a likely but not certain prediction. Further, since police cited this as one of the "amazing" predictions, it seems likely that the phrase "funny-looking" was probably also applicable to their confirmation. Perhaps all boots can be described as "funny-looking," but in this case the man in question had worn "an odd-looking pair of discarded firemen's boots."[57]

3. *The man with the boots had a dog.* Lucas calls this a "fair chance guess" since dogs are normally employed in searches. But note that the prediction does not apply to those who might have dogs with them but were not wearing boots. In any case, according to one newspaper report, only one dog had been used,[58] and *if* the police thought this prediction was correct, it was *presumably* with the man with the odd boots.

4. *A man with a crippled hand will find the body.* Lucas sarcastically calls this "a fantastic psychic hit!" agreeing that the finder had an injured finger. In fact, Steve Trew, the auxiliary policeman who first spotted the body, had damaged several fingers on his left hand in a drill-press accident at Peoria's Caterpillar Tractor plant. Clearly, Lucas has minimized the injury. This prediction is specific and not self-fulfilling.

5. *The body will be found near three roads.* Lucas sees this as self-fulfilling since cops trying to make this prediction fit could look down the road until they saw two other roads. This may be the case, but surely this prediction was perceived as "amazing" because the body *was* found near a single multi-road intersection rather than just on a road that intersected somewhere along the way with at least two other roads.

6. *The initial* S *will play an important role*. Lucas points out that though Steve Trew found the body, S is the most common letter in the alphabet (presumably as the first letter of a word) and could have been applied to many other things like "salt" on the road or "sticks" on the road. This seems a reasonable complaint. However, one might wonder how salt or a stick could as easily be interpreted as having played "an important role." The one point that both Lucas's and Alexander's touters overlook is that the letter S had *already* played an important role in the case, in that the primary suspect was named Stanley, a fact known by Alexander. Thus, Alexander had a ready-made "out" if no other S's materialized.

7. *The initial* B *is around the victim's body*. Lucas makes the same reasonable point, and in this case we are unclear as to why this was even considered a hit, since the particular B-word the cops spotted seems nowhere mentioned. What is remarkable is that a prediction so easily self-fulfilling was apparently a miss.

8. *The body would not be found in the state where she was born*. Lucas points out that newspaper stories mentioned the missing Illinois woman had been born in Mississippi. Certainly, Alexander may have seen this in the press, but Lucas does not tell us what papers carried this information, nor does he really establish any likelihood that Alexander might have read of it. Also, if she knew the woman was from another state, why did Alexander eliminate the possibility of her having gone home? Lucas's solution may be likely but is far from certain.

9. *Grabner's farm would play a part*. Lucas points out that no one would confirm this, but since the police did not indicate to Lucas that this was among her misses, either, at worst this might be simply vague enough to be easily self-fulfilled.

10. *There would be tree cuttings near the body*. Lucas says this was a complete miss. According to one newspaper report, Sergeant Fitzgerald earlier had said Alexander had predicted "the body would be covered by brush or leaves."[59] It was covered with leaves. In any case, why is this not at least self-fulfilling, since there were bound to be some tree cuttings *somewhere* near the body?

11. *The road splits near the body*. Lucas finds this a "good odds-on guess." Perhaps so, but far from a certainty.

12. *The road near the body is bumpy*. Lucas says this was not only a miss but a surprising one if police had three roads to choose from. We agree.

13. *The body will be off the main highway*. Lucas sees this as virtually meaningless since it is so vague. However, it could have been shown as false if the body had been found quite far from any highway. Also, to most people this probably first suggests that the body was not directly on but quite near the main highway. In fact, the body was found where "Illinois 121 merges into a four lane dual highway."[60] Though the statement is vague, it seems understandable why the cops considered this one a hit.

14. *A leg or foot on the body will be missing*. Lucas says this is a good guess since animals usually scatter bones. When a body has been lying around outdoors for months, it is not unlikely that it will become food for scavengers. But why not a missing hand or arm?

15. *The head will not be with the body*. Lucas says this is another good guess, given likely animal behavior. But is it? Do animals usually tear off the head this way? Lucas offers us no expert opinion on this.

16. *The body will be near a bridge*. Lucas says this is self-fulfilling when the body is next to a river with so many bridges, and even then the nearest bridge was over a quarter of a mile away. This indeed looks like a miss, but Lucas seems to be assuming the body would necessarily be found next to a river, which may be likely but surely was not otherwise certain.

17. *The body had been dragged from the place where the victim was killed*. Lucas says this was unconfirmed. In his notes on the case, Lucas says it was a "good odd-on guess," but it seems equally likely that the body might have been carried and dumped at its location, if the killing did not actually take place right at that site.

18. *Only part of the body will be showing*. Lucas says this was a good odds-on guess since the place had been searched earlier. However, this presumes that the body would have to have been where they had searched earlier and that Alexander knew they had already searched there.

19. *Cars stopping nearby will be important*. Lucas says this is a complete miss. However, it is unclear why Lucas concludes this rather than that it was merely unconfirmed. After all, the murderer might have dragged her to where he buried her to avoid being spotted by cars that surely occasionally stopped on one of the several roads there. In any case, the statement is really quite vague and could also be interpreted in terms of earlier events connected with the

crime. Why doesn't Lucas see this as potentially self-fulfilling rather than label it a clear miss?

20. *The body will be down an embankment.* Lucas thinks this is a good odds-on guess. Why? Surely there was not a better than 50 percent chance of this being the case? Or what does Lucas mean by "odds-on"?

21. *A faded sign will be important.* Lucas points out that lots of highway signs are faded, but in this case Sergeant Fitzgerald told Lucas the nearby one was not.

22. *The body will be across a road, down from the river.* Lucas found this a "meaningless prediction," presumably because of its vagueness. Yet in his notes, Lucas says it was an "odds-on guess from her previous knowledge." How can something meaningless also be an odds-on guess?

23. *Piles of salt or rock on the highway nearby will be important.* Lucas sees this as self-fulfilling, since there are many piles of salt along this stretch of highway and the nearest such pile was about a quarter of a mile away. Yet why doesn't Lucas call this one a miss, since no one seems to have suggested any way in which the salt pile might have been "important"?

24. *A church will play an important part.* Though there was a church-camp a half mile down the road, Lucas sees this as a common pseudo-psychic prediction that is almost self-fulfilling. We agree. After all, if there had been no church in the vicinity, the victim could have been an ardent churchgoer, could have gone to church the day before she died, the killer could have belonged to a church, et cetera.

How telling are Lucas's negative observations? Certainly, his points are important and greatly reduce the extraordinary impression these hits might first make upon a reader of them—that is, the evidential weight of these predictions is lower than many have claimed. But does this allow us to dismiss the case, as Lucas and many critics have? In the first place, even though twenty-four statements are discussed, only two (even though Lucas could apparently have cited four, numbers 10, 12, 19, and 21) were dismissed by Sergeant Fitzgerald as misses. Fitzgerald said right from the outset that he only credited Alexander with twenty-two "hits" and described her as "80 to 90 percent accurate."[61]

Second, when we look at the other twenty-two alleged hits in their entirety, a supporter of Mrs. Alexander can easily reach a conclusion opposite that of Lucas. For one thing, look at the number of cases Lucas describes as "odds-on" guess situations. In most cases, there is indeed a good chance of scoring a hit with an informed guess, but in most cases the odds of being correct in *each* case are probably less than 50 percent. The odds of hitting this many correctly would be computed by multiplying the odds for each against one another. So, figuring the odds for getting twenty-two correct out of twenty-four would still be winning against staggering odds. This does *not* mean that the results had to be paranormal, but it does mitigate against Lucas's cavalier dismissal of the whole based on weaknesses in the parts.

Third, if we look carefully at Lucas's specific alternatives, many of them seem to push rather hard for a way out of what manifestly seems at least a lucky guess. This is especially true when he speaks of odds-on guesses for which he really has no firm probability data anyway. His sometimes arbitrarily saying something could be "self-fulfilling" or an "odds-on guess" points up that his "outs" may be rationalizations, since "self-fulfilling" refers to vague generalities, while being "odds-on" should refer to some specific thing that is highly probable. His arguments may be plausible, but they are clearly after-the-fact (ex post facto) judgments.

Fourth, Lucas's bias seems to show most clearly in his too facile dismissal of Alexander's quite correct prediction that the finder of the body would have a crippled hand. Mere luck or not, this is a striking hit.

Fifth, Lucas seems to assume that the cops *wanted* to believe in Alexander and sought to find ways psychologically to credit her as successful. Many facts argue against this. For one thing, most of the officers quoted made a point of telling the reporters that they previously considered themselves nonbelievers or skeptics. Even after the body was found, not all who were impressed with Alexander credited her so easily. For example, Nick Graff, an investigator for the Tazewell County Sheriff's Office, probably voiced the feelings of some other officers when he said, "I personally think we would have found the body anyway. But she told us some things that no one could have known."[62] One is struck by the fact that most of the law officers interviewed about her role seem to have been won over rather grudgingly to her side. The fact that Lucas found a couple of the predictions unconfirmed, even though officers might easily have made them self-fulfilling if they had wanted to find confirmations, further argues against any strong bias in Alexander's favor.

In fact, all this nit-picking over the details of her predictions may be less central than it first appears. As Lucas correctly notes, when Greta Alexander originally drew a circle on the map as to where the body should be found, she actually missed the specific area by about three miles.[63] Also, her most remarkable hit, about the deformed hand, certainly was of no help to police hunting for the body. Perhaps most critically, Lucas seems to ignore the major problem that these twenty-four "predictions" are apparently really the later *recollections* Sergeant Fitzgerald had of what Alexander originally told the police. Examination of the newspaper reports at the time suggest some variation in the details of what Alexander supposedly said. There are even indications she may have scored some additional hits. For example, one story said she correctly told the police that "trail riders will play a role" and that "the body is across the road and down from the river."[64] The more we examine this case the more apparent it becomes that both proponents and critics simply produced rhetorical arguments based on limited and inadequate examinations of the facts.

What then can we conclude from this episode? First of all, we should not lose sight of the fact that Greta Alexander's involvement did contribute to the police's finding the body. Whether it was luck or whatever, the police probably would not have returned to a site they believed they had already searched adequately. Secondly, the actual odds of Greta Alexander's getting so many hits, especially the one about the deformed hand, strongly argue against this being a mere chance result. Third—and perhaps this is the most important neglected element—this case is far from being the only apparent success Greta Alexander has had. Though every one of her many cases can individually be challenged with *possible* (if not always plausible) alternative explanations for the results, her good (though far from perfect)[65] record of producing satisfied clients argues strongly that she has something *interesting*, if not psychic, going for her. And that *something* is worth learning more about.

We have called that special something the blue sense. We cannot discount that much of what psychics accomplish may be due to their simply being astute. Pocatello police Captain Lynn Harris said of Judy Belle's observations about the Bringhurst case: "I'm no trained psychologist, but if I went into any town, I could make educated guesses as to what happened. If the victim lived on the west side of town, it's likely the killer did, too."[66] Even police unconvinced of psychic powers frequently remark about some psychic's interpersonal skills. When Joe Austin, chief of homicide for the Anchorage, Alaska, Police Department, worked with Dixie Yeterian, he found her 180 degrees off. "We experimented with using her as an investigative tool, but it didn't pan out. We don't use psychics anymore. I don't think they work, frankly." But he did add: "She's very perceptive about people, though."[67] Similarly, Captain Gary Boswell of the Palm Springs, California, Police Department believes psychics have a place in dead-end investigations. He observes that they are often intelligent and perceptive people. "Whether they are psychic or not is another matter," he told us. However, he blames some of the problems on the credulity of some police who work with psychics, for he went on to say that "sometimes a new approach in an investigation can be useful. It all depends upon the investigator, whether he believes in it or not. If my wife was running the department, we'd all be using Ouija boards and crystal balls."[68]

Clearly, psychics are possible aids, not panaceas. At best, they may help without producing legal convictions at all. As Dixie Yeterian told us, "Most investigators would agree that my success rate is high in giving information leading to solutions. But as far as actually solving the cases, my rate is not high."[69] Not only do failures clearly occur, they should be *expected* to occur. Police should take this into account when deciding whether or not to pursue a psychic's hypotheses and lend manpower or resources to follow them up. As with the other fallible alternative aids we discussed, in the end it is a matter of rationally trying to weigh the potential costs against the potential benefits.

The problem has been exacerbated because many, if not most, psychics greatly exaggerate their own success rates. They often brag about being 80–90 percent right. Most of them probably fully believe this but when pressed will adjust the statement to mean that they produced something helpful in that percentage of the cases. For example, John Catchings, who has impressed a great many police departments with his many apparent hits, was quoted as saying, "I'm not always right. I'm only 80 to 85 percent accurate."[70] But in an apparently more reflective moment, he answered the question, "Are you ever wrong?" with "About twenty percent of the time I'm completely wrong. Another sixty percent I'm only partially right. Another twenty percent . . . I'm right on it."[71] As psychologist Louise Ludwig, who has worked with many psychic detectives, told us, a good psychic can hit 20–25 percent; on a good day, 40 percent;

and on the best day of his life, 80 percent. As she put it, "Psychics who claim to be right eighty percent are trying to get over their own insecurity by convincing themselves they're right all the time. Then they get stroked by people on the outside telling them how right-on they were. They get reinforcement from without and within."[72]

We need to remember that *if* police are dealing with a dead-end case, and *if* the costs of following up on the suggested avenue given them by a psychic with a good track record are small, even a 5 percent chance of success may be worth trying for. And for a family distraught by a lack of news, a psychic's hypotheses under similar conditions may be worth investigating even if the odds of a hit are only 1 percent. In the end, the truly skeptical but open-minded must weigh the probability of reasonably foreseeable benefits against the probability of reasonably foreseeable costs. We contend that in many instances, whatever the actual psychological mechanisms that may explain blue-sense successes, the chances for a hit exceed the chance level, and some psychic sleuths seem to perform well above it. Aristotle put it well when he urged that in all things, one's guide should be a reasonable moderation. So with psychics. After all, even if twelve eyewitnesses came forward to tell us that Jimmy Hoffa was buried under the foundation of a newly constructed building, that would not be conclusive evidence, and the costs of excavation to confirm their testimony would be prohibitive. As we saw when we examined the career of Peter Hurkos, particularly, police have sometimes gone too far in assigning scarce manpower and resources to follow up some purported psychic's "vision." But if a psychic with numerous police endorsements points at a bush and tells police to look in it because he says it contains the sought-after murder weapon, only an unreasonable person would find the cost of investigation so great that he would forego a peek into that bush.

Finally, it is most important to remember that psychics are not only fallible but that at best they are only potential investigative aids. Even calling them psychic "detectives" or "sleuths" may itself be misleading. The psychics really claim only to be extraordinary witnesses. At best, they should be viewed as consultants. Many of the psychics we interviewed repeatedly reminded us that they do not see themselves as *solving* crimes. The police must solve them. The psychic only tries to help by providing what often seems to be a better-than-chance set of directions which the police might pursue. Psychic Ingo Swann gave us a succinct statement of warning that all involved with psychics might well heed: "There is a great misconception about how ESP *should* work. The expectation is that it should be present along some kind of reproducible, mechanistic lines—when in fact it is a human ability present at its ultimate only if a lot of other things are present. A pole vaulter can make eighteen feet only with great preparation, but he cannot make eighteen feet a hundred successive times in a row even if he has the will to do so. I know of no human ability that is ideally present all the time; yet the attitude is prevalent that if a psychic is successful one time, he or she ought to be equally successful on demand."[73]

TEN

The Spook Circuit: Psychic Espionage

The work of psychic detectives in criminal investigations closely parallels the use of psychics in the sphere of international intrigue and the hoped-for development of military applications. Police search for evidence and suspects, intelligence agencies look for hidden bases and try to ferret out secret agents. Police would love to be able to read the minds of informers and suspects. So would the CIA. If the cops find psychics useful, it stands to reason that the Pentagon might, too.

As we noted earlier, many psychic detectives have claimed they worked with the FBI or CIA, sometimes on matters of international intrigue. Since these matters are, of course, usually "top secret," the psychic has a ready-made explanation for failure to present any corroborating evidence. An excellent example of what appears to be such puffery-without-proof is newspaperman Clifford Linedecker's biography of Ernesto O. Montgomery, *Psychic Spy: The Story of an*

Astounding Man.[1] A Jamaican psychic and faith healer, Montgomery claims that during World War II he worked with the "Psychic Division of British Intelligence," for whom he came up with many accurate prophecies. He even asserts that he had a vital secret role in predicting the weather to help set the time for the 1944 Normandy invasion. Since no military historian seems to have been aware of Mr. Montgomery's significance, he has apparently decided to push modesty aside and set the record straight.

Despite such pseudohistory, from time to time strange but authentic stories pop up in the press linking previously obscure psychics and occultists to major news events. Certainly a major story in 1988 was the revelation that President Ronald Reagan's White House schedule was in part guided by the advice of San Francisco astrologer Joan Quigley to Mrs. Nancy Reagan.[2] In fact, the media may have missed the deeper story of the President's many past involvements with astrology. Reagan indisputably had a long personal friendship from his acting days with Hollywood's "Astrologer to the Stars" Carroll Righter, whose syndicated astrology column Reagan acknowledged he and Nancy read every day.[3] Reagan's political ascent was embroiled in controversy when, during his California gubernatorial campaign, Governor Pat Brown accused Reagan of following the advice of astrologers. Matters became even hotter when Reagan had himself sworn in as governor in an after-midnight ceremony which many believed was based on advice from Righter.[4] Ironically, when Reagan complained in 1984 about his opponent Senator Mondale's and other Democrats' philosophy on the budget, he said, "We might be better off consulting astrologers about what the deficit will be in 1989."[5] Little did anyone then think Reagan might actually mean it.

What was far less publicized in the Reagan astrology story was the role claimed by another syndicated astrologer and former film actress, Joyce Jillson. Of special interest is Jillson's claim that she has been consulted by several police departments. According to one of her brochures for mail-order consultations, she has used her astrological approach for detective work in everything from "finding lost pets to tracking down desperate criminals."[6]

Before Don Regan's revelations about the Reagan astrology connection made big news in 1988, Jillson had already told a Los Angeles *Herald-Examiner* reporter back in 1980 that the Reagan campaign had then paid her $1200 to draw up horoscopes for eight candidates she was told were being considered for the vice presidency. Jillson said Reagan took these with him on a vacation in Mexico, pondered the charts, and came back agreeing that George Bush, a Gemini, would fit in best with Reagan, an Aquarius.[7] The Reagans denied Jillson's 1988 claim that she "spent a lot of time" at the White House after the assassination attempt on Reagan, and reporters seemed unaware of her 1980 claim.

Interestingly, Jillson's tale was echoed in an April 30, 1983, videotaped speech by a Georgia congressman, Democratic Representative Larry McDonald, to a meeting of the John Birch Society. He told those assembled that Reagan and his wife were both avid followers of astrology, and said that in 1980, during the Republican convention, "candidate Reagan had some of the various seers of the stars, those who draw up the horoscope menus, and they had a number of interviews with a whole group of them as to what they saw in the stars for the Republican convention. And guess what these seers of the horoscope had to say? That Mr. Reagan would be the nominee and that the Republicans could win the White House only if Mr. Reagan selected George Bush as his running mate."[8]

We may never know the full details of President Reagan's use of astrological counsel. According to Edward Helin of the Carroll Righter Foundation, Righter spoke frequently by phone with Reagan after he moved to the White House. Further, Helin claims to have heard Righter advise Reagan on many matters, including one case involving "major political decisions."[9] After Righter died on May 4, 1988, shortly before the Reagan astrology revelations broke, there were some speculations and allegations that Righter had past involvements with United States intelligence, including some as far back as 1940. In 1989, the *Pittsburgh Press* obtained heavily censored FBI files on Righter indicating that he had been investigated in 1987 "on a matter related to the national defense."[10]

As with psychic detectives, the role of astrologers in espionage work may involve disinformation. According to a 1988 letter to *The Times* of London from Miles Copeland, Sr., a former intelligence officer under Allen Dulles, the CIA set up a "Cosmic Operations Section" which ran for several years. Agents were taught "modern astrological techniques" and were subsequently planted on a number of world leaders, including Nkrumah of Ghana, Sukarno of Indonesia, and Mehmet Shehu of Albania, all of whom apparently took their charts quite seriously. In fact, Copeland wrote, "the CIA's hastily improvised arrangement of the stars" was used to persuade Nkrumah to visit China to get him out of the way when it was decided that General "Uncle Dan" Ankrah should take over the Ghanaian government. Similarly, many of Sukarno's decisions were made to play into CIA hands by providing him with the appropriate astrological advice. Copeland said the operation was discontinued when Allen Dulles learned that "we were bootlegging charts to certain members of our own White House staff."[11]

In 1987, the respected journal of political opinion *The New Republic* ran what to many must have seemed an incredible tale called "The Swami of Iranamok."[12] A black-bearded, then thirty-eight-year-old, Hindi-speaking Indian guru named Shri Chandra Swamiji Maharahj, who had reportedly miraculously cured movie star Elizabeth Taylor of a debilitating illness, became an important figure in the money-laundering scandals of the Iran-Contra or hostage-for-arms controversy. Already reportedly a confidant of top politicians in Indira Gandhi's Congress I Party, the Swami was described as having used "prestidigitation and feats of psychic power" to obtain the confidence of such world leaders as the Sultan of Brunei, Ferdinand and Imelda Marcos, the once Prime Minister of Fiji, and Zaire's President Mobutu Sese Seko. The Swami even claimed friendship with Richard Nixon.

The Swami reportedly demonstrated his mind-reading abilities for lawyer Steve Martindale at a Washington party in 1983. He asked Martindale to jot down a name, phone number, and secret wish on a piece of paper and then put it in his pocket. The guru dazzled Martindale by correctly guessing them all. Martindale says he saw him perform the same effect later on many world leaders.

The Swami impressed many international movers and shakers with his seeming psychic abilities and soon parlayed his many contacts into a sizable fortune by brokering deals and obtaining fees for arranging introductions among his powerful friends. For example, he was alleged to have received a fee of $500,000 for introducing Mohamed al-Fayed (the ex-brother-in-law of Saudi arms-dealer Adnan Khashoggi) to the Sultan of Brunei, said to be the richest man in the world.

In 1986, the Swami became involved in what was reportedly a blackmail scheme involving two Canadian financial advisers who threatened to blow the whistle on the CIA's dubious dealings with the Iranians. As these matters emerged and things began to fall apart for many like Khashoggi, the Swami returned to India. Though the Indian government was reported to be interested in tracing his seemingly unlimited access to foreign money, he soon vanished after posting bail with India's tax authorities, who were investigating him, and for some time retreated into obscurity as he observed "a holy vow of silence."

Another enigmatic case of a modern psychic's role in international relations is that of Israeli wonder-worker Uri Geller. As mentioned in the opening chapter, Geller made headlines in 1987 when he showed up at the Geneva arms-reduction talks and claimed some of the credit for the Soviet's next-day move to dismantle European-based medium-range missiles.[13] Whatever the facts of Geller's role at the talks, the week before he had been invited to address a Capitol Hill group by Senator Clairborne Pell, chairman of the Senate Foreign Relations Committee. On that occassion, Geller made a half-hour speech, followed by a question-and-answer period, in a special bug-proofed attic room in the Capitol. Known as "the vault," the room is normally used for top-secret briefings and document examinations. Geller reportedly spoke about what he claimed to have psychically learned of the Soviet intentions in the arm-controls negotiations. He also told this special audience of thirty-five—which included Representative Dante Fascell, chairman of the House Foreign Affairs Committee—of his belief that the Soviets are far ahead of the United States in psi research and predicted that within fifteen years, ESP could present an incredible threat to United States security.[14]

Geller's public association with top United States government echelons was not new. According to Ron McRae's book *Mind Wars*,[15] President Jimmy Carter had a private meeting with Geller in 1976 in Mexico City, soon after he became president-elect. Geller reportedly told Carter that the Soviets were screening children for paranormal powers. This incident reputedly induced the new President to order a high-level review of psychic research behind the Iron Curtain, completed in 1978. This assertion appears to be backed up by documents released in the early 1980s under the Freedom of Information Act, particularly a 1978 DIA report titled *Paraphysics R & D—Warsaw Pact*, which seems to be a direct result of Carter's order.[16]

According to espionage historian Richard Deacon, an informed source told him that Geller's activities in the United States were heavily monitored by the Soviets, who even set up a special committee operating out of Paris to study him and his experiments.[17] We are also told by several independent sources that Geller had been investigated by Israel's Mossad long before. In his book *The Geller Effect* Geller claims he has had off-and-on-again dealings with the FBI over the years, including an occasion when he was consulted about an alleged Soviet mole, a "sleeper," who an Eastern-bloc defector claimed was present in the top layer of Washington's administration. Geller says he came up with a name, but it was met with such incredulity that this was the last time this particular FBI agent ever asked him for help.[18]

As previously noted, Geller has apparently become a multimillionaire through his psychic consultations with oil and mining companies. Though critics have raised doubts about his successes, according to Australia's *The Skeptic*—a publication hardly friendly to Geller's claims—the Zanex mining company did pay Geller $250,000 (U.S.) plus an option to buy up to 1,250,000 Zanex shares at twenty cents each "for his advice on where to look for gold in the Solomon Islands and near Maldon in Victoria."[19] If Geller's life-style is any indication—he today lives with his family on a large and lovely country estate beside the river Thames in Berkshire, England, reputed to have a value of about £10 million—his claim that he is worth about $100 million appears credible. People often ask, "If you're so psychic, why aren't you rich?" Geller points out that he is.

Though Geller hints at some continuing involvement with psychic espionage[20] (a 1988 story appeared about an alleged death threat to him by the KGB),[21] he now seems more involved with his business ventures and pursues his role as a celebrity and entertainer. He intentionally works hard to present an ambiguous public image of a man half miracle worker, half charlatan, and total showman. As he neatly confided to reporter James Cook when interviewed for *Forbes* magazine, if people truly believed he had the powers he claims, he would have been dead long ago, for "whoever has people with such powers has an incredible weapon."[22]

Though Geller is still frequently being attacked with claims he is a total charlatan and rogue magician he has not ignored his critics, even though his detractors have largely ignored his rebuttals.[23] In fact, Geller recently filed two multi-million dollar lawsuits for alleged personal defamation against his major detractors, magician James Randi and the Committee for the Scientific Investigation of Claims of the Paranormal. As Geller told reporter Roy Stockdill, "Randi's been after me for seventeen years. In the past, when he's called me a fraud and a charlatan, I've chosen to ignore him. I don't have to prove anything. But this time he's gone too far."[24]

The suits, however, were dismissed on technical grounds.

Claiming that he is amused by the many magicians reproducing his key-bending and other effects, Geller insists that though magicians can simultate his results through trickery and can even produce many effects he cannot, he produces his own phenomena by psychic means. Whatever Geller's methods may be, the facts remain that he has produced some effects under conditions skeptics have yet to match, and, so far at least, he has not been indisputably "caught in the act."[25] Despite the continuing animosity of some conjurors (especially those who seem to have made a living from denouncing him), Geller has surprised many in the late 1980s by gaining some support and even a few public endorsements from professional magicians. As British magician David Berglas, current president of London's Magic Circle and then the acting chairman of the British branch of the Committee for the Scientific Investigation of Claims of the Paranormal, said in an article about Geller: "If he is a genuine psychic, and genuinely does what he claims to do by the methods he claims to use, then he is the only person in the world who can do it. Uri is the only one to have demonstrated consistently. He is a phenomenon, and we must respect that. If on the other hand, he is a magician, trickster or a con man, he is also phenomenal—the best there has ever been. So, whichever way you want to look at him, we must respect him as one or the other."[26]

Stories like these about the Swami and Uri Geller are nothing new. History is full of accounts of military leaders and political rulers employing prophets, soothsayers, and clairvoyants to spy psychically on enemies and to predict and even alter the outcomes of battles and events.

In the Bible (Kings 2:6), the Israeli Elisha's remote viewings of Syrian troop movements saved Israel from military defeat and precipitated the King of Syria's concern about who in his midst was a traitorous spy.

If Joan of Arc had been living today and working for the Pentagon, she would probably be termed clairvoyant and clairaudient. Unfortunately for her, she lived in the fifteenth century and her internal visions and voices only served to get her burned at the stake for being a witch.

John Dee, court astrologer and occultist for Elizabeth I, also acted as a secret agent for the realm, and it had been speculated by some that Dee's occult dabblings were in reality a cover for his intelligence-gathering mission. His psychic readings for European nobles netted valuable tidbits of information for the Crown. He advised Elizabeth on exploration ventures and accurately foretold that the Spanish were building larger ships to attack England.[27]

Modern governments have had their own psychic spies. In 1966, an article in the Czech military journal *Periskop* confirmed a long-term Czech interest in the military uses of psi. Among sources cited was a 1925 brochure-handbook titled *Clairvoyance, Hypnotism, and Magnetic Healing at the Service of the Military* by Karel Hejbalik. Hejbalik claimed that during the 1919 campaign against Hungary, he hypnotized two of his soldiers to improve their telepathic ability, then had them remote-view the enemy's strength and position. The article went on to say that during World War I the Czech army had used dowsers to locate traps, mines, and drinking water, with great success.[28]

Interestingly, forty years later in Vietnam, the U.S. Marines had its own group of mine-hunting dowsers. Dowsing for hidden mines, tunnels, and other objects was introduced to the marine corps by Falls Church, Virginia, dowser Louis J. Matacia in 1966. Matacia impressed the marines with demonstrations he gave at the Marine Corps Schools at Quantico. (Matacia today continues his work as a surveyor and dowser but also occasionally works as a psychic detective with his daughter Ginette.) After reporter Hanson W. Baldwin interviewed marines, including returning Vietnam veterans at Camp Pendleton, California, for *The New York Times*, he wrote that coat-hanger dowsing rods were "used in Vietnam with marked success in the last year, particularly by engineering units of the First and Third Marine Divisions, which are engaged in mine detection and tunnel destruction."[29] Similar acknowledgment of some success was made by *The Observer*, a weekly published for the U.S. forces in Vietnam, which described the operation and noted that "introduced to the Marines of the 2nd Battalion, 5th Regiment, the divining rods were greeted with skepticism, but did locate a few Viet Cong tunnels."[30]

During World War II, when the Soviet government officially

denied the existence of ESP, internationally famous mentalist and psychic Wolf Messing (whom we discussed in Chapter 2) was employed by the Ministry of Culture and toured the Soviet Union with his mind-reading act. Messing, a Polish Jew who fled Poland after the Nazi invasion, was reportedly held in great favor by Stalin, who was said to be intrigued by Messing's apparent ability to alter other people's perceptions by telepathy or suggestion. Stalin was also said to have used Messing as an oracle to predict the outcomes of military events and to spy psychically on the enemy. According to science writer Vadim Marin, Messing shocked those in a private Moscow club in 1940, when relations between Russia and Germany seemed excellent, by asserting that "Soviet tanks will be in Berlin." He also reportedly announced from the stage of the Novosibirsk Opera Theater in 1943, when the war with Germany looked gloomiest, that the war would end between May first and third in 1945. This prediction was off by one week.[31] Hitler, who many believed was deeply interested in the occult, was allegedly so spooked by Messing's talents that he put a bounty on the psychic's head after Messing predicted the death and defeat of the Führer.[32]

Another Jew who was sought and eventually executed by the Nazis was Stefan Ossowiecki, who it is claimed used his paranormal powers to aid the Polish underground. Among his alleged psychic feats of wartime detection was the locating of specific bodies in mass graves.[33]

British intelligence was able to take advantage of Hitler's belief in the occult when James Bond's creator, Ian Fleming, who at the time was with British Naval Intelligence, pulled off a particularly neat bit of psychic counterspying when he came up with the idea of passing on fake information gleaned from supposedly psychic sources. The Nazis had established a Pendulum Institute in Berlin to provide information to German Naval Intelligence. At the Institute, pendulum swingers would hold a pendulum over a map and dowse for enemy ships. Using his wide contacts in occult circles, Fleming managed to plant a false story that British intelligence was using their own pendulum swingers to track German U-boats. The story was leaked at a time when British sinkings of German subs were particularly high. The Germans fell for it, enforcing their commitment to their own swinging operations and resulting in what Fleming presumed would be all sorts of useless and time-wasting naval operations.[34]

The uses of psi by the Allies were not all for the purposes of disinformation, however. We had our own share of believers.

According to secret documents released by the British Army, the wife of Lord Hugh Dowding, head of the Royal Air Force, was able to pinpoint accurately and remote-view undiscovered enemy air bases.[35] In his book *British Agent* John Whitwell confirms that because of the dearth of information coming out of Germany after the British defeat at Dunkirk, some intelligence officials turned to crystal gazing. According to Whitwell, an enterprising fortune-teller had managed to convince several higher-ups of his fortune-telling abilities. For a short time, the unnamed crystal-reader's advice was influential in Western European intelligence circles, his advocates arguing that since no information was coming in, any kind was better than none.[36]

General George "Blood and Guts" Patton, who believed himself to be the reincarnation of a Roman general, was credited by his commanding officer and friend General Omar Bradley with having a "sixth sense" that saved his army on several occasions.[37]

According to Barbara Honegger, a former Reagan White House aide, in the early 1950s the State Department made "visualization exercises" part of its training curriculum in an effort to enhance the intuitive capabilities of its operatives; during the Eisenhower administration, the CIA set up an interagency committee to monitor psi research, a committee that she believes still exists sub-rosa. Honegger also claims that the Navy did its own testing of psychics to determine ship movements.[38] It is not known whether any pendulum swingers were used in the experiments, but New York psychic sleuth Shawn Robbins claims to have been one of the participants.[39]

A naval ESP test that received worldwide attention allegedly occurred aboard the U.S. nuclear submarine *Nautilus* in 1959. According to an article in the French magazine *Science et Vie*, top-secret tests were conducted in which telepathic "senders" on board the submerged submarine tried to beam mental messages to receivers on land. The purpose of this test was to develop a form of "mental radio," as a submerged submarine is unable to communicate with land by radio.

The report, which created quite a media splash, is believed by most experts to have been spurious, perhaps planted by disinformation experts to get the Soviets to pour rubles into fruitless research. If that was the case, it worked. The Soviets launched a series of submarine experiments of their own, and soon established several state-sponsored laboratories devoted to parapsychological research. [40]

The French, who some believe were behind the disinformation involved in the *Nautilus* story, got into the act again in 1979 when an article appeared in the May 18 issue of *Paris Soir* claiming that thousands of Soviet parapsychologists had been sent to consulates as telepathic agents. Their mission: to plant ideas favorable to the Eastern bloc in the minds of Western diplomats. This time, the Russians did not rise to the bait and lashed out in *Pravda* at the allegations.

The Russians have evinced a deep-seated historical interest in the paranormal. Atop a background of many Slavic folk beliefs about magic, witchcraft, and even vampires, Spiritualism was introduced to Russia through aristocratic followers of the French exponent of spiritism, Allan Kardec. Prince Wittgenstein introduced séances by various mediums before the Emperor Alexander II, including some by the great D. D. Home. Later, Alexander N. Aksakof, counselor to the Czar not only arranged séances but brought many Russian scientists to them. Starting in the 1920s, and probably impressed by stories of the "Mad Monk" Grigori Efimovich Rasputin's alleged hypnotic powers over the Empress Alexandra, Dr. Leonid L. Vasiliev, later chairman of the Department of Physiology at the University of Leningrad and a recipient of the Lenin Prize, began conducting experiments in controlling people's movements through mental commands. According to Vasiliev, the experiments proved successful over great distances, and were secretly funded through the Stalin years, when "telepathy" was a dirty (non-materialist) word.

It was after the appearance of the *Nautilus* story, however, that the Russians seem to have begun funding parapsychological research in a big way.

The Soviet thrust in psi experimentation seems to be in the area of long-distance control of thoughts and behavior in human beings. One Soviet psychic superstar is Nina Kulagina of Leningrad, who was reportedly thoroughly tested by respected scientists from the Institute of the USSR Academy of Science. In controlled laboratory experiments, Kulagina is said to have been able to psychokinetically move objects, affect compass readings, and even kill a frog by stopping its heart. Though much was written about her in the 1970s, with stories about scientists' endorsements of her powers in *Izvestia* and other media—including an appearance in which she demonstrated her powers on Soviet television—little had been heard about her in the West for nearly ten years until a remarkable article appeared about her in *Pravda* in 1988. This reported that after an article appeared in the Soviet journal *Man and Law*, claiming her a fraud, the psychic sued for defamation. At the trial, several scientists from the respected USSR Academy of Science testified in the psychic's defense, saying that they had tested her and found that her demonstrations of PK could in no way be explained away by clever manipulations as her detractors had claimed. The Soviet "people's court" ruled in her favor and ordered the journal to publish a retraction of its allegations of trickery and charlatanry. This decision was upheld upon appeal. [41]

Larissa Vilenskaya, a Russian émigré living in the United States since 1981, worked with top Soviet parapsychologist Edward Naumov and as a researcher at Moscow's Bioinformation Laboratory of the A. S. Popov Scientific and Technological Society of Radioelectronics and Communication. Vilenskaya has reported that the Soviet research on psi is geared to developing methods of influencing minds from a distance. [42] During a 1981 televised interview on *NBC Magazine with David Brinkley*, Vilenskaya stated that particularly gifted psychics are recruited by authorities and showed a film of one such subject who was asked to influence foreign political leaders negatively while listening to them on the radio. [43]

Dr. Milan Ryzl, a Czech biochemist who emigrated to the United States in 1967 after Czech secret police tried to recruit him as a spy, also finds a nefarious tone in Soviet psi research, saying its ultimate goal is thought control. He alleges he has visited Soviet labs where top-secret experiments in telepathic behavior control are being conducted. [44]

Estimates of the amount of money the Soviets have pumped into their parapsychology programs vary greatly, ranging from the tens to even hundreds of millions of dollars. But all agree that it has been many times that of the West. And the Soviets are not the only Eastern bloc nation to finance psi projects heavily. In Czechoslovakia, military interest in parapsychology has a strong historical basis, as was noted earlier. Today, Czech study in the field has been renamed "psychotronics," and the experiments have been carried out at the International Association for Psychotronics Research in Prague.

The leader in Czech research, Dr. Zdenek Rejdak, believes that the basis of all psi effects, including PK, is "psychotronic energy," a human force analogous to electromagnetic energy. A Czech engineer, Robert Pavlita, alleges success in harnessing and storing this energy in tiny machines which he calls "psychotronic generators." Pavlita has claimed that his generators are capable of moving distant objects and producing other psychokinetic effects, including the killing of small animals and insects.[45]

Bulgaria, long steeped in a gypsy tradition, has also committed itself to ESP research in a big way with the establishment of the Institutes of Suggestology and Parapsychology at Sofia and Petrich, headed by Dr. Georgi Lozanov. According to espionage expert Richard Deacon, the Bulgarian secret police have trained clairvoyants on staff as crime-busters and have some of the best clairvoyants and telepathy experts in the world.[46]

The most famous Bulgarian psychic is Vanga Dimitrova, a blind prophetess and clairvoyant living in Petrich, near the Greek border. Her alleged psychic feats have included reports of her paranormal detection, finding missing people, naming killers, et cetera. Her fame became so widespread that people flocked to her from all over Europe seeking readings. During the 1960s, Dimitrova was tested extensively by Dr. Lozanov, who proclaimed her genuine, and later by a special government commission of examiners. She passed with flying colors, and in 1966 she became a state-employed psychic, was given a government stipend, two secretaries, and even a special panel to interview those who applied to see her.[47]

Ironically, if all this Eastern-bloc research in parapsychology is a product of the disinformation intentionally planted by American intelligence through the *Nautilus* fiction, it spawned paranoia in those same circles.

Seven hundred pages of Defense Intelligence Agency (DIA) documents released under the Freedom of Information Act (FOIA) indicate that the DIA had an ongoing interest in parapsychological research since the early 1960s. Much of the material released was translations of Russian articles on such topics as psychotronics, bioenergetics, autosuggestion, and remote hypnosis, indicating that the DIA was concerned about Soviet developments in psi. One FOIA-released report was a 1976 study by E. C. Wortz et al., contracted by the CIA with AiResearch Manufacturing Company of California, a division of the Garrett Corporation, to evaluate the spectrum of Soviet parapsychological research. From an assessment of Soviet literature in the field, the report concluded that the Soviets had done considerable experimentation in PK, electrostatics, and remote viewing. Among the most interesting documents were those related to MKULTRA Subproject 136, which was the CIA's drug-testing and mind-control project. The subproject included an experimental analysis of psi, and a still partially censored internal CIA memo of 1961 states that the researchers (whose name remains classified information and so was blacked out in the released report) "went beyond the question of whether the phenomenon, extrasensory perception (ESP) exists." Funding was apparently laundered through an existing organization (whose name was also blacked out in the released document) for what is referred to as "security and cover purposes." The memo says this study was concerned with "the functional relationships between other personality factors and ESP skills" and "the factors that must be considered in using ESP as a method of communication." The memo pointedly notes that "any positive results along these lines would have obvious utility for the Agency," and closes by stating that a "request for covert security approval has been initiated."[48] If nothing else, this document clearly and flatly contradicts the claims that the CIA has never engaged in covert psi research.

Though there seems to have been some support for parapsychological research by the CIA in the 1960s, according to Ron McRae, it was in 1976 that then CIA Director George Bush was approached by a personal friend, ex-astronaut Edgar Mitchell, whose Institute for Noetic Sciences sought to encourage psi research. McRae reports that "Bush gave Mitchell permission to organize high-level seminars at the CIA to discuss possible intelligence applications of parapsychology." But even so, though scattered psi projects continue, parapsychological research "never got institutionalized at the CIA."[49]

Much alarmist information has been put out in recent years about the existing "psychic gap" between the Eastern bloc and the West. The statement is often bandied about, with little corroboration, that the United States is fifty years behind the Soviets in psychic research. The basis for alarm is the theory that any nation that could develop and control an arsenal of psychic weapons could achieve total world domination. Conventional weapon systems could be destroyed psychokinetically; nuclear silos could be pinpointed by remote viewing; computer and radar systems could be wiped out or altered from thousands of miles away, playing havoc with military guidance systems and destroying entire economies.

One architect of the current fear is Dr. Nikolai E. Khokhlov, a former KGB assassin who defected to the West in 1954 and is now a professor of psychology at California State University at San Bernardino.[50] Richard Deacon reports that Khokhlov testified during congressional hearings that Soviet mind-control programs had the backing of the military and scientists and that the Soviets had experimented with psychotronic weapons.[51] Over the years, Khokhlov expressed concern that the CIA and the rest of the intelligence community failed to take Soviet psi efforts seriously enough. TV reporter Garrick Utley in a 1981 segment on government psi research on *NBC Magazine,* on which Dr. Khokhlov appeared, said a 1976 "Khokhlov Report . . . was commissioned, was done and was submitted to the intelligence community," where it was summarized along with the report by Wortz et al., and "500 copies were circulated at high levels of the military and intelligence communities." According to Utley, "there was interest but little action."[52] In 1985, Khokhlov contended that the Soviets had already implemented attempts to influence the world through the use of electromagnetic waves and had been bombarding large portions of the United States with such signals since 1976.[53]

Another voice sounding the alarm about alleged Russian psi advantages is that of Dr. Andrija Puharich (whose researches with Peter Hurkos we discussed in Chapter 7). Puharich, a purported expert on military uses of psi, has put forth the theory that the Russians were using extremely low-frequency (ELF) sound waves to induce sickness and headaches in human beings. According to Puharich, the site selected for this ominous experiment was an area in Canada.[54]

Some degree of overblown apprehension and uncritical reporting about the actual state of psychic weaponry was probably present in articles in several official and semi-official military and strategy publications. In an essay for the December 1980 issue of *Military Review: The Professional Journal of the U.S. Army,* with the provocative title "The New Mental Battlefield: 'Beam Me Up, Spock,'" Colonel John B. Alexander (who retired in 1989) asserted that "psychotronic weapons already exist," that "there are weapons systems that operate on the power of the mind and whose lethal capacity has already been demonstrated," and that some persons seem able "to mentally retrieve data from afar while physically remaining in a secure location."[55] A reinforcing call for more attention to the threat of Soviet psi research came from military historian Dr. Roger A. Beaumont in the January 1982 issue of *Signal: Journal of the Armed Forces Communications and Electronics Association*.[56] September 1985 saw the *Journal of Defense and Diplomacy* publish the article "The Science of Psychic Warfare" by its science editor, Charles Wallach, in which he recommended that the United States initiate an independent "Psychic Service Corps" that should have "its own dedicated recruiting arm and training command."[57] And in 1986, *Military Intelligence*, a magazine put out by the U.S. Army Intelligence Center and School at Fort Huachuca, Arizona, published intelligence officer Captain Richard Groller's further call to psychic arms.[58] All of these raised the specter of impending psychic warfare. As one intelligence officer reportedly exclaimed—after seeing the results of CIA tests of remove viewing in which psychic descriptions of activities in the Soviet Union and China were confirmed by CIA agents in place there—"Hell, there's no security left!"[59]

But all this may seem mild compared to the bold and, to many, outrageous assertions of now retired Lieutenant Colonel Thomas E. Bearden, author of *Excalibur Briefing* and a specialist in "nuclear physics and intelligence analysis." Military paranoia seems manifest as Bearden tells us how the Soviets already have such weapons as a "photonic barrier modulator" capable of inducing physiological changes from a distance, and a "hyperspatial howitzer" that can telepathically transport nuclear explosions to far-reaching locations. Bearden even asserts that another Soviet psychic weapon sank the U.S. nuclear submarine *Thresher* in 1963, and that Legionnaires disease appears to have been a Soviet test of their new psychotronic weaponry.[60]

The concept of psychotronic weapons seems to have originated with Robert Pavlita's work, which is viewed with great suspicion among American parapsychologists. Yet a 1975 DIA report prepared by the Medical Intelligence and Information Agency and the office of the Surgeon General, *Soviet and Czechoslovakian Parapsychology*, demonstrates that the U.S. military and intelligence communities were concerned about these "generators." The report warns: "If Czech claims for these devices are valid, biological energy might be an effective anti-personnel weapon. . . . Soviet or Czech perfection of psychotronic weaponry would pose a severe threat to enemy military, embassy, or security functions."[61]

Another DIA document dating from 1972, *Controlled Offensive*

Behavior—*USSR*, is even more frightening. The 175-page report is a survey of Soviet research on mind control and quotes a 1970 U.S. military document which discusses the possibility of developing "apports"—a technique by which physical objects, such as documents, might be teleported from enemy territory.[62]

Part of the mutual concern and fear evinced by both superpowers might be a legacy of anxiety left by World War II and the subsequent development of nuclear weapons. Both the Nazi attack on Russia and the Japanese assault on Pearl Harbor were strategic surprises. And the destructive power of nuclear weapons, combined with technological advances in delivery systems, only adds to the fear. The horrifying possibility of a surprise nuclear attack and concerns about the ability to launch a nuclear response has led to an increasing emphasis on sophisticated surveillance and warning systems that can buy precious seconds. A psychic who could visualize such an attack the very moment it happened would constitute a cheaper and more effective warning system than any communication satellite.

International attention was drawn to Soviet military psi efforts in June of 1977 when *Los Angeles Times* reporter Robert C. Toth was detained and interrogated in Moscow by the KGB and accused of having received "state secrets" about parapsychology. It also called attention to the claims of another Soviet émigré, physicist August Stern, who defected in 1975 and claimed he had worked in a secret Siberian laboratory in search of "psi particles," an alleged physical basis for psychic energy.[63]

Although the CIA and the military deny they are funding psi research, a 1978 survey by the University of California–Davis psychologist Dr. Charles Tart showed that five out of fourteen active parapsychological research labs in the United States had been approached by information-gathering agents of the United States government.[64] Indeed, the Pentagon and the CIA had funded laboratory experiments since the early 1970's, and possibly long before that.

The focus of CIA and Defense Department interest seems to have been the experiments of physicists Dr. Harold E. Puthoff and Russell Targ at Stanford Research Institute (now SRI International) in Menlo Park, California.

Puthoff, a specialist in quantum physics, lasers, and optical devices, was formerly with the National Security Agency. He and Targ, whose specialties are lasers and microwave research, were conducting tests on the ability of select psychics to remote-view distant test sites. In these experiments (discussed in Chapter 3), a "sender" would be sent to a location and seemingly telepathically beam back an image of what he or she was seeing to the "receiver" in the lab, who would then sketch and describe what impressions were received. The scientists claimed extraordinary success in the experiments, saying that the psychic's drawings exhibited a remarkable degree of resemblance to photographs of the test sites.[65]

Given the obvious possible security and military applications of remote viewing, it is not surprising that the intelligence community would be interested in the SRI tests. A top-secret demonstration by two SRI star subjects, former police commissioner Pat Price and artist Ingo Swann (both of whom had previously done occasional psychic sleuthing), was arranged by the CIA and the National Security Council in 1973. Swann managed to describe correctly a target island in the South Indian Ocean. According to a military source claimed by reporter John Wilhelm, Price so accurately pictured a satellite interrogation station that eavesdropped on Soviet space vehicles and the code words involved that a security investigation was launched to make sure there had been no leak to Price or the SRI researchers.[66] The results, especially from a series of test runs called Project Scanate, were apparently impressive enough to elicit the funding for several SRI projects reportedly financed by the CIA, the DIA, and the Special Warfare Branch of the Naval Electronics Systems Command in the late 1970s. These researches are said to have required the psychics to remote-view military installations and secret locations inside the USSR, after being given only the geographical coordinates.[67]

Pat Price died of a heart attack in 1975, so his work at SRI was cut short. According to interviewed sources who asked for anonymity, while at SRI, Price became involved with the Patty Hearst kidnapping and produced information that proved of substantial help to the authorities in locating her. According to John Wilhelm, when Turkish terrorists kidnapped an Air Force officer in the early 1970s, Price and others at SRI were asked to try and remote-view his location. In this case, when intelligence operatives checked what the psychics "saw," it proved to be of no avail.[68]

Price was used by the CIA in other remote-viewing experiments in the 1970s, a fact seemingly confirmed in 1977 by then CIA Director Stansfield Turner. During a press conference, Turner told reporters that the Agency had found a man to whom the CIA scientists would show a picture of a place and he could then tell them about any activities going on there. He also acknowledged that his intelligence operatives had confirmed that the Soviets were spending time and money investigating psychic spying methods, including the study of persons who claimed to be able to read minds, tell the future, and "teleport" themselves to secret meetings. Turner told reporters that the CIA project was discontinued in 1975 when their psychic spook (apparently Price) died.[69]

The CIA-backed SRI programs were reportedly terminated in the late 1970s, but modest government support of SRI experiments, to the tune of several hundred thousand dollars a year, continued until recently. A big backer of these programs seems to have been President Jimmy Carter. As we saw earlier, Carter was reportedly impressed with Uri Geller and ordered a review of Soviet psi efforts. Carter was no stranger to anomalous science claims. Years before, when he was simply a Georgia citizen, he reported having seen an Unidentified Flying Object, and as President tried unsuccessfully to get NASA to take over the investigation of UFOs.[70]

In January 1980, when intelligence information about the condition of American hostages in Iran was minimal, it was decided to turn to SRI's psi program for possible help. According to our informants, a naval officer assigned to the National Security Council was sent to California to work with SRI remote-viewing attempts, mainly with psychic Keith Harary.

Asked about the health of the hostages, Harary focused in upon a man he said was suffering from a degenerative disease of the nervous system, involving a loss of muscle coordination. One of the hostages, Richard Queen, suffered from multiple sclerosis. Harary then accurately predicted that this man, apparently Queen, would be released sometime in July 1980.[71] The naval officer relayed the information to National Security Council Adviser Zbigniew Brzezinski and his associate David Aron. According to one informed source, the White House sent commendations back to SRI for the success, but this is a claim we were unable to confirm. In any case, the National Security Council seems to have been impressed enough after Queen's release to authorize further government work with Harary and later with Ingo Swann. The psychics were reportedly used to give their impressions about the health and location of the hostages and where they were in the complex, but they were never consulted about the raid. Harary is said to regret this bitterly, for he afterward felt he might have been able to warn them about the problems they encountered with the helicopters.

Interest in psi research did not end with the Carter administration. During the astrological administration of Ronald Reagan, the CIA took renewed interest in parapsychology. According to former Reagan White House aide and consciousness researcher Barbara Honegger, the CIA officer monitoring parapsychological research for the first time indicated in his "periodic report to the National Security Council that there is growing reason to take the field more seriously." This was a response to test results in Canada and the United States on the distant mental effects of certain frequencies of electromagnetic radiation. It was also during this period, Honegger says, that prominent psi researchers were funded by the Pentagon in an effort to evaluate the MX missile "shell-game mode." This was a $40 billion scheme by which the missiles would be secretly shifted between a series of silos, so that the Soviets would never know which targets to hit. Psychics were tested to see whether they could guess the positions of various targets. The program was scrapped, but Honegger said she did not know whether the results of the tests had any bearing on the decision.[72]

Some of this new interest was reflected in a 1981 staff report of the U.S. House of Representatives' Committee on Science and Technology. In this "Survey of Science and Technology Issues Present and Future," a remarkably upbeat perspective was presented in its discussion "Research on the Physics of Consciousness (Parapsychology)." The report stated that "experiments on mind-mind interconnectiveness have yielded some encouraging results." And relevant to psi sleuthing, it asserted: "In the area of investigative work, 'emotional imprints' have been used by skilled sensitives to race past events in archaeological and police investigations."[73] This was followed in 1983 by an unpublished report by the Science Police Research Division of the Congressional Research Service which called for more funding for psi research and argued that "whether or not psi is a real or usable phenomenon, the recognition that psi may be able to enhance the human condition could have far-reaching implications for science and the society it serves."[74]

In January 1982, Pentagon psychics were employed to help locate U.S. General James Dozier, who had been kidnapped by Italy's Red Brigade. Most of the psychic leads proved useless, but according to investigative reporter Steven Emerson in his book *Secret War-*

riors, the task force stumbled onto a psychic, a food-service supervisor named Gary, who at first produced what seemed to be incredibly accurate information. When tested with two hundred yes-no questions about Dozier's kidnapping, his answers were checked against what might be known through the media and what was only known to the special operations office. Gary astounded them by accurately describing closely held facts such as the dimensions of the trunk in which the terrorists had smuggled Dozier from his apartment and that Mrs. Dozier's earrings had been placed on the bathroom floor.

Gary was flown to Italy and produced some more remarkable information in preliminary tests there, but his "visions" about Dozier were mostly too vague, and those that could be checked out failed to prove useful. Other psychics were tried, and Emerson tells us the Pentagon even sent half a dozen to Italy, to no avail. Finally, relying on directions from an unnamed psychic who previously had worked with police departments in northern California, a five hundred-man battalion was dispatched and launched an assault on a house that matched the psychic's description. All they found was a very surprised Italian family.[75]

Though the efforts to remote-view General Dozier proved unsuccessful, proponents of the psychics were undeterred. In the early 1980s, the Army Intelligence and Security Command (IN-SCOM), under the direction of General Albert Stubblebine, brought in a battery of psychics to remote-view the interior of the house of Panamanian President Manuel Noriega. Working from photographs, the psychics described the contents of the house and the location of guard dogs and security cameras. The result was a top-secret two-page report, the details of which were never confirmed.[76]

Though Stubblebine had a reputation for brilliance and was mainly concerned with finding ways of using advanced concepts in experimental psychology to improve intelligence, he was soon considered a joke by some in military intelligence and pejoratively labeled a "spoonbender" because of his advocacy of psi. His interests were in the applied uses of alternative psychology, and in this he was not alone. The Army signed contracts with the Monroe Institute in Faber, Virginia, to develop the use of stereo sound waves to alter consciousness and relieve stress. Contracts with other firms were geared to intensify concentration and improve the accuracy of marksmen.[77]

If columnist Jack Anderson is to be believed, government

funding for such experiments has been much more intensive than the public has been led to believe. In one 1984 column Anderson stated flatly that "remote viewing has become almost universally accepted in the Intelligence community." Anderson described a remote viewing based on giving the psychic only map coordinates, apparently a reference to the Project Scanate series. In this case, the site was the Soviet's secret nuclear testing area at Semipalatinsk, Kazakhstan, and the psychic apparently gave a good description—except that he included a gantry and crane that the CIA had not seen there earlier. When a new set of spy satellite photos arrived, sure enough, the gantry and crane were indeed at the end of the field as the psychic had indicated. This greatly impressed the CIA—since no one there had earlier known of the presence of the equipment, the information could not have been leaked to the psychic. [78]

In this same column, Anderson said he had also learned that a Soviet TU-95 "Backfire" bomber had crashed in Africa, and the CIA wanted to take photos of the wreckage and purloin secret gear from it before it was found by the Soviets. He disclosed that an SRI remote-viewing project code-named "Project Grill Flame" succeeded in giving the CIA the plane's location within a few miles.

The next day, Anderson's column further revealed that Project Grill Flame's psychics had managed to breach the security of secret military installations by describing the contents of locked filing cabinets. Anderson also noted that SRI remote viewing had apparently discovered the rings around Jupiter years before astronomers saw them in satellite photographs. [79]

In a column the following month, Anderson reported that Project Grill Flame, which apparently had been initiated in 1978 and closed down in 1982, was actually continued through a bit of bookkeeping legerdemain; its budget was transferred from the DIA to the general Pentagon budget. [80]

Other reporters have echoed Anderson's assertions. During the 1984 Lebanon crisis, United States anti-terrorist experts were allegedly called upon to help locate hideouts and training sites of Hezbollah terrorists. In particular, the experts were interested in surgically striking at suspected terrorist leader Fadlallah without inflicting widespread damage. To effect this end, INSCOM psychics were called upon once more.

Given only a general description of Fadlallah's house in southern Beirut, the psychics were said to have impressed officials with detailed layouts, descriptions of door locks and wall decorations, and the number of occupants in the house. Some of the information was verified, but most of it was never confirmed.[81]

According to investigative reporter Howard Blum, a classified report prepared for the Defense Intelligence Agency describes how in the fall of 1985, in a lead-lined conference room of Washington's Old Executive Office Building, SRI scientists impressed Pentagon observers by having a psychic remote-view the country dascha of Mikhail Gorbachev. The viewer further shook up those assembled by specifying the longitude and latitude positions of submarines whose photos he was shown. Blum claims that this demonstration was so successful that the DIA and Naval Intelligence co-sponsored a program called Project Aquarius which was initiated less than six months later. This project lasted at least fourteen months during which psychics scanned the globe for Soviet submarines.[82]

According to one recent bizarre report, the CIA apparently has no age limit on the psychics it hires. In his February 15, 1989, column Jack Anderson reported that a nine-year-old psychic spy was named in a wrongful termination suit filed in federal court by former U.S. Customs Service agent Mark Woods. In 1982, Woods was fired after refusing to reveal to his customs boss the source of a tip he had gotten that the international terrorist "Carlos" (also called "The Jackal") planned to kill President Reagan. According to Anderson, until his firing Woods had otherwise been an exemplary customs agent and had earned many awards. For years, Woods maintained his silence, but in court papers divulged that his source was a nine-year-old Virginia Beach, Virginia, girl he claimed worked as a psychic for the CIA. In suing to get his job back, Woods asserted that he had refused his boss's order because of a warning from a CIA representative, Ursula Jahoda, against divulging the Agency's connection with the girl.

According to the court papers, the girl was one of the CIA psychics who had been consulted in the search for General James Dozier, who had been kidnapped by the Italian Red Brigade. She had also given the Agency advance information on the rise of Yuri Andropov in the Soviet Union, and had warned them about an impending assassination attempt on President Reagan on the White House lawn, which was forestalled when Reagan lighted the national Christmas tree from inside the White House.

Woods, who had gotten to know the family of the girl while he was a customs agent, said he was told by the nine-year-old that "Carlos" was in San Francisco and was planning to kill Reagan. Woods passed on the information to his boss, including the address where the terrorist could be found. The information was passed on to the Secret Service.

The basis of Wood's suit was that CIA representative Jahoda had assured him that in exchange for his silence, the Agency would make sure he kept his job, but that they reneged on the agreement. Anderson was unable to reach Jahoda, but the girl's mother told him that her daughter had nothing to do with the CIA.[83]

While the United States and the Soviet Union and its past allies were pursuing the applications of psi to intelligence, some similar activities may have taken place in the Far East.

China has a great historical tradition of supernaturalistic lore. Much of this remains intertwined with its folk medical traditions, the best known of these in the West today being acupuncture. China has a rich heritage of superstition among its 800 million peasants, but the elites have also had their share of occult activity. Until China's dynastic system was overthrown in 1911, many emperors had consulted stargazers and magicians. China's contemporary involvement with psi research must be understood in that context.

The great mystical guide to divination, the *I Ching*, or *Book of Changes*, has had an enormous influence on the thinking of the Chinese ever since its first publication perhaps as early as 1200 B.C. In his *History of the Chinese Secret Service*, Richard Deacon asserts that "when the ancient Chinese had an intelligence problem—that is to say, one they could not solve by normal processes—they would turn to the *Book of Changes*."[84]

According to Deacon, in the mid-1960s Taiwanese members of Chiang Kai-shek's Secret Service consulted the *I Ching* to ascertain whether or not Mao Tse-tung would succeed at the time of China's border clash with India. The hexagrams they produced by following the book's ancient ritual were interpreted to mean that Mao would win, but also indicated he would use caution.[85] A Chinese intelligence officer told Deacon that he had frequently, and usefully, consulted the *I Ching*. As he put it, "Espionage deals in facts, but you must remember that very often the facts do not fit into a pattern; they cannot be easily explained; they may even contradict one another." It was on such occasions of uncertainty that he and other intelligence officers would turn to the book for divination, not just for guidance but to immerse their minds in what they believe is its inherent wisdom. An answer or pattern would be found through using the book, "perhaps not the one we sought, or wanted to hear, but we should act on what it told us," he said. [86] Deacon's informant used as an example a case where he was confronted by evidence that there was a spy in their midst. The *I Ching* was interpreted by him to indicate that he incorrectly perceived the suspect, who was really an ally, and that they should give him trust and cooperation. As it turned out, the officer told Deacon, the suspect "turned out not to be a spy, but a double agent who had been posing as an enemy agent." [87]

Though there had been some interest in parapsychology in the first decades of this century, much of it following the lead of the West's psychical researchers, the Communist revolution in China brought with it a suppression of nonmaterialistic ideas like psi, which were considered symbols of idealism and a declining capitalism. Such un-Marxist ideas were particularly ruthlessly persecuted during the Cultural Revolution of the 1970s.

With the reforms of Deng Xiaoping following the overthrow of the People's Republic of China (PRC) Cultural Revolution, a side-effect was the revival of Chinese interest in the supernatural and paranormal. [88] This included some horrendous exploitation of the superstitious, especially in rural areas. Witch doctors and wizards began extorting money from the gullible in return for frequently catastrophic advice. According to a press report reaching the West about one such horrible episode, a Shandong Province fortune-teller posed as a mountain goddess and predicted bad luck would follow a wedding. Upon hearing her prophecy, the parents called off the marriage ceremony. Everyone was so distraught that the bride killed herself, and the groom went mad. [89]

Beginning with the discovery of twelve-year-old Tang Yu in Sichuan Province in late 1978, articles began to appear about young school-age children with what came to be called their bodies' "extraordinary human functions," or EHF. These children seemed to be able to demonstrate a wide variety of clairvoyant traits, including the ability to "read with the ears": the child would hold a folded piece of paper on which something had been secretly written up to his or her ear and tell what was written on it. Others reportedly could "read" such notes by placing them on their elbows or even by sitting on them. Some of these children achieved much publicity and celebrity. For example, Beijing's Wang sisters, Qian and Bin, got much attention when they demonstrated that they could apparently read notes inside boxes just by touching the boxes.

Scientists throughout China took great interest in these reports, and publications about experiments with the children started to appear, especially in Shanghai's *Nature Journal*. These reports often seemed quite fantastic but claimed careful, controlled and technologically sophisticated measurements of the "radiations" that seemed involved. Most of this work soon became intertwined with work in Chinese traditional medicine, especially the ancient Chinese breathing and healing regimen of *qigong*. As of 1989, *qigong*, which the Chinese classify as a "science of human physics," was an elective course in thirty-seven universities in the PRC.[90] Chinese researchers claimed they had found that adult *qigong* masters could produce these strange radiations even under laboratory conditions, and many thought they seemed capable of paranormal abilities. According to tradition, *qi* is a fundamental life force, sometimes also translated as "breath." Literally dozens of scientists, many of them physicists associated with Beijing University and the Chinese Academy of Sciences, began to try to find the relationship between *qi* and EHF.

In 1982 one of the authors (M.T.) went with a group of parapsychologists and physicians to the People's Republic of China for the U.S. Department of Defense's Advanced Research Projects Agency to look into surprising new reports of psi phenomena there. Mainly through the auspices of *Nature Journal*,[91] the group met with some of the top EHF researchers in Beijing, Xi'an, and Shanghai. After being told of extraordinary experiments, reportedly done with the utmost precautions against trickery, children were brought for demonstrations of their abilities, but their "amazing" powers were found to be utterly unconvincing, and, in one instance, a likely case of cheating.

The visiting group was told by Chinese officials of psi applications of all sorts. Most common were claims of medical healing and diagnosis, with frequent reports of children with seeming "x-ray vision" that purportedly allowed them to look into patients bodies and "see" what ailed their internal organs. Reports were given that described how psychics found natural resources and archaeological treasures. According to Ding Wei Xin, editor of the Chinese magazine *Paranormal Functions Probe*, paranormal powers have also been used behind the "Bamboo Curtain" in searching for criminals.[92] Thus, the PRC seems to have those who claim the blue sense.

Perhaps the most significant event concerning this revived interest in the paranormal, however, was the endorsement of these experimental directions by Dr. Qian Xueseng, one of the most politically powerful scientists in the PRC, whom many Chinese call their "Father of the Missile" for his outstanding space-science accomplishments. Through his sponsorship, research into *qigong* and EHF has become part of the Chinese program for training future astronauts.

Interestingly, both United States and Soviet astronauts had already been connected with psi studies. American astronaut Edgar Mitchell had conducted a much-publicized but unsuccessful telepathy test when he was in outer space, trying to transmit ESP symbols to the terrestrial psychic Olof Jonsson.[83] And Soviet defector Abraham Shifrin, a former adviser to the Soviet War Ministry, told reporters Douglas Starr and Patrick Quaid that he learned in 1963 from Solomon Gellerstein, director of a secret psi research lab in Moscow, that Gellerstein had personally trained three cosmonauts in telepathy. Starr and Quaid checked and found that his story was corroborated by a reference in a 1967 issue of *Soviet Maritime News* that "a psi training system had been incorporated in the cosmonaut's program."[94]

In 1984, Chen Hsin, vice-director of the Institute of Aerospace Medico-Engineering, and Mei Lei, vice-director of Space-Life-Science Commission, came to England's University of Cambridge to attend a joint meeting of the Parapsychological Association and the Society for Psychical Research. Reporting on the results of some of the psi experiments conducted under their auspices, they claimed that EHF had now been conclusively validated by their tightly controlled experiments. A description of their security precautions included double-blind conditions, continuous videotaping, special observers, et cetera.[95] To most Western psi researchers there, it all sounded too good to be true. Chen and Mei promised to send copies of the full research reports, which they had only summarized in their presentation, to the SRI scientists present, so the procedural details could be carefully and critically examined. For whatever reason, the reports were never sent.

Starting at about this time, a great controversy began in the PRC over the government's position on psi research when Yu Guangyuan, the vice-chairman of the Chinese Academy of Science, began public attacks on EHF claims. According to physicist Zha Leping, this produced confrontations between Qian Xueseng's pro-EHF faction and that of Yu Guangyuan,[96] which resulted in a 1982 party ruling that effectively silenced further communication regarding EHF research with the outside world while still allowing it quietly to continue. Zha tells us that between 1983 and 1986, work on EHF and *qigong* became less active and now was largely kept secret from the West. Sharp critical attacks on EHF also stopped, however.

According to Zha Leping, starting in 1983 the work on EHF began moving into the military sector, mainly at Beijing's "507 Institute" connected with the defense-related Spaceflight Department. Thus this work became isolated from civilian workers, since they had less access to the best psychic subjects, who gravitated to the well-funded military lab. A top example is psychic Zhang Baosheng, whom some have called "China's Uri Geller." Zhang moved to work exclusively at the 507 Institute in 1984. He has been periodically trotted out to demonstrate his abilities for political leaders. Qian Xueseng personally witnessed a demonstration he says he found convincing in which Zhang managed to remove twenty-three of a hundred tablets from an unopened jar. This might at first seem a likely conjuror's trick, but in 1987 a film showing his psychokinetic abilities was publicly awarded a scientific research prize by the Spaceflight Department. According to those who have seen the film, which was taken with a high-speed video camera, it shows a specially marked pill in a specially made and sealed glass container actually go through the container in various stages of penetration.[97] If this film has been correctly described—and this remains a big *if*—it would have to be extraordinary of Zhang to perform such a feat even if it was a trick.

In 1988, six members of the Committee for the Scientific Investigation of Claims of the Paranormal visited the PRC with the intention of investigating the EHF and gigong claims there. They were reportedly invited there by a Beijing newspaper, *Science and Technology Daily*. While there, they managed to examine stringently, the abilities of a number of psychics and *qigong* masters who offered themselves as test subjects. These tests all produced negative results.[98] As Zha Leping has correctly observed; however, this committee examined only self-proclaimed psychics and researchers who may have been quite unrepresentative of the best work Chinese officials who are proponents of psi have cited.[99] According to Zha, they actually had no contact with the major psi research centers, institutes, and universities conducting such work. They did not meet the Chinese scientists who have published psi-research reports in major science journals, or with any major psi subjects. Zha points out that this was "probably because they were invited by a group of journalists" rather than by the Chinese Academy of Science or the government's experimental scientists at the forefront of EHF and *qigong* research.

One of the positive results of the Committee's visit to the PRC was a heightened awareness of the need for tight controls before taking non-experimental demonstration very seriously. After the Committee's team departed, Wu Xiaoping went to see a demonstration being given by Zhang Baosheng. Wu brought a Beijing magician, Ti Yueli, with him to help control against possible trickery by Zhang. The results of this produced negative results by Zhang and some evidence that he may have tampered with seals on the bottles that were used.[100] Taken alone, this episode argues strongly against Zhang's having genuine psi. However, as with so much of the Chinese work, how can we properly account for the scientific reports, including the film of Zhang mentioned earlier, that claim a scrupulous adherence to extraordinary security measures?

If these reports are in error, those who wrote them, with what must then be manifestly misleading descriptions of what was actually done, must be guilty of fraud, too. That certainly could be the case, but is such an explanation really probable? A strong argument can be made that it is. Writing in the journal *Science, Technology & Human Values* about the problem of scientific corruption in China, Richard P. Suttmeier asserts that when comparing scientific practices in China with those sociologists say exist in the West, the actual norms of science in China seem quite different."[101] Suttmeier examines known cases of scientific deviance in China and finds that Chinese science practices, far more than those in Western science, are heavily influenced by norms from other social institutions including those from the pre-Communist academic structure, the political party, and those set by the particular work units involved. In other words, the standards for what is proper scientific behavior and what is judged as "corruption" or deviance in science, are quite different in the PRC from the standards observed in Western science. If Suttmeier's picture of Chinese science is accurate, and we find it convincing, this may go a long way toward explaining what we in the West view as not mere socially necessary embellishments but as widespread scientific corruption in Chinese reports of their psi experiments.

Whatever the scientific realities, it is clear that today EHF, *qigong*, and the psychics involved enjoy political support from some of the most influential members of the PRC's central committee. The main support seems to come from some of the older politicians, several of whom are said to have used the healing abilities of the gigong masters. Perhaps ironically, those who support it reportedly argue, in part, that the PRC should invest in this area because both the KGB and CIA are doing so.

While China has only recently come in contact with Western parapsychology, Japan has a much longer history of involvement.[102] Following an early period of mere description of alleged spontaneous cases from about 1820 to 1909, Japanese experimental research into psi began around 1910 with the work of Tomokichi Fukerai, a professor at the University of Tokyo, and Western-style psychical research was conducted between 1914 and 1936, after which it was cut short by the Japanese-Chinese conflict and later by World War II. Starting up again in 1950, it was highly influenced by the work of J. B. Rhine and those at Duke University's Institute of Parapsychology. The Japanese Society for Parapsychology was founded in 1963 and it now has about one hundred full and associated members. The leading figure in Japan's psi research is Soji Otani, a professor at the National Defense Academy, who visited the Duke laboratory for a year in 1963–1964.[103]

Like the Chinese, Japanese parapsychologists have shown a special interest in *qi* (which in Japan is called *ki*). In 1987, Otani gave his presidential address to the Japanese Society for Parapsychology on the topic "The Problem of Qi in Parapsychology." Another prominent Japanese psi researcher who also spent time at the Duke lab, and who like many Chinese researchers has been particularly interested in scientifically measuring *qi* radiation, is Hiroshi Motoyama. In addition to his science training, Motoyama is a Shinto priest, and his Institute for Religious Psychology and International Association for Religion and Parapsychology has offices in both Tokyo and Encinitas, California.[104]

In recent years, Japan has been undergoing an occult boom.[105] Despite a veneer of technological sophistication, many Japanese continue to accommodate traditional supernatural beliefs. Thus, in 1988, two Tokyo construction firms caused quite a stir among feminists when they asked women reporters not to attend a ceremony marking completion of a highway tunnel through a mountain. It seemed that their workers feared the local goddess might become jealous and would jinx the final part of the project.[106] And in 1987, newspapers reported that leading members of Japan's ruling party were lined up to meet with a soothsayer, Yoshiaki Murakami. Yoshiaki had correctly predicted the surprise choice of Prime Minister Yashuhiro Nakasone in 1982. Upon letting it be known that he heard the voice of God tell him the name of the next Prime Minister while he rode on the bullet train, his lair was visited by a steady stream of black limousines as politicians flocked to his Odawara home, fifty miles from Tokyo.[107]

Though there is no evidence of Japan's interest in psi as a tool for espionage, the government apparently takes it and its potential application seriously. In 1987, Soji Otani was appointed to a special body of the Ministry of Posts and Telecommunication called the Committee of Future Media for Communication. This panel consists of eight members with scientific specialties ranging from gravitational waves to brain physiology, as well as parapsychology. It is hard to imagine such a government appointment in the United States.

Since the advent of *glasnost* and improved Soviet-U.S. relations, there seems greatly lessened concern about the so-called psychic arms race. Few now demand a Manhattan Project for the paranormal, and some are beginning to echo nuclear physicist and parapsychologist Elizabeth Rauscher when she told a reporter in 1985: "Who wants to get into a mind race when we've already got this whole nuclear mess?"[108]

In the political spirit of recent years—except for the work being done in China—there has been increasing communication between East and West psi researchers. After leaving SRI in 1982, Russell Targ complained that the work there had been too preoccupied with military applications. In 1984, he and Keith Harary began a series of joint experiments with Soviet scientists into remote viewing, following an invitation from the Soviet Academy of Sciences. The Soviets apparently took psi research seriously, on what Harary described as "the highest levels," and he and Targ were told that their work had also been duplicated by researchers at the Armenian Academy of Science. The joint work included one transatlantic experiment. Harary went to a random site in San Francisco and was reportedly correctly "seen" by psychic healer Djuna Davitashvili—who had treated Brezhnev during his last years—as she sat in the living room of her Moscow apartment. Although Harary wrote in *U.S. News and World Report* that the Soviets sill appeared to be pursuing their interest in behavior manipulation at a distance,[109] Targ told *New Scientist* that there had been no suggestion of military applications in his dealing with the Soviets.[110]

Whatever one's view of the realities involved, things today have clearly cooled down. About ten years ago Representative Charles Rose, former chairman of the House Subcommittee on Intelligence Evaluation and Oversight and one who has seen many top-classified psi documents, was quoted as saying that the SRI tests could not have been faked. As he then put it, remote viewing "would be a hell of a cheap radar system, and if the Russians have it and we don't, we are in serious trouble." He openly wondered about the motives of skeptics in the Pentagon and CIA who sought to hinder psi research, and even warned, "We may have to investigate them."[111] Nowadays, his aide told a reporter, Rose rarely comments on psi research because he found that most voters seem to view it as a supernatural adventure unworthy of tax dollars.[112]

Concerned about the number of rumors and reports about the alleged military and intelligence uses of psi, the Army Research Institute contracted with the National Academy of Sciences in 1986 to have the National Research Council (NRC) assess the situation.[113] As we discussed in detail in Chapter 3, the eventual report, *Enhancing Human Performance*, condemned most psi research as being methodologically sloppy and/or nonrepeatable and was strongly responded to by the Parapsychological Association.[114] Incredibly, the NRC committee tells us they examined "only published reports that have undergone peer review" for their data base.[115] In other words, the report tells us nothing about the actual status of such reportedly classified studies as Project Scanate and Project Grill Flame, which we have been repeatedly told were the bases for studies like Stansfield Turner's and for Representative Rose's statements endorsing the SRI remote-viewing work. What may be the best-controlled and most convincing psi research, then, was apparently ignored by the NRC appraisers.[116] As with the Chinese work, we simply have no formal public assessment available to us of the intelligence-related psi studies that those who claim to have seen them report are utterly convincing.

Despite government denials, the evidence seems clear that there has been great interest in and at least modest support for psi research that might provide advantageous for intelligence. Clearly, in light of other governments' known efforts in parapsychology, those concerned with national security have needed both to monitor and investigate the potential of such alleged psychic technologies. Even philosopher Paul Kurtz, chairman of the debunking Committee for the Scientific Investigation of Claims of the Paranormal, told *New York Times* science reporter William J. Broad that "skeptics reluctantly endorse such research if only so the military can keep ahead of the remote possibility of enemy breakthroughs."[117] The irony is that by taking such an essentially defensive posture—mainly designed to avoid missing a long shot (a Type II error)—news of any government work quickly becomes distorted into claims of "proof" that government must believe psi is real. Sources, including stories from the tabloids, soon become part of the ever-widening rumor mill. And, as Starr and McQuaid found as they tried to track down the truth about secret government psi efforts: "The same rumors are cycled and recycled until by simple longevity, they seem to become fact."[118]

When one adds to all this the likelihood of at least some active disinformation being spread, the truth remains enveloped in a fog. However, one prediction seems reasonable: If glasnost and *perestroika* continue, it seems unlikely that the United States will want to encourage the Soviet Union to waste economic efforts on its psi research. All indications at present are that our government wishes democratization and economic success for the Russians. If so, we may see a halt to our own disinformation efforts.

As C. B. Scott Jones, a special assistant to Senator Clairborne Pell with good intelligence connections, has pointed out, in the face of recent improved Soviet-U.S. relations this must be a particularly confusing time for the paranoids who have been obsessed with the dangers of psychic weaponry. For those who believe the Soviets have psychotronic weaponry, current strategic arms-reductions talks could fatally disarm the West.[119] But the solid evidence we have suggests no such hyper-shrewd strategy by the one-time "Evil Empire." As Jones puts it, "It would take a conspiracy beyond the size I can imagine to explain how every potential fruit of psychical research has been hidden to keep the secret of the psychic-warfare arms race."[120] We agree.

ELEVEN

The Blue Sense and the Thin Blue Line

One-fourth of the 93 million households in the United States were touched by crime in 1988, according to a 1989 Bureau of Justice Statistics Bulletin. Other Justice Department statistics predict that at current crime rates, almost everyone will have to be a victim of some kind of crime in his or her lifetime.[1] Furthermore, in spite of technological strides in forensic investigative techniques, electronic surveillance, et cetera, the percentage of crimes solved by arrest has remained appreciably unchanged since the 1970s, and has even *decreased* in certain heavily urbanized areas. These facts, coupled with media saturation of stories dealing with drugs, child molestation, rape, and murder, have fueled a growing public anxiety about the effectiveness of local and federal police agencies to serve and protect.

Sociological and anthropological evidence seems to back up the generalization that stressful social situations are favorable to the emergence and acceptance of superstitious beliefs. Rosenthal and

Siegel suggest that "magic arises as a symbolic means of handling important environmental influences and for dealing with the anxiety, frustration, or threat which may result when people are confronted with important environmental forces which they cannot master."[2]

In *Journal of the Plague Year*, Daniel Defoe described how people ran to "fortune tellers, cunning men, and astrologers, to know their fortune . . . and this folly presently made the town swarm with a wicked generation of Pretenders to Magic."

It has been widely theorized by social researchers that where direct action and empirical techniques are available to deal successfully with a problem, they will be preferred to magical means. But where they are not, magical means will be used as a substitute. During drought conditions in the midwestern United States in 1988, several farmers resorted to hiring Indian rain dancers, something they probably would not have considered if other scientific options, like cloud-seeding, had been available. In other words, *any* action is better than none.

Corroboration of this theory was made by Vogt and Hyman in their comprehensive survey of the practice of water witching in the United States. Finding that there were some 25,000 people in the country practicing this ancient form of divination today, they postulated that the concentration of water witchers would be greatest in those communities in which the chances of locating water were the most uncertain. Their survey found that indeed this was true, in spite of the fact that positive results of water witchers were no better than chance.[3]

Belief in the use of diviners persists in the absence of quantifiable, objective success because it fulfills a psychological and sociological function and introduces a measure of predictability into an uncertain situation. Vogt concludes: "The *certain* answers provided by the dowser relieve the farmer's anxiety about groundwater resources and inspire confidence to go ahead with the hard work of developing farms."[4]

Stressful situations in which outcomes are uncertain lead to anxiety, and the less is known about the probable outcome, the more intense the anxiety. A person seeking to alleviate this anxiety will seek more information and some means of control. It is known that people in occupations that involve a great deal of physical or professional risk are notoriously superstitious. Sailors, athletes, farmers, gamblers, soldiers, miners, and actors are some such professions in which superstitious behavior is rampant. Football coaches will wear the same necktie while on a winning streak, sailors whistle for a wind; astrology has traditionally been popular among actors and actresses, including our former First Lady Nancy Reagan. Such magical belief, says Paul Blumberg, "institutionalizes optimism, makes predictable the unpredictable, and attempts to bring under control those things that knowledge and science have yet to control."[5]

We might add policemen to the list. The authors have encountered numerous psychics who list policemen among their regular private clients. The primary question most of them seem to want answered is about their personal survival on the job. This might explain why at least some policemen are so easily converted from skepticism to belief. Their anxiety about their personal safety and the frustration arising out of the uncertainty of the outcome of many of their cases—from the lack of clues or suspects and the possibility that they may have arrested the wrong man to the uncertainty of the judicial process—all that can lead to a propensity to believe. Thus even when a suspect has been found not guilty in a court of law, a psychic's testimony about the defendant may ease the anxiety of the arresting officer by corroborating the officer's suspicions of guilt.

By far the majority of investigations in which psychics are consulted are homicide and missing-person cases. It is these cases that produce the most grief and anxiety, and therefore the greatest psychological need for resolution. Unorthodox approaches that would not be considered under normal circumstances or in cases less urgent—theft, for example—are willingly employed when conventional methods have failed, to ensure that everything possible is done to assuage the family's guilt and fears.

Then, too, certain highly publicized cases—serial killings and missing children, for example—also strike emotional chords on the part of the public and can bring added pressure for a solution on the police. In such random killings, in which conventional motives are absent to tie the killer to the victim, the job of the police is particularly difficult. It should not be surprising, then, that departments stymied by a lack of clues and faced with high emotions in a community would be more willing to accept aid offered by a psychic than under other circumstances. It is also not surprising, considering the media attention such killings receive, that publicity-seeking psychics would be more than willing to offer it. "Serial homicide cases elicit calls from hundreds of psychics," says LAPD's Dr. Martin Reiser, "none of it correlating with anything."[6]

During the summer of 1980, Atlanta was held in the grip of fear in the wake of a series of brutal murders of black children in that Georgia city. The people were clamoring for a solution as each new murder was uncovered, but police had no leads. After Dorothy Allison appeared on the _Donahue_ TV show on September 9, public pressure was brought to bear on police officials to bring her to Atlanta.

When Allison arrived in October, she told a news conference, "I can guarantee he won't murder while I'm here. I will control him. I have seen who he is. I see where he is. I follow him." Baring her throat to the television cameras, she challenged the killer to "come and try to strangle me." She described the killer as a black male and vowed that she would stay in Atlanta until he was caught. When she nevertheless left several days later, several Atlanta public officials expressed annoyance at the media circus Allison had caused, and the police still had no suspects.

On November 11, Allison announced to the press that she had provided the police with detailed descriptions of two suspects in the killings and that she "strongly suspected a third." She said that the killers were working independently of one another and that a major break would come in the case on the following Wednesday. A break did not come until the following June, when Wayne Williams, a black man, was arrested and charged with the murders. Allison later claimed that she had given the name "Williams" to the police, a claim denied by Atlanta Police Chief George Napper.[7]

Allison was not the only psychic to be consulted on the case before it was over. Noreen Renier was brought a belt from one of the dead children by an agent of the FBI, and was paid three hundred dollars for a recorded psychometric reading. Whether the money had come out of FBI coffers or the agent's pocket is not clear, but FBI Agent Robert K. Ressler later recalled under oath that "to the best of [his] knowledge," he doubted that Renier had been "officially working for us on contract."

On November 20, UPI reported that another psychic, Pat Gagliardo of Norwich, Connecticut, had entered the case. Ms. Gagliardo apparently told police they would find clues to the killings in Lincoln Cemetery. Grasping at any straw held out to them, police went to the graveyard with a tracker and dogs and discovered some items they would not describe.[8]

The last psychic to get publicity from the Atlanta case was seeress Jeane Dixon, who announced in the February 16, 1981, issue of the *New York Post* that she was trying to "psych out the Atlanta killer."[9] And in his *Washington Post* syndicated column, William Raspberry revealed that the *Post's* astrologer, Svetlana, after casting the astrological charts of twelve of the Atlanta victims, concluded that the killer was probably a woman or a man dressed as a woman.[10]

According to some reports, as many as eight thousand communications were received by the Atlanta Police Department from psychics around the country who wanted to contribute their psychic impressions. In January 1981 Atlanta's then Deputy Chief of Police, M. G. Redding, who headed the Special Task Force investigating the murders, decided to contact William G. Roll, director of the Psychical Research Foundation in Chapel Hill, North Carolina. Though Redding was a strong skeptic, he wanted to leave no stone unturned, so he asked Roll to examine and analyze these psychic communications.

Initially, Roll was given a computer printout of about 1,300 volunteered statements that had come to the police from self-proclaimed psychics, but by July 1981 the quantity had grown to 2,394. Because Wayne B. Williams was arrested and charged on June 21, 1981, Roll's project was aborted, but not before he had performed an analysis of the data, concentrating on the points on which a majority of the psychics seemed to agree. At a 1983 convention of the Parapsychological Association, Roll reported numerous interesting correspondences between the aggregated descriptions and the facts brought out at Williams's trial, but acknowledged that these similarities might well have been due to factors other than psi.[11]

The Atlanta case is certainly not unique. Literally thousands of psychics came out of the woodwork in 1979 when the Yorkshire Ripper, Peter Sutcliffe, was conducting a reign of terror in Britain. Among those offering aid were British psychics Doris Stokes, who claimed in her book *Voices in My Ear* to have helped solve the crime, and Dutch *wunder* Gerard Croiset. Both psychics, despite later claims, failed miserably; none of their revelations came close to predicting the identity of the Ripper or the arrest of Sutcliffe in 1981.

Phil Jordan was called in by Michigan State Police in 1977 in response to intense community pressure for a solution of child killings in the Oakland area. After running out of leads, investigators contacted

SRI International and were given the names of five psychics from among whom they picked Jordan, primarily because of his law-enforcement background.

In what came to be labeled "Operation ESP," Jordan was driven to the abduction sites and given exhibits and photographs to psychometrize. Although coming to the overall conclusion that Jordan was sincere, a review of Jordan's impressions by a panel of five senior investigators concluded that the psychic's information was vague, contradictory, and basically useless. An interoffice memo dated September 27, 1977, stated: "The information obtained is not specific enough to aid in the ongoing investigation. Vague innuendos and baseless facts which are the result of some person's 'feelings' or ESP, if you will, simply cloud the facts and cause an investigator undue feelings of failure."[12]

The 1977 memo does not take into account the issue of dollars and man-hours that might be wasted following up empty psychic leads. A 1987 survey by British police reported that the child-murder of Sarah Jayne Harper had elicited six hundred unsolicited responses from psychics offering help. Calculating an average of six man-hours per psychic to assess the information, the survey concluded it would have taken "3600 detective man hours and 1200 control room man hours, a total of 4800 man hours would have been expended. Taking an average fixed cost of £7 per man hour this exercise would have cost £34000 from the inquiry budget." This calculation ignored the amount of time that would have been expended making inquiries based on the information, which was a "further unquantifiable figure."[13]

The greatest danger is when frustrated police forsake established investigation techniques for the advice of a psychic. A ludicrous example of this was a murder investigation in Cleveland, Ohio, in which one high-ranking police official sent a lieutenant and two detectives into the country on the testimony of a psychic to seek the identity of the killer from the first farmer they encountered plowing a field with a shepherd dog running behind him.[14]

This almost comic instance of wasted effort and resources by police is not unique. Television reporter Ward Lucas ran across a homicide case in Colorado in which a three-man police department ran randomly "from place to place, inspecting more than 120 different locations that were 'visualized' by an estimated 50 psychics who offered their help."[15] In spite of the squandering of taxpayers' dollars, that case was never solved.

In 1960, a psychic was consulted by the Missing Persons Unit of the New York Police Department in an attempt to find a missing judge. After being led to a location where the psychic said the judge's body would be, the credulous police used a bulldozer to dig a ditch "four feet deep for one square mile" in a vain search.[16]

A similar fiasco was averted in 1976 in Palm Springs, California, when Dorothy Allison was called into the investigation of the disappearance of a teenager by the boy's distraught parents. Allison told the parents their son was dead, and that his body was "under water" in an area that sounded vaguely like the Salton Sea, fifty miles south. After hearing about the case and contacting the family, an ESP believer in the Imperial County Sheriff's Department procured bulldozers to excavate the area, but was stopped by Palm Springs Police Captain Bill Valkenberg, who got word of the operation and immediately put a halt to the would-be costly operation. Valkenburg's skepticism proved well-founded when the missing boy was caught burglarizing a house two months later.

The 1979 California Department of Justice *Criminal Information Bulletin* emphasizes that while in some cases psychics may be of help to police, "the psychic does not replace sound investigative techniques but functions as an investigative tool."[17] Echoing that sentiment, Lieutenant Kurt Longfellow, who pioneered the Pomona Police Department's policy on psychics, says: "No matter what we do, it has to be turned into a conventional clue. We can wake up in the middle of the night with an idea about a case, but we have to convert that into something substantial we can take to court."[18]

Although some in law enforcement advocate bringing in a psychic at the beginning of an investigation, it is a general policy of police investigators who use psychics to do so only as a last resort, when all conventionally obtained leads are exhausted. Obviously, the first question for the investigator is how to pick the psychic he or she intends to use.

That process can be problematic—and hazardous—according to criminologist Robert Hicks. "The psychic does not fit any familiar category," he says. "Officers become adept at sizing up people and even pride themselves on their abilities to read characters. But the psychic appears intelligent, sincere, and therefore—dare I say it?—credible. Even more inviting, the psychic is neutral. The psychic has no personal involvement in the case and can make pronouncements indifferent to whomever is vindicated or suspected as a result. As for psychic ability, the officer cannot evaluate the skill. So what does the officer do? He executes the same process that he might follow in demonstrating to himself the veracity of any informant: he checks past successes."[19] Where does he go to do that? The primary source seems to be the media—both newspaper accounts and television and radio shows on which psychics appear to discuss their successes, often backed up by relatives of victims and police believers. Time and time again in our research, we were told by police detectives that they had enlisted the aid of a particular psychic after seeing him or her on television or reading a newswire story. The media, then, becomes the psychic's bona fides. "Press coverage equals veracity and legitimacy, including false claims of having helped the police," says Robert Hicks. "And if the psychic then appears on either the Phil Donahue or Oprah Winfrey programs, all doubt disappears. If it's on TV, it must be true."[20]

Aside from the practice of picking psychic media stars whose reputations have preceded them, advocates like Dr. Louise Ludwig suggest that police departments accumulate lists of "dependable" psychics. These lists can be made up from the recommendations of other detectives and police agencies; from parapsychological testing labs like SRI or psychic organizations, like the American Society for Psychical Research in New York, or from organizers of psychic fairs. Dr. Ludwig recommends police avoid any psychic who calls up and offers help. That person, more often than not, she says, is merely seeking publicity. She cites a recent case in which a then well-known, now disgraced, Los Angeles psychic called up a division of the LAPD with unsolicited "information" on the then still-at-large Hillside Strangler. To the dismay of police officials, a story appeared in the next day's edition of the Los Angeles *Times*, courtesy of the psychic, about how she had been "consulted" by the LAPD in the investigation.

Whitney Hibbard and Raymond Worring, authors of *Psychic Criminology: An Operations Manual for Using Psychics in Criminal Investigations*, also advocate police avoid psychics who are publicity-seekers, as well as cultists, frustrated housewives looking for a touch of the dramatic, any psychic who charges a fee other than expenses, and any psychic who claims more than 50 percent accuracy. They say that police should look for middle-class, upstanding citizens who are gainfully employed and are concerned about anonymity.[21]

Another factor in choosing a psychic, say those who have worked with them, is one of personal style. Lieutenant Kurt Longfellow recently recalled having worked successfully with psychic Armand Marcotte, but although Marcotte provided investigators with more accurate information than other psychics they had worked with, they had to abandon using him because of his "flamboyant" personality. "A lot of our investigators don't like to associate with people they consider 'abnormal.' We wouldn't be able to get our guys to sit down with someone like Armand. He was like a sideshow."[22]

The selection of the investigative team of detectives, argue proponents, is as important as the selection of the psychic. According to a 1979 article in *Police Chief* magazine, one of the most influential periodicals circulated among law enforcement officials, the team assigned to the psychic "should be composed of at least two or three officers who are fairly open-minded in regard to the existence of psychic ability. It must be remembered that while most psychics expect some skepticism concerning their abilities, hostile or overt skepticism may divert their attention and ultimately decrease their effectiveness."[23] That viewpoint is echoed by Noreen Renier, who states: "If the people I am working with are filled with doubts and animosity, I will pick up on these feelings and it will definitely hamper my work."[24]

After the investigative and psychic teams have been selected, the psychics should be tested, say the experts, by giving them sealed packets of solved cases, including victims' names, addresses, locations of the crimes, and photos of the victims. The psychics' impressions should then be judged for accuracy, to determine what relative weight their "impressions" should be given. Once the preliminaries are out of the way, the investigators and psychics get down to business. All working sessions should be taped to avoid false claims by either psychics or skeptics.

Under the guidance of Dr. Louise Ludwig of PSICOM, the Pomona Police Department in 1981 laid down official guidelines to be followed in the questioning of psychic witnesses:

1. Say *nothing* about your case to the sensitive except the following:
    a. Name the crime; homicide, robbery, rape.

b. Give the date of the crime.

c. Say how many victims were involved. Be specific: If one victim was killed and another wounded, say so. Give no other information about the victims or suspects.

d. State clearly the exact information you need for your case. Your requirements will vary from case to case and it is helpful to the sensitive if you are precise about what you need.

On some cases you may need to know who committed the crime, on others the motivation or the location of physical evidence or suspects. Whatever you need, be specific about it.

2. Give the psychometric objects to the sensitive.

3. After the sensitive has completed his report, give immediate feedback about all of the aspects of the case you know.[25]

The report goes on to lay out other instructions for the investigators, such as making sure the psychic does not interview suspects or witnesses; all contact with the case will be handled through a designated detective-bureau liaison; and that psychics are to be allowed to psychometrize objects independent of the investigator.

It should be understood by investigators that the pronouncements of a psychic are rarely literal, but are often symbolic and have to be interpreted. Thus, says Dr. Ludwig, "A 'row of white boxes' could mean a row of washing machines."[26]

Detective Sal Lubertazzi, Dorothy Allison's former sidekick and interpreter, knows just what Ludwig means. "Dorothy sees things, but she doesn't know geographical locations," he says. "Sometimes she'll say you have to go south (to find a body). If you do, and we don't find anything, I'll tell the police department to go north. It's kind of hard to explain."[27] Baltimore Detective Al Darden, who has also worked with Allison on many cases, agrees, saying, "I didn't know how to work with her then, but I do now. She might give you number 71, for example. In reality, it might be 17. You have to make facts out of what she says."[28]

Here, again, we have Martin Gardner's Catch-22, -23, and -24, and an obvious dilemma for law enforcement. If a row of white boxes might be washing machines, it could also be a graveyard, or a line of railroad boxcars. Is a police department supposed to commit significant personnel and time running from Laundromats to graveyards to railroad yards seeking clues?

No, says Dr. Martin Reiser. "If new evidence comes up, I'm willing to look at it, but I know of no case in which the use of a psychic has led to the solution of a crime. They are not qualified as investigators, they don't know the legal parameters, or how to handle evidence. 'Let's bring in another head,' that doesn't make sense to me."[29]

But there *are* cases in which that theory has seemed to make sense. Analyzing the Mary Cousett case, investigative reporter and skeptic Ward Lucas admitted that Greta had aided the investigation by her presence, in precipitating the police to re-search the area. "Their belief in the psychic's abilities caused them to reexamine their own case and repeat some vital, but seemingly unnecessary steps. In other words, whether they recognized it or not, Alexander became part of the 'brainstorming team.'"[30]

Similarly, Sergeant L. C. Stinett of the Maryland State Police credited the presence of John Catchings with helping find the body of Mary Cook Spencer in 1981 by allowing an additional search of the area that might not have been authorized without his coming. Stinett does not think Catchings led them to the body through psychic powers but through powers of observation, but it hardly matters. The result was the same.

We have encountered many such cases, in which areas were searched or re-searched when they might not have been, resulting in the discovery of a body or evidence, simply because of a psychic's insistence. It seems that in many instances when an investigation is at a dead end, a new perspective, provided by "another head," can cause detectives to look at the case from a different angle that had before eluded them.

Omar Khayyam Moore has theorized that some acts commonly accepted as magic, such as divination, can actually achieve tangible, efficacious results.[31] While studying the hunting techniques of Naskapi Indians, Moore found that when the supply of game became short, the Indians resorted to scapulimancy to determine the direction of their hunt. The shoulder of a caribou was held over hot coals and the cracks caused by the heat were then read like a map from which the direction of the hunt was gleaned.

Moore argued that the random cracks were functional in that if the Indians did *not* resort to divination, they would have a tendency to hunt where they had been successful before. This would lead them to areas already overhunted, thereby *decreasing* their likelihood of finding game. Also, the regularity of the hunters would have given the animals a chance of learning where they are most likely to be in danger. So by randomizing the direction of the hunt, the Indians were increasing their chances of success. It is noted that this method of hunting was only employed when there was no definite information to go on. When information was available, the Indians acted on it.

George Park, who also studied the Naskapi, theorized that their practice of divination was functional in that it had a *derandomizing* effect by establishing a consensus, thereby making action more predictable and regular.

These two points of view might not be as contradictory as they seem. While scapulimancy may randomize the direction of the hunt, the *interpretation* of the cracks in the bone provides a means of attaining a collective decision on the direction of the hunt.[32]

It is possible that both these processes can be at work when a psychic is introduced into a investigation. In the 1985 search for Mayme Knight, for example, John Catchings randomized police search efforts by leading them to an area they had not searched before simply because it was farther away than they thought an elderly, senile person could have wandered. In the Cousett case, Greta Alexander provided a consensus for the search party that eventually found the body.

One possibility that is seldom considered by critics or proponents of police use of psychics is that in certain instances, like the ones above, psychics might be functional in an investigation *regardless of whether they are psychic or not*.

As noted earlier, through the volume of their caseload, many psychics can be more expert than the police they work with. Even while expressing skepticism about the reality of psychic phenomena, many police investigators willingly admit that psychics are often discerning about human beings and their behavior.

Many psychics may be unconsciously adept at picking up physical cues from people. A psychic may unknowingly (or knowingly) elicit cooperation from a suspect by picking up subtle physical cues, such as facial expressions, verbal inflections, eye contact or lack of it, physical tenseness, et cetera. Although this may be erroneously taken for psychic power, it may nevertheless be an accurate barometer of truth and enable the sensitive to home in on a relevant line of questioning. A person particularly skilled at this might aid police by acting as a sort of lie detector even if the suspect has refused to submit to such a test.

Dorothy Allison was brought into the investigation of the murder of Russell Keller in Deadwood, South Dakota, by the dead man's family and Sheriff Charles Crotty. When Allison arrived, she met with Keller's family, and after speaking with Melvin Brown, the dead man's father-in-law, told Crotty, "Don't look any farther, he's involved." Brown, who was Keller's business partner and held a hundred-thousand-dollar insurance policy on his life, was already a suspect in the case. When Allison said Keller had known his killer, Brown broke down and cried. He was arrested, confessed, and later hanged himself in his jail cell, but information he gave before his death led to the conviction of three co-conspirators.

In an interview, Lawrence County Deputy Sheriff Dwane Russell admitted that an informant had already named Brown and the co-conspirators, but they needed corroboration. So police agreed to Allison's involvement to bring more psychological pressure on Brown in an effort to make him crack. "I'm not too sure that did it," Russell was quoted as saying, "but it put an added burden on him . . . My impression of [Allison] is that she'd probably make a fairly good detective if she was in police work. She had a good memory on her and a feeling for people."[33]

Another possible use of psychics that has been only partially explored by police is the exploitation of the "myth" of the psychic. According to Kenneth V. Lanning, of the FBI's Behavioral Science Section, the Bureau sometimes employs "proactive techniques" when conventional investigation has failed to produce results, high-risk techniques designed to manipulate a suspect through the use of the media. For instance, Bureau spokesman might put out information that a search party will be gathering to go over the scene of a crime and call for volunteers, on the hope that the suspect will show up. Such operations must be handled with the utmost care, says Lanning, as members of the media have a tendency to react angrily if they find out they have been hoodwinked, and although he knows of no instance in which a psychic has been used in this way, he says, "I see how it could be done."[34]

We uncovered at least one instance, in Beloit, Wisconsin, in

1981, in which it was done with media cooperation. One week after all leads on a double murder at a Radio Shack store came to naught, Beloit Police Chief John Mizerka announced that he was hiring a psychic to go over the murder scene. In case the killer left something behind besides vibrations, Mizerka announced that special photographic equipment would be brought in that he hoped would turn up valuable trace evidence.

When we subsequently inquired, Mizerka confessed that the police had used no special photographic equipment and had hired no psychic, although his department was contacted by several people identifying themselves as such and offering help after the story hit the papers. "The news story in our local media was a ruse manufactured to try to get the criminal to return to the crime scene," wrote Mizerka. "We conventionally photographed everyone who showed up at the Radio Shack. In the course of our investigation, we seriously considered the possibility that we had a typical serial killer on our hands. As such we had a psychological profile developed. Upon doing so we felt that we might be able to stimulate the killer to return to the crime scene. The story was so designed with the cooperation of our local media. Other media, like the Rockford [Illinois] paper, quickly joined in and seemed to manufacture what facts they could not pull from us or our local articles."[35]

The killer never did return to the scene of the crime, but Mizerka's psychological profile was validated when Raymond Lee Stewart was arrested by FBI agents on February 21 in Greensboro, North Carolina. In addition to the Beloit killings, Stewart was eventually convicted of four others in nearby Rockford, Illinois, during a one-week murder spree.

Another successful use of the myth of the psychic occurred in 1978 in Sturtevant, Wisconsin, in the case of the hit-and-run murder of Richard Rothering. Rothering had been standing alongside the highway, leaning against the door of his car, when a red pickup truck swerved into him, killing him instantly. Police had lots of conflicting descriptions of persons in the truck, but nobody got a license number. There things stood until 1983, when Sergeant Robert Mallwitz, who had become obsessed with Sturtevant's only unsolved homicide, called Greta Alexander. According to Mallwitz, Alexander gave him a description over the telephone of the truck and details of the accident she could not have possibly known. In addition, she came up with certain other "facts" that nobody else had; for instance, that there had been a woman in the truck; and a name, "Randy" or "Brandy."

Mallwitz went on the program *Crime Line Anonymous* on WISN, Channel 12, Milwaukee, and talked about Alexander's involvement in the case, and that, as a result, he was now looking for a female suspect. From that program, the case was picked up by television's *PM Magazine* and shortly thereafter Mallwitz received a phone call from a man saying that his girlfriend had seen the program and "panicked." Finding out that the frightened woman had fled to her aunt's home in Atlanta, Mallwitz attempted to contact her there, but was told by a sister that the woman had decided to "come clean" and had taken a bus back to Wisconsin.

When she was picked up at the bus station, the woman admitted to Mallwitz she had been in the car and named the driver, a man named Randy, who was picked up and charged with murder. Unfortunately, the woman changed her mind and refused to testify, resulting in the charges being dropped.

In an interview with the authors, Mallwitz confessed to having been "amazed" by Alexander's accuracy in the case. Whether or not her accuracy was due to psychic functioning is secondary to the point that the break in the case came through the scared woman's *belief* in psi and the fact that that belief was exploited through the use of the media.

As we earlier outlined in Chapter 8, there are other ways the "myth" of the psychic might be—and perhaps has been—advantageously utilized by police, such as producing a cover story for information otherwise obtained. Say the police have a criminal informant who is in danger from retaliation. Police might "launder" the information by putting out the story that a psychic was the source, thereby screening the true informant.

Such intentional disinformation might theoretically be employed on a national level. Say the United States has a spy satellite in place it does not wish the Soviets to know about. The intelligence it gathers might be attributed to the remote viewings of a psychic. Something of the sort might have been involved in Stansfield Turner's revelations about the CIA's use of psychic Pat Price in the 1970s.[36]

A psychic might be employed as an ally by a detective who has a theory about an unsolved case but who fails to convince his superiors of the plausibility of his conjectures. Such an investigator might take a psychic into his confidence in an attempt to sway the authorities into letting him continue his line of investigation. A possible corollary to this use of a psychic might be an instance in which a detective who has been ordered to remain silent about a case, but who wants to see certain facts come to the public's attention, "leaks" the information to the media through a psychic.

There are also psychological functions a psychic might serve in a criminal investigation—for the police as well as for families of victims. As noted earlier, families, suffering from guilt and anxiety need to be comforted by the feeling that they have made every effort to determine the fate of their loved ones and bring the cause of their grief to justice. Police, frustrated by their own fruitless efforts and a lack of clues, also need a sense of closure. By confirming details or a suspect, a psychic can provide corroboration for a detective that he has indeed solved the crime, even if no legal conviction is gained in the courts. At least the crime is solved in the cop's mind, if nowhere else. In talking with police, over and over again the authors encountered this dynamic to be at work. They knew the psychic was right, investigators would tell us, because he/she had the same suspect in mind as they did. "We know what happened, we know who did it, we just couldn't prove it."

Although rigid police attitudes toward the use of psychics seem to have loosened over the past few years, the official policies of a vast majority of departments remain negative. Unofficially, however, more police seem to be willing to experiment with psychics when all else has failed. As summed up by Sergeant Joseph Perkins, head of a Connecticut State Police task force looking into the disappearances of four Connecticut girls in 1979: "I have the philosophy that I don't care who solves a case as long as it gets solved. I've gone in closets with them and looked at candles. I put my head in a paper bag and looked for ghosts . . . Yet I still listen to them because someday one might come up with something."[37]

It is not difficult to see, however, that police detectives running around with their heads in paper bags might precipitate a crisis in public confidence. Departments must be careful to balance a policy of "no stone unturned" against the "giggle factor." It was for this reason that Pocatello, Idaho's, Chief of Detectives Lynn Harris instituted a strict "no psychics" policy after the still unsolved 1983 disappearance of 13-year-old Cindy Bringhurst. Brought in by the missing girl's parents, psychic Judy Belle announced that the girl was dead and worked up a composite sketch of the killer. "She told us, 'There's your man, go get him,'" Harris recalls bitterly. Later, in an interview with a local magazine, Belle made comments that reflected on the competence of the police because they could not find the man, yet, Harris said, "that picture was so generic, it could have fit ninety percent of the male population of Pocatello."[38]

Many proponents say the obvious solution to many of the problems police face in using psychics would be for the police to develop the blue sense of the cops themselves. The PSICOM program with the Pomona Police Department was geared toward that end—to heighten the intuitive powers of police investigators and loosen the grip of their rigid, analytical thinking. As Louise Ludwig says: "A lot of cops are good psychics themselves. It would be ideal if departments could help them develop that so they could have resident psychics and wouldn't have to call on outsiders."[39]

TWELVE

The Blue Sense and the Law: What Lies Ahead?

t is believed by some researchers in parapsychology that by the end of the century, not only will the reality of psi have been proved beyond a reasonable doubt, but that with the scientific refinement of training techniques developed through study and laboratory experiments, a cadre of top-notch, reliable psychics will emerge who will be employed in law enforcement, national security, and defense.[1]

The possibility was seen as long ago as 1928 by U.S. Supreme Court Chief Justice Louis D. Brandeis. In his dissenting opinion in *Olmstead v. United States*, a wiretap case, he wrote: "The progress of science in furnishing the government with means of espionage is not likely to stop with wiretapping. Ways may someday be developed by which the government, without removing papers from secret drawers, can reproduce them in court, and by which it will be enabled to expose to a jury the most intimate occurrences of the home. Advances in the psychic and related sciences may bring means of exploring unexpressed beliefs, thoughts and emotions."[2]

Because few of the accounts of psychic feats reported by the media are negative due to the fact that "sensational sells," and as the blitz of undocumented cases in the tabloids continues to assault us at every supermarket checkout stand as well as on various entertainment television "news" shows, public acceptance of the reality of psi will in all likelihood continue to grow. And since juries are made up of people, the courts will have to come to grips with the growing public belief. That was recently demonstrated in Philadelphia, when a judge set aside the $986,000 award a jury granted Judith Richardson Haimes for the loss of her psychic powers due to a hospital CAT-scan.[3]

As described earlier, psychics have been used by some attorneys to help them select juries. Some critics of psi have expressed outrage at this. When Phil Jordan was appointed an officer of the court in Binghamton, New York, to consult with Public Defender Robert L. Miller for jury selections, debunker James Randi complained that "the bar associations sit back while superstition and magic tricks take over the lives of those brought before the law, innocent, or guilty."[4]

Though disbelievers in psi may be upset by the invasion of psychics into the courtroom, in the case of Jordan, such criticism may well be based on an ignorance of the full nature of the jury-impaneling process. Attorneys are normally allowed to seek removal of potential jurors on two quite different grounds. The first, removal "for cause," exists when a lawyer can convince a judge that the potential juror should be dismissed on some accepted legal grounds, such as bias. Usually, any number of jurors can be removed when acceptably challenged "for cause." But attorneys are also allowed a set number of "peremptory" challenges (the number depends on the jurisdiction and the character of the crime), in which it is not necessary to present a "cause." In other words, an attorney might dismiss a potential juror for whatever reasons he deems fit, including the attorney's own intuition.

In 1987, one Rochester, New York, attorney, Hugh Silverstein, advertised his own psychic abilities, thus bypassing the need to hire any outside consulting clairvoyant. Silverstein contends his "intuitive abilities" have helped him pick clients and conduct effective cross-examinations.[5]

Because of the existing latitude allowed peremptory challenges, modern attorneys have frequently brought in a wide host of consultants, including psychiatrists, other behavioral scientists, and even psychics. Critics of jury selection by ESP need to remember that these psychics—whatever their powers—may actually be highly proficient "readers" of people. Ironically, many skeptics explain away psychics' apparent successes elsewhere by claiming that the psychics were merely astute observers of human behavior. If so, their use as jury consultants might be particularly appropriate. This is especially true when it is remembered that the effectiveness of behavioral scientists for similar consultations is also far from scientifically substantiated. "At best," Courtney J. Mullin concluded in his review of "normal" jury selection techniques, "when using the most sophisticated social science techniques, the gamble involved in jury selection will never be completely eliminated."[6]

It is instructive to compare Mullin's defense of these "normal" techniques with those who defend psychics. Mullin asserts that "attorneys have told me, whenever the outcome of the trial is 50/50, jury selection techniques push the trial outcome over into the winning category."[7]

In other words, the purpose in using a psychic or a psychologist in jury selection is to give an attorney a small extra edge. As long as uncertainty exists in the process, controversial methods will continue to be used. A psychic, indeed, might even have one factor operating in his or her favor in certain cases, in that if a potential juror believes in psi and observes that the psychic is aiding the attorney, that juror might be less effectively able to mask his or her bias, and thus might provide the attorney with grounds for dismissal "for cause."

Sometimes psychics have made news from the other side of the jury box. In 1986, a Denver woman was excused from jury duty when she told the judge she "knew" that the defendant was guilty. In this instance, the jury later concurred.[8] And in 1987, after psychic entertainer Marc Sky was rejected as a juror for a New Jersey trial, Sky told a reporter, "To tell the truth, I knew who was guilty and who was innocent before they even went to trial." Whether that boast was true or not, Sky's courtroom proclamation that he could "read minds" seems to have struck the judge as sufficient grounds for the psychic's dismissal.[9]

Media accounts of these instances of psychics being rejected for jury duty have suggested that the courts believed in their claimed powers. However, it must be remembered that jurors are routinely dismissed for *any* reason that might indicate they are unable to approach the trial with an open mind toward the evidence to be presented. Thus the alleged psychics could well have been dismissed simply because the judges viewed them as prejudiced rather than psychic.

Although psychic testimony is not now admissible as evidence in court, with the growth of public acceptance that could very well change, especially if a strong enough scientific case is made. According to acting justice of the New York State Supreme Court Howard E. Goldfluss: "Law enforcement agencies, juries, and judges are finally acknowledging that we don't have the answers to the unexplainable. It really shouldn't shock people that psychic phenomena have found a forum in the courts, requiring us to deal with novel and fascinating ideas."[10]

If these ideas are fascinating, they are hardly novel. Courtroom claims of self-defense against witchcraft and psychic attack go back thousands of years. And some contemporary attorneys, observing the growing public interest in psi, have sought to revive the "hexing" defense.

One such case took place in 1988, when Tommy Bradley went on trial for the 1986 stabbing death of a waitress in Alabama. After going into the local sheriff's office and telling detectives he had had visions from "God" about the murder of Tracy Schoettlin, including details of the crime only known to the police, Bradley was arrested for the crime. During the trial Dr. Keith Harary, director of the Institute of Advanced Psychology in San Francisco and himself a prominent psychic subject and occasional psychic sleuth, testified for the defense. Harary said that although he had not examined Bradley, who was diagnosed as a paranoid schizophrenic, it was possible for people to have information about crimes to which they couldn't have had access. Harary's testimony did not sway the jury, however, and Bradley was convicted of the crime.

But if the views of some parapsychology supporters are to be accepted, the fact that Bradley was diagnosed as a delusional schizophrenic did not necessarily negate the reality of his visions. As Montague Ullman, former director of psychiatry at New York's Maimonides Medical Center, has stated: "Those who have been upset or disturbed by their psychic experiences and who have sought professional help have often encountered frustrating responses. What they have reported honestly and out of conviction is rarely accepted as such. More often it is either discounted or, worse, labeled as a psychotic symptom. What a therapist fails to realize is that the law of parsimony does not prevail here. A person may have a lifelong history of severe mental disorders and, at the same time, experience some bona fide psi effects from time to time. In fact, there are times when the two seem intimately connected."[11]

The problem here is an obvious one: How do you know just when those "time-to-time" experiences occur? It does not take much imagination to see what kind of havoc this line of thought could wreak in our courtrooms. If psi is real, and certain people are able to manipulate other minds telepathically, the specters of death by hexing and black-magic curses loom nefariously in the wings. The old days of the witch trials might be revived.

In fact, such ideas were given an airing in the 1984 California murder trial of Michael Bear Carson and his wife Suzan. The Carsons' attorney pleaded self-defense for his clients, arguing that the pair had beaten and stabbed a woman to death because she was an "evil witch and a vampire" who had been trying to suck the "health and beauty" from Ms. Carson. During the trial the attorney, Marvin Rous, tried to prove the existence of psychic power and show that the Carsons were believers and feared for their lives. Among the expert witnesses called to bolster the defense were a self-proclaimed witch and two parapsychologists. Both defendants were convicted.

What does all this portend for our judicial system? "Lie detectors and truth serum have begun to get some acceptability scientifically, but a polygraph is still not recognized for evidentiary purposes," observes criminal attorney Michael Toomin. "Compare a polygraph to a psychic and you've got a pretty big chasm. There's no way a psychic's thoughts could be used as evidence."[12]

Similarly, Los Angeles Deputy District Attorney James W. Grodin observes: "It's kind of like what the law is going through with genetics. We have experts who can take a sample of semen from a rape victim and genetically compare it with the blood of a suspect and tell you with ninety-nine percent certainty that the man is guilty, but we are still fighting about it in court. Even though the technology is accepted as unerringly reliable by the scientific community, acceptance in the courtroom is moving pretty slow. Even if some expert somewhere down the line could show that a psychic tested out one hundred percent of the time—which is highly unlikely—it would be an uphill battle getting the person's testimony admitted."[13]

Other experts are not so sure. College administrator and law instructor Stanley L. Schall, a former PSICOM member, agrees that the main issue of the admissibility of psychic testimony is one of accuracy, but he does not believe that that in itself is enough to keep it out of the courtroom. "Evidential data to be used for court conviction must be highly reliable (beyond a reasonable doubt)," he writes. "Investigative information for search and arrest needs to be corroborated to be useful, and 'clues' employed in the early stages of investigation must be checked methodically. Thus, accuracy is sometimes crucial, but there is no need to exclude psychically derived information from investigative work solely because it is not perfectly reliable at the time it was given."[14]

Schall's argument was at least partially validated in the 1979 trial of Harold Ray "Butch" Memro, who was convicted of murdering seven-year-old Carl Carter, Jr., in South Gate, California. Memro became a suspect in the case after a drawing of the killer made by a psychic, "Joan," was shown to the boy's parents. Memro's attorney, public defender Peter Williams, argued that Memro's arrest and subsequent confession were illegal, as the basis of the arrest was the psychic's testimony, and therefore did not constitute "probable cause." Detectives in the case testified that although they had had little to go on before the involvement of Joan, the arrest was made on the basis of other factors, namely voluntary statements made by Memro *before* his arrest that he had taken the Carter boy "for a Coke" before his disappearance and then had seen him home. Carter had never returned home. In addition, police said they had observed pornographic photographs of young boys in Memro's apartment, and that Memro had admitted to them that he was a convicted sex offender currently on parole for child molestation from the California State Mental Hospital at Atascadero.

Superior Court Judge William McGinley, while agreeing that testimony from a psychic could not be used by an officer to justify an arrest, said that "it may be used to follow up additional leads." Finding that the arrest had been made on the basis of independent evidence gathered by the detectives, he ruled the arrest legal.[15] (Memro's conviction was overturned by the California Supreme Court, but not on the psychic issue. The Court found that Judge McGinley should have allowed more inquiry into Memro's allegations that his confession had been coerced.)

In Memro's case, the arrest was found to be legal *only* because the judge ruled that it was made on the basis of factors other than the psychic's drawing. But it can easily be seen that another judge might have ruled differently, and some attorneys fear that allowing psychic testimony into the trial process could be courting disaster. They argue that crucial evidence could be irreparably tainted, thus jeopardizing an entire case. This is the "fruit of the poisonous tree" concept.

Say a psychic with a good track record gives detectives detailed clues in a murder case, including the name and address of a suspect. On the basis of that, police search the man's house and find a knife with blood on it that matches the blood of the victim. In addition, they find a pair of shoes with mud on the soles that places the man at the location where the victim's body was found. The suspect is arrested and confesses, but as the arrest was illegal because of a lack of probable cause, none of the evidence—the knife, the shoes, et cetera—can be used, as they are the "fruit of the poisonous tree."

Several cases have been challenged on this basis in recent years. In 1978 in Chicago, hospital worker Allen Showery confessed to the murder of nurse Teresita Basa after being told by detectives that Basa had accused him by speaking through the body of a mutual acquaintance, Remibias Chua, while Mrs. Chua was in a trance. The voice had spoken in Tagalog, the native Philippine language of both Chua and Basa, although Mrs. Chua claimed that she had barely known the dead woman.

At the time Chua and her husband contacted police, months after the murder, detectives had run out their leads and the investigation was stymied. After interviewing the Chuas, detectives questioned Showery, who denied guilt. But when they confronted him with the fact that the "voice" had said that the woman Showery was living with had a ring that had belonged to the victim, Showery broke down and confessed that he had killed Basa and stolen the ring.

During the trial, Showery's attorney, Daniel E. Radakovich, tried to have the case dismissed on the basis that a voice from the grave was not probable cause for an arrest. But Cook County Circuit Judge Frank Barbaro ruled that Showery had spoken voluntarily to the detectives and had not been placed under arrest until after he had confessed.

But even though defense motions for dismissal were turned down and testimony about Mrs. Chua's psychic revelations was admitted, the ghostly specter of Teresita Basa caused problems for the prosecution. "Jurors dropped their teeth when they heard about the voice," then prosecutor Thomas J. Organ was quoted as saying. "Some put their heads in their hands, a couple laughed, one stood up."[16] The result was a hung jury and Showery wound up receiving a minimum fourteen-year sentence as part of a plea-bargaining deal.

If psychic testimony had an adverse effect on the jury in the Showery case, it is possible that it could work the opposite way in another case. Criminal attorney Ed Gensen says: "If I were trying a jury trial and I had independent evidence, I would throw in the psychic part . . . You just might get some crazy on the jury who'd believe in the damn psychic thing. You might sway him against the defendant because he'd say, 'See, the psychic says so.'"[17] But Gensen also sees a danger, in that such a decision by a juror might constitute cause for reversal by an appellate court, since it was based not on the evidence, but on a personal belief in ESP.

One Orange County, California, judge foresaw such a possibility of jury contamination in the 1989 trial of Randy Steven Kraft, accused of murdering sixteen young men in 1979. Kraft's attorney, C. Thomas McDonald, asserted that testimony from "Joan" would show a connection between one of the victims and a convicted sex molester, John McMillan, who committed suicide a week after Kraft's arrest. According to Joan, McMillan was part of a Satanic cult and had lured the victim, twenty-year-old marine Donnie Crisel, to a ritual site, where he had been sacrificed. As a result of Joan's revelations, Irvin police investigating the murder put three individuals under surveillance without result, and no evidence of any cult was uncovered in spite of a search by police helicopter at the psychic's direction. No connection between McMillan and Crisel was ever established and Judge Donald A. McCartin refused to allow the jury to hear Joan's testimony, deeming it irrelevant.

Here seems to be the crux of the matter. A psychic is not a detective, but, as we noted in Chapter 9, actually a kind of extraordinary *informant* and must be treated as such. Attorney Gensen says: "What's the difference between a psychic saying 'I think Joe's the criminal,' and my saying, 'I think Joe's the criminal'? It's hearsay either way, and a psychic's wouldn't be considered any more or less reliable than anybody else's."[18]

Presently, pronouncements by a psychic are not grounds for a search warrant. That situation could conceivably change if, in the future, some psychic tested under strict laboratory conditions were shown to be correct nearly one hundred percent of the time. While the likelihood of that happening in the near future—if ever—might seem remote to most of us, there are some parapsychologists who believe that that day is right around the corner.

Let us for the moment suspend disbelief and say that, through research and experimentation, a "superpsychic" is developed à la the "spook" the CIA sought to cultivate in the 1970s, who can remote-view distant locations with amazing accuracy, eavesdrop on private conversations, and telepathically pick up other people's thoughts. What would that person do to our judicial system? How would the existence of such powers be accommodated within the framework of the Constitution?

Let us suppose a man is arrested on suspicion of murder. The police, knowing that the man is a believer in psychic phenomena, bring in a well-known psychic and tell the suspect that no matter how much the man tries to cover up his guilt, the psychic will be able to read his thoughts. The suspect breaks down and confesses, as did Melvin Brown when Deadwood police brought in Dorothy Allison. Would this be constitutionally permissible?

Ronald J. Allen, professor of Northwestern University School of Law, does not think so. "If the police have reason to believe the suspect is susceptible to that interrogation method and use it to break down his will, there could be a Fifth Amendment claim."[19]

Veteran LA Deputy District Attorney James W. Grodin, however, disagrees. According to case law, police are allowed to lie to a suspect in order to get admissions from him. "Telling a suspect a psychic can read his every thought would be like telling him that his partner had already confessed, when he hadn't, or that they had his fingerprints at the scene of the crime."[20] In other words, the confession would probably hold up, *as long as the psychic was not really reading the man's mind.*

But what happens when our "superpsychic" is brought into the picture? After being read his Miranda rights, the suspect still refuses to talk, so the psychic is employed by police to pick up clues telepathically from the man's thoughts, which they are able to follow up and thus prove his guilt. This would undoubtedly be a violation of the suspect's Fifth Amendment rights protecting him from self-incrimination. "That would be like forcibly administering sodium pentothal," Grodin argues. "What if we could give people a pill so that they couldn't lie for twenty minutes? As the law stands, that would be a violation of constitutional law."[21] California criminal attorney Harold Weitzman puts it another way: "If psychics can do what they say, it would be the height of a Fourth Amendment violation. If there's any place you have a reasonable expectation of privacy, it's in your mind."[22]

Let's examine another possible scenario. Federal agents know that a high-level meeting of organized crime figures is taking place at a country estate surrounded by tight security that precludes any kind of electronic eavesdropping. A psychic with proven remote-viewing abilities is employed to enter the premises psychically and relate the conversation to the agents. Specific information is picked up about the movement of narcotics and tax fraud, and a subsequent investigation proves the information correct, leading to the arrest of several of the men. Is such psychic eavesdropping a Fourth Amendment violation?

The Fourth Amendment guarantees every United States citizen a Reasonable Expectation of Privacy (REP). This guarantee is in effect as long as the individual has indicated that he expects privacy and that such an expectation is reasonable and justifiable, considering the circumstances under which it occurs. For instance, when a person is under arrest, he must be aware that there is a distinct probability that what he says may be recorded; therefore, he has no reasonable expectation of privacy. In dealing with our "superpsychic," the central question would seem to be what would constitute "reasonable," and lately, that seems to be changing.

The Fourth Amendment forbids "unreasonable searches and seizures" of a person, his home, or personal effects. Historically, legal interpretations of this tenet were restricted to the time a person was at home, but with technological advances in electronic surveillance during the 1960s, the right of privacy was expanded to cover areas outside the home. In three pivotal decisions during that decade, the Supreme Court ruled that police were not allowed to eavesdrop on telephone conversations without a warrant from a magistrate and must show that they had "probable cause" to believe a crime was being committed.

But in January 1990, the Court broke from its previous stance. In the case of *Tyler* v. *Berodt*, it ruled that government agents could monitor conversations via cordless telephones without a judge's permission and without violating an individual's right to privacy.

In the case a Davenport, Iowa, couple, the Berodts, picked up a conversation on their cordless phone during which their neighbor,

Scott Tyler, seemed to be making a drug deal. The Berodts reported the conversation to the sheriff, who, without getting a warrant, asked the Berodts to tape any further conversation. Although Tyler was not trafficking in drugs, he was involved in a fraudulent business deal, and a subsequent investigation by police resulted in his conviction on fraud charges. The Tylers filed a federal suit against the Berodts and the Sheriff's Office for a violation of their Fourth Amendment rights. But a federal court in Iowa, and eventually the Supreme Court, ruled that because cordless telephone transmissions can be picked up outside the house, the Tylers had no right to assume that their conversation would not be overheard.

If our "superpsychic," while sitting at home, suddenly began to pick up a distant conversation in which a crime was being plotted and reported it to the police, would that constitute a violation of the conspirators' REP? Or would such conversations be considered the same as a cordless telephone transmission?

Farfetched? Probably. But as long as we've gone this far, let's take things a step further. Let us say that two men are sitting in a restaurant carrying on an illegal conversation. They are speaking in very low tones, and every time the waiter approaches the table they shut up, making their wish for privacy obvious. Police are viewing them from across the street with binoculars and are using a lip-reader to pick up what the men are saying. Is that legal, or an invasion of privacy?

Legal precedent states that a police officer may legally obtain evidence heard or seen through an open door or window, as long as he is standing on a public walkway. In a 1967 case, *People* v. *Regalado*, 224 CA. 2d. 586, it was deemed that although it was illegal for police to install an electronic listening device in a house, it was not illegal for officers to listen "at a door or common wall of an apartment, if the officers are legally there." According to the *California Search and Seizure Compendium*, "where a defendant has exhibited no reasonable expectation of privacy, the use of binoculars or aural aids is not prohibited, but where he had exhibited REP, the use of such aids is unconstitutional."[23]

Even though the two men in the above case were trying to cover up their conversation, the fact that they were in a public place, observable by police across the street, would negate any reasonable expectation of privacy. The use of binoculars and the expert skills of the lip-reader were merely enhancing the officers' senses of observation. Why, then, wouldn't the use of a psychic to pick up the men's conversation via remote viewing be considered merely an enhancement of the sense? What if the two men were carrying on their conversation not in a restaurant, but in an acoustically perfect museum in which a whispered conversation at one end of a large hall can be heard at the opposite end? Police in such a case would be within their legal rights to eavesdrop on the conversation. Could not a psychic, then, be considered a person who "hears" better than the normal person? Would it be legal for the psychic, who has the ability to eavesdrop telepathically, to sit in a car three blocks away and "listen in" on a conversation, as long as he was on public property?

Before we abandon our imaginative speculations, let's take a look at one more scenario. A psychic is in a convenience store making a purchase. While waiting at the checkout stand, he has a "vision" of the man in line in front of him robbing the place. Furthermore, he has a strong premonition that the store clerk will be killed during the robbery. He follows the would-be robber outside and takes down his license number, then goes to the police with the information. Because the psychic is well-known by the police as having been reliable in the past, they follow up the information and find that the owner of the car is a paroled felon with a record of armed robberies. They put his apartment under surveillance and observe the suspect meeting with two other ex-convicts with violent criminal records. They see the men cutting eyeholes into masks and getting ready to leave. Do they move in, or wait until the men attempt to pull off the robbery? Considering the psychic's vision of the dead store clerk, they decide not to wait for the suspects to get to the convenience store. Since consorting with known felons is a violation of parole, police enter the premises and find weapons, narcotics, and evidence of conspiracy to rob the convenience store. Since the only information that led police to put the man under surveillance was that provided by the psychic, would the arrests be held valid? Was that tip sufficient grounds to develop probable cause? Did an emergency situation exist, i.e., the possibility that the store clerk might be killed?

The answer to all these questions is that, at the present time, there is no answer. Nor is there likely to be one until a psychic comes along with accuracy that approaches a hundred out of a hundred times. And if that ever happens, the ramifications would extend far beyond the legal system. Says D. A. Grodin: "If they had *one psychic* in the United States who could do that, the crime rate would go down. There would be no secrets. It would be the ultimate 1984."[24]

THIRTEEN

Psychics, Criminal Investigation and the Limits of Science

Those who may have expected our analysis of psychic sleuths and the blue sense to result in a simple universal judgment of either validation or dismissal will be disappointed. Many proponents we interviewed assumed that any objective examination of the available facts would overwhelm us with evidence favoring psychic detectives. On the other hand, many critics presumed that a dispassionate analysis would inevitably disclose the flimsiness of these claims and allow us to dismiss them all. Instead, we unearthed new evidence supporting *both* sides in the controversy. We hope we have shown that much of the debate has been extremely simplistic. For many specific cases, clear answers are possible. Some highly touted cases we examined (like some of those involving Peter Hurkos or Gerard Croiset) turn out to be pure bunk. But investigation also shows that some critics' dismissive analyses have been seriously flawed. While we have cast new light on many past case reports, we do not claim any final answers. Our more limited goals have been (1) to obtain a fuller description of the events themselves, (2) evaluate the existing arguments on all sides, (3) cast some new light on the controversy, and (4) produce new and better questions and directions for future research.

Evidence is always a matter of degree. And evidence of the blue sense does not yet meet the heavy burden of proof many scientists demand for validation of what they see as such extraordinary claims. To the hard-line skeptic, the case for the blue sense remains *not proved*. However, as we have repeatedly noted, *non*proof does not constitute *dis*proof. The case for the blue sense may not be totally convincing, but it is far more substantial than many critics have presumed. And not all scientists take the hard-line position. Extraordinariness is also a matter of degree, and among the sciences it is mainly psychology that judges the blue sense contrary to orthodoxy. For the many scientists less impressed by the materialistic orientation dominant in today's psychology, intuition remains a largely mysterious and perhaps even transcendent human capacity. Thus, informed scientists can still reasonably differ about the nature of the blue sense.

Criminal investigation, like the rest of life, remains more art than science. Those who insist that criminology must be thoroughly scientific forget that the fundamental goals of criminology are nonscientific. Science, which simply maps the way the world *is*, should not be evaluative. That is, there is nothing in science that says murderers should be caught, bodies should be found, or that criminals should be punished. These are *human* and not really scientific goals. They are not built into scientific method. More important, however, we cannot conduct science to its fullest with inadequate data. Sherlock Holmes liked to remind Dr. Watson "how dangerous it always is to reason from insufficient data." As the great fictional detective aptly put it in "The Adventure of Wisteria Lodge": "It is a capital mistake to theorize before one has data. Insensibly one begins to twist facts to suit theories, instead of theories to suit facts."

As we have seen, many who have argued both for and against the blue sense have not been properly informed of the facts. This has often generated more heat than light. But even where the available facts are known and agreed upon, there are many cases where analysts can reasonably differ. At this point, critics of the blue sense who demand an immediate scientific decision on the existing evidence simply cannot be satisfied. The existing data—large as we have shown them to be—simply remain inadequate for us to reach a sound rational judgment that is simply pro or con. It remains wise to *doubt* the blue sense, but it is scientific folly to *deny* it categorically.

Those who demand immediate closure on these questions should heed Thomas Edison's reminder that "we do not know one millionth of one percent about anything." In a similar spirit, philosopher Alfred North Whitehead observed: "The universe is vast . . . At this moment scientists and skeptics are the leading dogmatists." Scientists cannot believe that everything is possible the way metaphysicians might. But J. B. S. Haldane was probably close to the truth (and may have been thinking of the Hamlet principle we discussed in Chapter 3) when he said, "The universe is not only queerer than we imagine, it's queerer than we *can* imagine."

Because we have found that the validity of psi (and therefore the blue sense) simply cannot be established or dismissed beyond a reasonable doubt, we have turned to the more answerable question of its utility. These are thoroughly separate questions. Even some parapsychologists, like J. G. Pratt, who believe that psi is real, have argued that it may be quite unlawlike, as if the universe simply occasionally hiccuped. If psi in fact exists but without any predictable empirical pattern, it would be mostly inconsequential to science (which is primarily interested in lawlike phenomena). Similarly such random instances of psi would not have any potential applications since we never would know when it might appear. Ironically, then, while unpatterned *real* psi might be useless, the myth of psi (i.e., an *unreal* psi)—as we have repeatedly shown—may still prove useful.

Whether proponents or critics like it or not, certain basic social facts exist and must be dealt with: (1) Unsolved crimes, missing persons, and other mysteries we want solved continue to occur. (2) Information for their purely rational and scientific solution is often simply inadequate, yet great social and psychological pressures may exist for their solution. (3) Many people assert they have psychic powers and offer their aid to police. Some of these psychics can show evidence of apparent past successes. (4) Many police investigators, like most other people, are inclined to believe in such intuitive abilities. (5) Some police investigators, whether or not they believe in psychic powers, are simply open-minded or desperate enough to try a psychic even as a long shot. As a result of these facts, psychics are going to be used by some police detectives and others needing information no matter what we or any critics might say. Given this social reality, the central question for us must be: How can we improve this situation?

First and foremost, we need to encourage increased rationality and more informed opinion. To a large degree, this simply means getting those involved to emphasize common sense, an attitude of moderation and balance, and a concern for truth, including the encouragement of the true skepticism that is at the heart of science. This means doubt not only toward the claims of the psychics but also some degree of doubt toward those who might prematurely close the door on the new and revolutionary. Scientific skepticism is a two-edged sword. Francis Bacon was correct in reminding us that "there is a superstition in avoiding superstitions." Real science should produce humility rather than arrogance toward nature. As the philosopher Miguel de Unamuno said, "True science teaches, above all, to doubt and to be ignorant."

All this means we must recognize the limits of our knowledge, but it also means that we should appreciate that even incomplete knowledge is better than *no* knowledge. In *The Psychology of Science*, psychologist Abraham Maslow reminded us that when confronted with a fifty-fifty decision choice, even if our theory gives us only a fifty-one percent chance of being right, we have an edge. The use of the blue sense may only give us a similar small advantage, but it perhaps remains better than nothing. Good science means not only doubt but moderation. Sigmund Freud correctly observed that "it is a mistake to believe that science consists in nothing but conclusively proved propositions, and it is unjust to demand that it should. It is a demand only made by those who feel a craving for authority in some form and a need to replace the religious catechism by something else, even if it be a scientific one."

Second, we need to improve our data base in ways that will allow us to refine our knowledge. We hope that this book will be a beginning toward that end, but a great deal more needs to be done. Science has sometimes been defined as "refined common sense." Ironically, refinement has often resulted in sense that is no longer common (like science's conclusion that the earth is not flat and that tables are not really solid). Both critics and proponents have appealed to what they say is common sense in their arguments over the blue sense, but the data are simply inadequate for the refined analysis we need. The major problem is the absence of a proper baseline against which we can judge any claims of success, especially a lack of information about the character and number of both successes and failures by psychic detectives.

A major obstacle to obtaining the needed data base has been police fear of the "giggle factor." News of a psychic's failure usually results not only in criticism but also in public ridicule. Knowing this, many police departments have tried to keep their attempts at using psychics secret from the media, sometimes even when the psychic proved successful. Though it is perhaps understandable that police may be likely to deny having used a psychic if the psychic failed, there is also evidence that they may want to avoid giving public credit to a psychic even when there are private admissions of the psychic's usefulness. Police who use psychics need to come out of the closet and provide scientific evaluators with the needed score sheets.

In addition to improving our data base on the psychics themselves, scientists need to engage in studies actually comparing them against the other techniques now being used for criminal investigation. As we saw in Chapter 9, scientists find that the current alternative procedures, such as psychiatric profiling, hypnosis, and polygraphs, leave much to be desired. In addition, there are newer techniques, such as psycho-linguistic analysis, that show promise but also contain some of the methodological problems that may be found in interpreting reports from psychics. Any analysis of the utility of psychics needs to be grounded in better comparative data, too.

We also need to encourage the psychics to strive for greater professionalization and the creation of ethical standards. One of the surprises we found in our interviews with psychics is how few of them even knew of one another. Many individually told us they felt a need for some sort of organization, if only so they might be able to refer police in other countries or states to competent colleagues. Many psychics also told us that they were concerned about the bad apples among people working in this field and expressed a hope that there might eventually be licensing for their profession. Ironically, many critics have expressed opposition to licensing. For example, on January 26, 1985, California's Bay Area Skeptics passed a resolution showing their opposition to the Concord, California, City Council's proposed ordinance to regulate psychics working in that community. Their opposition was based on their conviction that "there are no standards or criteria by which they [the psychics] could be judged." This goes too far, for there *are* standards that the community's skeptics could have suggested the City Council might use. This might mean some compromise between the skeptics and the psychics as to the criteria. But even if they only agreed that those without past criminal records should be allowed to practice, surely that would result in some improvement over the current situation existing in some places where rogue psychics are completely free to bilk gullible clients.

Many critics make the mistake of viewing all psychics as crooks or fools. All professions include some scam artists, but we found most professional psychics sincere and concerned individuals anxious to help others. And many are offended by the black sheep in their midst. The mass media seldom tells us of these professional complaints. For example, during the publicity given astrologer Joan Quigley's book about her role as adviser to Nancy Reagan, what was reported about the many complaints among astrologers? Many of them were outraged, pointing out that Quigley's disclosures clearly violated her client's right to expect professional confidentiality. Not only was it unethical, many astrologers also realized it was bad for business. It might be far wiser for critics to join with honest psychics to help them police their own.

Finally, the police need better information to help them sort through the many offers of psychic help extended to them. Like the psychics, many police departments have also been working in the dark. They usually know little about the experiences other departments have had with psychics, including the psychics they themselves employ. This book should give them a better basis for assessing and foreseeing the likely costs and benefits derived from using psychics. But this is just the beginning. New information about psychic sleuths comes into the Center for Scientific Anomalies Research (CSAR) clearing house continually. CSAR welcomes inquiries as well as new data. With the continued cooperation of both police and psychics, we may yet be able to solve the riddle of the blue sense.

The Center for Scientific Anomalies Research (CSAR) began its Psychic Sleuths Project in 1980. It has become an international clearing house for data on police use of psychics. This book is the first public report on the information so far collected at the Center, which now has data on over two hundred psychics who have worked with police and law-enforcement agencies. We urge both police agencies and psychics who work with them to contact the Center to help build this data bank and share information. Psychic success stories often seem to reach the national media, but stories of failures seem less likely to leave the region. We also invite readers of this book to help us by sending information about local news stories that involve psychic detectives. All should write to: CSAR; PO Box 1052; Ann Arbor, Michigan, 48103, USA.

Notes

Notes for Chapter 1

[1] Charles Bosworth, "Psychic Help: Searchers Find Body of Slain Alton Woman," *St. Louis Post Dispatch*, November 15, 1983, p. 3A.

[2] Telephone interview with Mel Ramos, August 28, 1989.

[3] Some of the major network broadcasts worth special note would include the following: In November of 1989, Geraldo Rivera devoted his syndicated talk show to the subject of psychic detectives and featured guests Nancy Czetli, Dr. Alex Tanous, and a New York City psychic who uses the name "Yolana"; on December 21, 1989, ABC broadcast the full hour documentary special "Psychic Detectives"; and on February 10, 1990, CBS aired a *48 Hours* show on "Psychics and Skeptics" that featured an opening and closing segment on Nancy Czetli.

[4] Interview with Dr. Martin Reiser, July 14, 1989.

[5] Jan Klunder, "'Psychic Vision' Woman Wins False Arrest Suit Against LAPD," *Los Angeles Times*, March 27, 1987, pp. 1, 6; and Richard Varenchik, "L.A. Court Vindicates Psychic Vision," *Fate*, August 1987, pp. 42–48.

[6] Thomas J. Gordon and Jerry J. Tobias, "Managing the Psychic in Criminal Investigations," *Police Chief*, May 1979, p. 58.

[7] Anonymous, "Use of Psychics in Law Enforcement, *Criminal Information Bulletin* [State of California Department of Justice], February 7, 1979, p. 26.

[8] Charles Roscoe Farabee, Jr., *Contemporary Psychic Use by Police in America* (M.S. Thesis, Department of Criminology, California State University, Fresno, 1981), p. 56.

[9] Interview with Dr. Louise Ludwig, October 12, 1989.

[10] Interview with Lieutenant Kurt Longfellow, August 31, 1989.

[11] Vernon J. Geberth, *Practical Homicide Investigation* (New York: Elsevier, 1983), p. 420.

[12] Joseph R. Kozenczak, and Karen M. Henrikson, "Still Beyond Belief," *Policing*, Vol. 5, No. 2, 1989, p. 145.

[13] Letter from Uri Geller, August 8, 1989. *See also* Uri Geller and Guy Lyon Playfair, *The Geller Effect* (London: Jonathan Cape, 1986), pp. 74–88.

[14] Jacob Young, Barbara Rosen, and Jane Whitmore, "The Senator and the Psychic: A New Medium in the Quest for World Peace?" *Newsweek* (International Edition), May 11, 1987, p. 21. *Also see* John Witherow and Jon Connell, "Did Uri Bend the Will of Gorbachev?" *The Sunday Times* [London], May 3, 1987, p. 1; and David Horovitz, "Uri Geller Used to Bend Mind of Soviet Negotiator," *The Jerusalem Post*, May 3, 1987, p. 1.

[15] Interview with Special Agent Kenneth Lanning, July 13, 1989.

[16] Vicki Guarino, "$25,000 Awarded: Psychic Wins Suit Against Detractor," *The Mail Tribune* [Medford, OR], September 14, 1986, p. 3A. Ms. Renier's award was upheld on appeal.

[17] Much on this has appeared over the years in Jack Anderson's columns in *The Washington Post*, e.g., *see* his "CIA Toys with Extrasensory Weapons," March 30, 1981; "Pentagon, CIA Cooperating on Psychic Spying," May 3, 1984; and "Spy Race with Soviets," February 15, 1989. The best-balanced source on this topic remains Martin Ebon's *Psychic Warfare: Threat or Illusion?* (New York: McGraw-Hill, 1983). *See also* Ron McRae, *Mind Wars: The True Story of Secret Government Research into the Military Potential of Psychic Weapons* (New York: Simon & Schuster, 1984); and John White, ed., *Psychic Warfare: Fact or Fiction?* (Wellingborough, Northamptonshire: Aquarian Press, 1988).

[18] James Coates, "Psychic Spy Died, No Word Since," *Detroit Free Press*, August 10, 1977, p. 6A.

[19] Steven Emerson, *Secret Warriors: Inside the Covert Military Operations of the Reagan Era* (New York: G. P. Putnam's Sons, 1988), "Kidnapping in Italy," pp. 58–70.

[20] Cf. Art Levine, Charles Fenyvesi, and Steven Emerson, "The Twilight Zone in Washington," *U.S. News and World Report*, pp. 24–26, 30; and Emerson, *Secret Warriors*, p. 197.

[21] Emerson, *Secret Warriors*, p. 113.

[22] USAF Senior Noncommissioned Officers Academy, Associate Program, Vol. 2: *Management, Concepts, Theories, and Practices* [#008C 02 8205, Course 8C] (Extension Course Institute, Air University, 1985), p. 65.

[23] Interview with Special Agent Kenneth Lanning, July 13, 1989.

[24] George Gallup, Jr., and Frank Newport, "Gallup Poll: Normal and Paranormal," *St. Louis Post-Dispatch*, August 5, 1990, pp. 1, 10.

[25] Andrew Greeley, "Mysticism Goes Mainstream," *American Health*, January/February 1987, p. 47.

[26] Anonymous, "Woman Claims CAT Scan Ended Her Psychic Powers: Gets $1 Million for Suffering," *Los Angeles Times*, March 29, 1986, p. 3; and "Psychic's $986,000 Award Voided; Blamed X-Ray for Loss of Powers," *Los Angeles Times*, August 9, 1986, p. 20.

[27] Mary Ann Galante, "Psychics: Lawyers Using Seers to Help Select Juries, Find Missing Children," *The National Law Journal*, January 27, 1986, p. 32. *Also see* Howard E. Goldfluss, "Courtroom Psychics," *Omni*, July 1987, p. 12.

[28] Galante, *Psychics*, p. 32.

[29] Interview with Lieutenant Kurt Longfellow, August 31, 1989.

[30] Interview with Dr. C. B. Scott Jones, July 18, 1989.

Notes for Chapter 2

[1] Eric J. Dingwall, *Ghosts and Spirits in the Ancient World* (London: Kegan Paul Trench Trubner & Co., 1930), pp. 82–83; and Dennis Bardens, *Ghosts and Hauntings* (New York: Taplinger Publishing Co., 1965), p. 41.

[2] Cf. Willoughy-Meade, *Chinese Ghouls and Goblins* (New York: Frederick A. Stokes, 1926), pp. 19–20.

[3] W. H. C. Tenhaeff, "The Employment of Paragnosts for Police Purposes," *Proceedings of the P.I. (Parapsychological Institute of the State University of Utrecht)*, No. 1. December 1960, p. 15.

[4] Cited in Keith Thomas, *Religion and the Decline of Magic* (New York: Charles Scribner's Sons, 1971), pp. 215–216.

[5] *Ibid.*, p. 216.

[6] *Ibid.*, p. 217.

[7] *Ibid.*

[8] *Ibid.*, p. 243.

[9] *Ibid.*

[10] *Ibid.*, p. 221.

[11] *Ibid.*, p. 222.

[12] *Ibid.*, p. 220.

[13] The details of this case and Aymar's involvements are well detailed in Christopher Bird, *The Divining Hand* (New York: E. P. Dutton, 1979), pp. 97–104. Critics of dowsing have sometimes misrepresented the details of this episode. For example, a brief but almost totally inaccurate version of this episode is presented by debunker James Randi in *Flim-Flam! The Truth About Unicorns, Parapsychology and Other Delusions* (New York: Lippincott & Crowell, 1980), p. 4. For what is probably the best skeptical look at Aymar, *see* Rossiter W. Raymond, "The Divining Rod," *Journal of the Franklin Institute*, 119, 1885, pp. 1-18.

[14] Andrew Lang, "The Divining Rod," *Cornhill Magazine*, 47, January 1883, p. 89.

[15] Earl Wesley Fornell, *The Unhappy Medium: Spiritualism and the Life of Margaret Fox* (Austin: University of Texas Press, 1964).

[16] Representative examples can be found in: F. W. H. Myers, "On Indications of Continued Terrene Knowledge on the Part of Phantasms of the Dead," *Proceedings of the Society for Psychical Research*, 8, 1892, pp. 243–244; and Eugene Osty, *Supernormal Faculties in Man* (London: Methuen & Co., 1923), pp. 30–31.

[17] Emma Hardinge Britten, *Modern American Spiritualism* (New Hyde Park, New York: University Books, 1979 [orig. 1870]), p. 531.

[18] Excellent surveys can be found in Peter Underwood, *Jack the Ripper: One Hundred Years of Mystery* (New York: Javelin Books, 1988); and Donald Rumbelow, *The Complete Jack the Ripper* (Boston: New York Graphic Society, 1975).

[19] Underwood, *Jack the Ripper*, p. 86.

[20] London: John Long, Ltd., 1935.

[21] New York: William Morrow and Co., 1969.

[22] Stephen Knight, *Jack the Ripper: The Final Solution* (London: Grafton Books, 1976).

[23] D. J. West, "The Identity of 'Jack the Ripper': An Examination of an Alleged Psychic Solution," *Journal of the American Society for Psychical Research*, 35, 1949, pp. 76–80.

[24] Melvin Harris, "I Captured Jack the Ripper," in his *Investigation of the Unexplained* (Buffalo, New York: Prometheus Books, 1986), pp. 59–65.

[25] Underwood, *Jack the Ripper*, p. 97. Interesting further defense of Lees's version of the events can be found in Peter Underwood, *Queen Victoria's Other World* (London: Harrap, 1986), Chapter 6: "Robert James Lees—Medium and Mentor," pp. 96–108.

[26] Quoted in Underwood, *Jack the Ripper*, p. 87.

[27] From the full text of the letter quoted in Edward T. Woodhall, *Crime and the Supernatural* (London: John Long, Ltd., 1935), pp. 33–34.

[28] *Ibid*. According to one of Conan Doyle's biographers, Charles Higham, Sir Arthur, in his police advisory role as deputy lieutenant of Surrey, may have played a larger role in finding Mrs. Christie than has generally been disclosed. Cf. Charles Higham, *The Adventures of Conan Doyle: The Life of the Creator of Sherlock Holmes* (New York: W. W. Norton and Co., 1976), p. 343.

[29] Woodhall, *Crime and the Supernatural*.

[30] Details of this episode and the many séances were documented by one of the participants, W. Tylar, in *The Spirit of Irene* (Bournemouth: William Tylar, 1923).

[31] Woodhall, *Crime and the Supernatural*, p. 113.

[32] New York: Taplinger, 1974.

[33] Piet Hein Hoebens, with Marcello Truzzi, "Reflections on Psychic Sleuths" in Paul Kurtz, ed., *A Skeptic's Handbook of Parapsychology* (Buffalo, NY: Prometheus Books, 1985), pp. 636–638.

[34] Cf. Albert Hellwig, *Okkultismus und Verbrechen. Eine Einführung in die kriminalistischen Probleme des Okkultismus für Polizeibeamte, Richter, Staatsanwälte, Psychiater und Sachverständige* (Berlin: Dr. P. Langenscheidt, 1929), pp. 131–141. See also his *Okkultismus und Strafrechtspflege* (Bern-Leipzig: Verlag Ernst Bircher AG, 1924). Parapsychologist Fanny Moser cited this Ballenstedt case as a prime example of a spurious psychic success in her *Der Okkultismus, Täuschungen und Tatsachen* (Munich: Ernst Reinhardt, 1935), p. 617.

[35] Cornelius Tabori (translated and edited by Paul Tabori), *My Occult Diary* (New York: Living Books, 1966). Strangely, in this book Thoma's first name is given as Ludwig.

[36] Tartaruga, *Kriminal-Telepathie und -Retroskopie; Telepathie und Hellsehen im Dienste der Kriminalistik* (Leipzig, 1922).

[37] Hellwig, *Strafrechtspflege*, p. 87. It is unfortunate that Hellwig's writings on psychic criminology remain untranslated into English, for they are perhaps the most important books yet published on the subject. Hellwig was a moderate skeptic who remained open to the possibility of psychic powers. His work was praised by friends and foes for its thoroughness, fairness, and accuracy.

[38] For further difficulties with Tabori, see Hoebens with Truzzi, "Psychic Sleuths."

[39] Quoted in Paul Tabori, *Crime and the Occult* (New York: Taplinger, 1974), pp. 135–136). See also Anonymous, "Psychic Sleuth Solved Murder by Divination"

in Perrott Philips, *Out of This World*, Vol. 21 (London: Phoebus Publishing Co., 1981), pp. 85–86.

[40] The contemporary report on this is to be found in Argentina's Hungarian newspaper *Magyar*, February 10, 1935.

[41] Cf. Alan Hynd, "Mind-Reader Who Trapped Alberta's Mad Murderer," *Fate*, March 1958, pp. 49–54, reprinted from *Liberty of Canada*. *See also* Michael Gier and Kurt Singer, "Brain Waves Don't Lie," *Tomorrow*, 5, 5, Autumn 1957, pp. 10–21; Colin Wilson, *The Psychic Detectives: The Story of Psychometry and Paranormal Crime Detection* (London: Pan Books, 1984), pp. 184–187; and John Robert Columbo, "Mannville/The Murderer and the Mentalist" in his *Mysterious Canada* (Toronto: Doubleday Canada, 1988).

[42] Quoted by Wilson, *Psychic Detectives*, p. 184.

[43] Philip H. Godsell, "From the Files of the Mounted Police: How a Mentalist Solved a Murder," *Fate*, January 1959, pp. 36-43. *See also* John Robert Columbo, "Beechy/'Murder on His Mind,'" in *Mysterious Canada*, p. 299; and George Woodbury, "Stranger Than Fiction: The Mind-Reader Murder Case," *Manchester Union-Leader*, June 27, 1969.

[44] These included Dr. H. Thouless and Dr. B. P. Weisner, who wrote the foreword to Marion's autobiography. *See also* Harry Price, *Confessions of a Ghost Hunter* (London: Putnam and Co., 1936), pp. 272–277; and S. G. Soal, *Preliminary Studies of a Vaudeville Telepathist* (University of London Council for Physical Investigation, Bulletin III, 1937).

[45] *London Forum*, June 1934, pp. 387–394. This case is cited by Harry Price, "Mediums Who Aid the Police," in his *Fifty Years of Psychical Research* (New York: Longmans, Green, 1939), p. 222.

[46] Frederick Marion, "Experiments in Criminology," in his *In My Mind's Eye* (New York: E. P. Dutton, 1950), pp. 196-206.

[47] *Ibid*., pp. 199-200.

[48] *Ibid*.

[49] Anonymous, "Girl Psychic Finds Missing Articles," *New York Times*, February 25, 1924, p. 8.

[50] New York: Open Court, 1907. Abbott is especially respected by magicians for his many inventions and creations for conjurers. There was probably no skeptic then more knowledgeable about the methods of false mediums.

[51] Woodhall, *Crime and the Supernatural*, p. 211. For an interesting but more skeptical view of Dennis, *see* Milbourne Christopher, *ESP, Seers & Psychics* (New York: Thomas Y. Crowell, 1970), pp. 83-90. Unfortunately, magician/historian Christopher, who witnessed her on stage, does not deal with her many detective episodes.

[52] Fred Archer, *Crime and the Psychic World* (New York: William Morrow, 1969), p. 35.

[53] Anonymous, "Girl Psychic Finds Missing Articles."

[54] Anonymous, "Wonder Girl to Appear in Pictures," *New York Times*, August 26, 1922, p. 6.

[55] Anonymous, "Psychic Aids a Detective," *New York Times*, February 26, 1924, p. 21.

[56] Anonymous, "Call Girl Psychic a Fortune Teller," *New York Times*, March 7, 1924, p. 32.

[57] Anonymous, "She Disclosed Chiefly Our Credulity," *New York Times*, March 24, 1924, p. 14.

[58] Anonymous, "Girl Psychic Guilty of Fortune Telling," *New York Times*, March 22, 1924, p. 13.

[59] Anonymous, "Girl Psychic Fined," *New York Times*, March 28, 1924, p. 7.

[60] Quoted in Joseph F. Rinn, *Sixty Years of Psychical Research* (New York: Truth Seeker Co., 1950), p. 464.

[61] Cf. Woodhall, *Crime and the Supernatural*, pp. 218–223; and Archer, *Crime and the Psychic World*, pp. 35-36.

[62] "Final Curtain," *The Billboard*, March 27, 1948.

[63] An organization in New York City organized by the well-known psychical researcher and writer Hereward Carrington.

[64] Mary Ellen Frallic, "The Psychic Who Solves Crimes," *Fate*, July–August 1952, pp. 95–103.

[65] Mabel Love, "The Woman Who Solves Crimes," *Tomorrow*, 7, 2, Spring 1959, pp. 9–18.

[66] Robert Fink, as told to Virginia A. Santore, "The Disappearance of Carol Allen," *Fate*, September 1965, pp. 53–57.

[67] Jack Harrison Pollack, "Florence Sternfels: The Amazing Mind Reader Who Solves Crimes," *Parade Magazine*, April 26, 1964, pp. 4–5.

[68] *Ibid.*, p. 5.

[69] *Ibid.*

[70] Love, "The Woman," pp. 13–15.

[71] Frallic, "The Psychic," p. 98.

[72] Pollack, "Florence Sternfels," p. 4.

[73] *Ibid.*, pp. 11–12.

[74] Fink, "Carol Allen."

[75] P. H. Hendrickson, "The Body in the House Next Door," *Fate*, May 1965, pp. 78–82. This case is also discussed briefly in Long John Nebel, with Sanford M. Teller, *The Psychic World Around Us* (New York: New American Library, 1969), pp. 149–150.

[76] Quoted in Love, "The Woman," p. 10.

[77] Excerpts from the book were published in the Soviet journal *Science and Religion*, Nos. 1-7, 1965.

[78] These alleged tests are also described in detail in Tatiana Lungin, ed. by Scott Rogo, *Wolf Messing: The True Story of Russia's Greatest Psychic* (New York: Paragon House, 1989), pp. 57–60; Sheila Ostrander and Lynn Schroeder, "Wolf Messing, the Psychic Stalin Tested" in their *Psychic Discoveries Behind the Iron Curtain* (New York: Bantam Books, 1970), pp. 42–58; and Ludmilla Zielinski, "The Magnificent Messing" in Martin Ebon, ed., *Psychic Discoveries By the Russians* (New York: New American Library/Signet, 1971), pp. 163–171.

[79] Quoted in Ostrander and Schroeder, *Psychic Discoveries*, p. 44.

[80] Vladimir Reznichenko, "The Boy in the Crystal Coffin," in Sheila Ostrander and Lynn Schroeder, ed., *The ESP Papers: Scientists Speak Out from Behind the Iron Curtain* (New York: Bantam Books, 1976), p. 33.

[81] Ostrander and Schroeder, *Psychic Discoveries*, pp. 53–54. It should be noted that Messing's solution to this mystery may have been more mundane than here related. According to his own account of this affair, his friend Tatiana Lungin tells us, Messing said he was unable to pick up the thoughts of the young boy and asserted, "This case didn't require my sixth sense; I knew I could solve it rationally and psychologically." Quoted in Lungin, *Wolf Messing*, p. 47.

[82] Charles Reynolds, "Hanussen Lecture," presented at London's Magic Circle, 1989. *See also* Franz J. Polgar, with Kurt Singer, "The Sinister Hanussen," in their *The Story of a Hypnotist* (New York: Hermitage House, 1951), p. 70.

[83] John Goodwin, *This Baffling World* (New York: Hart Publishing Co., 1968), p. 268.

[84] Reynolds, "Hanussen Lecture."

[85] Anonymous, "Trial of a Mind Reader," *Fate*, February 1959, p. 30.

Notes to Chapter 3

[1] Jack Cowan, "Weber Forbids Psychics," *News Democrat* [Belleville, IL], November 18, 1983, pp. 1A, 5A.

[2] Re this general argument, cf. Marcello Truzzi, "The Occult Revival as Popular Culture: Some Random Observations on the Old and the Nouveau Witch," *Sociological Quarterly*, 13, 1972, pp. 16–36.

[3] Re critical examinations of CSICOP's biases, cf. T. J. Pinch and H. M. Collins, "Private Science and Public Knowledge: The Committee for the Scientific Investigation of Claims of the Paranormal," *Social Studies of Science*, 14, 1984, pp. 521–546; Roy Wallis, "The Origins of CSICOP," *New Humanist*, 100, 3, 1985, pp. 14–15; Jerome Clark, "Censoring the Paranormal," *Omni*, February 1987, p. 33; George Hansen, "CSICOP and Skepticism: An Emerging Social Movement," *Proceedings of Presented Papers, The Parapsychological Association, 30th Annual Convention, August 5–8, 1987, at Edinburgh University* (Parapsychological Association, 1987), pp. 317–331; and Robert Anton Wilson, *The New Inquisition* (Phoenix, AZ: Falcon, 1986).

[4] CSICOP, "CSICOP Blasts Police Department for Use of Psychic Detectives," Press Release, Buffalo, NY, December 10, 1982, p. 1.

[5] *Ibid.*

[6] *Ibid.*, p. 3.

[7] University of Texas at Austin, News & Information Service, "Science and Pseudoscience—Part II," Press Release, Austin, TX, April 27, 1983, p. 1.

[8] Cf. Alan Gauld, *The Founders of Psychical Research* (New York: Schocken Books, 1968). *Also see* Renée Haynes, *The Society of Psychical Research, 1882–1982: A History* (London: MacDonald and Co., 1982).

[9] Most scientists surely expect future discoveries of some scientific processes still unknown or unrecognized as of today—and it was in appeal to this realm of the scientifically yet unknown that the term *paranormal* was introduced. Unfortunately, many people, especially critics, have used the term to refer to any public beliefs generally considered wild, crazy, or tinged with the supernatural. Using that definition, it is easy to attack claims of the paranormal. An excellent demonstration of this tactic can be found in the writings of the well-known critic of psychical research, science writer Martin Gardner. [Martin Gardner, *The WHYS of a Philosophical Scrivener* (New York: Quill, 1983), particularly Chapter 3 "Why I Am Not a Paranormalist," pp. 49–66.] But that is not the meaning of *paranormal* as psychical researchers have used and developed it. [A representative modern definition of *paranormal* can be found in Michael A. Thalbourne's *A Glossary of Terms used in Parapsychology* (London: Heinemann, 1982), which was published on behalf of the Society for Psychical Research: "Term applied to any phenomenon which in one or more respects exceeds the limits of what is deemed physically possible on current scientific assumptions." For further consideration of the term *see* E. W. Mabbett,

"Defining the Paranormal," *Journal of Parapsychology,* 46, 1982, pp. 337–354.]
Ironically, Gardner has himself pointed out "the kind of confusion that is
inevitable whenever a philosopher, following Humpty [Dumpty], takes a useful
word, with a commonly understood meaning, and gives it a new and novel
meaning." [Gardner, *The WHYS,* p. 45.] Though Gardner claims to use the term
"the way it is used today in ordinary discourse" [*Ibid.*, p. 51.], he apparently
recognizes that some proponents do not, for he also states: "If by *paranormal*
you mean all the laws and theories not yet discovered, then all scientists believe
in the paranormal . . . In this sense of *paranormal* I am a paranormalist of the
most extreme sort. I firmly believe there are truths about existence as far
beyond our minds as our present knowledge of nature is beyond the mind of a
fish." [*Ibid.*]

[10] Though critics of psychical research often see all such efforts as oriented toward the
supernatural and like to speak of things like clairvoyance as apparent "miracles,"
the distinction between the supernatural and the paranormal is well established
among theologians. If a candidate for sainthood in the Catholic Church were
believed merely to demonstrate some paranormal abilities, that would not be
considered supernatural and would not count as "evidence" for the miracles
required for elevation to sainthood.

[11] After the German term *Parapsychologie,* coined by Max Dessoir in 1889.

[12] Cf. Michael A. Thalbourne and Robert D. Rosenbaum, "The Origin of the Word
'Parapsychology,' *Journal of the Society for Psychical Research,* 53, 802, 1986,
pp. 225–229.

[13] The Parapsychological Association (PA), an organization that carefully screens
members for their scientific credentials, was created in 1957 and gained
affiliation with the American Association for the Advancement of Science (AAAS)
in 1969. Unless someone is a member of the PA, his/her claim to being a
parapsychologist should be questioned.

[14] J. B. Rhine, *Extra-Sensory Perception* (Boston: Boston Society for Psychical
Research, 1934; reprinted by Branden Press, 1964). The best history of early
parapsychology is Seymour H. Mauskopf and Michael McVaughn's *The Elusive
Science: Origins of Experimental Psychical Research* (Baltimore: Johns Hopkins
University Press, 1980).

[15] One skeptical psychologist when asked his opinion of ESP is said to have replied,
"Error Some Place!" Cf. Charles Honorton, "Paranormal Communication: 'Error
Some Place!'" *Journal of Communications,* 25, 1, 1975, pp. 103-116.

[16] Cf. Mahlon W. Wagner and Mary Monnet, "Attitudes of College Professors
Toward Extra-Sensory Perception," *Zetetic Scholar,* No. 5, 1979, pp. 7–16; and
James McClenon, *Deviant Science: The Case of Parapsychology* (Philadelphia:
University of Pennsylvania Press, 1984).

[17] B. P. Weisner and R. H. Thouless, "The Present Position of Experimental
Research into Telepathy and Related Phenomena," *Proceedings of the Society
for Psychical Research,* 47, Part 166, 1942, pp. 1–19.

[18] Whitney S. Hibbard and Raymond W. Worring, *Psychic Criminology: An Operations Manual for Using Psychics in Criminal Investigations* (Springfield, IL:
Charles C. Thomas, 1982).

[19] John A. Swets and Daniel Druckman, ed., *Enhancing Human Performance:
Issues, Theories, and Techniques* (Washington, DC: National Academy Press,
1988). This study was funded by the Army Research Institute and conducted by
a special committee of the NRC with Professor Ray Hyman as chairman of the
subcommittee examining parapsychology.

[20] *Ibid.*, p. 22. The chairman of the NRC subcommittee on parapsychology, and the person most responsible for this section of the report, was the psychologist Dr. Ray Hyman, a longtime critic of psi research. This report was released through a press conference, and its conclusions received widespread attention, especially in the scientific press. In July 1988, a *Reply to the National Research Council Study on Parapsychology: A Special Report Prepared for the Board of Directors of the Parapsychological Association, Inc.* [Reprinted in *The American Journal of Psychical Research*, 83, 1, 1989, pp. 31–49.], by psychologist Dr. John A. Palmer, parapsychologist Charles Honorton, and statistician Dr. Jessica Utts, was distributed. It criticized the NRC report for examining less that 10 percent of psi research, making no attempt to balance its committee with scientists neutral or favorable to the issues, failing to follow its own guidelines for research evaluation, and selectively omitting important evidence favorable to psi. Unlike the NRC report, the PA's reply went almost unnoticed by the media. This debate continued when a select group of critics and proponents were brought together by the U.S. Congress's Office of Technology Assessment (OTA), which issued its *Report of a Workshop on Experimental Parapsychology* on February 22, 1989. [Reprinted in *The American Journal of Psychical Research*, 83, 4, 1989, pp. 317–339.] This OTA report raised many serious questions about the NRC report's conclusions, but its distribution was extremely limited, so the NRC report's conclusions were probably widely accepted and may have done much to undermine further scientific investigation into the question of psi.

If the NRC study had merely asserted that there was "inadequate" scientific evidence for the existence of psi, instead of flatly asserting that there was "no" evidence, many parapsychologists might have agreed with that conclusion. But by stating that "*no* scientific evidence" for psi exists, they may have effectively discouraged some future efforts to investigate. It is important to note that the authors of the NRC study limited it to examination of published experimental reports that underwent peer review and which they deemed to be adequately documented. The study ignored any evidence from spontaneous cases such as those usually encountered with psychic detectives since they viewed such reports as anecdotal (inadequately documented) and thus scientifically irrelevant.

[21] This confusion is well exemplified by the fact that people frequently ask, "Do you believe in parapsychology?" when what they really mean to ask is "Do you believe in psi?"

[22] There is some evidence that there is far more homogeneity of opinion among critics than among proponents of psi. Cf. Susan Blackmore, "What Do We Really Think: A Survey of Parapsychologists and Sceptics," *Journal of the Society for Psychical Research*, 55, 814, 1989, pp. 251–261.

[23] Cf. Parapsychological Association, *Report I: Terms and Methods in Parapsychological Research*, 1985. [Position paper.] It was, in fact, the PA's lack of prior commitment to the question of psi's reality that allowed it to become affiliated with the AAAS. Parapsychology stands for a scientific research program to investigate the question of whether or not psi exists, and, if it exists, how it functions.

[24] Andrew MacKenzie, "How Common Are Psychic Experiences?" *Fate*, November 1987, pp. 42–50.

[25] Joseph H. Rush, "Spontaneous Psi Phenomena: Case Studies and Field Investigations," in Hoyt L. Edge, Robert L. Morris, Joseph H. Rush, and John Palmer,

Foundations of Parapsychology: Exploring the Boundaries of Human Capability (Boston: Routledge & Kegan Paul, 1986), pp. 48–69.

[26] Ian Stevenson, "Changing Fashions in the Study of Spontaneous Cases," *Journal of the American Society for Psychical Research*, 81, 1, 1987, pp. 1–10; and "Why Investigate Spontaneous Cases?" *Journal of the American Society for Psychical Research*, 81, 2, 1987, pp. 101–109. *See also* Stevenson's earlier "The Substantiality of Spontaneous Cases," *Proceedings of the Parapsychological Association*, 5, 1968, pp. 91–128.

[27] Louisa E. Rhine, "Research Methods with Spontaneous Cases," in Benjamin B. Wolman, ed., *Handbook of Parapsychology* (New York: Van Nostrand Reinhold Co., 1977), p. 78.

[28] Cf. Rémy Chauvin, *Parapsychology: When the Irrational Rejoins Science* (Jefferson, NC: McFarland & Co., 1985).

[29] David Marks and Richard Kammann, *Psychology of the Psychic* (Buffalo, NY: Prometheus Books, 1980).

[30] Thanks for this cogent example to psychologist Lee Nisbet.

[31] J. B. Rhine and S. R. Feather, "The Study of Cases of 'Psi-Trailing' in Animals," *Journal of Parapsychology*, 39, 1975, pp. 135–142. We should note that many incidents of animal "homing" that Rhine and others studied involved much longer distances than a mere fifty miles. For a recent such Russian case of a pet that apparently found its way home from over four hundred miles away, *see* Anonymous, "Cat Treks 720 Km Back to Moscow," *Toronto Star,* November 3, 1989.

[32] Re science and the problem of burden of proof, *see* Marcello Truzzi, "Editorial: On Pseudo-Skepticism," *Zetetic Scholar*, No. 12/13, 1987, pp. 3–4.

[33] H. A. Murray and D. R. Wheeler, "A Note on the Possible Clairvoyance of Dreams," *Journal of Psychology*, 3, 1936, pp. 309-313.

[34] *Ibid.*, p. 312.

[35] *Ibid.*, p. 313.

[36] This is an early example of what parapsychologists later came to call "psi- missing," a phenomenon statistically equally anomalous to "psi- hitting."

[37] Martin Gardner, *Science: Good, Bad, and Bogus* (Buffalo, NY: Prometheus Books, 1981), pp. 83–84. Quoting Rhine saying that "scoring rate is hampered as the experiment is made more complicated" and that "precautionary measures are usually distracting in themselves," Gardner argues that this Catch-23 "makes it impossible to establish psi powers by tests that are convincing to the goats [non-believers] who are the vast majority of professional psychologists." For the details of these issues, *see* James C. Carpenter, "Intrasubject and Subject-Agent Effects in ESP Experiments," in Benjamin Wolman, ed., *Handbook of Parapsychology* (New York: Van Nostrand Reinhold Co., 1977), pp. 202–272. On the debate itself, *see* H. M. Collins and T. J. Pinch, "The Construction of the Paranormal: Nothing Unscientific Is Happening," in H. M. Collins, ed., *Sociology of Scientific Knowledge: A Sourcebook* (Bath: Bath University Press, 1982), pp. 151–183.

[38] On the Maimonides work, *see* Irvin L. Child, "Psychology and Anomalous Observations: The Question of ESP in Dreams," *American Psychologist*, 40, 1985, pp. 1219–1230. For an impressive recent development from this line of experimentation, *see* Charles Honorton et al., "Psi Communications in the Ganzfeld: Experiments with an Automated Testing System and a Comparison with a Meta-Analysis of Earlier Studies," *Journal of Parapsychology*, 54, 1990, in press.

[39] The main early technical papers using remote viewing can be found in Charles T. Tart, Harold E. Puthoff, and Russell Targ, *Mind at Large* (New York: Praeger, 1979). Popular accounts are in Russell Targ and Harold E. Puthoff, *Mind-Reach: Scientists Look at Psychic Ability* (New York: Delacorte/Eleanor Friede, 1977); and Russell Targ and Keith Harary, *Mind Race: Understanding and Using Psychic Abilities* (New York: Villard Books, 1984). The major criticisms of remote viewing can be found in David Marks and Richard Kammann, *Psychology of the Psychic*, Martin Gardner, *Science: Good, Bad, and Bogus*, and Ray Hyman, *The Elusive Quarry: A Scientific Appraisal of Psychical Research* (Buffalo, NY: Prometheus Books, 1989).

[40] Ray Hyman and Charles Honorton, "A Joint Communiqué: The Psi-Ganzfeld Controversy," *Journal of Parapsychology*, 50, 1986, p. 351.

[41] *Enhancing Human Performance*, p. 200. The studies are still dismissed by the report on the grounds of what Professor Ray Hyman calls the "dirty test tube" argument, which states that when the results are "obtained under conditions that fail to meet generally accepted standards," science can ignore the claimed results. Critics claim that this is a spurious argument since it makes little sense to speak of dirt in a test tube when we cannot offer some plausible reason why it might be a contaminant. To claim there is dirt in the test tube, there must be some sort of description of the "dirt," which reasonably might produce the error. Otherwise the argument is unfalsifiable and becomes pseudoscientific.

[42] *Ibid.*, p. 22.

[43] Cf. International Security and Commerce Program, Office of Technology Assessment, United States Congress, "Report of a Workshop on Experimental Parapsychology," *American Journal of Psychical Research*, 83, 4, 1989, pp. 317–339.

[44] Psi proponents also contended that while this critical panel examined some research few parapsychologists considered significant, it failed to examine several experiments psi researchers believe among the strongest or most convincing. Cf. John A Palmer, Charles Honorton, and Jessica Utts, "Reply to the National Research Council Study on Parapsychology," *Journal of the American Society for Psychical Research*, 83, 1989, pp. 31–43. *Also see* Scott Jones, "Enhancing Human Performance: Responding to a Flawed Report," *Body, Mind, Spirit*, April 22, 1988, pp. 16, 80; and Dean I. Radin, "Parapsychology Bushwhacked," *Fate*, February 1989, pp. 36–43. *See also* John A. Swets and Robert A. Bjork, "Enhancing Human Performance: An Evaluation of 'New Age' Techniques Considered by the U.S. Army," *Psychological Science*, 1, 2, 1990, pp. 85–96.

[45] On the controversy around meta-analysis, *see* Kenneth W. Wachter, "Disturbed by Meta-Analysis?" *Science*, September 16, 1988, pp. 1407–1408. For the method itself, *see* Frederic M. Wolf, *Meta-Analysis: Quantitative Methods for Research Synthesis* (Beverly Hills, CA: Sage Publications, 1986).

[46] Charles Honorton, "Meta-Analysis of Psi Ganzfeld Research: A Reply to Hyman," *Journal of Parapsychology*, 499, 1985, pp. 51–91. *Also see* Robert Rosenthal, "Meta-Analytic Procedures and the Nature of Replication: The Ganzfeld Debate," *Journal of Parapsychology*, 50, 1986, pp. 315–336.

[47] No formal meta-analysis has yet been conducted on the now available remote-viewing data. A list of known studies through 1982 is in: George P. Hansen, Marilyn J. Schlitz, and Charles C. Tart, "Remote-Viewing Research 1973–1982," in Targ and Harary's *Mind Race*, pp. 265–269. They found that fifteen out of twenty-eight formal published studies and eight out of eighteen unpublished

studies obtained statistically significant psi results. This led them to conclude that "the success of remote viewing is not due to reporting bias, in which vast numbers of unsuccessful experiments go unreported" (*ibid.*, p. 265). For a parallel example of formal meta-analysis dealing with the file-drawer problem, *see* Dean I. Radin, Edwin C. May, and Martha J. Thompson, "Psi Experiments with Random Number Generators: Meta-Analysis Part 1," *Proceedings of Papers Presented at the 28th Annual Convention of the Parapsychological Association, Vol. 1* (Parapsychological Association, 1985), pp. 199–233.

[48] This was Dr. Brink's doctoral dissertation (for Brink's LLD degree) done under the jurist Professor W. P. J. Pompe at the State University at Utrecht: *Enige aspecten van de paragnosis in het Nederlands Strafproces* [Some Aspects of Extra-sensory Perception in the Netherlands Criminal Proceedings], (Utrecht: Durkkerij Storm, 1958).

[49] F. Brink, "Parapsychology and Criminal Investigation," *International Criminal Police Review*, 134, January 1960, pp. 3–9.

[50] Though he indicates that all the subjects were willing to have their names published, Dr. Brink kept them anonymous. The famous subject is described as frequently appearing in the media and practicing "psychical magnetism," so most probably was Gerard Croiset.

[51] Brink, "Parapsychology," p. 9

[52] Ward Lucas, "Police Use of Psychics: A Waste of Resources and Tax Money," *Campus Law Enforcement Journal*, 15, 4, July–August, 1985, p. 15–21. Aside from his work as a reporter, Ward Lucas is also a skilled psychic entertainer, so has a particularly good background allowing him to recognize psychic fraud.

[53] *Ibid.*, p. 16

[54] Reports of these experiments were widespread in the media. For example: "Police Are Calling on Psychics for Aid," *New York Times*, November 26, 1978, p. 61; Al Seckel, "Skeptical Eye: Sensing Just How to Help the Police," *Los Angeles Times*, November 16, 1987, Metro Section, Part 2, p. 5.

[55] Martin Reiser, Louise Ludwig, Susan Saxe, and Clare Wagner, "An Evaluation of the Use of Psychics in the Investigation of Major Crimes," *Journal of Police Science and Administration*, 7, 1, 1979, pp. 18–25.

[56] *Ibid.*, p. 24. For related criticism of the Reiser study, *see* Charles R. Swanson, Jr., "Psychics and Criminal Investigation," in *Criminal Investigation*, 3rd edition, (New York: Random House, 1984), pp. 709–710.

[57] CSICOP, "CSICOP Blasts Police Department." *See also* Kendrick Frazier, "Psychics and crime," *The Skeptical Inquirer*, 3, 4, 1979, 7; and "CSICOP Cautions Against Use of Police Psychics," *The Skeptical Inquirer*, 5, 4, 1981, pp. 6-7.

[58] Reiser et al., "Use of Psychics," p. 24.

[59] The psychics used were selected by Dr. Louise Ludwig "from among those considered to be the most reputable and able in the Los Angeles area who were willing to participate" (*ibid.*, p. 18).

[60] *Ibid.*, p. 19.

[61] Martin Reiser and N. Klyver, "A Comparison of Psychics, Detectives, and Students in the Investigation of Major Crimes," in Martin Reiser, *Police Psychology: Collected Papers* (Los Angeles, CA: Lehi Publishing Co., 1982), pp. 260–267.

[62] *Ibid.*, p. 264.

[63] *Ibid.*, p. 265.

[64] For an excellent overview of theory in parapsychology, *see* Douglas Stokes,

"Theoretical Parapsychology," in Stanley Kripner, ed., *Advances in Parapsychological Research*, 5, (Jefferson, NC: McFarland & Co., 1987), pp. 77–189.

[65] Cf. Robert G. Jahn and Brenda J. Dunne, *Margins of Reality: The Role of Consciousness in the Physical World* (New York: Harcourt Brace Jovanovich, 1987). For a recent popular account, *see* Steve Fishman, "The Dean of Psi," *OMNI*, September 1990, pp. 42–46, 88, 90, 92.

[66] For a good review, *see* Charles Honorton and Diane C. Ferrari, "Future Telling: A Meta-Analysis of Forced Choice Precognition Experiments," *Journal of Parapsychology*, 53, 1989, in press.

[67] This term seems to have been coined by parapsychologist Dr. Jeffrey Mishlove in his article "Psionic: The Practical Applications of Psi," in *Applied Psi*, 3, 1984, pp. 10–16. *Applied Psi* first came out as a newsletter in 1982, was retitled *Intuition* in 1988, and is now published quarterly by The Center for Applied Intuition in San Francisco. It has frequently included articles about psychic detection. *See also* Jeffrey Mishlove, "Applied Parapsychology," *Psi Research*, June 1984, pp. 4–15.

[68] On Geller's successes, *see* John Chadwick, "The Geller Effect on Exploration," *International Mining*, May 1987, pp. 50–54; and James Cook, "Closing the Psychic Gap," *Forbes*, May 21, 184, pp. 90–95. The success of Rossville, Georgia, psychic R. C. "Doc" Anderson in locating oil wells was presented in the syndicated television special "Unknown Powers." Re Anderson, *also see* Robert E. Smith, *The Man Who Sees Tomorrow* (New York: Paperback Library, 1970).

[69] Beverly Jaegers gave commodity broker John Peter Dixon advice to buy coffee when it was down. It then went up dramatically and Dixon made $1.2 million, for which he gave Jaegers $57,500 for a house she wanted. *See* Shirley Hoffman, "Psychic Is Given $60,000 House for Helping Tycoon Make a Million," *The Star*, June 29, 1976; Linda Redeffer, "Bevy Jaegers—the Future Is Hers to See," *The Times West*, March 4–11, 1981; and Jim Creighton, "The Psychic Teacher," *St. Louis Post Dispatch*, September 30, 1977, pp. 3F–4F. As reported on the television science show *Nova* in January of 1984, Keith Harary, then with the applied psi firm Delphi Associates, made nine (out of nine) correct predictions about the silver market and made over $100,000 for Delphi's clients. For details on this episode, *see* D. Scott Rogo, "Psychics Beat the Stock Market," *Fate*, July 1984, pp. 63–68. For examples of psi used in gambling, *see* D. Scott Rogo, "ESP at the Races," *Fate*, pp. 56–63; and Jack Lewis, "ESP Wins in Las Vegas," *Fate*, October 1987, pp. 61–63.

[70] Deborah Caulfield, "The Psychic Who Came in from the Cold," *Fate*, September 1981, pp. 79–86.

[71] An exception here is D. J. West's short study "The Identity of 'Jack the Ripper': An Examination of an Alleged Psychic Solution," *Journal of the Society for Psychical Research*, 35, 1949, pp. 76–80.

Notes to Chapter 4

[1] Russell Targ and Keith Harary, *Mind Race: Understanding and Using Psychic Abilities* (New York: Villard Books, 1984), p. 130.

[2] *Ibid.*, pp. 147–148

[3] On this issue of public confusion between illusion and reality, *see* Ian Mitroff and Warren Bennis, *The Unreality Industry: The Deliberate Manufacturing of*

Falsehood and What It Is Doing to Our Lives (New York: Birch Lane Press, 1989).

[4] For examples of this problem, *see* Curtis D. MacDougall, *Superstition and the Press* (Buffalo, NY: Prometheus Books, 1983), especially pp. 522–547.

[5] Anonymous, "Police File Against Psychic for Howard Hughes Claim," United Press International news release, July 30, 1987 (via Lexis).

[6] Anonymous (UPI), "Voice Tipped Police Search in Slay Case," *The Tennessean*, March 6, 1978, pp. 1, 6; Don Holt and Pamela Ellis Simons, "Crime: A Tip from Beyond?" *Newsweek*, September 18, 1978, pp. 35–36; John O'Brien and Edward Baumann, "Accused of Murder by a Voice from the Grave," *Ebony*, June 1978, pp. 56–63; and Lesley Sussman, "Did Voice from Grave Name Killer?" *Fate*, July 1978, pp. 61–67.

[7] Interview with Nancy Czetli, December 17, 1989.

[8] Quoted by Roberta Grant, "Psych Out! The Woman Who Catches Killers with Her Mind," *Redbook*, May 1989, p. 141. On Czetli's earlier cases, see the article by her later husband, Steven N. Czetli, "Nancy Anderson: Psychic Sleuth," *Your Virginia State Trooper Magazine*, Spring 1982, pp. 23–31.

[9] Gayle Crakovic, "Mind Over Murder: Psychic Aid in Investigation," *Law and Order*, September 1986, pp. 44–47. A later version of this same article appeared as "Mind Over Murder! Psychic Aid in Investigations," *Police Times*, March–April 1987, pp. 1, 6, 8; John Jeter, "Psychic Tie Aids Arrest of Suspect in 2 Killings," *Chicago Sun Times*, October 25, 1987; and Gayle Crakovic, "Will County Psychic Aids Investigation: Work in Murder Case Earns Honors," *Herald-News* [Joliet, IL], November 15, 1987, p. 13; and Molly Woulfe, "Television Viewers Can See Lockport Psychic: Ward Stars as Himself in ABC's 'Crime Busters,'" *Herald-News*, May 25, 1989.

[10] References to cases with Greta Alexander are particularly voluminous. Major pieces about her include an eight-part series of articles about her work by Rick Baker in the Peoria, Illinois, *Journal Star*, August 19–26, 1979; Max D. Isaacson, "Greta Alexander, Delavan Psychic," *Fate*, January 1981, pp. 56–63; and John M. McGuire, "Is She Psychic? Or Is She Fake?" *St. Louis Post-Dispatch*, November 27, 1983, pp. 3C, 10C.

[11] Robert V. Cox and Kenneth L. Peiffer, Jr., *Missing Person: The True Story of a Police Case Resolved by the Clairvoyant Powers of Dorothy Allison* (Harrisburg, PA: Stackpole Books, 1979). More has probably been written about Allison than any other female psychic detective. Major pieces would include Dorothy Allison and Scott Jacobson, *Dorothy Allison: A Psychic Story* (New York: Jove Publications, 1980); Joseph P. Blank, "The Woman Who Sees Through Psychic Eyes," *Reader's Digest*, December 1978, pp. 107–113; Kristin McMurran, "Some Days, Say Police, This New Jersey Psychic Can Indeed See Forever," *People*, July 16, 1979, pp. 95ff.; Mary Jo Patterson, "Dorothy Allison: The Extrasensory Detective," *Police Magazine*, March 1981, pp. 46–49; and Kenneth L. Woodward, "The Strange Visions of Dorothy Allison," *McCall's*, September 1978, pp. 28–38.

[12] Richard G. Case, "The Psychic of Candor," *Syracuse Herald American*, January 4, 1976, pp. 4–9; Phil Jordan, "Psychic's Search for a Missing Child," *Fate*, August 1977, pp. 60–65; Frank Zahour, "Psychic Reads Minds, Finds Hidden Objects and Makes Furniture Rise in Air," *National Enquirer*, February 21, 1978, p. 2; Lawrence Cortesi, "Psychic Searches for Missing Boy," *Fate*, December 1986, pp. 60–69; and Tommy McIntyre, *Wolf in Sheep's Clothing: The Search for a Child Killer* (Detroit: Wayne State University Press, 1988), pp. 201–208.

[13] Charles Roscoe Farabee, *Contemporary Psychic Use by Police in America* (M.S. Thesis, Department of Criminology, California State University, Fresno, 1981), pp. 51–52.

[14] Quoted in Russell Targ and Harold Puthoff, *Mind-Reach: Scientists Look at Psychic Ability* (New York: Delacorte Press/Eleanor Friede, 1977), p. 47. For details on Price's psychic sleuthing, *see* David Hammond, *The Search for Psychic Power* (London: Hodder and Stoughton, 1975), pp. 93–103.

[15] Interview with Judy Belle, August 31, 1989. *Also see* Anna Phillips, "Psychic Cop Helps Solve Crimes with ESP: Deputy Coroner Can Feel the Victim's Pain," *National Enquirer,* undated clipping.

[16] Farabee, *Psychic Use by Police,* pp. 49–50.

[17] Brad Steiger, "Employing Psi Against Crime," in his *The Psychic Feats of Olof Jonsson* (New York: Popular Library, 1971), pp. 129–133; and "Psychic Olof Jonsson Solves Mass Murder," *Fate,* July 1972, pp. 77–85.

[18] Clifford Linedecker, *Psychic Spy: The Story of an Astounding Man* (Garden City, NY: Doubleday, 1975).

[19] Alexander Tropkin, "Psychic Plays Detective," *Soviet Life,* April 1990, pp. 60–62.

[20] A. F. Leber, "Psychic Rescue Squads: Extraordinary Talents of Ordinary People," *Fate,* September 1975, pp. 46–52; Jim Creighton, "The Psychic Detectives," *St. Louis Post Dispatch,* September 30, 1977, pp. 3–4; Shirley Hoffman, "Psychics Lead Police to Murder Victims' Bodies," *The Star,* October 12, 1976, p. 3; Tom Tiede, "Look Out Crooks; This Team Can Read Minds," *Cedar Rapids Gazette,* May 18, 1980, p. 8C; Rick Desioge, "Psychic Powers Help Police Solve Crimes," *Courier News,* October 19, 1977, p. 5A; and Laile Bartlett, *Psi Trek* (New York: McGraw-Hill, 1981), pp. 97–102.

[21] Anonymous, "Psychics Assist Police," *The Plain Dealer* [Cleveland, OH], October 1, 1986.

[22] *Encyclopedia of Associations, 24th Edition* (Detroit: Gale Research, 1990), p. 706.

[23] Interviews with Stephan Schwartz, November 1989.

[24] *Ibid. Also see* Ann Druffel, "The Psychic Laboratory of the Mobius Society," *Fate,* June 1988, pp. 91–103, and July 1988, pp. 63–77; and Jeffrey Mishlove, "An Interview with Stephan Schwartz: The Mobius Group," *Applied Psi Newsletter,* 1, 3, 1982, pp. 5–6.

[25] Interviews with Fred Hansen, August 1989. The "USA" publishes an occasional newsletter, *The Sensitive Times.*

[26] Donald J. Burnett, Chief of Police, Police Department of the City of Pomona, California, "Memorandum on Departmental Policy on the Use of Psychics," September 10, 1981.

[27] Abigail Rockmore, producer, "Dream Murder," segment of ABC News's *20/20* television show, August 6, 1987. Show transcript #730 (New York: Journal Graphics, 1987).

[28] Interview with Dixie Yeterian, August 24, 1989.

[29] Re Dykshoorn, *see* M. B. Dykshoorn, as told to Russell H. Felton, *My Passport Says Clairvoyant* (New York: Hawthorn, 1974); and Piet Hein Hoebens, "The Mystery Men from Holland, 3: The Man Whose Passport Says Clairvoyant," *Zetetic Scholar,* November 10, 1982, pp. 7–16; and Dan Greenburg, "I Don't Make Hocus Pocus," *Playboy,* February 1976, pp. 70–72, 167–168, 170–172. Re the Mattacias, *see* "About the Psychic," *Caledonian-Record* [St. Johnsbury, VT], September 15, 1988, p. 1; and Hanson W. Baldwin, "Dowsers Detect Enemy's Tunnels: Coat Hangers Also Used by Marines to Find Mines," *New York Times,* October 13, 1967.

[30] *Sentinel* Staff, "Search Made in Area for Missing Teen-Ager," *Daily Sitka Sentinel* [Alaska], February 27, 1987, p. 5. Formerly Frances Cannon, Ms. Baskerville claims to have found over five hundred persons. She runs The Baskerville Foundation for Psychical Research, has produced recordings, and was working on a Broadway musical.

[31] Quoted in Jenny Scott, "Police Psychic: Visions of Crime?" *The Sunday Record* [Northern New Jersey], June 24, 1984, p. A22.

[32] Letter to Dr. Edwin C. May, December 22, 1988.

[33] Interviews with Noreen Renier, December 1989. *See also* Susan Tyler Hitchcock, "Psychis 'Tunes In' to Help Police Solve the Unsolvables," *Virginia Police Journal*, 17, 2, Summer 1982, pp. 21–22; Mimi Tandler, "Noreen Renier: Psychic Detective," *Frontiers of Science*, November–December 1980, pp. 25–28; and Laura Ost, "Students Get Good Vibes in Psychic Teacher's Class," *Orlando Sentinel* [Florida], July 28, 1986, pp. B-1, B-6.

[34] Tandler, "Noreen Renier," pp. 27–28.

[35] Interview with Kathlyn Rhea, December 1989. *See also* Kathlyn Rhea, with Maggie O'Leary, *The Psychic Is You: How to Develop Your Psychic Ability* (Milbrae, CA: Celestial Arts, 1979), especially "The Psychic Detective," pp. 31–41.

[36] Interview with Dr. Louise Ludwig, October 12, 1989.

Notes to Chapter 5

[1] Anonymous, "Woman's body Within 15 Yards of Where Psychic Said It Would Be," Associated Press news release, January 2, 1985 (via Lexis).

[2] Keith Anderson, "Dallas' Psychic Detectives," *Dallas Morning News*, April 29, 1984, pp. 1F–2F, 6F; and Anonymous (AP), "Psychic Leads to Body," *Houston Texas Chronicle*, July 22, 1981. Re other Catchings cases, *see* Paul F. Levy, "Psychic Leads Police to Murder Victim Missing 3 Months," *National Enquirer*, February 17, 1981; Anonymous, "Psychic," United Press International news release, July 30, 1981 (via Lexis); Anonymous, "Texas Psychic Says Girl Strangled to Death," United Press International news release, February 14, 1982 (via Lexis); Anonymous, "Psychic Seeks Killer with Mind Over Matter," United Press International news release, February 18, 1985 (via Lexis); Jane Martin, "Mind Over Matter Can Be Touchy Subject to Police," *St. Louis Globe-Democrat*, August 30–31, 1986; Anonymous, "Psychic Assists Police," *The Plain Dealer* [Cleveland, OH], October 1, 1986.

[3] Tom Suk, "Psychic Leads Police Here to Body in River Brush; 'Incredible,' Official Says," *The Des Moines Register*, June 13, 1979, pp. 1, 4; James McCandlish, "From 350 Miles Away . . . Psychic Directs Police by Phone to Missing Man's Body," *National Enquirer*, December 4, 1979, p. 60; Curtis Fuller, "She Walked with Him," *Fate*, October 1979, pp. 29–30; and Max D. Isaacson, "Greta Alexander, Delavan Psychic," *Fate*, January 1981, pp. 56–63.

[4] Interview with Detective Tim McFadden, December 11, 1989. On this case, *see also* Tom Dempsey, *The Use of Psychics by Police as an Investigative Aid: An Examination of Current Trends and Potential Applications of Psi Phenomena to Law Enforcement*, M. S. Thesis, Department of Criminal Justice, California State University, Long Beach, 1981, pp. 56–58.; and Kathyln Rhea, with Maggie O'Leary, *The Psychic Is You: How to Develop Your Psychic Ability* (Milbrae, CA: Celestial Arts, 1979), Chapter 4: "The Psychic Detective," pp. 31–41.

[5] Ken Grayzel, "Psychic Detectives," manuscript, March 1978, made available through the courtesy of James Randi, archives of the Psychic Sleuths Project, Center for Scientific Anomalies Research. *Also see* Jenny Scott, "Police Psychic: Visions of Crime?" *The Sunday Record* [Northern New Jersey], June 24, 1984, pp. A1, A22–A23.

[6] Robert Sheaffer, "Psychic Vibrations," *The Skeptical Inquirer*, Winter 1981–82, p. 17.

[7] Anonymous, "Island Psychic Offers Help, Healing Power," *Galveston Daily News*, April 19, 1988.

[8] Lawrence Cortesi, "Psychic Search for Missing Boy," *Fate*, December 1986, pp. 60–69; and John Blackburn, "Psychic Tells Police Exact Spot—And They Find Missing 5-Year-Old," *National Enquirer*, September 23, 1975, p. 17.

[9] Interview with Detective Stanley White, September 1989.

[10] Mark Jones, "Psychics and Police Mix It Up in L.A.," *Fate*, October 1979, p. 69.

[11] Mitch Weiss, "Psychic Pinpoints Purloined Persian: Says Others Alive," *The Plain Dealer* [Cleveland, OH], January 19, 1989.

[12] Kendrick Frazier, "Psychic Vibrations," *The Skeptical Inquirer*, Winter 1978, p. 13. Re Lydecker, *also see* Dick Peck, "Clairvoyant Leads Deputies to Woman Missing 3 Days," *Sarasota Herald Tribune*, April 13, 1983, pp. 1A, 10A; and Anonymous, "Cops Stunned as Psychic Leads Them to Woman Lost for 4 Days in Swamp," *The Star*, May 10, 1983.

[13] M. B. Dykshoorn, as told to Russell H. Felton, *My Passport Says Clairvoyant* (New York: Hawthorn, 1974).

[14] Cf. Piet Hein Hoebens, "The Mystery Men from Holland, 3: The Man Whose Passport Says Clairvoyant," *Zetetic Scholar*, November 10, 1982, pp. 7–16.

[15] Reported in the *Chicago Daily News*, June 3, 8, 1971, as cited in Curtis D. MacDougall, *Superstition and the Press* (Buffalo, NY: Prometheus Books, 1983), pp. 538–539.

[16] Claire Gilbert, "The Psychic Investigator," *Police Review*, January 1987, pp. 22–23. For a critical view of Nella Jones, *see* Melvin Harris, *Investigating the Unexplained* (Buffalo, NY: Prometheus Books, 1987).

[17] John M. McGuire, "Is She Psychic? Or Is She Fake?" *St. Louis Post-Dispatch*, November 27, 1983, p. 10C.

[18] On the debate over the findings, *see* Betty Lou White, "Psychics Find Egyptian Ruins," *Fate*, April 1981, pp. 36–41. On the project itself, *see* Stephan A. Schwartz, *The Alexandria Project* (New York: Delacorte Press/ Eleanor Friede, 1983). For Schwartz's later comments on the Alexandria project and an overview of the various Mobius activities, *see* Ann Druffel, "The Psychic Laboratory of the Mobius Society, Parts One and Two, *Fate*, June 1988, pp. 91–103, and July 1988, pp. 63–77. *See also* Jeffrey Mishlove and Kathy Goss, "An Interview with Stephan Schwartz, *Applied Psi Newsletter*, 1, 3, 1982, pp. 5–6. Re other works on psychic archaeology, *see* Stephan A. Schwartz, *The Secret Vaults of Time: Psychic Archaeology and the Quest for Man's Beginnings* (New York: Grosset and Dunlap, 1978); Jeffrey Goodman, *Psychic Archaeology: Time Machine to the Past* (New York: Berkeley Books, 1978); David E. Jones, *Visions of Time: Experiments in Psychic Archaeology* (Wheaton, IL: Quest/Theosophical Publishing House, 1979); and Joseph K. Long, ed., *Extrasensory Ecology: Parapsychology and Anthropology* (Metuchen, NJ: Scarecrow Press, 1977).

[19] Paul Bannister, "Psychic Solves Gem Theft," *National Enquirer*, July 13, 1982; and John Godwin, *Occult America* (Garden City, NY: Doubleday, 1972), pp. 124–127.

[20] Interviews with Ingo Swann, December 1989.

[21] Reported in *Wall Street Journal*, April 28, 1977, as cited in MacDougall, *Superstition*, p. 534.

[22] John Chadwick, "The Geller Effect on Exploration," *International Mining*, May 1987, pp. 50, 53–54; Philip Rennie, "Zanex, Uri Geller and Psychic Geology in the Solomons," *Ryders: The Business Journal*, January 1986, pp. 36–37; and James Cook, "Closing the Psychic Gap," *Forbes*, May 21, 1984, pp. 90–91. *Also see* Uri Geller and Guy Lyon Playfair, *The Geller Effect* (London: Jonathan Cape, 1986).

[23] Christopher Bird, *The Divining Hand* (New York: E. P. Dutton, 1979), pp. 215–222. It is curious that anecdotal tales of lost objects found through psychics are extremely common while authenticated reports are rare. Typical of the former might be the claims found in Kathryn Hilton, "Psychic Finder of Lost Things," *Fate*, January 1988, pp. 92–100; or P. C. Candargy, "The Story of a Stolen Fur," *Annals of Psychical Science*, 4, 22, 1906, pp. 229–235.

[24] Interview with Judy Belle, August 31, 1989.

[25] Interview with Detective David Frost, September 1, 1989.

[26] Interview with Sergeant Mark Anderson, August 27, 1989.

[27] Roberta Grant, "Psych Out! The Woman Who Catches Killers with Her Mind," *Redbook*, May 1989, p. 142.

[28] *Ibid.*

[29] Mary Ann Galante, "Psychics: Lawyers Using Seers to Help Select Juries, Find Missing Children," *The National Law Journal*, January 27, 1986, p. 33.

[30] James Crenshaw, "Court Admits Psychic Evidence," *Fate*, November 1979, p. 50. Re Joan, *also see* Jerry Hicks, "Kraft Jury Not Allowed to Hear Psychic Testify," *Los Angeles Times*, February 16, 1989, Part 2, p. 4.

[31] Bill Heffernan, "Psychic Sculptor Helps Police by Shaping Faces from Unidentified Skulls," *National Enquirer*, Jan. 2, 1979.

[32] Interview with Detective Frank Donlon, August 25, 1989.

[33] Whitney S. Hibbard and Raymond Worring, *Psychic Criminology: An Operations Manual for Using Psychics in Criminal Investigations* (Springfield, IL: Charles C. Thomas, 1981), p. 72.

[34] Some of the problems with the other names Hurkos gave in this case will be discussed in Chapter 7.

[35] See Harris, *Investigating the Unexplained,* on Nella Jones's testimony.

[36] Marcello Truzzi, "Anti-Matter: Psychic Sleuths," *Omni*, August 1982, p. 92; and his "Summary Report on Dorothy Allison's Claims Re Atlanta Murders Perpetrator," Research Memo, Psi Sleuths Project, Center for Scientific Anomalies Research, March 21, 1982. For Allison's version of the events, *see* Donna Leusner, "Psychic Says She 'Sighted' Atlanta Slayer; Nutley Woman Gave Name, Sketch to Police," *Newark Star Ledger,* March 4, 1982; and Pat Malone, "Psychic's Eerie Sketch of Atlanta Killer Was Drawn a Year BEFORE Murders," *The Star,* March 30, 1982, p. 23. On Allison and the Atlanta murders, *also see* Chet Dettlinger with Jeff Prugh, *The List* (Atlanta: Philmay Enterprises, 1983), pp. 83–92.

[37] Kay Bartlett, "Seer Turns Her Powers on Wall Street—But Still Has Time for the Enquirer," *Los Angeles Times*, February 28, 1988, p. 4. For her predictions for this past decade, *see* Shawn Robbins, as told to Milton Pierce, *Ahead of Myself: Confessions of a Professional Psychic* (Englewood Cliffs, NJ: Prentice-Hall, 1980).

[38] Antoinette May, "Premonitions: Coincidence or Prophecy?" *Living: The Magazine of the San Francisco Examiner & Chronicle*, February 21, 1982.

[39] Mel Ziegler, "Surprisingly Accurate Forecasts: The Earthquake Lady," *San Francisco Chronicle*, August 12, 1976, p. 2; Bruce Henderson and Anita Hoffman, "'Earthquake Lady' Hits the Mark," *Los Angeles Free Press*, March 23, 1978, p. 20; and Bob Temmey, "Gov't. Credits Psychic with Amazing Earthquake Forecasts," *National Enquirer*, November 1, 1977.

[40] Detailed testimony on this was given by an FBI agent at the libel trial brought by Renier against one of her more zealous detractors. *See* "Deposition of Robert Ressler," Circuit Court of the State of Oregon for the County of Jackson, Case No. 85-3781-J-1, Norman Renier, Plaintiff, vs. John Douglas Merrell, Defendant, September 5, 1986. *See also* Art Levine, C. Fenyvesi, and S. Emerson, "The Twilight Zone in Washington," *U.S. News and World Report*, p. 25.

[41] Anne Richardon, "Ruckersville Psychic on Trial of Rapist," *The Daily Progress* [Charlottesville, VA], December 11, 1979.

[42] Robert Sheaffer, "Psychic Vibrations." Re Hughes's psychic sleuthing, *see* Brad Steiger, "Irene Hughes and the Canadian Kidnappings," *Fate*, July 1971, pp. 36–44; David Techter, "One of Our Aircraft Is Missing . . . Can a Psychic Help?" *Fate*, November 1968, pp. 37–42; Alan Vaughn, "Interview: Irene F. Hughes," *Psychic*, November–December 1971, pp. 5–7, 32–35; and Henry Wood, "Psychic Will Try to Find Slaying Suspect's Sons," *Chicago Tribune*, February 23, 1979. *Also see* Brad Steiger, *Irene Hughes on Psychic Safari* (New York: Paperback Library, 1972), pp. 7–12.

[43] Tom Gorman, "Psychic's Foreboding Turned All Too Personal," *Los Angeles Times* (San Diego County edition), September 14, 1989, Part 2, p. 1; and Anonymous, "Psychic Won't Be Charged in Shooting Death of Spouse," *Los Angeles Times* (San Diego County edition), October 1, 1989, Part 2, p. 6. *Also see* Tom Gorman, "Seeing Is Believing for Skeptics of Psychic," *Los Angeles Times*, April 30, 1989, Part 2, p. 1.

[44] Rick Baker, "Greta Alexander Convinces Washington, D.C., Police," *Journal Star* [Peoria, IL], August 20, 1979, pp. A1, A11.

[45] Mark Jones, "Psychics and Police," 1979, p. 64.

[46] *Ibid.*, p. 70.

[47] Interview with Kathlyn Rhea, December 11, 1989.

[48] Galante, "Psychics," p. 32.

[49] *Ibid.*

[50] *Ibid.*

[51] Glen Crane, "Anti-Matter: Psychic Lawyers," *Omni*, January 1987, p. 86.

[52] *Ibid.*

[53] Interview with Raymond Worring, December 1989.

[54] Interview with Jenita Cargile, December 1989.

[55] Mark Elliot Jones, "Anti-Matter: Psychic Cops," *Omni*, August 1984, p. 94.

[56] Richard Guarino, "The Police and Psychics," *Psychic*, June 1975, pp. 9–15. There are some indications that this percentage may actually be substantially higher. *See* Eleanor L. Myers, "ESP and Law Enforcement Seminar Survey," research report (SRI International, Menlo Park, CA), July 1979; and Carl Cowan and Joan Luxenberg, "Mind Science in Police Science: Applications for Parapsychology," paper presented at the Annual Meeting of the American Society of Criminology, Philadelphia, PA, November 8, 1979.

[57] Michael Riley and David Thompson, "Hearing Voices of Reason?" *U.K. Police Review*, January 16, 1987, pp. 121–122; and Anonymous, "Detectives Examine Role Played by Psychics," *Psychic News*, February 7, 1987, p. 5.

[58] David Kerr, "Investigation of the Homicide Scene," in Samuel R. Gerber and Oliver Schroeder, Jr., *Criminal Investigation and Interrogation* (Cincinnati, OH: W. H. Anderson, 1972, Revised Reprint), p. 159.

[59] Interview with Dr. Martin Reiser, July 14, 1989.

[60] Interview with officer Tom Macris, December 11, 1989.

[61] *Ibid.*

[62] Interview with Armand Marcotte, September 7, 1989.

[63] Anonymous, "Use of Psychics in Law Enforcement," *Criminal Information Bulletin* (State of California Department of Justice), February 7, 1979, p. 25.

[64] Thomas G. Gordon and Jerry J. Tobias, "Managing the Psychic in Criminal Investigations," *The Police Chief*, May 1979, p. 58.

[65] U.S. Department of Justice, Bureau of Justice Statistics, *Report to the Nation on Crime and Justice* [NCJ-105506, March 1988] (Washington, D.C.: U.S. Government Printing Office, 1988), p. 29.

[66] Donald J. Burnett, "Memo [on department policy guidelines on use of psychics]," Police Department of the City of Pomona, September 10, 1981, p. 1.

[67] Peter W. Greenwood, Jan. M. Chaien, and Joan Petersilia, *The Criminal Investigation Process* (Lexington, MA: D. C. Heath, 1977), p. 35.

[68] Interview with Detective Lynn Harris, August 27, 1989.

[69] Jane Martin, "Mind Over Matter Can Be Touchy Subject to Police," *St. Louis Globe-Democrat*, August 30–31, 1986.

[70] Quoted in Steven N. Czetli, "Nancy Anderson: Psychic Sleuth," *Your Virginia State Trooper Magazine*, Spring 1982, p. 27.

[71] Letter from Ingo Swann, October 3, 1989.

[72] Interview with Sergeant Robert Mallwitz, September 15, 1989.

Notes on Chapter 6

[1] Piet Hein Hoebens, "Gerard Croiset: Investigation of the Mozart of 'Psychic Sleuths'—Part I," *The Skeptical Inquirer*, Fall 1981, p. 18.

[2] Though Croiset usually later spoke of his psychic abilities as clairvoyance rather than spirit mediumship, he apparently did claim to contact dead spirits when advising some clients; for example, *see* Dora M. Pettinella, "Croiset Locates a Suicide," *Fate*, April 1977, pp. 43–45.

[3] George Zorab, "Parapsychological Developments in the Netherlands," *European Journal of Parapsychology*, 1, 3, 1976, p. 71.

[4] Cf. R. D. Pauwels, "Gerard Croiset: Psychic Healer," *Journal of the Society for Psychical Research*, 35, 1949, pp. 44–45.

[5] Jack Harrison Pollack, *Croiset the Clairvoyant: The Story of the Amazing Dutchman* (Garden City, NY: Doubleday, 1964), p. 281.

[6] Norma Lee Browning, *The Psychic World of Peter Hurkos* (Garden City, NY: Doubleday, 1970), p. 170. Browning incorrectly asserts that Tenhaeff "was not a professor at the University of Utrecht," but she apparently did not understand that his was an endowed chair and thus paid for by a sponsor.

[7] Jack Harrison Pollack, "Holland's Incredible Mind Readers, Part I," and "Crime Busting with ESP, Part II," *This Week Magazine*, February 19, 1961, pp. 4–5, 7–8, and February 26, pp. 20–21, 23.

[8] Pollack, *Croiset the Clairvoyant*.

[9] Quoted by Hoebens, "Gerard Croiset," p. 18.

[10] In addition to Pollack's discussion of this somewhat farcical episode, see Murray Teigh Bloom, "Is It Judge Crater's Body:" Harper's Monthly, November 1959, pp. 41–47; and Anonymous, "Weird Clue in the Crater Mystery," Life, 47, November 16, 1959, pp. 42–44.

[11] For details on this episode, see Anonymous (UPI), "Clairvoyant Locates Body of Girl," St. Louis Post-Dispatch, May 7, 1976; and Tom Smith, "Famed Psychic Amazingly Pinpoints Location of Missing Girl's Body—After Search by 750 Policemen Fails," National Enquirer, July 20, 1976, p. 44.

[12] Anonymous, "'Killed Because He Knew Too Much': Drugs Crusader Executed," Sunday Sun, January 22, 1978, p. 27; and Anonymous, "Mackay 'Shot in Spine, Buried," The Telegraph [Brisbane], January 21, 1978.

[13] Jack Harrison Pollack, "Croiset Aids FBI in Civil Rights Murders," Fate, February 1966, pp. 74–80.

[14] W. H. C. Tenhaeff, Ontmoetingen met Paragnosten [Encounters with Psychics], (Utrecht: Bijlevald, 1979).

[15] Referred to in Piet Hein Hoebens, "Croiset and Professor Tenhaeff: Discrepancies in Claims of Clairvoyance," The Skeptical Inquirer, 6, 2, 1981–1982, p. 33.

[16] F. Brink, Enige aspecten van de paragnosie in het Neterlandse Strafproces (Utrecht: Drukkerij Storm, 1958). For a summary, see his "Parapsychology and Criminal Investigation," International Criminal Police Review, 134, January 1960, pp. 3–9.

[17] Pollack, Croiset the Clairvoyant, p. 9; and W. H. C. Tenhaeff, "Aid to the Police," Tomorrow, Autumn 1953, pp. 10–18.

[18] C. Pelz, "Herr Croiset, Sie Können nicht hellsehen," Kosmos, 1959/1960.

[19] Th. van Roosmalen, "Ervaringen met Paragnosten en die zich zo noemen," Algemeen Politieblad, 109, 1960, pp. 3–9.

[20] Piet Hein Hoebens, "The Mystery Men from Holland: The Strange Case of Gerard Croiset," Zetetic Scholar, No. 9, 1982, p. 22.

[21] Cf. Piet Hein Hoebens, "Jack Harrison Pollack as an Ear-Witness," Research Report to Marcello Truzzi for the Center for Scientific Anomalies Research's Psychic Sleuths Project, 1982; also see Hoebens, "Mozart of 'Psychic Sleuths.'"

[22] Hoebens, "Mozart of 'Psychic Sleuths,'" p. 26.

[23] Ibid.

[24] Ibid.

[25] Ibid.

[26] Piet Hein Hoebens, " Croiset: Double Dutch," The Unexplained, No. 132, 1983, p. 2633.

[27] Hoebens, "Croiset and Tenhaeff," p. 37.

[28] Ibid., p. 36.

[29] Roy Stemman, "Croiset: The Psychic Detective," The Unexplained, No. 25, 1981, p. 489.

[30] Hoebens, "Mystery Men from Holland," p. 22.

[31] This conference paper is summarized in Tenhaeff's article "Aid to the Police."

[32] Pollack, "Crime Busting with ESP," p. 20.

[33] C. E. M. Hansel, ESP: A Scientific Evaluation (New York: Charles Scribner's Sons, 1966), pp. 197–201.

[34] Tenhaeff quotes what he misrepresented as the full text of Van Maaldrink's supportive letter in his 1957 Dutch-language Beschouwingen over het gebruik van Paragnosten (Utrecht: Bijleveld, 1957).

[35] Quoted by Piet Hein Hoebens, "The Wierden Case," Research Report to Marcello Truzzi for the Center for Scientific Anomalies Research's Psychic Sleuths Project, 1982.

[36] Hoebens, "Mystery Men from Holland."

[37] W. H. C. Tenhaeff, "The Employment of Paragnosts for Police Purposes," *Proceedings of the Parapsychological Institute of the State University of Utrecht*, No. 1, December 1960, pp. 15–32.

[38] Hoebens, "Mystery Men from Holland."

[39] Quoted by Hoebens from van Roosmalen's Dutch article "Ervaringen met Paragnosten en die zich zo noemen," *Algemeen Politieblad*, 109, 1960, pp. 3–9.

[40] *Ibid.* Reported by Hoebens in "Croiset and Tenhaeff," pp. 33–34; also by George Zorab, "Review of Jack Harrison Pollack's *Croiset the Clairvoyant*," *Journal of the Society for Psychical Research*, 43, 1965, pp. 209–212.

[41] See Hans Bender, "Paräkognition im qualitativen Experiment: zur Methodik der 'Platzexperimente' mit dem Sensitiven Gerard Croiset," *Zeitschrift für Parapsychologie und Grenzgebiete der Psychologie*, 1, 1957, pp. 5–36; U. Timm, "Die statistische Analyse qualitativer paragnostischer Experimente," *Zeitschrift für Parapsychologie und Grenzgebiete der psychologie*, 8, 1965, pp. 78–122; and U. Timm, "Neue Experimente mit dem Sensitiven Gerard Croiset," *Zeitschrift für Parapsychologie und Grenzgebiete der Psychologie*, 9, 1966, pp. 30–59. See also Jack Harrison Pollack, "Croiset's Amazing Chair Tests," *Fate*, December 1964, pp. 29–38; and Aristide H. Esser and Lawrence LeShan, "A Transatlantic 'Chair Test,'" *Journal of the Society for Psychical Research*, 45, 1969, pp. 167–171.

[42] Zorab, "Pollack's *Croiset*," p. 211. For additional criticisms, *see* W. Gubisch, *Hellscher Scharlatane Demagogen* (Munich/Basle: Ernst Reinhardt Verlag, 1961); and Pelz, "Herr Croiset."

[43] Zorab, "Pollack's *Croiset*," p. 211.

[44] Piet Hein Hoebens, "Comparison of the 'Denver' Chair Test: A Critical Examination of the Methods of W. H. C. Tenhaeff," *Journal of the Society for Psychical Research*, 53, 1986, pp. 311–320; *see also* the special note following Hoebens's paper: "The Denver Chair Test: Comments from Jule Eisenbud," pp. 321–324.

[45] Hoebens, "Croiset: Double Dutch," p. 2633.

[46] *Ibid.*

[47] W. H. C. Tenhaeff, "Der Paragnost," *Esotera*, September 1980, pp. 816–829.

[48] Hoebens, "Croiset and Tenhaeff," pp. 35–36.

[49] Hoebens, "Mystery Men from Holland," p. 21.

[50] Hoebens, "Croiset and Tenhaeff," p. 37. Hoebens also calls our attention to the fact that Croiset often had "assistants" or "secretaries," such as Dick West, with him, something seldom mentioned by his supporters.

[51] For an example of one of Zorab's investigations into Croiset that produced positive results, *see* George Zorab, "A Case of Clairvoyance?" *Journal of the Society for Psychical Research*, 388, 1956, pp. 244–248.

[52] For example, *see* J. Kistemaker and W. Gorter, "Correspondence: Croiset the Clairvoyant," *Journal of the Society for Psychical Research*, 43, 1966, pp. 331–332.

[53] Cf. Donald Hudson, "Psychic Pinpoints Missing Girls' Graves—From 4,000 Miles Away . . . Using Only Their Photographs," *National Enquirer*, June 30, 1974; and Colin Wilson, "The Long-Distance Psychic Detective," in his *Mysterious Powers* (New York: Danbury Press, 1975), p. 127.

[54] Piers Paul Read, *Alive: the Story of the Andes Survivors* (Philadelphia: J. B. Lippincott, 1974), pp. 348–349.

Notes for Chapter 7

[1] Peter Hurkos, *Psychic* (New York: Popular Library, 1961). Since Hurkos was barely literate, this book actually seems to have been largely produced by his then-friend and attorney V. John Burggraf, who shares the copyright and to whom Hurkos dedicates the book.

[2] Norma Lee Browning, *The Psychic World of Peter Hurkos* (Garden City, NY: Doubleday, 1970).

[3] Norma Lee Browning, *Peter Hurkos: I Have Many Lives* (Garden City, NY: Doubleday, 1976).

[4] This is the date Norma Lee Browning tells us she obtained from the medical authorities, and that Hurkos was in the hospital for twenty-six days. However, Hurkos's own version of these events varies. In his autobiography, he speaks of it happening in June of 1943 (p. 11) and says he was in the hospital for "four long months" (p. 17).

[5] Piet Hein Hoebens, "The Mystery Men from Holland, 1: Peter Hurkos' Dutch Cases," *Zetetic Scholar*, No. 8, 1981, pp. 12–13. *Also see* his "Peter Hurkos—Psychic Superstar," Research Report to Marcello Truzzi for the Center for Scientific Anomalies Research's Psychic Sleuths Project, 1982, p. 2; and "Less Sensitive by Half?" *The Unexplained*, No. 138, 1983, p. 275.

[6] Hurkos, *Psychic*, pp. 29–31.

[7] Hoebens, "Psychic Superstar," p. 3; and "Less Sensitive," pp. 2754–2755.

[8] Hoebens, "Dutch Cases," p. 13.

[9] Browning, *Psychic World*, pp. 56–57.

[10] Hoebens, "Dutch Cases," p. 14. The quote about Goozens refers to Hurkos's description of him in his *Psychic*, p. 26.

[11] Hurkos, *Psychic*, p. 37.

[12] Browning, *Psychic World*, p. 56. Browning's version seems more likely, but Hurkos's earlier claim of having been in Buchenwald does not seem just a simple mistake in the name, since he goes into some detail about his impressions of the death camp in his autobiography.

[13] Milbourne Christopher, *Mediums, Mystics, and the Occult* (New York: Thomas Y. Crowell, 1975), p. 67.

[14] Browning, *Many Lives*, p. 84.

[15] Theodore T. Beck, "Holland's 'Radar-Man,'" *Fate*, November 1953, p. 29.

[16] Hurkos, *Psychic*, p. 57.

[17] John Kobler, "Man with the X-Ray Mind," *True*, June 1956, p. 76.

[18] Jess Stearn, *The Door to the Future* (New York: Macfadden Bartell, 1964), p. 215.

[19] Hurkos, *Psychic*, pp. 46–48.

[20] Hoebens, "Dutch Cases," p. 15.

[21] Hoebens, "Psychic Superstar," p. 2756.

[22] *Ibid.*, pp. 2756–2757. Hurkos's own version of the events appears in his *Psychic*, pp. 64–67. A similar version of this tale in which a few more details are given is in Kobler, "X-Ray Mind," pp. 37, 73.

[23] Hoebens, "Dutch Cases," p. 17.

[24] Hurkos, *Psychic*, p. 76. It was around this time that rumors circulated that Hitler was alive and in Argentina. Historians today agree that Hitler died in April 1945.

[25] *Ibid.*

[26] Nat Freedland, *The Occult Explosion* (New Your: G. P. Putnam's Sons, 1972), p. 194.

[27] Hoebens, "Psychic Superstar," p. 2756. Hurkos also directly mentions that he received a papal commendation, this time apparently unconnected with any priest's murder, however, but "for some cases in which I had helped people" (*Psychic*, p. 72). That story is probably false for the same reasons.

[28] Hurkos, *Psychic*, pp. 90–93.

[29] Hoebens, "Dutch Cases," p. 14.

[30] Cited by Hoebens, *ibid.*, as in *De Telegraaf*, August 23, 1958.

[31] Hurkos, *Psychic*, p. 48.

[32] Hoebens, "Dutch Cases," p. 12.

[33] Browning, *Psychic World*, p. 71.

[34] Hurkos, *Psychic*, p. 107.

[35] Browning, *Psychic World*, p. 22.

[36] For a good description of some of his performance disasters by a fellow performer, see the chapter "Peter Hurkos—Psychic Sleuth" in Christopher, *Mediums, Mystics*, pp. 66–76.

[37] Hurkos, *Psychic*, p. 127.

[38] Stearn, *Door to Future*, p. 218; and Browning, *Psychic World*, p. 81.

[39] Andrija Puharich, *The Sacred Mushroom* (Garden City, NY: Doubleday, 1959).

[40] Andrija Puharich, *Beyond Telepathy* (Garden City, NY: Doubleday, 1962).

[41] Browning, *Psychic World*, p. 72.

[42] James G. Bolen, "Interview: Peter Hurkos," *Psychic*, March–April 1970, p. 6.

[43] Hurkos, *Psychic*, p. 106.

[44] Hoebens, "Less Sensitive," p. 2755.

[45] Browning, *Psychic World*, p. 72.

[46] *Parapsychology Bulletin*, No. 53, May 1960, p. 3.

[47] Stearn, *Door to Future*, p. 211.

[48] Charles T. Tart and Jeffrey Smith, "Two Token Object Studies with Peter Hurkos," *Journal of the American Society for Psychical Research*, 62, 1968, pp. 143–157.

[49] Kobler, "X-Ray Mind." Those in the narrower occult-oriented community had already read of him three years before in *Fate* magazine in the article by T. Beck, "'Radar-Man.'" The earliest U.S. article about Hurkos we have located appeared in *Fate* a few months before that as a short filler piece about Hurkos's allegedly helping a Monsieur Fernand Dubois in 1952 in Lille, France, by psychically recovering gold Dubois had buried but which had been removed. *See* Harold T. Wilkins, "Clairvoyant Recovers Lost Gold," *Fate*, July 1953, p. 25.

[50] Kobler, "X-Ray Mind," p. 73.

[51] Norma Lee Browning, "The Strange Powers of Peter Hurkos," *Chicago Sunday Tribune Magazine*, February 19, 1961, p. 18. Oddly, this article on Hurkos appeared the same Sunday that the first article on Croiset appeared in the competing Sunday supplement *This Week*.

[52] Ronald A. Schwartz, "Sleight of Tongue," *The Skeptical Inquirer*, 3, Fall 1978, pp. 47–75.

[53] Hurkos, *Psychic*, pp. 133–134.

[54] Browning, *Psychic World*, pp. 84–85.

[55] For discussions of this case, *see* S. H. Posinsky, "Communication—The Case of John Tarmon: Telepathy and the Law," *The Psychiatric Quarterly*, 35, 1, January 1961, pp. 165–166; Walter J. McGraw, "Where Peter Hurkos Failed," in Martin Ebon, ed., *The Satan Trap: Dangers of the Occult* (Garden City, NY: Doubleday & Co., 1976), pp. 13–72; and Stearn, *Door to Future*.

[56] Quoted in Stearn, *Door to Future*, p. 201.

[57] American Civil Liberties Union, *40th Annual Report* (New York, 1960), pp. 57–58. *See also* Curtis Fuller, "Peter Hurkos and the Jackson Family Murders," *Fate*, October 1960, pp. 49–54 [also reprinted in *The Best of Fate: Murder Most Eerie; Homicide and the Paranormal* (Norfolk, VA: Donning, 1982), pp. 175–181].

[58] Browning, *Psychic World*, p. 87.

[59] McGraw, "Where Hurkos Failed," p. 17.

[60] Quoted in Stearn, *Door to Future*, p. 202.

[61] McGraw tells us that Dr. Riesenman said Hurkos spoke of three men, the third being someone called "Mike." *See* McGraw, "Where Hurkos Failed," p. 17.

[62] Stearn, *Door to Future*, p. 202.

[63] Browning, *Psychic World*, p. 90.

[64] Posinsky, "John Tarmon," p. 165.

[65] Browning, *Psychic World*, p. 93.

[66] Hurkos, *Psychic*, p. 155.

[67] Christopher, *Mediums, Mystics*, p. 71.

[68] Browning, *Many Lives*, p. 89.

[69] Gerold Frank, *The Boston Strangler* (New York: New American Library, 1966), p. 90.

[70] Gerold Frank gave him the pseudonym "Thomas O'Brien," and that name has been reused in much of the other writings about this case.

[71] "Boston: Hunt for the Strangler," *Time*, February 24, 1964, p. 31.

[72] This is the version from Gerold Frank. Hurkos told Norma Lee Browning that he was on his way to start living in California right after his divorce came through from Maria.

[73] Paul Mandel, "How a Seer Helps Stalk a Boston Strangler," *Life*, 56, March 6, 1964, p. 50.

[74] According to Christopher, (*Mediums, Mystics*, p. 73), Hurkos was acquitted. Despite this, Hurkos was finally convicted but was not imprisoned, reportedly paying a fine of $1,000. *See*: Anonymous, "Hurkos Guilty, Posed as FBI Man," *New York Herald Tribune*, Nov. 15, 1964; and James Randi, *Flim Flam* (New York: Lippincott and Crowell, 1980), p. 272.

[75] Reasonable questions still exist about this case, and DeSalvo may actually not have been telling the truth in his confession, but there are many inconsistencies in Hurkos's story about what he actually said, and some of Hurkos's apologists have tried to indicate that Hurkos's descriptions of the killer actually fit DeSalvo better than they did the salesman.

[76] Quoted in Arnold Rosenfeld, "Peter Hurkos: Showman or Psychic?" *Detroit Free Press*, July 6, 1989, p. 10A.

[77] Browning, *Psychic World*, p. 135.

[78] Walker Lundy, "Dutch Seer Arrives to Trace Six Slayings," *Detroit Free Press*, July 22, 1969, p. 3A; and Dennis Chase, "Hurkos Begins Slayings Probe," *Ann Arbor News*, July 22, 1969, p. 15.

[79] An excellent overview of this case is Edward Keyes, *The Michigan Murders* (New York: Pocket Books, 1976). *See* Chapter 12 for some otherwise unreported details on Hurkos's involvement.

[80] "Mystic Agrees to Probe Six Slayings at a Cut Rate," *Detroit Free Press*, July 16, 1969, p. 3A; and "Seer Wants Cooperation," *Ann Arbor News*, July 15, 1969, p. 27. According to Keyes (*Michigan Murders*, p. 175), Hurkos originally asked the citizens' committee for $5,000 plus expenses.

[81] Arnold Rosenfeld, ". . . And a Man Who Claims He Can Describe the Killer," *Detroit Free Press*, July 6, 1969, p. 10A.

[82] Lundy, "Six Slayings."

[83] "Mystic Works Two Hours on Killings, Awes Police," *Detroit Free Press*, July 23, 1969, p. 3A.

[84] "Mystic Vibrating, But No Help Yet," *Detroit Free Press*, July 24, 1969, p. 6A.

[85] "Hurkos Probe at an Impasse," *Ann Arbor News*, July 25, 1969, p. 15.

[86] Chase, "Slayings Probe."

[87] Dennis Chase, "Identification of Suspect Is Claimed for Hurkos," *Ann Arbor News*, July 24, 1969, p. 25.

[88] "Hurkos Probe Impasse"; and Keyes, *Michigan Murders*, p. 185.

[89] "Mystic Vibrating," p. 6A.

[90] Keyes, *Michigan Murders*, p. 197.

[91] *Ibid.*, p. 225.

[92] Walker Lundy, "Mystic Huffs Off After Sheriff's Snub," *Detroit Free Press*, July 28, 1969, p. 4B.

[93] Keyes, *Michigan Murders*, p. 205.

[94] Browning, *Many Lives*, pp. 11–12.

[95] Vincent Bugliosi with Curt Gentry, *Helter Skelter* (New York: Bantam Books, 1975), p. 76.

[96] *Ibid.*, p. 212.

[97] Quoted in Mary Ann Galante, "Psychics: Lawyers Using Seers to Help Select Juries and Find Missing Children," *National Law Journal*, January 27, 1986, p. 32.

[98] Browning, *Many Lives*, p. 209.

[99] *Ibid.*, p. 208.

[100] Bugliosi with Gentry, *Helter Skelter*, p. 76.

[101] Browning, *Many Lives*, p. 223.

[102] Stearn, *Door to Future*, p. 223.

[103] Telephone conversation with C. B. Scott Jones, February 15, 1990.

[104] Alexander wrote about this episode in a June 1988 letter to the *Los Angeles Times*, which is mostly quoted in Kendrick Frazier, "Hurkos, in Death as in Life, He Encourages Idea He's Psychic," *The Skeptical Inquirer*, 13, Winter 1989, pp. 116, 118.

[105] Letter to Marcello Truzzi from Chief Fetzer dated May 15, 1981. Notes from telephone conversation from call to Fetzer dated May 27, 1981.

[106] This Geraldo Rivera show was aired on October 2, 1987.

[107] The quote from President and Mrs. Reagan on Hurkos's brochure was: "We want you to know how deeply grateful we are . . . your support and encouragement mean so much to us, and we will do our best to keep faith with you." The quote from President Johnson said: "Thank you for your help. It has meant much to me. I am grateful."

Notes on Chapter 8

[1] Media coverage of this hoax was particularly extensive. For general surveys, *see* D. Scott Rogo, "The Psychic With 20/20 Hindsight," *Fate*, August 1981, pp. 70–75; and Kendrick Frazier and James Randi, "News and Comments: Predictions After the Fact: Lessons of the Tamara Rand Hoax," *The Skeptical Inquirer*, February 1981, pp. 4–7.

[2] Quoted in Committee for the Scientific Investigation of Claims of the Paranormal [CSICOP], "U.S. Overrun by Psychic Charlatans: Skeptical Group to Discuss 'Psychic Detectives' at Press Conference in Atlanta," Press Release, Buffalo, NY, December 9, 1982, pp. 2–3.

[3] On these excesses, see the essays by Ray Hyman, "Pathological Science: Towards a Proper Diagnosis and Remedy," *Zetetic Scholar*, No. 6, 1980, pp. 31–39; and "Proper Criticism," *Skeptical Briefs*, 3, May 1987, pp. 4–5. Both are reprinted in Ray Hyman, *The Elusive Quarry: A Scientific Appraisal of Psychical Research* (Buffalo, NY: Prometheus Books, 1989), pp. 243–250, 437–441.

[4] On the distinction between nonbelief and disbelief, *see* W. V. O. Quine and J. S. Ullian, *The Web of Belief* (New York: Random House, 1978), p. 12. *Also see* Marcello Truzzi, "On Pseudo-Skepticism," *Zetetic Scholar*, Nos. 12/13, 1987, pp. 3–4.

[5] Paul Kurtz and Andrea Szalanski, "'Psychic Detectives,'" *Miami Herald*, April 28, 1984, p. 4E. *See also* CSICOP, "Psychic Charlatans," and CSICOP, "CSICOP Blasts Police Department for Use of Psychic Detectives," Press Release, Buffalo, NY, December 10, 1982.

[6] *See* Charles Sanders Peirce, "The First Rule of Reason," in C. Hartshorne and P. Weiss, eds., *Collected Papers of Charles Sanders Peirce* (Cambridge, MA: Harvard University Press, 1966), p. 56.

[7] For an excellent review of the fraud issue within parapsychology, *see* George P. Hansen, "Deception by Subjects in Psi Research," *Journal of the American Society for Psychical Research*, 84, 1990, pp. 25–80. Much of this discussion also seems to presume the relative absence of fraud in other areas of science, something recent history of science brings into serious question. *See* William Broad and Nicholas Wade, *Betrayers of the Truth: Fraud and Deceit in the Halls of Science* (New York: Simon and Schuster, 1982); and Alexander Kohn, *False Prophets: Fraud and Error in Science and Medicine* (New York: Basil Blackwell, 1986).

[8] Leonard Zusne and Warren H. Jones, *Anomalistic Psychology: A Study of Extraordinary Phenomena of Behavior and Experience* (New York: Lawrence Erlbaum Associates, 1982), p. 7.

[9] In a recent overview of this issue in the sciences, it was stated flatly: "There is no criterion of impossibility, no final test." Philip J. Davis and David Park, eds., *No Way: The Nature of the Impossible* (New York: W. H. Freeman and Co., 1987), p. xvi.

[10] Mario Bunge, "Comments on 'Pathological Science,'" *Zetetic Scholar*, No. 6, 1980, p. 46; reprinted in Hyman, *Elusive Quarry*, p. 258.

[11] For example, one hard-line critic of parapsychology speaks of psychics' "laws of denial" which he asserts make some psi claims impossible. Milton A. Rothman, *A Physicist's Guide to Skepticism* (Buffalo, NY: Prometheus Books, 1988), especially "Laws of Denial: Precision," pp. 137–144.

[12] For example, Rothman's position is in marked contrast with that of the current editor of *The Skeptical Inquirer*, who acknowledged the principle of Hamlet when he wrote of "the tentative nature of all scientific knowledge and the need for humility about all current understanding." Kendrick Frazier, "The 'Whole Earth' Review of the Fringe," *The Skeptical Inquirer*, Winter 1986–1987, p. 198. Rothman explicitly rejects Frazier's position as an overstatement. Rothman, *Guide to Skepticism*, p. 137.

[13] On this subject, *see* Thomas S. Kuhn, *The Essential Tension* (Chicago: University of Chicago Press, 1977). Note, too, that by following both these principles,

science can avoid what we described in Chapter 3 as the Type I error (by following Laplace's dictum) and the Type II error (by following Hamlet's).

[14] Named after William of Ockham (frequently misspelled "Occam"), an influential fourteenth-century British philosopher, Occam's Razor is often modernized as "Entities are not to be multiplied without necessity." Modern philosophy indicates that what constitutes "simpler" may actually be a very complex issue. *See* Mario Bunge, *The Myth of Simplicity* (Englewood Cliffs, NJ: Prentice-Hall, 1963).

[15] Re authenticity versus validity, *see* Richard de Mille, "Explicating Anomalistic Anthropology with Help from Castaneda," *Zetetic Scholar*, Nos. 3/4, 1979, pp. 69–70. Though usually thought to be a relatively simple matter, the question of what constitutes validity is actually quite complex and multidimensional. *See* David Brinberg and Joseph E. McGrath, *Validity and the Research Process* (Beverly Hills, CA: Sage Publications, 1985).

[16] Kendrick Frazier, "How to Cover 'Psychics' and the Paranormal," *Bulletin of the American Society of Newspaper Editors*, April 1982, p. 18. Though skeptics often picture psychics as inauthentic con artists, according to the scientific investigations we have studied, the reality is far more complex, with most psychic readers believing in their abilities and viewing themselves as helpful quasi-therapists for their clients. For some of the available ethnographic literature, *see* Geri-Ann Galanti, *The Psychic Reader as Shaman and Psychotherapist: The Interface Between Clients' and Practitioners' Belief Systems in Los Angeles*, doctoral dissertation, Department of Anthropology, University of California, Los Angeles, 1981; Funmilayo M. Jones, *Strategies and Techniques Used in Occasion Maintenance: An Examination of Reader-Client Relationships in a Tearoom*, doctoral dissertation, Department of Sociology, Boston University Graduate School, 1981; Brain Rusted, "'The Palm at the End of the Mind,' or Narrative Fortune Telling as Urban Folk Therapy," *New York Folklore*, 10, 1/2, 1984, pp. 21–38; John Heeren and Marylee Mason, "Talk about Visions: Spiritual Readings as Deviant Work," *Deviant Behavior*, 2, 1981, pp. 167–186; and David Lester, "Astrologers and Psychics as Therapists," *American Journal of Psychotherapy*, 36, 1, 1982, pp. 56–66. For studies of inauthentic psychic readers, *see* Charlotte R. Tatro, "Cross My Palm With Silver: Fortunetelling as an Occupational Way of Life," in Clifton D. Bryant, ed., *Deviant Behavior: Organizational and Occupational Bases* (Chicago: Rand McNally, 1974), pp. 286–299; and Jacqueline Boles, Phillip Davis, and Charlotte Tatro, "False Pretense and Deviant Exploitation: Fortunetelling as a Con," *Deviant Behavior*, 4, 1983, pp. 375–394.

[17] Persi Diaconis and Frederick Mosteller, "Methods for Studying Coincidences," *Journal of the American Statistical Association*, 84, 1989, pp. 853–861. A non-technical summary of this study is Gina Kolata, "1-in-a-Trillion Coincidence, You Say? Not Really, Experts Find," *New York Times*, February 27, 1990, pp. B5, B8. *Also see* Ruma Falk, "On Coincidences," *The Skeptical Inquirer*, Winter 1981–1982, pp. 18–31. Both these papers define "coincidence" as meaningful and surprising cases of events found together. We are using the term in the standard dictionary manner of any events found together apparently by chance, whether or not surprising.

[18] W. Clement Stone and Norma Lee Browning, *The Other Side of the Mind* (New York: Paperback Library, 1967), p. 103.

[19] Melvin Harris, *Investigating the Unexplained* (Buffalo, NY: Prometheus Books, 1986), p. 36.

[20] J. Kenneth Evans, "Psychic's Success Impresses Police," *Pittsburgh Post Gazette*, February 5, 1988.

[21] Interview with Corporal Willis Greenaway, September 7, 1989.

[22] Piet Hein Hoebens, with Marcello Truzzi, "Reflections on Psychic Sleuths," in Paul Kurtz, ed., *A Skeptic's Handbook of Parapsychology* (Buffalo, NY: Prometheus Books, 1985), p. 640.

[23] Frances Martin, "Do Psychics Help Police?" *Charlottesville Observer*, August 15–21, 1985.

[24] Joseph R. Kozenczak and Karen M. Henrikson, "Still Beyond Belief," *Policing*, Vol. 5, No. 2, p. 145.

[25] Interview with Dr. Martin Reiser, July 14, 1989.

[26] Janny Scott, "Police Psychic: Visions of Crime?" *Sunday Record* [Northern New Jersey], June 24, 1984, p. A–22.

[27] *Ibid*.

[28] Dorothy Allison and Scott Jacobson, *Dorothy Allison: A Psychic's Story* (New York: Jove Publications, 1980).

[29] Quoted in Scott, "Police Psychic," p. A–23.

[30] D. H. Rawcliffe, *Illusions and Delusions of the Supernatural and the Occult* [originally *Psychology of the Occult*] (New York: Dover, no date indicated [originally 1959]), p. 371.

[31] *See* Ray Hyman's exemplary articles, "'Cold Reading': How to Convince Strangers That You Know All About Them," *The Zetetic* [later renamed *The Skeptical Inquirer*], No. 1, Spring–Summer 1977, pp. 18–37; and "The Psychic Reading," in T. A. Sebeok and R. Rosenthal, eds., *The Clever Hans Phenomenon: Communication with Horses, Whales, Apes and People* (New York: New York Academy of Sciences, 1981), pp. 169–181. Both are reprinted in Hyman, *Elusive Quarry*, pp. 402–419, 424–436. For an excellent but more technical study, *see* Edna Aphek and Yishai Tobin, *The Semiotics of Fortune-Telling* (Philadelphia, PA: John Benjamins, 1989).

[32] For example, *see* D. H. Dickson and I. W. Kelly, "The 'Barnum Effect' in Personality Assessment: A Review of the Literature," *Psychological Bulletin*, 57, 1985, pp. 367–382; and Adrian Furnham and Sandra Schofield, "Accepting Personality Test Feedback: A Review of the Barnum Effect," *Current Psychological Research and Reviews*, 6, 2, 1987, pp. 162–178.

[33] *See* Ricky Jay, *Learned Pigs & Fireproof Women* (New York: Villard Books, 1986).

[34] Oskar Pfungst (edited by Robert Rosenthal), *Clever Hans: The Horse of Mr. Van Osten* (New York: Holt, Rinehart and Winston, 1965). *Also see* Marcello Truzzi, "Reflections on Paranormal Communication: A Zetetic Perspective," in Sebeok and Rosenthal, *Clever Hans Phenomenon*, pp. 297–309.

[35] The term was first introduced by psychologist Donald G. Paterson in an unpublished paper ("Character Reading at Sight of Mr. X According to the System of Mr. P. T. Barnum"), cited by his colleague Paul Meehl in "Wanted—A Good Cookbook," *American Psychologist*, 11, 1956, p. 266. *Also see* Dickson and Kelly, "'Barnum Effect'"; Furnham and Schofield, "Personality Test Feedback"; and, for a popular account, C. R. Snyder and Randee Jae Shenkel, "Astrologers, Handwriting Analysts and Sometimes Psychologists Use . . . the P. T. Barnum Effect," *Psychology Today*, March 1975, pp. 52–54. Contrary to what might be expected, there seems to be no connection between being fooled by the Barnum Effect and either general credulity or belief in the paranormal. *See* Lionel Standing and Gregory Keays, "Do the Barnum Effect and Paranormal Belief Involve a General Gullibility Factor?" *Psychological Reports*, 61, 1987, pp. 435–438.

[36] A very substantial literature on cold reading exists in the conjuring literature mostly available only through magic dealers. A great deal of this consists of elaborate stock spiels, and it is widely believed among magicians that some of the best customers for these books (with titles like *How to Answer Questions* and *Secrets of a Psychic Medium*) include private psychic readers outside the conjuring community.

[37] Paul Kurtz and Andrea Szalanski, "'Psychic Detectives,'" *Miami Herald*, April 28, 1984, p. 4E.

[38] Reported in Daniel Goleman, "As a Therapist, Freud Fell Short, Scholars Find," *New York Times*, March 6, 1990, p. B9. Details are in Patrick Mahony, *Freud and the Rat Man* (New Haven, CT: Yale University Press, 1986). It is worth noting that many psychic and spiritualist readers view themselves as being "poor people's psychiatrists."

[39] *See* Marcello Truzzi, "Sherlock Holmes: Applied Social Psychologist," in M. Truzzi, ed., *The Humanities as Sociology* (Columbus, OH: Charles E. Merrill Publishing Co., 1973), pp. 93–126.

[40] *See* Eugene J. Webb et al., *Unobtrusive Measures: Nonreactive Research in the Social Sciences* (Chicago: Rand McNally, 1966).

[41] Quoted in Glen Warchol, "Psychic Investigators," *Twin City Reader*, November 29–December 5, 1989, p. 12.

[42] Hoebens with Truzzi, "Psychic Sleuths," p. 634. Very similar observations are made in Jim Lippard, "Psychic Detectives," *Phoenix Skeptics News*, May/June 1988, pp. 4–7.

[43] Quoted in Edmund Mahony, "Psychics' Aid Rarely Helps Solve Crimes," *Hartford Courant*, November 4, 1979.

[44] Quoted in Martin Reiser, Louise Ludwig, Susan Saxe, and Clare Wagner, "An Evaluation of the Use of Psychics in the Investigation of Major Crimes," *Journal of Police Science and Administration*, 7, 1, 1979, p. 19.

[45] Kurtz and Szalanski, "'Psychic Detectives,'" p. 4E.

[46] Ward Lucas, "Police Use of Psychics: A Waste of Resources and Tax Money," *Campus Law Enforcement Journal*, July–August 1985, p. 16. A related observation was made by James Randi, who stated that "conversations with police officials . . . revealed that 'psychics' give them literally hundreds of 'facts' about each case, some of which are bound to 'fit'—but none of which lead to solutions." Quoted in Committee for Scientific Investigation of Claims of the Paranormal, "U.S. Overrun by Psychic Charlatans: Skeptical Group to Discuss 'Psychic Detectives' at Press Conference," Press Release, Buffalo, NY, December 9, 1982. p. 2.

[47] Hoebens with Truzzi, "Psychic Sleuths," pp. 640–641.

[48] Lucas, "Police Use of Psychics," p. 16. On the general psychology of the self-fulfilling prediction, *see* Russell A. Jones, *Self-Fulfilling Prophecies: Social, Psychological and Physiological Effects of Expectancies* (New York: Lawrence Erlbaum Associates, 1977).

[49] Hoebens with Truzzi, "Psychic Sleuths," p. 641.

[50] *See* Bernard Holland, "A Record Reader Sees What Others Only Hear," *New York Times*, November 18, 1981, p. 23; Anonymous, "Skeptical Eye: A Record Claim," *Discover*, January 1982, pp. 10–11; and Alex Evans, "The Man Who Reads Phonograph Records," *Fate*, June 1982, pp. 71–73.

[51] Hoebens with Truzzi, "Psychic Sleuths," p. 642.

[52] Quoted by Keith Anderson, "Dallas' Psychic Detectives," *Dallas Morning News*, April 29, 1984, p. 2F.

[53] L. K. Summers, book review of *Psychic Criminology, Law and Order,* November 1982, p. 71.

[54] Piet Hein Hoebens, "The Mystery Men From Holland, 3: The Man Whose Passport Says Clairvoyant," *Zetetic Scholar,* No. 10, 1982, pp. 7–16.

[55] M. B. Dykshoorn, as told to R. H. Felton, *My Passport Says Clairvoyant* (New York: Hawthorn, 1974). Dr. Dykshoorn told me his doctorate is an honorary one in civil law bestowed upon him by New York City's Catholic University in 1987.

[56] *Ibid.,* p. 16.

[57] Hoebens, "The Man Whose Passport," p. 9.

[58] Dykshoorn, "My Passport," p. 70. Note that Dykshoorn carefully prefaces his assertion with "I believe that . . ." In fairness to him, it is possible that he does, but those who read his book are clearly meant to believe it is a fact and not just Dykshoorn's opinion.

[59] Hoebens, "The Man Whose Passport," p. 10.

[60] Ted L. Gunderson with Roger McGovern, *How to Locate Anyone Anywhere Without Leaving Home* (New York: E. P. Dutton, 1989); Louis J. Rose, *How to Investigate Your Friends and Enemies* (St. Louis, MO: Albion Press, 1981); and Michael J. Zoglio, *Tracing Missing Persons: A Professional's Guide to Techniques and Resources* (Doylestown, PA: Tower Hill Press, 1980).

[61] Examples include: Lee Lapin, *How to Get Anything on Anybody* (San Francisco, CA: Auburn Wolfe Publishing, 1983); Ralph D. Thomas, *How to Find Anyone Anywhere* (Boulder, CO: Paladin Press, 1983); Scott French and Lee Lapin, *Ninja 1990: How to Get Anything on Anybody, 2* (Foster City, CA: Crocker-Edwards Publishing, 1985); Bill Pryor, *Secret Agent,* Vol. 1 (Fountain Valley, CA: Eden Press, 1986); Ronald G. Eriksen, II, *How to Find Missing Persons: A Handbook for Investigators* (Port Townsend, WA: Loompanics Unlimited, 1982); and John D. McCann, *Find 'Em Fast: A Private Investigator's Workbook* (Boulder, CO: Paladin Press, 1984).

[62] Duke McCoy, *How to Organize and Manage Your Own Religious Cult: A Psycho-Political Primer* (Port Townsend, WA: Loompanics Unlimited, 1980).

[63] These books are generally available only through magic-supply houses like Calgary's Micky Hades Enterprises, which continues to reprint many of the early works once put out by Nelson Enterprises, a firm that largely catered to the pseudo-psychic marketplace. Two of the most interesting such volumes are *Confessions of a Psychic: The Secret Notebooks of Uriah Fuller* and *Further Confessions of a Psychic,* put out by magician-publisher Karl Fulves in 1975 and 1980 and pseudonymously authored by a magician better known as a prominent critic of psychic claims. An enlightening look at some rogue pseudo-psychics can be found in M. Lamar Keene, as told to Allen Spraggett, *The Psychic Mafia* (New York: Dell Publishing Co., 1976).

[64] Ken Grayzel, "Psychic Detectives," manuscript, March 1978, p. 5. made available through the courtesy of James Randi, archives of the Psychic Sleuths Project, Center for Scientific Anomalies Research.

[65] *See* Will Goldston, "The Cornells and Their Ghastly Publicity Stunt," in his *Sensational Tales of Mystery Men* (New York: Magico Magazine, 1981 reprint), pp. 39–41. Also mentioned in Fred Archer, *Ghost Writer* (London: W. H. Allen, 1966), p. 102.

[66] *See* Hoebens with Truzzi, "Psychic Sleuths," p. 641.

[67] Letter from Martin Ebon to Marcello Truzzi, January 9, 1980.

[68] For a comprehensive look at the problems, *see* John T. Noonan, Jr., *Bribes* (New York: Macmillan Publishing Co., 1984).

[69] Re these allegations against Allison, *see* Mary Jo Patterson, "Dorothy Allison: The Extrasensory Detective," *Police*, March 1981, p. 49.

Notes for Chapter 9

[1] Interview with Lieutenant Marvin Goss, August 25, 1989.
[2] William Schofield, *Psychotherapy: The Purchase of Friendship* (New Brunswick, NJ: Transaction Publications, 1986 edition).
[3] Dixie Yeterian, *Casebook of a Psychic Detective* (New York: Stein and Day, 1982), p. 192.
[4] Gustav Jahoda, *The Psychology of Superstition* (New York: Jason Aronson, 1974), p. 133. A very similar situation exists in another area of applied psi: dowsing. Even if the dowser fails to find any water, his clients usually are glad they used him. Cf. Evon Z. Vogt and Ray Hyman, *Water Witching USA*, 2d ed. (Chicago: University of Chicago, 1979), pp. 190–220. Interestingly, this need for information may be active even at the animal level. In a rat study by W. F. Prokasy ["The Acquisition of Observing Responses in the Absence of Differential External Reinforcement," *Journal of Comparative Physiological Psychology*, 49, 1956, pp. 131–134], a maze was set up that led to two goal boxes. In either box, the chance of food was even, but on one path, information was consistently provided whether there was food in the box or not. After a period of time, the rats developed a preference for the passage that provided information, even though their chances of obtaining food were no greater than in the other half of the maze.
[5] *See* George C. Homans, "Anxiety and Ritual: The Theories of Malinowski and Radcliffe-Brown," *American Anthropologist*, 43, 1941, 2, Part 2, pp. 104–172.
[6] Peter K. Manning, *Police Work: The Social Organization of Policing* (Cambridge, MA: MIT Press, 1977), Chap. 9: "Uncertainty, Sanctity, and Myth: Police work as Ritual," pp. 300–335.
[7] *Ibid.*, p. 300.
[8] Peter W. Greenwood, Jan M. Chaiken, Joan Petersilia, et al., *The Criminal Investigation Process* (Lexington, MA: D.C. Heath, 1977), p. 43.
[9] *Ibid.*, pp. 42–43.
[10] David E. Kerr, "Investigation of the Homicide Scene," in Samuel R. Gerber and Oliver Schroeder, Jr., eds., *Criminal Investigation and Interrogation* (Cincinnati, OH: W. H. Anderson, 1972), p. 159.
[11] Interview with Sergeant David Frost, August 3, 1989.
[12] Quoted in Steven N. Czetli, "Nancy Anderson: Psychic Sleuth," *Your Virginia State Trooper*, Spring 1982, p. 25.
[13] Yeterian, *Psychic Detective*, pp. 79–80.
[14] William B. Sanders, *Detective Work: A Study of Criminal Investigations* (New York: Free Press, 1977), p. 23.
[15] This distinction between "data" and "information" follows that found in William R. Burnham, "Modern Decision Theory and Corrections," in Don M. Gottfredson, ed., *Decision Making in the Criminal Justice System: Reviews and Essays* (Rockville, MD: National Institute of Mental Health, 1975), pp. 94–95.
[16] Sanders, *Detective Work*, p. 27.
[17] Kerr, "Homicide Scene," p. 160.

[18] Whitney S. Hibbard and Raymond W. Worring, *Psychic Criminology: An Operations Manual for Using Psychics* (Springfield, IL: Charles C. Thomas, 1981), p. 4.

[19] A judge asked for a warrant based on a psychic's vision may not grant it on those grounds but may be influenced enough to grant it on weaker but other legally permissible grounds. Several years ago, one judge created a huge public outcry when he let it be known that he used astrology to help him decide the severity of his sentencings.

[20] On this issue of thresholds, *see* Laurent Beauregard, "Skepticism, Science, and the Paranormal," *Zetetic Scholar*, No. 1, 1978, pp. 3–10; and the rebuttal by Ray Hyman, "Believers Versus Skeptics: Comments on Laurent Beauregard's Paper," *Zetetic Scholar*, No. 2, 1978, pp. 113–119.

[21] Though some humanistic social scientists reject the idea of an objective and "value-free" science, that is not the position of most positivists, and they are the major critics of psi. For the extreme positivist, validity of psi must be the exclusive issue here.

[22] There is a surprising paucity of criminological studies on private investigators in the United States. *See* T. Becker, "The Place of Private Police in Society: An Area of Research for the Social Sciences," *Social Problems*, 21, 1974, pp. 438–453. Some related materials can be found in Clifford D. Shearing and Philip C. Stenning, eds., *Private Policing* (Beverly Hills, CA: Sage Publications, 1987). On private investigators in Great Britain, however, *see* Hilary Draper, *Private Police* (New York: Penguin Books, 1978); and Nigel South, "Private Eyes: Private Spies?" in his *Policing for Profit: The Private Security Sector* (Newbury Park, CA: Sage Publications, 1988).

[23] Marvin Scott, "She Finds Lost People," *Parade*, December 24, 1989, pp. 14–15. *See also* Marilyn Greene and Gary Provost, *Finder: The True Story of a Private Investigator (New York: Crown Publishers, 1988).*

[24] Scott, *Lost People* p. 14.

[25] The literature on detection of deception from nonverbal clues is immense and spans the literatures of both social psychology and communications research. A leading work is Paul Ekman's *Telling Lies: Clues to Deceit in the Marketplace, Politics, and Marriage* (New York: W. W. Norton, 1985). A good review of the literature can be found in Bella M. DePaulo, J. I. Stone, and G. D. Lassiter, "Deceiving and Detecting Deceit," in Barry R. Schlenker, ed., *The Self and Social Life* (New York: McGraw-Hill Book Co., 1985), pp. 323–370. Contrary to what might be expected, there seems to be little relationship between sensitivity to nonverbal behavior and the ability to spot lies. *See* Glenn E. Littlepage, R. McKinnie, and M. A. Pineault, "Relationship Between Nonverbal Sensitivities and Detection of Deception," *Perceptual and Motor Skills*, 57, 1983, pp. 651–657.

[26] Scott, "Lost People," p. 14.

[27] This interpretation is strengthened when we consider details of some of her cases. For example, when she found a lost deer hunter in about six hours after the Civil Air Patrol had unsuccessfully searched for him for four days, she claimed her most valuable tool was her trained "air-scent" dogs. Unlike most dogs who followed a scent on the ground, where there are footprints, she told Scott ("Lost People," pp. 14–15) that her German shepherds "follow a scent deposit left in the air by human beings—a scent not discernible to people." Surely the claim that a person's scent will stay stable in the air for a period of four days is itself extraordinary enough that scientists might label any such scent itself quite paranormal.

[28] Stephen G. Michaud, "The F.B.I.'s New Psyche Squad," *New York Times Magazine*, October 26, 1986, p. 40.

[29] *Ibid.*, p. 42.

[30] *Ibid.*, p. 50.

[31] On the psychology of intuition, *see* Malcolm R. Westcott, *Toward a Contemporary Psychology of Intuition: A Historical, Theoretical and Empirical Inquiry* (New York: Holt, Rinehart and Winston, 1968); and Tony Bastick, *Intuition: How We Think and Act* (New York: John Wiley and Sons, 1982).

[32] Joseph J. Cocozza and Henry J. Steadman, "Prediction in Psychiatry: An Example of Misplaced Confidence in Experts," *Social Problems*, 25, 3, 1978, p. 275. For an excellent general critical survey of the failures of modern mental science, *see* Martin L. Gross, *The Psychological Society* (New York: Random House, 1978).

[33] David Faust and Jay Ziskin, "The Expert Witness in Psychology and Psychiatry," *Science*, July 1, 1988, p. 31. On this general debate, *see* Daniel Goleman, "Psychologists' Expert Testimony Called Unscientific," *New York Times*, October 11, 1988, pp. 19, 23; and John Bales, "Expert Witness Controversy Continues," [American Psychological Association's] *Monitor*, January 1989, p. 21. There is some indication that actuarial predictions made here are better than clinical ones. The Quantico profilers seem aware of this and have based their work more on actuarial data than clinical interpretations. Nonetheless, this still leaves the problem already mentioned of the representativeness of the samples on whose behaviors they base their projections. On this issue, *see* Robyn M. Dawes, David Faust, and Paul E. Meehl, "Clinical Versus Actuarial Judgment," *Science*, March 31, 1989, pp. 1688–1674.

[34] David and Herbert Spiegel, "Forensic Uses of Hypnosis," in Irving B. Weiner and Allen K. Hess, eds., *Handbook of Forensic Psychology* (New York: John Wiley & Sons, 1987), pp. 490–507.

[35] Interview with Captain Bill Valkenburg, October 11, 1989.

[36] J. N. Gilbert, *Criminal Investigation* (Columbus, OH: Merrill, 1980).

[37] A. M. Weitzenhoffer, "Hypnotism and Altered States of Consciousness," in A. A. Sugarman and R. E. Tartar, eds., *Expanding Dimensions of Consciousness* (New York: Springer Publishing Co., 1979), p. 353.

[38] Graham F. Wagstaff, "Forensic Aspects of Hypnosis," in Nicholas P. Spanos and John F. Chaves, eds., *Hypnosis: The Cognitive-Behavioral Approach* (Buffalo, NY: Prometheus Books, 1989), p. 353.

[39] Martin T. Orne et al., "Reconstructing Memory through Hypnosis: Forensic and Clinical Implications," in Helen M. Pettinati, ed., *Hypnosis and Memory* (New York: Guilford Press, 1988), p. 55.

[40] Some examples of Kreskin's press-covered cases include: Dan Gordon, "Entertainer Using Talents in Murder Probe; Kreskin No Stranger to Crime Solving," *Reno Evening Gazette*, March 27, 1976, p. 9; Anonymous, "Probing People's Subconscious for the Picture of the Murderer," *Nevada State Journal*, March 29, 1976, p. 12; Anonymous, "Kreskin Joins Hunt for L.A. Strangler," *New York Post*, December 23, 1977; and Anonymous, "Hillside Strangler vs. Great Kreskin," *Los Angeles Times*, December 23, 1977.

[41] Interview with Kreskin, October 24, 1989.

[42] For a recent overview, *see* Stanley Krippner and Leonard George, "Psi Phenomena as Related to Altered States of Consciousness," in Benjamin B. Wolman and Montague Ullman, eds., *Handbook of States of Consciousness* (New York: Van Nostrand Reinhold, 1986), pp. 332–364.

[43] Cf. Martin Reiser, *Handbook of Investigative Hypnosis* (Los Angeles, CA: LEHI

Publishing Co., 1980); and his "Investigative Hypnosis," in David C. Raskin, ed., *Psychological Methods in Criminal Investigation and Evidence* (New York: Springer Publishing Co., 1989), pp. 151–190.

[44] Reiser, *Investigative Hypnosis*, 1989, p. 175.

[45] *Ibid.*, p. 180.

[46] Benjamin Kleinmuntz and Julian J. Szucko, "Lie Detection in Ancient and Modern Times," *American Psychologist*, 39, 7, 1984, pp. 766–775.

[47] John M. Roberts, "Oaths, Autonomic Ordeals, and Power," in *American Anthropologist*, 67, 6, Part 2, 1965, pp. 186–212.

[48] William G. Iacono and Christopher J. Patrick, "What Psychologists Should Know About Lie Detection," in Weiner and Hess, *Forensic Psychology*, p. 462.

[49] David C. Raskin, "Polygraph Techniques for the Detection of Deception," in Raskin, *Psychological Methods*, p. 248.

[50] Raskin (*ibid.*, p. 283) categories countermeasures as *general* (which includes drugs, relaxation techniques, hypnosis, biofeedback training, and mental dissociation from the examination), and *specific* (which includes physical and mental maneuvers in response to both control and relevant questions). There is in fact a substantial "underground" literature on this subject. For example: Vlad Kalshnikov, *Beat the Box: The Insider's Guide to Outwitting the Lie Detector* Mount Ida, AR: Deep Cover Press, 1983); and Scott French and Paul Van Houten, *Never Say Lie: How to Mislead Anyone/Anything/Anytime—And Get Away With It!* (Boulder, CO: CEP, Inc., 1987).

[51] Paul Ekman and Maureen O'Sullivan, "Hazards in Detecting Deceit," in Raskin, *Psychological Methods*, pp. 317–322.

[52] Iacono and Patrick, "Lie Detection," p. 486.

[53] Phillip W. Davis and Pamela McKenzie-Rundle, "The Social Organization of Lie-Detector Tests," *Urban Life*, 13, 2/3, 1984, p. 186.

[54] Quoted in Anonymous, "Psychic on the Mark in Search for Body," *New-Democrat* [Belleville, IL], November 15, 1983, p. 1A.

[55] Charles Bosworth, "Police Credit Psychic in Finding of Body," *St. Louis Post-Dispatch*, November 15, 1983, p. 1.

[56] Ward Lucas, "Police Use of Psychics: A Waste of Resources and Tax Money": *Campus Law Enforcement Journal*, July–August 1985, pp. 15–21. Ward Lucas was kind enough to share with us the notes he made on his conversation with Sergeant William Fitzgerald, who was the Alton, Illinois, Police Department's principal contact with Alexander and Lucas's source of information about her specific predictions, which were only rather vaguely given in most newspaper reports.

[57] Anonymous, "Search for Body."

[58] *Ibid.*

[59] John M. McGuire, "Is She Psychic? Or Is She a Fake?" *St. Louis Post-Dispatch*, November 27, 1983, p. 30.

[60] Anonymous, "Search for Body."

[61] Quoted in McGuire, "Is She Psychic?"

[62] *Ibid.*

[63] *Ibid.*, and Lucas, "Use of Psychics," pp. 18–19.

[64] Anonymous, "Search for Body."

[65] For some of Alexander's past misses, *see* Harry Eagar, "How Psychic Is Greta Alexander? Not Very, Her Track Record Shows," *Des Moines Register*, September 30, 1981. Careful reading of this article suggests that Eagar treats some of her past predictions unfairly, as when in one case Alexander said she saw "a

gunshot" and Eagar seems to dismiss this by noting of the located dead hostage that, "instead of 'a shot,' he was the victim of a least five bullets."

[66] Interview with Captain Lynn Harris, August 1989.

[67] Interview with Chief Joe Austin, September 1989.

[68] Interview with Captain Gary Boswell, October 11, 1989.

[69] Interview with Dixie Yeterian, August 24, 1989.

[70] Quoted in Carolyn Mark, "He Solves Murders . . . and Finds Thimbles," *The Austin Citizen*, April 22, 1981.

[71] Quoted in Jim Atkinson, "The Long Arm of the Oracle," *Texas Monthly Magazine*, July 1981, pp. 41–42.

[72] Interview with Dr. Louise Ludwig, October 12, 1989.

[73] Letter from Ingo Swann, October 3, 1989.

Notes for Chapter 10

[1] Clifford Linedecker, *Psychic Spy: The Story of an Astounding Man* (Garden City, NY: Doubleday, 1976).

[2] Steven V. Roberts, "White House Confirms Reagans Follow Astrology, Up to a Point," *New York Times*, May 3, 1988, pp. 1, 15; Martin Gardner, "Seeing Stars," *New York Review of Books*, June 30, 1988, pp. 43–45; and Joan Quigley, *"What Does Joan Say?" My Seven Years as White House Astrologer to Nancy and Ronald Reagan* (New York: Birch Lane Press, 1990).

[3] Angela Fox Dunn, "Meet 'Dutch Reagan,'" *Detroit Free Press*, November, 9, 1980, pp. 1B, 4B. *See also* Ronald Reagan, with Richard G. Huber, *Where's the Rest of Me? The Autobiography of Ronald Reagan* (New York : Karz Publishers, 1981 edition).

[4] George Draper, "Astrology Furor: The Stars That Shine on Reagan," *San Francisco Examiner*, November 29, 1966.

[5] Quoted in William Safire, "On Language; Forgive Me, But . . . ," *New York Times*, October 21, 1984, Section 6, p. 14.

[6] Quoted from 1989 brochure for her "Joyce Jillson Research Project."

[7] *See* Ted Schulz, "Reagan and Astrology," *Whole Earth Review*, Fall 1986, p. 14.

[8] Anonymous, "Congressman Spoke of Reagan Astrology 5 Years Before Reagan Book," Associated Press story, May 13, 1988 (via Lexis).

[9] Ken Potter et al., "The REAL Secret Astrologer Who Guided President—The Untold Story: New White House Astrology Bombshell," *National Enquirer*, May 24, 1988, p. 40.

[10] United Press International news story reproduced in *Inner Dimensions*, February 1989.

[11] Miles Copeland, "Letters: How CIA Sought Help From Stars," *The Times* [London], May 21, 1988.

[12] Michael Isikoff and Mark Hosenball, "The Swami of Iranamok," *The New Republic*, November 9, 1987, pp. 21–23.

[13] *See* Jacob Young, Barbara Rosen, and Jane Whitmore, "The Senator and the Psychic; A New Medium in the Quest for World Peace?" *Newsweek* [International Edition], May 11, 1987, p. 21. As with many of Geller's claims, this one produced some criticisms. *See* John Lofton, "Mystical Capitol Caper," *The Washington Times*, May 20, 1987; and "How Princess Michael Got Uri Geller to Bend Russian Minds for U.S. Ambassador," *News of the World*, May 3, 1987, pp. 28–29.

[14] *See* Niles Lathem, "Uri Geller Bends Pols' Ears on Soviets," *New York Post*, April 28, 1987; and John Harney, "Red Spying May Soon Be All in Their Minds," *New York Post*, April 30, 1987, p. 20.

[15] Ron McRae, *Mind Wars* (New York: St. Martin's Press, 1984), pp. 71–73. Also reported on in William J. Broad, "Pentagon Is Said to Focus on ESP for Wartime Use," *New York Times*, January 10, 1984, pp. 17, 18.

[16] Anonymous, *Paraphysics R & D: Warsaw Pact*, Defense Intelligence Agency Task No. PT-1810-18-76 (DST-1810SS-202-78), March 30, 1978. This document as released is highly censored, including the name of its author(s).

[17] Richard Deacon, *The Israeli Secret Service* (New York: Taplinger, 1978), p. 296.

[18] Uri Geller and Guy Lyon Playfair, *The Geller Effect* (New York: Henry Holt and Co., 1987), p. 81.

[19] Anonymous, "Zanex Pays Geller Over $350,000," *The Skeptic: Newsletter of the Australian Skeptics*, 6, 2, June 1986, p. 1.

[20] Some details on this and his many other activities can be found in the cover story about Geller in the German magazine *Esotera* of February 1987, pp. 20–27.

[21] Lawrence Stone, "Geller Plays It Safe in His British Fortress Home: KGB Death Threat to Uri the Spoon-Bender," *Sunday Mirror*, February 7, 1988.

[22] Quoted in James Cook, "Closing the Psychic Gap," *Forbes*, May 21, 1984, p. 91.

[23] The principal attack on Geller is magician James (The Amazing) Randi's *The Truth About Uri Geller*, 2d ed. (Buffalo, NY: Prometheus Books, 1982,). Geller's major rebuttal statements appear in Geller and Playfair, *Geller Effect*. A purported response to his rebuttal was issued in 1987 by the Committee for the Scientific Investigation of Claims of the Paranormal, titled *What the World Media Thinks About Geller Today*. This compilation of clippings in large part ignores the details of Geller's rebuttals and mostly repeats the old charges.

[24] Quoted in Roy Stockdill, "Uri Sues Magician for £45m," *News of the World*, November 5, 1989, p. 29.

[25] The closest thing to an alleged "smoking gun" in the case against Geller is C. Eugene Emery, Jr., "Catching Geller in the Act," *The Skeptical Inquirer*, 12, Fall 1987, pp. 75–80. However, careful reading of the article reveals that the principal evidence claimed is based on a combination of the author's memory of the events and a tape recording. The photograph Emery presents to support his contention that Geller's spoon was bent prior to his alleged exercise of PK in fact does not necessarily show a bent spoon and depends upon Emery's questionable inferences about what we might see with an unbent spoon, and he specifically acknowledges that the bend is "not present in photographs taken before the reporter/photographer was distracted, is partly hidden by Geller's left hand." His memory, like all memories, is fallible, and when one of us (M.T.) asked to hear a copy of the tape involved, the request was declined on the grounds of the rights of newspaper confidentiality. Though Emery does make a reasonable case, it is far from an argument making its point beyond a reasonable doubt. A somewhat similar alleged debunking of Geller, but one that relies even more upon the hardly impartial testimony of its author, is Michael Hutchinson, "A Thorn in Geller's Side: Uri Geller Is Caught in the Act," *The British & Irish Skeptic*, 2, 4, July–August 1988, pp. 9–11.

[26] David Berglas, "'Magicians are the Most Narrow-Minded People in the World'— Famed Magician," *Psychic News*, December 13, 1986.

[27] Richard Deacon, *Spyclopedia: The Comprehensive Handbook of Espionage* (New York: Silver Arrow Books/William Morrow, 1987), pp. 95–96; and his *John Dee:*

Scientist, Geographer, Astrologer and Secret Agent to Elizabeth I (London: Muller, 1968).

[28] The translated article appeared as Zdenek Rejdak, "Parapsychology—War Menace or Total Peace Weapons?" in Sheila Ostrander and Lynn Schroeder, eds., *The ESP Papers: Scientists Speak Out from Behind the Iron Curtain* (New York: Bantam, 1976), pp. 116–124. *Also see* Richard Deacon, *With My Little Eye: The Memoirs of a Spy Hunter* (London: Frederick Muller, 1982), p. 238; and his *The Israeli Secret Service*, pp. 293–194.

[29] Hanson W. Baldwin, "Dowsers Detect Enemy's Tunnels," *New York Times*, October 13, 1967. For a detailed account, *see* Christopher Bird, "The U.S. Marines Learn to Dowse," in his *The Divining Hand* (New York: E. P. Dutton, 1969), pp. 199–214; and Louis J. Matacia, *Dowsing Introduced to the United States Armed Forces*, booklet printed for presentation to the American Society of Dowsers, Annual Convention, October 4–6, 1968 (Oakton, VA: Louis J. Matacia, 1968).

[30] Anonymous, "Shades of Black Magic: Marines on Operations Divine for VC Tunnels," *The Observer*, March 13, 1967 (reproduced in Bird, *Divining Hand*, p. 206). For an excellent review on dowsing, *see* George P. Hansen, "Dowsing: A Review of Experimental Research," *Journal of the Society for Psychical Research*, 51, 1982, pp. 343–367.

[31] Barbara Honneger and Jeffrey Mishlove, "Security Implications of Applied Psi: An Historical Summary," *Applied Psi News*, November–December 1982, p. 3.

[32] Vadim Marin, "Messing Predicts," in Ostrander and Schroeder, *ESP Papers*, pp. 38–40. Hitler's bounty on Messing is referred to in Sheila Ostrander and Lynn Schroeder, *Psychic Discoveries Behind the Iron Curtain* (New York: Bantam, 1971), p. 42.

[33] Deacon, *My Little Eye*, p. 236. For details re Ossowiecki, *see* Andrzej Borzymowsi, "Startling Experiences of Poland's Most Famous Psychic," in Ostrander and Schroeder, *ESP Papers*, pp. 3–16.

[34] Re Flemming and the Pendulum Institute scam, *see* Deacon, *My Little Eye*, pp. 252–254. The literature alleging Hitler's deep involvements with occultism is now substantial. The best overview is probably found in Nicholas Goodrick-Clarke, *The Occult Roots of Nazism: The Ariosophists of Austria and Germany, 1890–1935* (Wellingborough, Northamptonshire: Aquarian Press, 1985). Some of the other, less scholarly, works include: Nigel Pennick, *Hitler's Secret Sciences: His Quest for the Hidden Knowledge of the Ancients* (Suffolk: Neville Spearman, 1981); Jean-Michel Angebert, *The Occult and the Third Reich* (New York: Macmillan, 1974); Dusty Sklar, *Gods and Beasts: The Nazis and the Occult* (New York: Thomas Y. Crowell, 1977); Francis King, *Satan and Swastika: The Occult and the Nazi Party* (Frogmore, St. Albans, England: Mayflower, 1976); and J. H. Brennan, *The Occult Reich* (New York: Signet/New American Library, 1974).

[35] Honegger and Mishlove, "Applied Psi," p. 2.

[36] John Whitwell, *British Agent* (London: William Kimber, 1966), p. 165.

[37] Honegger and Mishlove, "Applied Psi," p. 2.

[38] *Ibid.*

[39] *Ibid.*, p. 4.

[40] For the best discussion of this whole episode, *see* Martin Ebon, *Psychic Warfare: Threat or Illusion?* (New York: McGraw Hill, 1983), Chapter 3: "The Great 'Nautilus' Hoax," pp. 22–32.

[41] Anonymous, "An 'Affair' About Telekinesis," *Pravda*, February 1988. On Kulagina

generally, *see* Ebon, *Psychic Warfare*, Chapter 6: "If Thoughts Can Kill . . . ," pp. 63–78.

[42] Larissa Vilenskaya, "Epilogue: Psi Research in the Soviet Union: Are They Ahead of Us?" in Russell Targ and Keith Harary, *The Mind Race* (New York: Villard Books, 1984), pp. 247–269. *Also see* D. Scott Rogo, "An Interview with Larissa Vileñskaya: Inside Look at Soviet Parascience," *Fate*, June 1982, pp. 64–70.

[43] The film of this unidentified psychic was shown on *NBC Magazine with David Brinkley* on March 13, 1981.

[44] Milan Ryzl, "Parapsychology in Communist Countries of Europe," *International Journal of Parapsychology*, 10, 3, 1968.

[45] Re Pavlita's generators, *see* Deacon, *My Little Eye*, pp. 260–261; Stanley Krippner, "A First Hand Look at Psychotronic Generators," in John White and Stanley Krippner, eds., *Future Science: Life Energies and the Physics of Paranormal Phenomena* (New York: Doubleday Anchor, 1977), pp. 420–430; and Stanley Krippner, *Human Possibilities: Mind Exploration in the USSR and Eastern Europe* (New York: Anchor Press/Doubleday, 1980), pp. 55–56.

[46] Deacon, *Israeli Secret Service*, p. 296.

[47] Ostrander and Schroeder, *Psychic Discoveries,* "Vanga Dimitrova, the Bulgarian Oracle," pp. 265–288.

[48] "Memorandum for the Record; Subject Project MKULTRA, Subproject 136," August 23, 1961. FOIA-released documents on MKULTRA include numerous others related to psi research. On the project in general, *see* John Marks, *The Search for the "Manchurian Candidate": The CIA and Mind Control* (New York: Times Books, 1979; and Alan W. Scheflin and Edward M. Opton, Jr., *The Mind Manipulators* (New York: Paddington Press, 1978). *See also* David B. Clemens (Institute for Advanced Mind Science), "Parapsychology and the C.I.A.," in W. G. Roll, R. L. Moris, and R. A. White, eds., *Research in Parapsychology 1981* (Metuchen, NJ: Scarecrow Press, 1982, pp. 192–193.

[49] McRae, *Mind Wars*, p. 103.

[50] On Khokhlov's remarkable story, *see* John Barron, *KGB:The Secret Work of Soviet Secret Agents* (New York: Bantam, 1974); and Nikolai Khokhlov, *In the Name of Conscience* (New York: David McKay, 1959).

[51] Richard Deacon, *The Truth Twisters* (London: Macdonald, 1987), p. 192.

[52] Quotes from the transcript of *NBC Magazine with David Brinkley* of March 13, 1981, NBC Television Network. *See also* Nikolai Khokhlov, "The Relationship of Parapsychology to Communism." Paper presented at the Foundation for Research into the Nature of Man, September 1, 1966.

[53] Douglas Starr and E. Patrick McQuaid, "Psi Soldiers in the Kremlin," *Omni*, August 1985, p. 104.

[54] Re Puharich's extraordinary claims, *see* Deacon, *My Little Eye*, 1982, p. 242; and Guy Lyon Playfair, "The Third World War?" *The Unexplained*, No. 64, 1981, p. 1269.

[55] John B. Alexander, "The New Mental Battlefield: 'Beam Me Up, Spock,'" *Military Review*, December 1980, pp. 47–54.

[56] Roger A. Beaumont, "C[nth]?: On the Strategic Potential of ESP," *Signal: Journal of the Armed Forces Communications and Electronics Association*, January 1982, pp. 39–45.

[57] Charles Wallach, "The Science of Psychic Warfare," *Journal of Defense and Diplomacy*, September 1985, pp. 38–44.

[58] Richard Groller, "Soviet Psychotronics—a State of Mind," *Military Intelligence*, October–December 1986, pp. 18–21, 58.

[59] Reported in Henry Gris and William Dick, *The New Soviet Psychic Discoveries* (Englewood Cliffs, NJ: Prentice-Hall, 1978), p. 292. This appears to refer to Ingo Swann's remote viewings, since almost the same episode is described in John L. Wilhelm, *The Search for Superman* (New York: Pocket Books, 1976), pp. 197–198.

[60] Thomas E. Bearden, "Soviet Psychotronic Weapons: A Condensed Background," in John White, ed., *Psychic Warfare: Fact or Fiction?* (Wellingborough, Northamptonshire: Aquarian Press, 1988), pp. 156–168; and *Excalibur Briefing* (San Francisco: Strawberry Hill Press/Walnut Hill, 1980). Writing papers with titles like "Solution of the Fundamental Problem of Quantum Mechanics," Colonel Bearden is unlikely to be accused of modesty.

[61] Louis F. Maire, III, and J. D. LaMothe, *Soviet and Czechoslovakian Parapsychology Research*, Defense Intelligence Agency Task PT-1810-12-75 (DST-18105-387-75) September 1975, p. 34.

[62] John D. LaMothe, *Controlled Offensive Behavior—USSR*, Defense Intelligence Agency Task No. T72-01-14 (ST-CS-01-169-172), July 1972, p. 27.

[63] *See* Robert C. Toth, "Times Correspondent in Russia 'Detained' by KGB," *Los Angeles Times*, June 12, 1977, pp. 6, 7; and Flora Lewis, "Emigre Tells of Research in Soviet Union in Parapsychology for Military Use," *New York Times*, June 19, 1977, pp. 1, 20. Stern was working as a senior psychologist at the Free University of Amsterdam when interviewed in 1985. *See* Starr and McQuaid, "Psi Soldiers," pp. 106–108.

[64] Charles T. Tart, "A Survey on Negative Uses, Government Interest and Funding of Psi," *Psi News: Bulletin of the Parapsychological Association*, 1, 2, 1978, 2.

[65] Russell Targ and Harold Puthoff, *Mind-Reach: Scientists Look at Psychic Ability* (New York: Delacorte Press/Eleanor Friede, 1977). *Also see* Charles T. Tart, H. E. Puthoff, and R. Targ, eds., *Mind at Large: Institute of Electrical and Electronic Engineers Symposia on the Nature of Extrasensory Perception* (New York: Praeger, 1979).

[66] John Wilhelm, "Psychic Spying? The CIA, the Pentagon and the Russians Probe the Military Potential of Parapsychology," *Washington Post*, August 7, 1977, pp. B1, B5.

[67] *Ibid.*; and Jack Anderson, "Pentagon, CIA Cooperating on Psychic Spying," *Washington Post*, May 3, 1984, p. B15.

[68] John Wilhelm, "Psychic Spying?" p. B5.

[69] James Coates, "Psychic Spy Died, No Word Since," *Detroit Free Press*, August 10, 1977, p. 6-A.

[70] On these episodes, *see* Philip J. Klass, "NASA, the White House, and UFOs," *The Skeptical Inquirer*, Spring/Summer 1978, pp. 72–81.

[71] Our information about this episode largely stems from one of the author's (M.T.'s) involvement with an aborted CBS-TV *60 Minutes* episode on the topic. Some of this material was later reported in Art Levine, Charles Fenyvesi, and Steven Emerson, "The Twilight Zone in Washington," *U.S. News and World Report*, December 5, 1988, p. 30. In that report, the success of the remote viewing of Queen was diminished by quoting an unnamed White House witness as saying, "I was unimpresed" because the psychic's (presumably Harary's) description of Queen's condition struck him as vague.

[72] Honegger and Mishlove, "Applied Psi," p. 4. Re the distant projection of such electromagnetic fields to the brain to control behavior, *see* Kathleen McAuliffe, "The Mind Fields," *Omni*, February 1985, pp. 41–44, 96–104; and Larry Collins, "Mind Control," *Playboy*, January 1990, pp. 158, 204–208.

[73] Committee on Science and Technology, U.S. House of Representatives (Ninety-Seventh Congress, 1st Sess., Serial G), *Survey of Science and Technology Issues Present and Future* (Washington, D.C.: U.S. Government Printing Office, June 1981), p. 59.

[74] Quoted in Anonymous, "'Psi' R&D: Congress Gets Favorable Report," *Science & Government Report*, 13, 16, October 1, 1983, p. 3.

[75] Steven Emerson, *Secret Warriors: Inside the Covert Military Operations of the Reagan Era* (New York: G. P. Putnam's Sons, 1988), pp. 64–66. The use of the psychics and the failed assault on the house were reported at the time by Pierre Salinger on the ABC-TV evening news.

[76] *Ibid.*, p. 111.

[77] *Ibid.*, pp. 103–104.

[78] Jack Anderson, "The Race for 'Inner Space,'" *San Francisco Chronicle*, April 23, 1984.

[79] Jack Anderson, "Secret Psychic Research," *San Francisco Chronicle*, April 24, 1984.

[80] Jack Anderson, "Pentagon, CIA Cooperating on Psychic Spying," *Washington Post*, May 3, 1984, p. B15.

[81] Emerson, *Secret Warriors*, p. 197.

[82] Howard Blum, *Out There: The Government's Secret Quest for Extraterrestrials* (New York: Simon and Schuster, 1990), pp. 35–39.

[83] Jack Anderson, "Spy Race With Soviets," *Washington Post*, February 15, 1989.

[84] Richard Deacon, *A History of the Chinese Secret Service* (London: Frederick Muller, 1974), p. 28.

[85] *Ibid.*, pp. 29–30.

[86] *Ibid.*, pp. 30–31.

[87] *Ibid.*, p. 31.

[88] *See* Zheng She, "Parapsychology, Is It Real?" *China Reconstructs*, January 1981, pp. 50–51; Anonymous, "The Parapsychology Controversy," *China Reconstructs*, June 1982, p. 51; Martin Ebon, "Parapsychology in Contemporary China," *Parapsychology Review*, 12, 5, 1981, pp. 1–5; and "China Opens Door to the Paranormal," *Fate*, February 1982, pp. 69–76; Kathy Goss, "Studying Psi in China," *Applied Psi Newsletter*, 1, 6, 1981, pp. 1–44; James McClenon, "Children with Extraordinary Talents," *Fate*, June 1987, pp. 68–76; Paul Dong, "Summary Report on Qigong Investigation in Mainland China," *Psi Research*, September–December, 1985, pp. 133–138; and Marcello Truzzi, "Chinese Parapsychology: A Bibliography of English Language Items, Parts I and II," *Zetetic Scholar*, No. 10, 1982, pp. 143–145; and No. 12/13, pp. 58–60.

[89] Michael Weisskopf, "Superstition: China Hopes to Quell Practice of Sorcerers, Wizards," *Ann Arbor News*, April 6, 1984, p. B10. *See also* Chung Yu Wang, "China's Unwanted Heritage," *Tomorrow*, 4, 1, 1955, pp. 55–63.

[90] Andrew Giarelli, "Qigong," *World Press Review*, April 1989, p. 44. *Also see* "T. C. Koh, "Qigong—Chinese Breathing Exercise," *American Journal of Chinese Medicine*, 10, 1982, pp. 86–91.

[91] Details of this can be found in Marcello Truzzi, "China's Psychic Savants," *Omni*, January 1985, pp. 62–66, 78–79.

[92] James Alcock et al., "Preliminary Testing," *The Skeptical Inquirer*, Summer 1988, p. 371.

[93] *See* Ebon, *Psychic Warfare*, pp. 172–175; and McRae, *Mind Wars*, pp. 66–67.

[94] Starr and McQuaid, "Psi Soldiers," p. 104.

[95] Chen Hsin and Mei Lei, "Study of the Extraordinary Function of the Human Body

in China," paper distributed at the Annual Meeting of the Parapsychological Association, August 16–20, 1982.

[96] Zha Leping, "Recent Parapsychological Studies in P. R. China as Known to Me," paper distributed at the Annual Meeting of the Parapsychological Association, 1989, pp. 5–6. *See also* Zha Leping and Tron McConnell, "Parapsychology in the People's Republic of China: 1979–1989," *Journal of the American Society for Psychical Research*, in press.

[97] Zha Leping, "Studies in China," pp. 13–14.

[98] *See* Paul Kurtz, Testing Psi Claims in China: Visit by a CSICOP Delegation," *The Skeptical Inquirer*, Summer 1988, pp. 364–366; and Alcock et al., "Preliminary Testing," pp. 367–375.

[99] Zha Leping, "Studies in China," pp. 16–17.

[100] Wu Xiaping, "Report of a Chinese Psychic's Pill-Bottle Demonstration," *The Skeptical Inquirer*, Winter 1989, pp. 168–171.

[101] Richard P. Suttmeier, "Corruption in Science: The Chinese Case," *Science, Technology & Human Values*, Winter 1985, pp. 49–61.

[102] On the history of psi research in Japan, *see* Soji Otani, "History of Parapsychology in Japan," *Psychologia*, 10, 1967, pp. 51–57; and his "Past and Present Situation of Parapsychology in Japan," in A. Angoff and B. Shapin, eds., *Parapsychology Today: A Geographic View* (New York: Parapsychology Foundation, 1973), pp. 32–42.

[103] Anonymous, "Japanese Parapsychologist," *Parapsychology Bulletin*, August 1964, p. 1.

[104] On Motoyama, *see* Anonymous, "Parapsychology and Religion—A New Approach," *Parapsychology Bulletin*, November 1962, p. 1. *Also see* Hiroshi Motoyama, "The Motoyama Device: Measuring Psychic Energy," White and Krippner, *Future Science*, pp. 444–450.

[105] James McClenon, "Parapsychology in Japan," *Parapsychology Review*, July–August 1989, p. 14.

[106] Anonymous, "In Japan, Technology Collides With Superstition," *Providence Journal* [Rhode Island], March 13, 1988.

[107] Anonymous, "Japanese Want to See Seer: Soothsayer Believed to Hold Political Secrets of the Future," *The Plain Dealer* [Cleveland, OH], August 22, 1987.

[108] Quoted in Starr and McQuaid, "Psi Soldiers," p. 108.

[109] Keith Harary, "A Conversation with Keith Harary: 'Almost Everyone Has Psychic Abilities," *U.S. News and World Report*, May 7, 1984, p. 73.

[110] Targ quoted in Anonymous, "Strange Case of the Psychic 'Spy,'" *New Scientist*, November 22, 1984, p. 3.

[111] Quoted in McRae, *Mind Wars*, p. 48.

[112] Paul Engstrom, "Psychic Spying Debate," *San Jose Mercury News*, May 27, 1984.

[113] Ed Rogers, "National Academy to Assess Potential for 'Psychwars,'" *Washington Times*, March 3, 1986.

[114] *See* John A. Swets, ed., *Enhancing Human Performance: Issues, Theories, and Techniques* (Washington, DC: National Academy of Sciences, 1988); and John A. Palmer, Charles Honorton, and Jessica Utts, "Reply to the National Research Council Study on Parapsychology," *Journal of the American Society for Psychical Research*, 83, 1989, pp. 31–43. *See also* John A. Swets and Robert A. Bjork, "Enhancing Human Performance: An Evaluation of 'New Age' Techniques Considered by the U.S. Army," *Psychological Science*, 1, 2, 1990, pp. 85–96. This article notes the critical reactions to the NRC report but rather surprisingly fails to respond to the main charges critics raised.

[115] Swets, ed., *Human Performance*, p. 179.

[116] The main member of the NAS committee responsible for the psi assessment was University of Oregon psychologist Ray Hyman, who was granted top-security clearance to look at the military research. When asked about whether he found John Wilhelm's criticism of Project Scanate to be correct, he indicated he had not read carefully the full report.

[117] William J. Broad, "Pentagon Is Said to Focus on ESP for Wartime Use," *New York Times*, January 10, 1984, p. 17.

[118] Starr and McQuaid, *Human Performance*, p. 106.

[119] C. B. Scott Jones, Essay review of *Psychic Warfare: Fact or Fiction? Journal of Parapsychology*, 53, 1989, pp. 141–150.

[120] *Ibid.*, p. 149.

Notes for Chapter 11

[1] U.S. Department of Justice, *Report to the Nation on Crime and Justice*, Second Edition (Washington, DC: U.S. Department of Justice, Bureau of Justice Statistics, March 1988), p. 29.

[2] Theodore Rosenthal and Bernard J. Siegel, "Magic and Witchcraft: An Interpretation from Dissonance Theory," *Southwestern Journal of Anthropology*, 15, 1959, p. 144.

[3] Evon Z. Vogt and Ray Hyman, *Water Witching USA*, Second Edition (Chicago: University of Chicago Press, 1979).

[4] Evon Z. Vogt, "Water Witching: An Interpretation of a Ritual Pattern in a Rural American Community," in William A. Lessa and Evon Z. Vogt, eds., *Reader in Comparative Religion* (N.Y.: Harper and Row, 1965), p. 375.

[5] Paul Blumberg, "Magic in the Modern World," *Sociology and Social Research*, 47, 2, 1963, p. 158.

[6] Interview with Dr. Martin Reiser, July 14, 1989.

[7] Interview with Police Chief George Napper, March 16, 1982.

[8] Summarized in Curtis D. MacDougall, *Superstition and the Press* (Buffalo, NY: Prometheus Books, 1983), p. 544.

[9] Summarized in *ibid.*

[10] Summarized in *ibid.*

[11] William G. Roll and Roger C. Grimson, "A Majority-Vote Study of Impressions Relating to a Criminal Investigation," paper presented at the annual meetings of the Parapsychological Association, 1983.

[12] "Subject: Operation ESP," Michigan State Police, Interoffice Correspondence memorandum, from D/Sgt. Roger Rivard to F/Lt. Robert H. Robertson, September 27, 1977. Also interview with Captain R. H. Robertson, January 23, 1981.

[13] Michael Riley and David Thompson, "Hearing Voices of Reason?" *UK Police Review*, January 16, 1987, p. 122.

[14] David E. Kerr, "Investigation of the Homicide Scene," in Samuel Gerber and Oliver Schroeder, eds., *Criminal Investigation and Interrogation* (Cincinnati, OH: Anderson, 1972), p. 159.

[15] Ward Lucas, "Police Use of Psychics: A Waste of Resources and Tax Money," *Campus Law Enforcement Journal*, July–August 1985, pp. 20–21.

[16] Richard Guarino, "The Police and Psychics," *Psychic*, June 1975, p. 14.

17 Anonymous, "Use of Psychics in Law Enforcement," *Criminal Information Bulletin*, February 1979, p. 25.

18 Interview with Lieutenant Kurt Longfellow, August 31, 1989.

19 Robert Hicks, "The Psychic World of Law Enforcement," paper presented at the annual conference of the Committee for the Scientific Investigation of Claims of the Paranormal, November 5, 1988, p. 10.

20 *Ibid.*, pp. 14–15.

21 By these standards, most of the "psychic superstars" would seem to be eliminated from contention, as many of them have sought media attention, claimed accuracy rates above 80 percent, and charged handsomely for their services.

22 Interview with Lieutenant Kurt Longfellow, August 31, 1989.

23 Thomas J. Gordon and Jerry B. Tobias, "Managing the Psychic in Criminal Investigations," *Police Chief*, May 1979, pp. 58–59.

24 Quoted in Vernon J. Geberth, *Practical Homicide Investigation: Tactics, Procedures, and Forensic Techniques* (New York: Elsevier, 1983), p. 421.

25 Donald J. Burnett, Police Chief, "Policy Memorandum on the Use of Psychics," City of Pomona Police Department, September 10, 1981.

26 Interview with Dr. Louise Ludwig, October 12, 1989.

27 Mary Jo Patterson, "Dorothy Allison: The Extrasensory Detective," *Police Magazine*, March 1981, p. 48.

28 *Ibid.*, p. 48.

29 Interview with Dr. Martin Reiser, July 14, 1989.

30 Ward Lucas, "Police Use of Psychics," pp. 20–21.

31 Omar Khayyam Moore, "Divination—a New Perspective," *American Anthropologist*, 59, 1957, pp. 69–74.

32 George K. Park, "Divination and Its Social Contexts," *Journal of the Royal Anthropological Institute*, 93, 1963, pp. 195–209.

33 Jenny Scott, "Police Psychic: Visions of Crime," *The Sunday Record* [Northern New Jersey], June 24, 1984, p. A-22.

34 Interview with Special Agent Kenneth Lanning, July 13, 1989.

35 Letter from Chief of Police John M. Mizerka to Marcello Truzzi, March 3, 1981.

36 James Coates, "Psychic Spy Died, No Word Since," *Detroit Free Press*, August 10, 1977, p. 6–A.

37 Edmund Mahony, "Psychics' Aid Rarely Helps Solve Crimes," *Hartford Courant*, November 4, 1979.

38 Interview with Detective Lynn Harris, August 27, 1989.

39 Interview with Dr. Louise Ludwig, October 12, 1989.

Notes for Chapter 12

1 Stanley L. Schall and William H. Kautz, "Legal Issues Related to Psi Applications in Law Enforcement," *Applied Psi*, 3, Winter 1984/1985, p. 12.

2 Quoted in Stanley L. Schall, "Legal Issues Related to the Use of Psi," *Archaeus*, 3, Summer 1985, p. 53 (from 277 U.S. 438 at 474).

3 Lee Nisbet, "Psychics in the Courtroom," *The Humanist*, July–August 1977, p. 47.

4 James Randi, "Justice by Horoscope," *The Skeptical Inquirer*, Spring–Summer 1978, p. 9.

5 Marjie Lundstrom, "Psychics Winning Growing Acceptance by U.S. Law Enforcement Agencies," *The Denver Post*, December 2, 1987.

6 Courtney J. Mullin, "Jury Selection Techniques: Improving the Odds of Winning,"

in Gerald Cooke, ed., *The Role of the Forensic Psychologist* (Springfield, IL: Charles C. Thomas, 1980), p. 159.

[7] *Ibid.*

[8] Lundstrom, "Psychics."

[9] Anonymous, "Psychic Flunks Jury Duty," *Weekly World News*, February 24, 1987.

[10] Howard E. Goldfluss, "Courtroom Psychics," *Omni*, July 1987, p. 12.

[11] Russell Targ and Keith Harary, *The Mind Race* (New York: Villard, 1984), p. 241.

[12] Bernadette Doran, "Psychic Sleuths," *Student Lawyer*, 7, 3, November 1978, p. 51.

[13] Interview with Deputy District Attorney James Grodin, May 1, 1990.

[14] Schall and Kautz, "Legal Issues," p. 7.

[15] Mary Ann Galante, "Psychics: Lawyers Using Seers to Help Select Juries, Find Missing Children," *The National Law Journal*, January 27, 1986, p. 33.

[16] *Ibid.*, p. 3.

[17] Quoted in Doran, "Psychic Sleuths."

[18] *Ibid.*, p. 51.

[19] Goldfluss, "Courtroom Psychics."

[20] Interview with Deputy District Attorney James Grodin, May 1, 1990.

[21] Goldfluss, "Courtroom Psychics."

[22] *Ibid.*

[23] Carl Cappozzola, *California Search and Seizure Compendium*, Section 0, p. 3.

[24] Interview with Deputy District Attorney James Grodin, May 1, 1990.

Bibliography

General English Language References on Psychic Detectives and Items On Two or More Psychic Sleuths

Anderson, Keith. "Dallas' Psychic Detectives." *Dallas Morning News*, April 29, 1984, pp. 1F–2F, 6F.
———"Psychics' Misses Outnumber Hits, Say Debunkers." *Dallas Morning News*, April 29, 1984, p. 2F.
Anonymous. "Use of Psychics in Law Enforcement." *Criminal Information Bulletin* [State of California Department of Justice], February 1979, pp. 23–26.
Anonymous. "Detectives Examine Role Played by Psychics." *Psychic News*, February 7, 1987, p. 5.
Anonymous. "BC Skeptics—In the News." *BC Skeptics Newsletter* [British Columbia], undated clipping, 1987, p. 5.
Anonymous. "Psychical Help Sought in Probe of Murders." *Durham Morning Herald*, February 10, 1981.
Anonymous. "Police Are Calling on Psychics for Aid." *New York Times*, November 26, 1978.
Anonymous. "Cloudy Crystal Balls." *Saturday Review*, 7, June 1980, p. 6.
Anonymous. "Psychic Detectives." *Alpha*, 1, April–May 1978, p. 3.

Anonymous. "Psychics Join Hunt for Premier's Killer." *Psychic News*, November 28, 1987, pp. 1, 5.

Anonymous. *Do As I Say and You Will Find the Body,"* in Perrott Philips, ed. *Out of this World*, Vol. 4. London: Phoebus Publishing Co., 1981, pp. 97–102.

Archer, Fred. *Crime and the Psychic World*. New York: William Morrow and Co., 1969.

———*Ghosts, Witches—and Murder!* London: W. H. Allen, 1972.

Balton, Michael. "Researchers to Study Police Use of ESP." *Law Enforcement News*, March 23, 1981, pp. 1, 12.

Barrett, William F. *Psychical Research*. New York: Henry Holt and Co., 1911.

———and Theodore Besterman. *The Divining Rod*. New Hyde Park, NY: University Books, 1968, pp. 3–4, 27–32.

Bartlett, Laile E. "Detection: The Phantom Sleuth." Chapter 5 in *Psi Trek*. New York: McGraw-Hill, 1981, pp. 75–102.

Bell, A.H. "Tracing the Lost," in his (edited) *Practical Dowsing*. London: G. Bell, 1955, pp. 92–94.

Bird, Christopher. *The Divining Hand*. New York: E. P. Dutton, 1979.

Brink, Filippus. "Parapsychology and Criminal Investigation." *International Criminal Police Review*, 134, January 1960, pp. 3–8.

Carpenter, Sally. "Some Texas Police Officers Accepting Help From Psychics." *Dallas Times-Herald*, September 21, 1980.

Clark, Jerome. "How Psychic Were the 'Superpsychics?'" *Fate*, March 1982, pp. 78–79.

Cohen, Daniel. *ESP: The Search Beyond the Senses*. New York: Harcourt, Brace, Jovanovich, 1973, pp. 123—132.

Comings, Mark. Review of *Psychic Criminology: An Operations Manual for Using Psychics in Criminal Investigations*. Applied Psi Newsletter, 1, 3, July–August 1982, p. 7.

Committee for the Scientific Investigation of Claims of the Paranormal. "U.S. Overrun by Psychic Charlatans: Skeptical Group to Discuss 'Psychic Detectives' at Press Conference in Atlanta." Press Release, Buffalo, NY, December 9, 1982.

——— "CSICOP Blasts Police Department for Use of Psychic Detectives." Press Release, Buffalo, NY, December 10, 1982.

Cooke, John. "Los Angeles Police Dept. Probes Psychic Powers . . . After They Solve Baffling Crimes." *National Enquirer*, April 24, 1979, p. 6.

Couttie, Bob. "Misdetection." Chapter 6 in *Forbidden Knowledge: The Paranormal Paradox*. Cambridge: Lutterworth Press, 1988, pp. 45–55.

Cowan, Carl, and Joan Luxenburg. "Mind Science in Police Science: Applications for Parapsychology." Paper presented at the Annual Meeting of the American Society for Criminology, November 8, 1979, Philadelphia, PA.

Crane, Glen. "Anti-Matter: Psychic Lawyers." *Omni*, January 1987, p. 86.

Daiger, Michael. "Psychic Gang Busters—Police Departments' Secret Service." *Psychic World*, May 1977, pp. 22–34.

Dempsey, Tom. "The Use of Psychics by Police as an Investigative Aid: An Examination of Current Trends and Potential Applications of Psi Phenomena to Law Enforcement." Master's Thesis, Department, of Criminal Justice, California State University, Long Beach, December 1981.

Doran, Bernadette. "Psychic Sleuths." *Student Lawyer*, November 1978, pp. 25–26, 51–53.

Druffel, Ann. "The Psychic Laboratory of the Mobius Society." *Fate*, June 1988, pp. 91–102, and July 1989, pp. 63–77.

Editors of *Fate*. *Murder Most Eerie: Homicide and the Paranormal*. Norfolk/Virginia Beach, VA: Donning, 1982.

Farabee, Charles Roscoe, Jr. *Contemporary Psychic Use by Police in America*. M.S. Thesis, Department of Criminology, California State University, Fresno, 1981.

Flammarion, Camille. *Death and Its Mystery Before Death*. New York: Century, 1921, pp. 185, 215–219.

Frazier, Kendrick. "How to Cover 'Psychics' and the Paranormal." *Bulletin of the American Society of Newspaper Editors*, April 1982, pp. 17–19.

———"Psychics and Crime." *The Skeptical Inquirer*, Summer 1979, p. 7.

———"CSICOP Cautions Against Use of Police Psychics." *The Skeptical Inquirer*, Summer 1981, pp. 6–7.

Freedland, Nat. *The Occult Explosion*. New York: G. P. Putnam's Sons, 1972.

Galante, Mary Ann. "Psychics: Lawyers Using Seers to Help Select Juries, Find Missing Children." *The National Law Journal*, January 27, 1986, pp. 1, 32–33.

Geberth, Vernon J. "Psychics," in his *Practical Homicide Investigation: Tactics, Procedures, and Forensic Techniques*. New York: Elsevier, 1983, pp. 420–424.

Goldfluss, Howard E. "Forum: Courtroom Psychics." *Omni*, July 1987, p. 12.

Gordon, Henry. "How Psychics Help Lawyers Select Juries." *The Ontario Skeptic*, 1, 4, Winter 1987/88, p. 7.

Gordon, Thomas J., and Jerry J. Tobias. "Managing the Psychic in Police Investigation." *The Police Chief*, May 1979, pp. 56–59.

Grayzel, Ken. "Psychic Detectives." Unpublished (?) manuscript, circa 1978.

Grimson, Roger. "The Atlanta Child Murders: Impressions by Psychics and Others." Paper presented at the Conference on Psi, Science and Survival of the Psychical Research Foundation, Chapel Hill, NC, October 22, 1983.

Guarino, Richard. "The Police and Psychics." *Psychic*, June 1975, pp. 9, 14–15.

Hammond, David, with David Frederick Brown. *The Search for Psychic Power: The Evolution of the Mind*. London: Hodder and Stoughton, 1975.

Hanauer, Joan. Untitled article on ABC's TV special "Psychic Detectives," UPI, December 20, 1989 (via Lexis).

Hansel, C. E. M. *E.S.P.: A Scientific Evaluation*. New York: Charles Scribner's Sons, 1966, pp. 197–203.

Harris, Melvin. *Investigating the Unexplained*. Buffalo: Prometheus Books, 1986, pp. 35–59.

Harrison, Lee. "Enquirer Psychic Crime Squad is Ready to Help Police Solve Cases." *National Enquirer*, June 14, 1977.

Hibbard, Whitney S., and Raymond W. Worring. *Psychic Criminology: An Operations Manual for Using Psychics in Criminal Investigations*. Springfield, Illinois: Charles C. Thomas, 1981.

Hicks, Robert. "The Psychic World of Law Enforcement." Paper presented at the annual conference of the Committee for the Scientific Investigation of Claims of the Paranormal, Chicago, IL, November 5, 1988.

Hines, Terence. "Psychic Crime Detection." In *Pseudoscience and the Paranormal: A Critical Examination of the Evidence*. Buffalo, NY: Prometheus Books, 1988, pp. 46–48.

Hitching, Francis. *Dowsing: The Psi Connection*. Garden City, NY: Anchor Books, 1978, pp. 32–35, 57–59, 182, 205–206, 265.

Hoebens, Piet Hein. Miscellaneous research reports on psychic detection cases for the CSAR Psychic Sleuths Project. Archives of the Center for Scientific Anomalies Research, 1981–1984.

Hoebens, Piet Hein, with Marcello Truzzi. "Reflections on Psychic Detectives," in

Paul Kurtz, ed., *A Skeptics Handbook of Parapsychology*. Buffalo, NY: Prometheus, 1985, pp. 631–643.

Hunt, D. *Exploring the Occult*. New York: Ballantine Books, 1965, pp. 114–117.

Jones, Mark. "Psychics and Police Mix It Up in L.A." *Fate*, October 1979–pp 64–71.

———"Police Find It Pays to Take Psychics out of Woodwork." *The Jersey Journal*, December 6, 1978, p. 23.

Jones, Mark Elliot. "Anti-Matter: Psychic Cops." *Omni*, August 1984, p. 94.

Kitaev, Nikolai, and Nikolia Ermakov. "Usage of Parapsychology in Criminal Investigation." *International Journal of Paraphysics*, 12, 5/6, 1978, pp. 111–116.

Klein, Aaron. "Out of Sight." Chapter 1 in his *Beyond Time and Matter*. Garden City, NY: Doubleday, 1973, pp. 13–25.

Korem, Dan. "Psychic Detectives." Part I in *Powers: Testing the Psychic & Supernatural*. Downers Grove, IL: Intervarsity Press, 1988, pp. 61–83.

Kozenczak, Joseph R., and Karen M. Henrikson, "Still Beyond Belief," *Policing*, 5, 2, 1989, 131–149.

Kurtz, Paul, and Andrea Szalanski. "Psychic Detectives." *Miami Herald*, April 28, 1984, pp. 1E, 4E.

Laubscher, B. J. F. "Psi in Traditional Bantu Culture." In J. C. Pynton, ed., *Parapsychology in South Africa*. Johannesburg: South African Society for Psychical Research, 1975, pp. 7–14.

Lippard, J. M. "Psychic Detectives. *Phoenix Skeptics News*, May/June 1988, pp. 4–7.

Lucas, Ward. "Police Use of Psychics: A Waste of Resources and Tax Money." *Campus Law Journal*, 15, 4, July–August 1985, pp. 15–21.

Lundstrom, Marjie. "Psychics Win Spurs with Officer." *Denver Post*, December 27, 1987, pp. 1A, 4A.

Luxenburg, Joan, and Carl Cowan. "Police and Paraphysical Phenomena." Paper presented at the Annual Meeting of the Academy of Criminal Justice Sciences, March 12–14, 1980, Oklahoma City, OK.

MacDougall, Curtis D. "Clairvoyance." Chapter 26 in *Superstition and the Press*. Buffalo, NY: Prometheus, 1983, pp. 532–544.

MacGregor, Rob, and Trish Janeshutz. "Psychic Crimebusters." *Fate*, September 1985, pp. 43–50.

Mahony, Edmund. "Psychics' Aid Rarely Helps Solve Crimes." *Hartford Courant*, November 4, 1979.

Martin, Deirdre, and Mark Levine, "Unlikely Allies: Psychics & Law Enforcement Agencies," *Law Enforcement Technology*, September 1990, 58–60 & 63.

May, Meredith. "Police Consult Psychics." *The Daily Californian* [Berkeley, CA], April 20, 1990, p. 15.

Mishlove, Jeffrey. *The Roots of Consciousness: Psychic Liberation Through History, Science and Experience*. New York: Random House/Bookworks, 1975.

———and Kathy Goss. "An Interview with Stephan Schwartz." *Applied Psi Newsletter*, 1, 3, July/August 1982, p. 5.

Myers, Eleanor L. "Results of the ESP and Law Enforcement Survey: Conducted at the ESP and Law Enforcement Seminar, Santa Barbara, CA, June 27–28, 1979." Research paper (Xerox) at SRI International, July 1979.

———"The Use of Psychics to Aid Police Investigators in Solving Crimes." *Applied Psi Newsletter*, 1, 3, July/August 1982, pp. 1–2.

Nebel, Long John, with Sanford M. Teller. *The Psychic World Around Us*. New York: New American Library, 1969, pp. 141–163.

Nicely, Steve. "Disc Jockey, Psychics Have Fun Divining Name of J. R.'s Assailant." *Kansas City Times*, November 22, 1980, p. B–11.

O'Hanlon, Kevin, "Cops Turn to Psychics to Solve Tough Ones," *Argus Leader* (Sioux Falls, SD), May 6, 1985.

Osis, Karlis. "The Application of ESP to Crime Detection." Unpublished manuscript, circa 1983.

————"The Application of ESP to Criminal Investigations, Locating Missing Persons, and Cases of Airplane Disasters." In C. B. Scott Jones, ed., *Proceedings of a Symposium on Applications of Anomalous Phenomena, November 30– December 1, 1983, Leesburg, Virginia*. Alexandria, VA: Kaman Tempo, 1984, pp. 241–179.

Ostrander, Sheila, and Lynn Schroeder. *Psychic Discoveries Behind the Iron Curtain*. New York: Bantam Books, 1970, pp. 53–55, 97, 277–284.

Pollack, Jack Harrison. *Croiset the Clairvoyant: The Story of the Amazing Dutchman*. Garden City, NY: Doubleday, 1964.

Price, Harry. "Mediums Who Aid the Police." In his *Fifty Years of Psychical Research: A Critical Survey*. New York: Longmans Green and Co., 1939, pp. 220—222.

Randi, James. "Atlanta Child Murderer: Psychics' Failed Visions." *The Skeptical Inquirer*, Fall 1982, pp. 12–13.

Randles, Jenny, and Peter Hough. *Death by Supernatural Causes*. London: Grafton Books, 1989, pp. 194–206.

Reiser, Martin, L. Ludwig, S. Saxe, and C. Wagner. "An Evaluation of the Use of Psychics in the Investigation of Major Crimes." *Journal of Police Science and Administration*, 7, 1, 1979, pp. 18–25.

————with N. Klyver. "A Comparison of Psychics, Detectives, and Students in the Investigation of Major Crimes." In M. Reiser, *Police Psychology: Collected Papers*. Los Angeles: LEHI Publishing Co., 1982, pp. 260–267.

Riley, Michael, and David Thompson. "Hearing Voices of Reason." *UK Police Review*, January 16, 1987, pp. 121–122.

Rodr, Frantisek. "Psychotronics and the Law." *Proceedings of the Second International Congress on Psychotronic Research*, 1975, pp. 250–252.

Roll, W. G., "Public Safety Agencies: Should We Become Involved?" *Research in Parapsychology*, 1981, pp. 19–20.

————and Roger C. Grimson. "A Majority-Vote Study of Impressions Relating to a Criminal Investigation." *The Parapsychological Association 26th Annual Convention. Presented Papers, August 9–13, 1983*, pp. 186–203.

Rudley, Stephen. *Psychic Detectives*. New York: Franklin Watts, 1979. [Book for young readers.]

S., A.P., "Missing Persons?" *Prediction*, January 1970, pp. 11–12.

Schall, Stanley L. "Legal Issues Related to the Use of Psi." *Archaeus*, 3, Summer 1985, pp. 47–52.

————and William H. Kautz. "Legal Issues Related to Psi Application in Law Enforcement." *Applied Psi*, 3, Winter 1984/85, pp. 7–12.

Seckel, Al. "Skeptical Eye: Sensing Just How to Help the Police." *Los Angeles Times*, November 16, 1987, Metro Section, Part 2, p. 5.

Stearn, Jess. "The Crime Busters" and "The Psychic Machine." Chapters 12 and 13 in *The Door to the Future*. New York: Macfadden-Bartell Books, 1964. [orig. 1963] [Reprinted as "Crime Busters with a Sixth Sense" in Brant House, ed., *Strange Powers of Unusual People*. New York: Ace Books, 1963, pp. 44–63.

Stith, Pat. "Raleigh Police Chief Finds Merit in Psychics, Biorhythms." *Triangle* [Raleigh, NC], September 2, 1986, pp. 1C–2C.

Stone, Clement W., and Norma Lee Browning. *The Other Side of the Mind*. New York: Paperback Library, 1967, pp. 92–103.

Summers, L. K. Review of *Psychic Criminology*. *Law and Order*, November 1982, p. 71.

Sutton, R. "A Look at Police Parapsychology." *Behind the Badge*, 2, 1, 1981, pp. 95–101.

Swanson, Charles R., Jr., Neil C. Chamelin, and Leonard Territo. "Psychics and Criminal Investigation." In their *Criminal Investigation*, 3rd Edition. New York: Random House, 1984, pp. 708–711.

Tabori, Cornelius (translated and edited by Paul Tabori). *My Occult Diary*. New York: Living Books, 1966. Abridged as "Psychic Crime Hunters." *Fate*, January 1953, pp. 79–105.

Tabori, Paul. *Crime and the Occult*. New York: Taplinger, 1974.

Tenhaeff, W. H. C. "The Employment of Paragnosts for Police Purposes." *Proceedings of the P.I. [Parapsychological Institute of the State University of Utrecht]*, No. 1, December 1960, pp. 15–31.

Thomas, Keith. "Cunning Men and Popular Magic." In his *Religion and the Decline of Magic*. New York: Scribner's, 1971, pp. 212–252.

Trubo, Richard. "Psychics and the Police." *Psychic*, 6, 2, May–June 1975, pp. 8, 10–12.

Truzzi, Marcello. "Anti-Matter: Psychic Sleuths." *Omni*, August 1982, p. 92.

V., J. G. Book Review of Fred Archer's *Crime and the Psychic World*. *Spiritual Frontiers*, 1, Autumn 1959, pp. 254–255.

Vaughn, Alan. Book review of Whitney S. Hibbard and Raymond W. Worring's *Psychic Criminology*. *Journal of the American Society for Psychical Research*, 78, 3, 1984, pp. 280–282.

Walther, Gerda. "Crime Detection by Clairvoyance." *Tomorrow*, 1, 1, Autumn 1952, pp. 30–37.

Warchol, Glen. "Psychic Investigators." *Twin Cities Reader*, November 29, 1989, pp. 12–13.

Wilcox, Tamara. *Mysterious Detectives: Psychics*. Milwaukee, WI: Raintree, 1977. [Book for young readers.]

Wilson, Colin. *The Psychic Detectives*. London: Pan Books, 1984.

Wolkimer, R., and J. Wolkimer. "Clairvoyant Crime Busters." *McCalls*, September 1978, pp. 162–164.

Woodhall, Edward T. *Crime and the Supernatural*. London: John Long, Ltd. 1935.

Index

Abbott, David P., 28, 30
Adell, Larry, 126
Adell, Robert, 126
Aksakof, Alexander N., 199
Albro, Lawrence, Jr., 10, 86
Alexander, David, 127
Alexander, Greta, 1–2, 38, 60–61, 64, 67–69, 71, 76, 85, 92, 178–85, 232, 235–36
Alexander, John B., 203
Alghinin, Shamil, 63
Allaway, Thomas Henry, 22–23
Allen, Nathan, 32
Allen, Ronald, J., 247
Allison, Dorothy, 3, 6, 54, 61, 63, 67–68, 72–73, 82, 140–42, 153–54, 169, 225, 228, 231, 234, 247
Anderson, "Doc," 55
Anderson, Jack, 209–12
Anderson, Mark, 79
Archer, Fred, 19, 21
Aron, David, 207
Ashman, Chuck, 127
Astrology, 190, 256
Atkins, Susan, 125
Austin, Joe, 186
Ayers, John, 30
Ayers, Raymond, 74
Aymar, Jacques, 16–17, 67

Babyak, Mark, 7
Ball, Lucille, 116
Barbaro, Frank, 245
Barnard, Patrick, 63
Bass, Teresita, 59, 245
Baskerville, Frances, 67, 88
Bearden, Thomas, E., 204
Beaumont, Roger A., 204
Belgardt, Gerhard, 36
Belk, William Henry, 114
Belle, Judy, 62, 67, 69, 78–79, 92, 162, 185, 237–38
Belli, Melvin, 10, 86
Bem, Daryl, 148
Bender, Frank, 80–81
Bender, Hans, 55, 97, 104
Bennett, Tony, 129

Benton, Jack, 140
Berglas, David, 195
Berluti, Adam, 145
Bernhardt, Clarissa, 83–84
Berodts, The, 248–49
Bessemans, Albert, 115
Bird, Christopher, 78
Blue sense, definition of, 11
Blum, Howard, 211
Blumberg, Paul, 224
Booher, Vernon, 26
Boswell, Gary, 186
Bottomly, John, 119–20
Bouverie, Alice, 114
Bradley, Omar, 198
Bradley, Tommy, 242
Brandeis, Louis, D., 239
Brando, Marlon, 116
Brejack, George, 153–54
Bringhurst, Cindy, 92, 237
Brink, Filippus, 51, 97
Broad, William J., 221
Broman, Carol, 6, 140
Brown, Melvin, 234, 247
Brown, Pat, 190
Browning, Norma Lee, 95, 107, 109–10, 114, 116–19, 121, 124–27, 137
Brussel, James, A., 171
Brzezinski, Zbigniew, 207
Bubar, David Nobel, 151–52
Buel, Francis, 61, 141–42
Bugliosi, Vincent, 125
Bunge, Mario, 134
Burggraf, John, 119
Burks, Arthur, 32
Burnett, Donald J., 91
Bush, George, 191, 202

Cammaert, Captain, 111–12
Carey, Constable, 26–27
Cargile, Jenita, 88
"Carlos" ("The Jackal"), 211–12
Carrington, Hereward, 30
Carson, Michael Bear and Suzan, 243
Carter, Carl, Jr., 80, 244
Carter, Jimmy, 84, 193, 207

Catchings, John, 64, 68, 70–71, 148, 186, 232–33
Cate, Basil, 71
Center for Scientific Anomalies Research (CSAR), 256–57
China, 212–18
Christie, Agatha, 21–22
Chua, Remibias, 245
CIA (Central Intelligence Agency), 7, 189–92, 201–12
Clogg, Mitchell, 33
Clover, Hans, 143
Collins, John Norman, 124
Committee for Scientific Investigation of Claims of the Paranormal (CSICOP), 3, 132
Conan Doyle, Arthur, 21–22
Cook, James, 194
Copeland, Miles, Sr., 191
Courtney, Alan, 116
Cousett, Mary L., 1, 38, 178–79, 232
Cracknell, Robert, 63
Crane, Jim, 120
Crisel, Donnie, 246
Croiset, Gerard, 3, 39, 63, 93–107, 127, 131, 150–51, 161, 226, 251
Croiset, Gerard, Jr., 63, 106
Cronin, John, 31
Crotty, Charles, 234
Czartoryski, Count, 34
Czetli, Nancy M., 59–60, 67–68, 79, 87, 92, 133, 137–39, 162–63

Darden, Al, 231
Davis, James, 85
Davis, Linda, 84–85
Davis, Phillip W., 177
Davitashvili, Djuna, 220
Deacon, Richard, 193, 201, 203, 212–13
Dean, Beverlee, 55
Dee, John, 196
Dellaert, Rene, 115
den Hollander, A. M., 102
Dennis, Eugenie, 28–31
DeSalvo, Albert, 121
Diaconis, Persi, 136
Dibler, Colleen, 73
Diller, Phyllis, 129
Dimitrova, Vanya, 201
DiNatale, Phillip, 121
Ding, Wei Xin, 214
DiVirgilio, Ramon, 71
Dixon, Jeane, 130, 226
Donlon, Frank, 81, 156
Dozier, James Lee, 8, 208–9, 211
Driesch, Hans, 25
Drost, August, 23–24
Dubois, Phoebe, 32
Dulles, Allen, 191
Dunninger, Joseph, 58
Duval, Anna Mary, 81

Dykshoorn, Marinus, 3, 63, 67, 75, 150
Dylan, Bob, 129
Dymond, Frances, 63

Ebon, Martin, 152–53
Edalji, George, 21
Eekhof, Commander, 104–5
Eisenbud, Jule, 104
Ekman, Paul, 177
Emerson, Steven, 208–9
Etheridge, Owen, 2
Experiments, 48–55

Fascell, Dante, 193
Faurot, Joseph, 29
Faust, David, 172
Ferraro, Angelo, 142
Fetzer, Dix R. M., 127–28
Fink, Carol Ann, 33
Fink, Robert, 31, 33
Finke, Allen Glenn, 79–80
Fischel, Michael F., 24
Fitzgerald, William, 1–2, 179, 183
Fleming, Ian, 197
Foley, Mary, 29
Folger, Abigail, 125
Ford, Gerald, 83
Ford, Glenn, 85, 116, 119
Foster, Charles, 18
Fox, Kate and Margaret, 17
Frallic, Mary Ellen, 31
Frank, Gerold, 119–20
Frazier, Kendrick, 135
Freedland, Nat, 112
Freud, Sigmund, 26, 145, 254
Fromme, Lynne "Squeaky," 83
Frost, David, 79, 162
Frykowski, Voyteck, 125
Fukerai, Tomokichi, 218
Fuller, Melvin, 122–23

Gacy, John Wayne, 6, 61, 140
Gagliardo, Pat, 225
Gandhi, Indira, 83
Gardner, Martin, 47, 231
Garnier, Pierre, 16
Garrett, Eileen, 39
Gerberth, Vernon J., 5
Geller, Uri, 6, 55, 78, 114, 160, 193–95, 207
Gellerstein, Solomon, 215
Gensen, Ed, 246
Gibson, Walter, 34
Gladstone, Professor, 26–27
Gluhack, Louie, 80
Goldfluss, Howard E., 242
Goldston, Will, 152
Goodman, Dean, 75
Goozens, Hirt, 109
Gorbachev, Mikhail, 211
Goss, Marvin, 156

Graff, Nick, 184
Greco, Gary, 130–31
Greenaway, Willis, 138–39
Greene, Marilyn, 169–70
Grodin, James, W., 243, 247, 250
Groller, Richard, 204
Gros, Ray, 62, 68
Gull, William, 20–21

Haimes, Judith Richardson, 9, 240
Haldane, J. B. S., 253
Hamilton, George, 85
Hancock, William, 26
Hansel, C. E. M., 101–2
Hansen, Fred, 65
Hanussen, Erik Jan, 34–36, 58
Harary, Keith, 39, 55, 57, 59, 128, 170, 207, 219–20, 242
Harding, Thomas, 15
Harris, Jean, 10, 86
Harris, Lynn, 92, 185, 237–38
Harris, Melvin, 20, 137
Harper, Sarah Jane, 227
Harvey, Douglas, 124
Hasperhoven, G., 102
Hauptmann, Bruno, 46
Hawn, Goldie, 85
Hearst, Patty, 61, 73, 83, 206
Heilijgers, Cor, 63
Hejbalik, Karel, 196
Helin, Edward, 191
Hellwig, Albert, 23–24
Hibbard, Whitney S., 81, 165, 229
Hicks, Robert, 145, 228–29
Hinckley, John Warnock, 130
Hitler, Adolph, 25, 34–35, 112, 197
Hoebens, Piet Hein, 23, 94, 98–100, 102–6, 109, 112–13, 139, 145, 147–48, 150
Hoellard, A. P. H., 27
Hoffa, Jimmy, 127, 187
Holliday, Stanley, Jr., 1, 178
Home, D. D., 199
Honegger, Barbara, 198, 208
Honorton, Charles, 49
Houdini, Harry, 30
Huff, Pat, 75
Hughes, Howard, 59
Hughes, Irene F., 68, 84
Hurkos, Bea van der Berg, 108, 110
Hurkos, Peter, 3, 39, 63, 68, 73–74, 81, 107–28, 131, 135, 137, 149–51, 161, 187, 251
Hurkos, Stephany Courtney, 121, 128
Hyman, Ray, 49

Ilg, Alfred, 13
Imkin, Edna, 71

Jacksons, The, 117–18
Jack the Ripper, 18–21
Jacques, Terri, 119

Jaegers, Beverly, 55, 64, 69, 88, 133
Jahn, Robert G., 54
Jahoda, Gustav, 160
Jahoda, Ursula, 211–12
Jenkins, Donald, 139
Jillson, Joyce, 190–91
Joan, 80, 244, 246
Johnson, Martin, 97
Jones, C. B. Scott, 11, 127, 221
Jones, Nella, 63, 76, 82
Jones, Warren H., 133
Jongsma, W., 98–99
Jonsson, Olaf, 39, 63, 215
Jordan, Phil, 10, 61, 73–74, 86, 226–27, 240

Kammann, Richard, 142
Kasabian, Linda, 125
Kaufmann, Ted, 67
Kele, Janos, 24–25
Keller, Joe, 32
Keller, Russell, 234
Kelly, George, 149
Kennedy, George, 85–86
Kennedy, Tommy, 61, 74
Kerler, W. de, 24
Kerr, David E., 162, 164
Khokhlov, Nikolai, E., 203
Khue, P. M., 78
Kikuchi, Miwa, 96
Kinkade, Kebrina, 85
Knecht, Peter, 125
Knight, Mayme, 70–71, 233
Knight, Stephen, 20
Kobler, John, 110, 116
Kozenczak, Joseph, 6, 140
Kraft, Randy Steven, 246
Krasny, Walter, 123–24
Krenwinkel, Patricia, 125
Kreskin, 174–75
Kulazina, Nina, 199–200
Kursics, Michael, 141–42
Kurtz, Paul, 39, 132, 221

LaBianca, Leno and Rosemary, 125
Lang, Andrew, 17
Lange, Kelly, 130–31
Langsner, Maximillian, 26
Lanning, Kenneth, 6, 9, 234
Lanzer, Ernst, 145
LaPlace, Pierre Simon de, 133–34
Lavorini, Ermano, 99
Lees, Eva, 20
Lees, Robert James, 18–21
Legal issues, 239–50
LeLorrain, Pierre, 13
Lewis, Leslie, 88–89
Lie detectors, 176–77
Lindbergh baby, 46
Linedecker, Clifford, 189
Linscott, Steve, 66

Lipe, Tom, 117
Little, Joan, 9
Lombroso, Cesare, 55, 148, 176
Longfellow, Kurt, 5, 9, 11, 65–66, 228, 230
Lozanov, Georgi, 201
Lubertazzi, Sal, 231
Lucas, Ward, 51–52, 146–47, 179–85, 227, 232
Ludwig, Louise, 5, 65, 69, 229–31
Luttikhuizen, (farmer), 28
Lydecker, Beatrice, 75

Maar, Herk de, 94
MacDonald, A. B., 26
Mackay, Donald, 96
MacKenzie, Flora, 63
MacKenzie-Rindle, Pamela, 177
Macris, Tom, 62, 80, 89–90
Maharahj, Shri Chandra Swamiji, 192–93
Mahony, Patrick, 145
Mallwitz, Robert, 92, 235–36
Manning, Peter K., 161
Manson, Charles, 81, 83, 125, 158
Marcos, Ferdinand, 127, 192
Marcotte, Armand, 90, 230
Marin, Vadim, 197
Marion, Frederick, 27–28
Martindale, Steve, 192
Maslow, Abraham, 254
Matias, Delvis, 153
Mattacia, Ginette and Louis, 67, 196
Mauck, Carroll K., 87, 162
Maurice, Dick, 129–31
May, Edwin D., 54
McCartin, Donald A., 246
McClelland, William, 138–39
McDonald, C. Thomas, 246
McDonald, Larry, 191
McDougall, William, 41
McFadden, Dennis, 40
McFadden, Tim, 72
McGinley, William, 80, 244
McKillip, Don, 174
McLauchlin, Scotty, 27
McManus, Jack, 86–87
McMillan, John, 246
McRae, Ron, 193, 202
Megalis, 24
Mei Lei, 215
Memro, Harold Ray "Butch," 80, 244
Merrell, John, 7
Mesmer, Franz, 175
Messing, Wolf, 33–34, 197
Metesky, George, 171
Michaud, Stephen A. 171
Mihalasky, John, 8
Miller, Dolly, 32
Miller, Robert, 10, 86, 240
Mindemon, Yap, 108
Mitchell, Edgar, 63, 202, 215
Mitchell, Michelle, 174

Mittelman, Georg, 24
Mizerka, John, 235
Mobius Group, 64–65
Mondale, Walter, 84, 190
Montgomery, Ernesto, 63, 189–90
Moore, James, 80
Moore, Omar Khayyam, 232
Morgan, David, 76
Morsche, Gerda ter, 94
Mosrie, Arif, 85
Mosteller, Frederick, 136
Motoyama, Hiroshi, 218
Mulholland, William, 122–23
Mullin, Courtney J., 241
Murakami, Yoshiaki, 219
Murray, H. A., 46
Myersburg, Barbara, 85

Nakasone, Yashuhiro, 219
Napflin, Clothilde, 63
Napper, George, 82, 225
Nash, John A., 31
Naumov, Edward, 200
Nazarenko, Dina, 63, 68
Nicolich, Gustavo, 106
Noriega, Manuel, 8, 209

Organ, Thomas J., 246
Orne, Martin T., 173
Osis, Karlis, 25, 55
Ossowiecki, Stefan, 197
Osty, Eugene, 103
Otani, Soji, 218–19
Ott, Mary, 33
Ottervanger, Ph. B., 97

Papapetro, Maria, 63
Parent, Steven Earl, 125
Park, George, 233
Pathes, Alfred, 24
Patton, George, 198
Paul, Jerry, 9
Pavlita, Robert, 201, 204
Pell, Claiborne, 6–7, 11, 193
Perkins, Joseph, 237
Peters, Edward S., 64
Phillips, John and Michelle, 125
Phillips, Karen, 66
Pickering, Edward, 31
Piest, Robert, 140
Polanski, Roman, 125–26
Police, 91, 92, 224–38
Pollack, Jack Harrison, 94–98, 101–2, 106
Ponce, Fernando, 80
Price, Pat, 7, 39, 49, 55, 62, 206, 236
Principle of Hamlet, 134
Principle of Laplace, 133–34
Psychic detection
    legal issues, 239–50
    and police, 91, 92, 224–38

pseudo-psychics, 129–54
psychic espionage, 189–221
psychic sleuths' activities, 70–92
psychic sleuths in history, 12–36
psychic spectrum, 57–69
search for legitimacy, 37–56
success stories, 155–66
Psychic Detective Bureau, 64
Puharich, Andrija, 114–15, 120, 128, 203
Puthoff, Harold, 49, 205

Qian Kueseng, 215–16
Quaid, Patrick, 215, 221
Queen, Richard, 207
Quigley, Joan, 190, 256
Quinn, Ed, 130

Raboid, Rajah, 58
Radakovich, Daniel E., 245
Radcliffe-Brown, A. R., 160
Ramos, Mel, 2
Rand, Tamara, 129–31
Radi, James, 3, 131, 194–95, 240
Raspberry, William, 226
Rasputin, Grigori Efimovich, 199
Rauscher, Elizabeth, 219
Rawcliffe, D. H., 142
Reagan, Nancy, 190, 224, 256
Reagan, Ronald, 7, 84, 128–30, 190–91, 208, 211–12
Reams, Deanna, 59
Redding, M. G., 226
Reese, Melvin David, 118
Regan, Don, 190
Reiser, Martin, 4, 52–53, 89, 141, 146, 175, 232
Rejdak, Zdenek, 200
Renier, Noreen, 7, 63, 67–69, 84, 90, 133, 139, 225, 230
Ressler, Robert K., 7, 225
Retrocognition, 82
Rezmichenko, Vladimir, 34
Rhea, Kathlyn, 62, 69, 71–73, 80, 86–87, 90
Rhine, Joseph Banks, 41, 43, 45–47, 97, 115, 218
Rhine, Louisa, 43, 45
Richardson, George F., 32–33
Riesenman, F. Regis, 117–18
Righter, Carroll, 190–91
Rinn, Joseph F., 30
Rivera, Geraldo, 128
Robbins, Shawn, 83, 198
Roberts, John M. 176
Roberts, Kelly, 68, 84–85
Robinson, James B., 139–40
Rodriguez, Jeana, 73
Roll, William G., 226
Rosana, Charles B., 17
Rose, Anne, 75
Rose, Charles, 7, 220
Rosenfield, Arnold, 122
Rosenthal and Siegel, 222–23
Rothering, Richard, 235

Rous, Marvin, 243
Rumola, Michael J., 141
Russell, Dwane, 234
Ryzl, Milan, 200

Sadat, Anwar, 84
Salmi, Albert, 116
Sanders, William B., 163–64
Sandridge, Donald, 179
Santiago, Victoria de, 72
Schall, Stanley L., 244
Schermann, Raphael, 24
Schilling, Leonetta, 79
Schneider, Peter, 33
Schoettlin, Tracy, 242
Schultz, Dutch, 31
Schultz, Sigrid, 26
Schwartz, Ronald A., 116
Schwartz, Stephen, 64–65, 76–77
Sebok, Sandor, 25
Sebring, Jay, 125
Semenov, Nikolai, 34
Senf, Mr., 99–100
Shade, Jim, 74
Shehu, Mehmet, 191
Shifrin, Abraham, 215
Showery, Allan, 59, 245–46
Silver, Ed, 121, 123–24
Silverstein, Hugh, 240
Sims, William, 80
Sinatra, Frank, 116
Sinatra, Frank, Jr., 120
Sky, Marc, 241
Slater, Oscar, 21
Slesers, Anna, 119
Smith, Etta Louise, 4, 66
Smith, Irvin, 60, 79
Smith, Jeffrey, 116
Solleveld, Father, 112
Son of Sam, 61
Soshnick, Julian, 120
Sothern, Ann, 85
Soviet Union, 7, 219–21
Spacek, Sissy, 58
Spencer, Mary Cook, 148, 232
Spiegel, David, 173
Spiegel, Herbert, 173
Spilsbury, Bernard, 30
Stalin, Josef, 34
Starkey, Charlotte, 22
Starr, Douglas, 215, 221
Stallone, Sylvester, 129
Stearn, Jess, 110, 115, 119
Steers, Jean, 62–63, 74
Stemman, Roy, 100
Stern, August, 205
Sternfels, Florence, 31–33
Stewart, Raymond Lee, 235
Stinnet, L. C., 148, 232
Stockdill, Roy, 195

Stokes, Doris, 3, 63, 226
Stubblebine, Albert, 8, 209
Stuldrecher, C. J. F., 108–9, 113
Sukarno, 191–92
Summers, L. K., 149
Superstition, 222–24
Sutcliffe, Peter, 82, 226
Suttmeier, Richard P., 217
Swan, T. C., 92
Swann, Ingo, 49, 55, 77, 92, 187, 206–7
Szimon, Stephan, 25

Tabori, Paul, 23
Tahi, Istvan, 25
Tanous, Alex, 39
Targ, Russell, 49, 205, 219
Tarmon, John A., 117–18
Tarnower, Herman, 10, 86
Tart, Charles T., 115–16, 205
Tartaruga, Dr., 24
Tate, Sharon, 81, 125–26
Taylor, Bill, 27
Taylor, Elizabeth, 83, 192
Tenhaeff, Wilhelm H. C., 13, 55, 95–106, 115, 127
Thoma, Leopold, 24
Thomas, Keith, 14–16
Thomas, W. I., 164
Thompson, James, H. W., 121
Thoones, Anthonius, 98
Thouless, R. H., 41
Timmerman, Brian, 72, 141
Toland, John, 35
Tonet, Sylvester, 137–38
Toomin, Michael, 243
Toth, Robert C., 205
Trew, Steve, 2, 180–81
Turner, Stansfield, 7, 206–7, 220
Tyler, Scott, 248–49

Ullman, Montague, 242
Unamuno, Miguel de, 254
Underwood, Peter, 21
Uribe, Melanie, 4
Utley, Garrick, 203

Valkenberg, Bill, 173, 228
Van den Bos-Theunissen, Mrs., 95
Van Maaldrink, E. D., 101–2
Van Prong, Henri, 100
Van Roosmalen, Th., 103

Van Straaten, René, 109
Van Tossing, Bernhard, 110
Van Woerden, Speijart, 111–12
Vasiliev, Leonid, L., 199
Vicaro, Donald, 142
Vidi, Luce, 24
Vierbloom, Piet, 111
Vilenskaya, Larissa, 200
Vogt and Hyman, 223
Von Strahl, Lotte, 63, 85–86
VoSum, Captain, 78

Wagstaff, Graham F., 173
Wallace, Jean, 26
Ward, Bill, 60, 67, 69, 78
Warmouth, Ron, 77
Watson, Charles "Tex," 81, 125
Watson, Jim, 64
Weber, Don W., 38
Weisner, B. P., 41
Weitzenhoffer, A. M., 173
Weitzman, Harold, 248
West, Donald J., 20, 56
Wheeler, D. R., 46
White, Stanley, 74
Whitehead, Alfred North, 253
Whitman, Hugh, 88–89
Whitmore, Gifford, 32
Whitwell, John, 198
Wilhelm, John, 206
Wilkins, Irene, 22–23
Williams, Peter, 244
Williams, Wayne B., 225–26
Wissell, Henry, 31
Wolf, Richard, 9
Wolverton, Keith, 87
Woodhall, Edwin T., 19, 22–23
Woods, Jack, 27
Woods, Mark, 211–12
Worring, Raymond, 81, 87, 165, 229

Yeterian, Dixie, 2, 66–67, 81, 156, 160, 162–63, 186
Yu Guangyuan, 215–16

Zha Leping, 215–17
Zhang Baosheng, 216–17
Ziskin, Jay, 172
Zorab, George, 94, 97, 104–5
Zuane, Leonard, 133